D0018786

Also by Michael S Lief and H. Mitchell Caldwell

Ladies and Gentlemen of the Jury:
Greatest Closing Arguments in Modern Law (with Ben Bycel)

And the Walls Came Tumbling Down:
Greatest Closing Arguments Protecting Civil Liberties

THE
DEVIL'S
ADVOCATES

*Greatest Closing Arguments
in Criminal Law*

Michael S Lief
H. Mitchell Caldwell

A LISA DREW BOOK
SCRIBNER
New York London Toronto Sydney

A Lisa Drew Book / Scribner
A Division of Simon & Schuster, Inc.
1230 Avenue of the Americas
New York, NY 10020

First Lisa Drew / Scribner trade paperback edition September 2007

SCRIBNER and design are trademarks of
Macmillan Library Reference USA, Inc., used under license
by Simon & Schuster, the publisher of this work.

A LISA DREW BOOK is a trademark of Simon & Schuster, Inc.

For information about special discounts for bulk purchases,
please contact Simon & Schuster Special Sales at
1-800-456-6798 or business@simonandschuster.com.

Text set in Bembo

Manufactured in the United States of America

1   3   5   7   9   10   8   6   4   2

The Library of Congress has cataloged the hardcover edition as follows:

Lief, Michael S
The devil's advocates : greatest closing arguments in criminal law / Michael S Lief,
H. Mitchell Caldwell.
p. cm.
"A Lisa Drew Book."
Includes index.
1. Trials—United States. 2. Criminal justice, Administration of—United States—
History—Sources. I. Caldwell, Harry M. II. Title.
KF220.L54 2006
345.73'07—dc22

2005057584

ISBN-13: 978-0-7432-4669-9 (pbk)

This book is dedicated to the memory of Shirley Weber Lief, 1906–1986, the card-playing, joke-telling, cigarette-smoking, most loving grandmother a guy could have. And to Sergeant Bernard Solomon Sands, USMC, 1933–1991, who loved "brawling, books, booze, and broads," not necessarily in that order. He would have enjoyed this book. Semper Fi, Mac!

—MSL

For Joyce, my rock and my rudder.

—HMC

Acknowledgments

The following law students contributed mightily to this book: Charity Hansen, Kasey Swisher, Tammy Tsoumis, Maralee Downey, Amanda Harvey, and Christopher Sun. And a special thank-you to Denise Coulter for her invaluable assistance with the Ossian Sweet–Clarence Darrow chapter.

We would be remiss in not thanking Candace Warren, Marc Rivera, and Casey Critchlow for their skill and patience in processing draft after draft.

Contents

THE
DEVIL'S
ADVOCATES

Introduction

THE CLOSING ARGUMENT CHRONICLES

In book one of our series, *Ladies and Gentlemen of the Jury,* we focused on compelling trials that featured the greatest closing arguments in American history: Clarence Darrow saving the lives of Leopold and Loeb, Gerry Spence bringing the nuclear power industry to its knees, William Kunstler taking on the Establishment. We also featured the successful prosecutions by Robert Jackson of the Nazi hierarchy, Vincent Bugliosi of Charles Manson, and Aubrey Daniel for the My Lai massacre.

Book two, *And the Walls Came Tumbling Down,* concentrated on landmark trials and their culminating arguments that redefined civil rights in America and profoundly affected the lives of all Americans: from the *Amistad* case, in which John Quincy Adams brought the injustice of slavery to the center stage of American politics, to the prosecution of Susan B. Anthony, which paved the way to success for women's suffrage, to the Larry Flynt trial, in which the porn king became the unlikely champion for free speech. In this book we also included the trial brought by Karen Ann Quinlan's family asking the court to let their hopelessly comatose daughter die, and the McCarthy-era blacklist case in which master lawyer Louis Nizer whipped the forces of innuendos and lies.

And now in book three, *The Devil's Advocates: Greatest Closing Arguments in Criminal Law,* we turn our attention solely to crimes. There's something intriguing about *real* crimes, real killers and madmen and traitors, not just the celluloid creations of the Hollywood dream machine.

It is that intrigue that led us to write this book. As in our previous efforts, we are motivated by the belief that there truly is a best seat in the house to understand terrible crimes: it's in the jury box. Victims may have understood why they were suffering so at the hands of others, but they rarely receive the opportunity to enlighten us. Killers and madmen may understand their motivation, but they often have strong incentives to lie to us. Eyewitnesses may present us with a thread of the tapestry, but not enough to give us a clear view of the whole.

But jurors! Jurors are presented with the most complete retelling, through the presentation of days, weeks, even months of testimony and evidence. And, at the end of the process, the lawyers present their arguments, summing up all that has gone before, weaving together each testimonial thread, combining the warp and woof of eyewitnesses and experts until—violà!—the advocates step back and allow the tapestry to tell the story and persuade the captive audience. However, the audience has a far more active part to play than those seeing a theatrical production, for they will determine the outcome: Freedom or captivity? Life or death?

The Devil's Advocates focuses attention on the types of crimes and trials that have so captivated the public, cases that have also helped to illuminate underlying principles of the American criminal justice system.

The United States of America is largely defined by how we treat those accused of criminal acts. Owing in large part to our English common-law traditions, America has continued to define and refine a system that presumes innocence until and if the state can establish beyond any reasonable doubt a person's guilt. And along the path beginning even before the birth of this nation, lawyers, judges, and legislators, as well as circumstances, have worked to hone America's justice system. In this collection we have compiled eight remarkable, landmark cases, each of which either identified a protection or better focused a right that we as Americans have all come to expect.

We begin with the right to sanctuary. That is the guarantee that once an accused is taken into custody he or she will be safely sheltered from outside forces. Such guarantees are often hard-earned, as when a Tennessee sheriff turned a blind eye to a mob hell-bent on wrenching a man from jail and lynching him.

We then turn to the Fourth Amendment guarantee to be free from unreasonable search and seizure. While the Founding Fathers contemplated such protection, it went largely vacuous until in the late 1950s, when a single mother protested a warrantless search of her home. From such modest beginnings emerged the backbone of the American criminal justice system, the exclusionary rule, which excludes illegally seized evidence from trial.

Five years after establishing the exclusionary rule, the Supreme Court, frustrated at continued police violation of a suspect's right to counsel and right to be free from self-incrimination, constructed the Miranda standard, which mandated that the police inform suspects of basic rights prior to interrogation.

There is also a basic right to be left alone, to live an unconventional life, even a strange life, free from the scrutiny of the state. That right was dramatically illustrated when self-willed outsider Randy Weaver was targeted by government agents, who would eventually shoot and kill his wife and son.

Also depicted is the most basic of rights, the right to a lawyer, a zealous advocate to represent even the despised and the vilified. It was for John Adams, who would later become the second president of the United States, to inaugurate a tradition that everyone, including the British redcoats involved in the Boston Massacre, must be represented. It remains one of history's great ironies that Adams, a leading voice for America's independence from England, would risk his life and imperil his professional career as well as political future by defending the British soldiers who had shot and killed five American patriots.

No book on memorable and significant criminal trials would be complete without including Clarence Darrow. And in 1925, the great American lawyer represented an African-American family who had the temerity to defend themselves in their home from a mob intent on running them out or worse. Darrow, as only he was capable, honed and refined the concept of self-defense.

American criminal justice was also refined on the eve of the Civil War when Congressman Daniel E. Sickles, laboring under a severe emotional strain, shot and killed the son of Francis Scott Key on a crowded, sunny Sunday afternoon in Washington, D.C.'s Lafayette Square, resulting in the concept of temporary insanity as a defense in criminal trials.

We end with the treason trial of Aaron Burr. One of the most controversial and larger-than-life figures in all of American history, Burr was accused of plotting to break away the Western territories of the United States and to form a new country with himself as its head. Burr's trial forced the justice system to fashion the vague constitutional guidelines outlawing treason into workable standards for all such trials to follow.

These arguments—and the cases motivating them—provide the reader with a ringside seat to real-life passion and drama, as well as to the shaping of the modern legal system we alternately praise and curse today.

CHAPTER ONE

When Mob Rule Trumps Rule of Law

The U.S. Supreme Court steps in when local authorities don't act to prevent lynchings

If the life of one whom the law has taken into its custody is at the mercy of the mob, the administration of justice becomes a mockery.

—*U.S. Supreme Court chief justice Melville Fuller*

Atticus Finch, attorney at law, sits in a chair propped against the front door of the jail in Maycomb, Alabama, reading a newspaper by the light of a makeshift lamp. The mob approaches . . . angry men looking for Southern justice. Finch calmly folds his newspaper and drops it in his lap; he seems to be expecting them. "He in there, Mr. Finch?" one man asks. And so the exchange begins, the angry white mob ready to storm the jail and lynch his client, a black man accused of raping a white girl. Finch stands his ground and eventually disperses the angry crowd. The accused will survive the night and will make it to his trial.

This scene in Harper Lee's classic novel, *To Kill a Mockingbird,* presented a rosier outcome than was often found in the American South of the late nineteenth and early twentieth centuries. The rule of law, so often taken for granted by modern Americans, took a backseat to lynch law, the rule of the mob, to whom guilt or innocence were of little consequence. There was no sanctuary in the criminal justice system, no Atticus Finch to stand guard through the night. Many lawyers, police officers, and public officials often stepped aside in the face of vigilante justice, giving their tacit—if not outright—stamp of approval to the "law" of the mob.

Perhaps the most abhorrent aspect of this conduct was the failure to protect the accused by those elected to do so. Like Atticus Finch, the sheriff or police chief must provide sanctuary whereby an accused can safely await his trial, his due process. When those to whom we entrust the public safety abdicate their role of public protector, the system has failed at its most fundamental level.

Strange Fruit

The phrase *lynch law* was coined during the American Revolution, when Colonel Charles Lynch and his men dispensed their own brand of summary justice to loyalists accused of plotting against the colonists. Lynch law gained its horrific racist association in the post–Civil War South, where the defeat of the Confederacy and the emancipation of the slaves shocked Southern society. The Fourteenth and Fifteenth Amendments to the U.S. Constitution conferred new rights upon the former slaves: citizenship and the right to vote. At the same time, in an effort to reunite the country, Reconstruction imposed and maintained a strong (and deeply resented) Northern presence in the South. Although this represented great progress for the freed slaves, it came at a high price: the challenge to white supremacy incited many to threats and violence as a means of protecting their social status. With the end of Reconstruction in the late 1870s came both a growing Northern indifference to the plight of Southern blacks and a renewed Southern determination to keep Northerners and blacks from interfering in their social and political affairs.

It is in this environment that lynch law flourished. From the 1870s on, mob violence—lynchings—became a primary means of asserting white dominance and reaffirming blacks' inferior station in the old (and new) Southern hierarchy. Lynch mobs were generally composed of rural Southerners, men whose status was most directly threatened by the progress and newfound prosperity of free blacks.

Although lynching is most often associated with death by hanging, the actual process was far more violent and sadistic, often including torture, dismemberment, burning, and even castration. All this took place not under the cover of darkness, the participants hiding their identities, but in full view, often as a community affair. Adults cheered and children played, while blacks were beaten, whipped, covered in coal tar, and set aflame. It was not uncommon for pieces of the corpse to be distributed as souvenirs. Many lynchings were documented in photographs— some sold as postcards—broken victims surrounded by hundreds of gleeful faces, hands raised in celebration, grins from ear to ear; men, women, and children rejoicing in the torture and execution of another human being.

Between 1882, when reliable statistics were first collected by the

Tuskegee Institute (a school founded in the late 1880s in Tuskegee, Alabama, to educate newly freed slaves), and 1968, when lynching had for the most part ended, a reported 4,743 men, women, and children died at the hands of lynch mobs. Of those victims, 3,446 were black. These numbers are almost certainly understated, as they represent only *reported* lynchings; many, especially in small and isolated communities, went unreported.

And with rare exception, the lynch mob went about its business with impunity, without fear of legal repercussions. Indeed, many Southern officials condoned the lynchings, incorporating racial hatred successfully into their political platforms. The strong influence of public opinion on local courts made indictment of mob participants nearly impossible. If the lynchers were, by some anomaly, indicted, convicted, and sentenced, a pardon would usually follow. The key figures in the judicial process—judges, jurors, and lawyers—were all white and often sympathetic to the lynch mob.

The prospects for a black defendant were grim: the law offered little or no protection; there was no guarantee of due process, no guarantee one would live to see a trial, and no guarantee that the trial's outcome would prevail even if a trial was held. Mob rule supplanted rule of law. So it was until 1906, when in Hamilton County, Tennessee, a man was lynched in open defiance of the U.S. Supreme Court. In the words of Supreme Court chief justice Melville Fuller, "If the life of one whom the law has taken into its custody is at the mercy of the mob, the administration of justice becomes a mockery." And that, the Supreme Court decided, could and would not be allowed.

The Crime

January 23, 1906, 6 p.m., Nevada Taylor, an attractive, twenty-one-year-old white woman, left the W. W. Brooks grocery store, where she worked as a bookkeeper, and boarded one of Chattanooga's new electric trolleys. At six thirty, Taylor stepped off the trolley near Thirty-fifth Street in the shadow of Lookout Mountain and started her short walk home. The night was unusually dark. She heard footsteps behind her, and before she could turn to see who was there, something was wrapped around her throat. Choking, she tried to cry out for help. "If you scream, I'll kill you," the attacker warned. After ten minutes, it was over; violated and choked unconscious, she was less than a hundred yards from the safety of her home. A few minutes later, at six forty-five, Taylor regained consciousness. Alone in the dark, she stumbled home, where she told her father and siblings what had happened. The sheriff and the family doctor were summoned, and the physician confirmed her worst fears—she had been raped.

Within the hour, Sheriff Joseph Franklin Shipp assembled a group of his best men and a couple of bloodhounds. The posse combed the scene of the crime, searching the area for the attacker, witnesses, and any evidence.

The Investigation

Sheriff Shipp was a much admired Civil War veteran, whom everyone called Captain. Born and raised in Jasper County, Georgia, Shipp enlisted in the Confederate Army in 1862 and, during his three years as a soldier, was wounded on three separate occasions. Mustered out as a captain in 1865, Shipp returned to his parents' home in Georgia, where he worked for several years in his father's cotton gin business. It was there he met and married his wife, Lily, and began a family that would eventually include seven children. In 1874, the Shipps moved to Chattanooga to build and operate a water-pump manufacturing plant. The business proved a huge success and Shipp quickly became one of the wealthiest men in the city. In 1904, he was elected to a two-year term as Hamilton County sheriff. Described by local newspapers as "a natural born leader" and a "tender and devoted husband and a loving father," he was an astute politician, an active community leader, and a "take charge kind of fellow." He fired all the deputies who had campaigned against him and replaced them with loyal supporters.

Late in his first term as sheriff, the *Chattanooga Times* wrote that the city was in the midst of a "negro crime wave." For Shipp, facing reelection, the assault on Nevada Taylor couldn't have come at a worse time. On December 26, the *Times* ran the front-page headline: "Desperadoes Run Rampant in Chattanooga; Negro Thugs Reach Climax of Boldness."

Shipp felt pressured to crack down on the "negro thugs," and the attack on Nevada Taylor—only two months short of the election—brought public passions to a fever pitch. Shipp needed a quick and satisfactory resolution to the Taylor rape.

Unfortunately, the victim was able to provide only the most general description of her attacker: he was about her height, or maybe a little taller; he wore black clothes and had a hat; his arms were muscular; and he had a "soft, kind voice." Although she thought the man was a Negro, she was unsure, as she never got a good look at him.

The investigation was at a standstill. Although every person in the area of the attack had been questioned, no witnesses had been found. Everyone pointed out how incredibly dark it had been the night of the rape. Bloodhounds followed the scent left by the rapist on the victim's clothes, but lost the trail at the streetcar tracks. The only piece of evidence recovered was a leather strap, twenty-five inches long and a little less than an inch wide, with a split in one end and a narrow edge at the other. When the narrow end was inserted into the split, it produced a makeshift noose. Shipp showed the strap to Nevada Taylor, but she was unable to say whether it was the restraint used by her attacker. However, a comparison of the strap width to the red marks on Taylor's neck confirmed that it most likely was used on her. Unfortunately, the sheriff had no idea to whom the strap belonged.

The Reward

Sheriff Shipp was desperate. With every passing hour, the likelihood of finding credible evidence or witnesses decreased. The local newspapers published detailed accounts of the crime and the struggling investigation, adding to the public outcry. Shipp announced a $50 reward to anyone providing information leading to the arrest and conviction of the assailant. By that evening, thanks to generous contributions from community members, the total reward stood at $375—more than many citizens of Chattanooga earned in an entire year.

The reward seemed to jog the memory of Will Hixson, a white man who worked near the scene of the crime. Hixson called the sheriff to verify the size of the reward; satisfied it was legitimate, Hixson claimed that he was at the trolley station near Taylor's stop the night of the rape. According to Hixson, a black man was standing nearby "twirling a leather strap around his finger." A few minutes after six, a streetcar came by and Hixson could make out the man's face by its lights, a man to whom he had given a match earlier that day. Hixson said the man fled when he realized he had been seen. About half an hour later, Nevada Taylor's trolley arrived. Hixson identified the strap recovered by Sheriff Shipp as identical to the one he saw the black man twirling the night of the rape. Although he didn't know the black man's name, Hixson assured the sheriff that he'd be able to identify him if he saw him again.

The Arrest

The sheriff and Hixson spent an hour looking for the suspect, without success. Later that evening, Hixson called Sheriff Shipp again; he had spotted the man walking around town with another black man. The sheriff and his deputies rushed to meet Hixson, then began searching the homes nearby. They found a black man who fit the victim's description:

Ed Johnson. Hixson confirmed that Johnson was the man he had seen near the scene of the rape, and Johnson was arrested and immediately charged.

Back at the jail, a confused and frightened Ed Johnson repeatedly denied any involvement in the rape. He asserted and reasserted his alibi: he was miles away from the scene of the crime, having a drink at the Last Chance Saloon. Johnson said a dozen men could vouch for him, most of them black men who frequented the saloon, and provided the sheriff with a list of the alibi witnesses. Shipp personally questioned Johnson for more than three hours. According to local newspapers, Johnson was "subjected to some severe sweating and tested in many ways." Much to Shipp's chagrin, Johnson maintained his innocence.

Ed Johnson was a man of no great importance in Chattanooga. With just a fourth-grade education, he was said to be "not an intelligent" person. Unmarried, childless, at twenty-four he was a carpenter who had worked much of the past year building and roofing houses. In the evenings he would do odd jobs, cleaning and tending pool tables at the Last Chance Saloon. The only family he had were his mother, "a Christian woman," his father, nicknamed Skinbone, and his sister. To the local community, Johnson was just a black man who had raped a white woman, a crime punishable by death.

The Mob

News of Johnson's arrest spread like wildfire. A large group met at a local saloon, then made their way to the county jail, fifteen hundred strong, brandishing guns and ropes. They demanded Johnson be handed over; Shipp's deputies told the mob that he was not even in the jail, but had been moved to another facility. Unconvinced, the mob launched a barrage of stones, bricks, and pieces of iron; soon, every glass window in the jail was broken. Leaders of the mob grabbed a nearby steel post and began battering the front door. Other men grabbed sledgehammers from the local hardware store and attempted to dislodge the hinges that secured the steel door to the walls. By 9:30 p.m., the mob had nearly destroyed the steel door and could see the deputies inside, guns drawn.

At that volatile moment, Hamilton County judge Sam McReynolds arrived on the scene. At thirty-five, Judge McReynolds was the youngest judge in Hamilton County. McReynolds despised mob violence and believed in upholding the rule of law, but he was also a politically ambitious man who was dangerously close to the time for reelection. He chose his words carefully as he addressed the crowd.

Men, the Negro suspected of assaulting the young lady at St. Elmo is not here. He has been sent away to Knoxville. You might search the jail all night and you would not find him. I appeal to you as a friend, and I am sure you are all friends of mine, to quietly disperse to your homes and refrain from violence. The accused rapist is not here. . . . I know that you want justice and punishment. I do as well. But this is not the way. . . . I have called for a special session of the county grand jury. . . . Following an indictment, I will give the criminal trial precedence over all other trials. I hope that before week's end, the rapist will be convicted, under sentence of death, and executed according to law before the setting of Sunday's sun.

In fact, Judge McReynolds had ordered Sheriff Shipp to move Johnson, fearing a lynching, but had actually ordered Johnson moved to Nashville, not Knoxville, misleading the crowd to prevent any possible interception. To convince the skeptics, the judge allowed the mob to choose several representatives to enter the jail and confirm Johnson's absence. They searched for forty minutes without finding Ed Johnson. The mob slowly left the badly damaged jail; no one was arrested for the damage done. Even though they had not seized the prisoner, they had sent a powerful warning to Sheriff Shipp and Judge McReynolds: quick conviction and quick execution, or the mob would take matters into their own hands.

The Identification

Not satisfied with Hixson's identification alone, Shipp wanted some corroborating evidence. He asked Nevada Taylor to travel to Nashville to take a look at the man charged with attacking her. Shipp directed her to a special room, designed for eyewitness identifications. Shipp brought Johnson and one other young black man into the room, where a bright light was trained on them, making it impossible for them to see the witnesses. The sheriff had the men speak and walk around. Nevada Taylor carefully studied the men, their voices, their movements, their clothing.

"Does either one of them look familiar?" Shipp asked.

Taylor said that the man on the left [Johnson] was "like the man as I remembered him. He has the same soft, kind voice."

"Are you sure that he is the man?" Shipp asked again.

"From that Negro's general figure, height, and weight, from his voice, as I can distinctly remember it, from his manner of movement and action, and from the clothing he wears, it is my best knowledge and belief that the man who stood on your left [Johnson] was the one who assaulted me."

That was good enough for Shipp. He sent a telegram to Judge McReynolds: "Nevada Taylor has identified suspect. Proceed with grand jury."

However, Shipp was concerned that the evidence against Johnson was still rather weak; a confession would help sew the case up. The sheriff was determined to get a confession. After being beaten and denied food and water, Johnson would still not confess, holding steadfast to his story: he had not raped Nevada Taylor.

The Charges

Judge McReynolds began grand jury proceedings as soon as he received Shipp's telegram, believing time was of the essence to prevent an outbreak of violence. The grand jury was to evaluate the prosecution's evidence and decide if there was probable cause for the case to advance to trial. The grand jury, composed of twelve white men purportedly chosen at random from property and voting records, heard Hixson's identification and Taylor's identification; they returned with a unanimous indictment of Johnson.

Judge McReynolds held a private meeting with Sheriff Shipp and Hamilton County district attorney Madison Whitaker. Such a private meeting would be prohibited today by the American Bar Association's code of professional conduct as "ex parte" (private) communications between a judge and an attorney in an ongoing case, but in 1906 such meetings were both acceptable and commonplace. The men agreed on several key points: First, the trial must take place as soon as possible, perhaps within the week, as it was an election year and McReynolds had promised the people swift justice. Second, there was the issue of security. Worried about another mob attack, the judge said he'd ask the governor for assistance, and the sheriff agreed to ask the police department for men to help guard the prisoner. Third, Johnson must be defended by a white attorney; a black lawyer would undoubtedly face the wrath of the mob. Tennessee was one of the few states at the time requiring appointed counsel in capital cases.

The Lawyers

The actual task of appointing counsel was left in the hands of Judge McReynolds; he appointed three: Robert T. Cameron, W. G. M. Thomas, and Lewis Shepherd.

Cameron was a lawyer not known for his skill or success in the courtroom. In fact, he had only tried a handful of cases, all involving small civil disputes. He spent most of his time finding clients for "big name" attorneys who would cut him a slice of the profits if one of his referrals produced a courtroom win. Because Cameron was considered little more than a paralegal, there was little doubt he was ill-equipped to handle a case of this magnitude.

W. G. M. Thomas, on the other hand, was an accomplished trial attorney. However, all of his success came from high-profile civil litigation. A Vanderbilt grad, he and his brother had a prominent firm specializing in defending insurance companies. He had little to no experience in criminal cases, much less death penalty cases, and was stunned by his appointment.

Shepherd was the sole source of criminal trial experience on the Johnson defense team, and his presence was entirely the result of his own efforts. After hearing of the appointment of the other attorneys, he approached Judge McReynolds and told him that the Johnson case was important and that the judge needed to appoint a seasoned member of the criminal bar to help out. McReynolds agreed and promptly appointed Shepherd.

Shepherd, a former judge, prosecutor, and experienced trial lawyer, doubtless knew criminal law and procedure better than anyone else in the county and was likely the most prominent member of the local bar. A flamboyant character, he lived for the challenge of the unwinnable case.

Judge McReynolds told the defense they had a week to prepare for trial. The attorneys were shocked. They needed at least a month! The judge was unswayed. One week—be prepared, he said, adding his personal opinion that there wasn't much to debate in this case anyway.

With Shepherd's guidance the defense team mapped out a plan: interview their client; visit the crime scene to get an idea of lighting conditions and try to uncover more witnesses; find alibi witnesses who would support Johnson's story; and learn all the evidence that the prosecution had against their client. The defense team soon found themselves the target of threats and intimidation. Their neighbors, churches, clients— even family members—were furious with them for taking the case. Both Cameron and Thomas published public statements emphasizing that they were required by Judge McReynolds to take the case and begging for public acceptance to complete the task that was forced upon them. Shepherd was unfazed, accustomed as he was to ruffling feathers.

Shepherd recognized that the defense team would need help gathering evidence and witness information, especially from members of the black community, who would be apprehensive about coming forward to aid Johnson. So he turned to Noah Parden, Chattanooga's premier black attorney.

Shepherd had the utmost respect for Parden. The two had worked together on several occasions and were not only colleagues but friends. Parden initially refused to have anything to do with the Johnson case. Aware of the potential consequences, he told Shepherd, "No, thank you . . . I like my practice here just fine." Any effort by a black attorney to help Ed Johnson would be seen by those high up in the Hamilton County justice system as an act of insubordination, a violation of the well-established Southern hierarchy. Any interference was unwelcome, especially from someone they considered socially and intellectually inferior, i.e., a black man.

Parden knew it was hard enough to make a decent living as a black attorney without having prosecutors, judges, and the police personally bent on destroying his career. However, after a couple hours spent in deep discussion with Shepherd, Parden agreed to interview Johnson's alibi witnesses and convince them to testify. His only condition: he wanted his involvement in the case to remain an absolute secret. Shepherd agreed. He understood that Parden was risking not only his reputation but his livelihood.

The defense team repeatedly begged for more time, telling the judge they had not yet even interviewed their own client, but their requests were denied, McReynolds insisting that the trial take place as soon as possible to satisfy the public's demand for a swift punishment. Not until the day before the trial was to begin was the defense team finally able to speak with Johnson about the events of January 23. Shepherd and Thomas traveled to the Nashville jail and asked him to recount his activities on the night of the rape. The two lawyers listened intently to Johnson, who told them, "But I don't understand. I never done what they say. I swear to God I didn't. I never seen the woman they brought up here before. I didn't even know where she lived. I just want to go home." They believed him.

The Trial

In the early-morning hours of February 6, 1906, a police patrol wagon, curtains drawn, made its way through downtown Chattanooga, surrounded by a heavily armed escort. Ed Johnson was back, Chattanooga was ready for the trial; for many, it merely represented a formality preceding the execution.

By 9 a.m., the courtroom was packed. On the left side of the room, Hamilton County district attorney Madison "Matt" Whitaker and his assistants sat facing Judge McReynolds, while the defense team—Shepherd, Cameron, and Thomas—were seated at an identical table on the right. Ed Johnson was seated behind them, a sheriff's deputy on either side of him.

McReynolds banged his gavel and asked if both sides were ready to proceed. The state was ready, but the defense once again said they needed more time. Thomas stood and addressed the court, saying he wanted the record to reflect that the defense team had privately been told by the judge that any motion for continuance or change of venue would be denied.

Even with the greatest diligence, we have not been able to investigate every phase of the case or to run down all reported facts. We have worked day and night in the interest of truth and justice. I slept one hour one night and went forty-eight hours without removing my shoes.

Your Honor knows what occurred between us yesterday. As appointees for a man arrested for the worst crime known to men, whose life is involved in the issue in the interest of justice, we do not believe we have had sufficient time to develop the facts to our satisfaction.

We do not believe that this is the time or Chattanooga the place, in view of [the attempted lynching], for this trial to take place. The defendant ought to be tried at a later date and in some other county. We argue this not for the sake of delay, but that justice may be done.

We have understood that Your Honor does not agree with us on any of these points. We, therefore, bow to Your Honor's view in the matter.

With the defense requests denied yet again, jury selection began, and in short order twelve white, male faces stared at the defendant from the jury box. Although the U.S. Supreme Court had ruled that blacks could not intentionally be excluded from the jury pool, no black man had ever served on a criminal jury in Hamilton County. Women were considered emotionally unfit for jury service. Both sides waived opening statements and proceeded without delay to the production of evidence and witnesses.

The prosecution's first witness was the victim, Nevada Taylor. The courtroom was silent as she slowly made her way to the witness stand. Whitaker thanked her for her courage: "If it were up to me, I would not require your testimony in such an open forum before so many people. But the law states that every criminal has a right to face his accuser in public court. It is a law that should be amended." With that Whitaker began his direct examination. The audience listened in sympathetic silence. After some preliminary questions Whitaker moved to the events of January 23, 1906:

WHITAKER: Okay, Miss Taylor, I'm going to ask you now about the night of January twenty-third. Are you ready for that?

TAYLOR: Yes.

WHITAKER: Tell us, the best you can, what happened that night. Walk us through your evening.

TAYLOR: On the night of January twenty-third, I left work at six and went to St. Elmo on the car, leaving the transfer station at six. I reached what is known as the Cemetery Station at nearly six thirty o'clock and started home, a distance, if it is measured, of nearly two and one-half blocks. I heard something behind me, but I did not think they were following me. I felt the strap around my neck before I thought anyone was going to do me any harm. I was by myself and was going toward the cemetery gate along the sidewalk on the west side of the street, near the broad fence which surrounds the marble yard.

WHITAKER: What happened then, Miss Taylor?

TAYLOR: I reached up and pulled the strap loose and screamed. He pulled the strap tight.

WHITAKER: Is this that strap? [Whitaker handed Taylor the strap that had been found.]

TAYLOR: I think that strap is the one he used.

WHITAKER: Please continue. What happened next?

TAYLOR: He pulled me back to the fence, a distance of ten or twelve feet, and then threw me over the fence. I swung clear of the boards. I know I didn't touch them. The Negro, for I could see it was a Negro man, then got over the fence. I pulled the strap loose again and screamed again. Then the Negro put the end of the strap through the hole in the other end and pulled it tight around my neck. He then put his hand on my face to see if my tongue had been forced out of my mouth and then choked me until I was insensible. Before he choked me with his hand, he waited a minute as if he were listening to find out if anybody were coming. He then told me in a kind, gentle voice that if I screamed again, he would cut my throat. I saw him face-to-face by the dim light cast by the block signal box on the pole owned by the Rapid Transit Company. It is from this light that I got my best view of him.

WHITAKER: And then you blacked out?

TAYLOR: Yes, sir.

WHITAKER: What do you remember when you regained consciousness?

TAYLOR: No one came by that I know of at the time. I reached home after coming to myself about six forty-five o'clock, my home being about one and a half blocks from the scene of the crime. My father, two brothers, and three sisters were at home when I got there, and I told them what happened. They telephoned Sheriff Shipp, and Dr. Wilson was summoned to attend me.

WHITAKER: Do you remember anything else about the Negro brute who assaulted you?

TAYLOR: He had on a dark sack coat.

WHITAKER: Miss Taylor, would you know the man again if you were to see him?

TAYLOR: I think so.

WHITAKER: Is that man present in this courtroom today?

TAYLOR: I believe *he* is the man [pointing to Ed Johnson, the only black person in the courtroom].

Whitaker then questioned Taylor about her trip to Nashville and her identification of Johnson.

TAYLOR: I went to Nashville with Sheriff Shipp and saw two Negroes brought out in the sheriff's office where I could see them. I sat in the obscurity and they were in the light. Sheriff Shipp talked to them, and one of them, from his voice, his size, his face, and everything combined, I thought was the Negro who assaulted me. He, at first, had the same soft voice he used in talking to me, and later he changed it, making it deeper. I looked at the Negroes and listened to them. Though this Negro tried to change his voice, I believe that I recognized it. His hat, the one he had on the night of the assault, and the one he had on at the Nashville jail, was a soft, dark hat. The brim looked like it had been rolled at one time and had become straightened out.

WHITAKER: Miss Taylor, do you have any doubt in your mind that this Negro is the brute who assaulted you?

TAYLOR: There is no trouble in my mind about this Negro being the right man. I want the guilty man punished and I don't want an innocent man punished.

Whitaker again thanked Taylor for her courage in testifying and told the judge he had no further questions. McReynolds asked the defense if they had any questions. Thomas rose and slowly approached Taylor, aware that he must tread softly when dealing with her. Shepherd had warned him that the defense team must not attack any portion of the victim's testimony, nor belittle her in any way. Instead, Thomas—chosen because he had the least intimidating demeanor among Johnson's attorneys—was to elicit information from Taylor that would be helpful to the defense later on. Before beginning his cross-examination, he apologized profusely for having to question her about the horrific event, assuring her that it was painful for him to do so. Thomas asked Taylor what time it was when she stepped from the trolley car the night of the attack.

TAYLOR: About six thirty o'clock.
THOMAS: Your house is how far from the station?
TAYLOR: Two and one-half blocks.
THOMAS: Are there any buildings or trees blocking the line of sight between your house and the train station?
TAYLOR: There are a few trees between them. But you can see my father's house from the depot.
THOMAS: Could you see your house from the station that night?
TAYLOR: I could see the lights from the house. It was too dark to see the house itself.

And with that modest and careful cross-examination, Nevada Taylor was dismissed. The courtroom had been quiet and respectful throughout her testimony, but, for the balance of the trial, the spectators acted as if this death penalty case were a sporting event, cheering when the prosecution made a good point, booing when the defense attempted to counter. The circuslike atmosphere drew no comment from Judge McReynolds; not once did he reprimand the observers or assert control over the proceedings.

The prosecution next called Taylor's treating physician, Dr. Wilson. Wilson confirmed that the strap in evidence matched the marks left on Taylor's neck.

Will Hixson was next. His testimony was vital to the prosecution's case—he provided the link between Ed Johnson and the leather strap used in the attack on Taylor.

WHITAKER: How old are you, Mr. Hixson?
HIXSON: Twenty-two.
WHITAKER: Where do you work?

HIXSON: Chattanooga Medicine Company.

WHITAKER: Have you ever seen the defendant in this case, Ed Johnson, before?

HIXSON: I believe so.

WHITAKER: Have you ever seen this strap before?

HIXSON: That one or one like it.

WHITAKER: Tell the jury what you told the sheriff.

HIXSON: At five fifty o'clock on the evening of the assault, I saw the defendant with a strap in his hand closely resembling the strap you showed me, near the scene of the crime. I know the Negro's face, for I have known him for about a month when he worked on the rock church four or five blocks away from where I saw him that night.

WHITAKER: Wasn't it very dark?

HIXSON: I saw him in the light made by two electric cars which passed each other at the Cemetery Station, where Miss Taylor alighted from the car. I saw his face well and could not be mistaken in it. This defendant here is the Negro I saw. The Negro looked at me full in the face for a minute and then turned away and walked up toward the cemetery gate. I saw him before, on Monday morning, for he asked me for a match at that time. I helped find Johnson, for I remembered seeing the Negro with the strap on the night of the crime. I hunted for him from Wednesday morning at ten until Thursday at one or two. I finally saw him at the rock church talking to a Negro.

WHITAKER: What did you do then, Mr. Hixson?

HIXSON: I telephoned Sheriff Shipp and he came out with some deputies. However, I followed the Negro, who turned and walked away when he saw me. He led me to Red Row [a black residential area], where I lost him. The sheriff and I found the Negro to whom Johnson was talking, in Red Row, and arrested him. We then went on and found Johnson riding on a wagon in front of Foust's stockyard. Deputy Kirkland arrested him.

When Cameron stood to cross-examine Hixson, the gloves came off. Cameron lit into Hixson, attacking not only the witness's testimony but his motivation for giving such testimony. Wasn't the $375 reward the only reason Hixson had come forward? Cameron challenged. That wasn't true, Hixson answered.

CAMERON: So you don't want the reward?

HIXSON: Of course I do.

Cameron also questioned Hixson about a conversation he had had the day after the assault on Taylor with Harvey McConnell, a black man who supervised work at the church where Ed Johnson was employed part-time. During this conversation, Cameron asked, didn't Ed Johnson walk by? Hixson denied knowing McConnell or ever speaking with him. Hixson also denied telling McConnell or anyone else before Ed Johnson's arrest that he would collect the $375 reward.

A shaken Hixson was excused and the prosecution called their next witness, Sheriff Joseph Shipp. On direct examination Shipp gave the jurors a quick run-through of the entire case. He detailed the attack, identified the leather strap, recounted the information conveyed to him by Hixson leading to Johnson's arrest, told how Johnson had supposedly changed the pitch of his voice when he'd realized Taylor was listening to him for identification purposes, and told the jury of the apparent inconsistencies in Johnson's story.

> **SHIPP:** The first story Johnson told me was he had gone to the Last Chance Saloon the night of January twenty-third about six and remained there until close-up. Later, he said he had gone to the church Tuesday morning but it was too cold to work. So he went to the saloon at twelve and remained there until it closed up at night. In Nashville, Johnson said he went to the saloon at four and remained there until ten.

On cross-examination, the sheriff did concede that Taylor's identification of Johnson was "not exactly positive." He also confirmed that, even under a great deal of pressure, Johnson had firmly maintained his innocence, admitting his frustration at his inability to elicit a confession from Johnson.

The state's final witnesses were two of the sheriff's deputies, Kirkland and Baker. Their testimony paralleled Sheriff Shipp's concerning the leather strap and Johnson's different stories about his alibi the night of the attack. When the prosecutor finished with the second deputy, he turned to Judge McReynolds and declared that the state rested.

Even though the hour was late and the parties were tired, Judge McReynolds was determined to speed the trial along. He directed the defense to call its first witness. Shepherd stood and announced that Ed Johnson would testify on his own behalf. Shepherd began with basic questions about Johnson's background. He wanted the jury to have some sense of Ed Johnson as a man rather than as an accused rapist. Shepherd then moved to the night of the crime. Johnson passionately reasserted his innocence, claiming he had never even seen Taylor until that very morning in court when she'd taken the stand to testify, as he was completely unable to see her during the lineup. He denied telling Sheriff Shipp and his deputies different stories about his whereabouts the day of the attack. He maintained that Sheriff Shipp and his deputies just misunderstood what he was telling them.

SHEPHERD: Tell the jury how you spent [the day of the rape].

JOHNSON: I had been working on the rock church at St. Elmo since the day after Labor Day. On Monday, it rained and we did not go to work that day. On Tuesday, I went out to the church. I got there before eight and left there about eight. It was too cold to work. I stayed around home for an hour or better. Then I went up to the Last Chance Saloon and stayed there until about two. I went back home and came back to the saloon about four thirty in the afternoon. I stayed there until ten that night. At noon that day, the saloon owner's son sent me over to his house to water a pony. Then I helped fix some chicken nests until about twelve thirty, and I came back to the saloon. At two, I left the saloon and went home and got dinner. I got back at four thirty and stayed until ten that night.

SHEPHERD: What did you do at the saloon?

JOHNSON: I worked for the porter of the pool room. I kept pool tables there two or three times a week.

SHEPHERD: What did you do that Tuesday?

JOHNSON: When I got there, John Duckworth [a deputy sheriff], Jeff Lee, Mr. Jones [the owner], Uncle Ike Kelly, Joe Graves, and perhaps others were already there. Jeff asked me to fix the fire upstairs because it was getting cold in the pool room. Mr. Jones told me to light the lamps.

SHEPHERD: How much money did you make that night?

JOHNSON: Maybe one dollar or a dollar fifty.

SHEPHERD: Did you ever leave the saloon that night for any extended period of time?

JOHNSON: Mr. Jones sent me out for firewood a couple of times.

Johnson provided the names of nine different individuals who could verify that he was at the saloon throughout the evening of January 23. Johnson also denied ownership of the leather strap—testifying that he didn't own a strap, or even a belt, only his suspenders.

During cross-examination, prosecutor Whitaker went on the attack. He questioned Johnson about changing his voice when he realized he was being identified by the victim. Johnson said he "didn't notice or remember" changing his voice, although he did admit that he was aware of her presence and her purpose. Johnson also denied knowing Hixson or ever associating with him. According to the defendant, he had never asked Hixson for a match.

It was 8 p.m. by the time the prosecutor was through with Johnson. Judge McReynolds, however, did not call for a recess, directing the defense to call their next witness. So began the string of witnesses who would attempt to corroborate Johnson's whereabouts the night of the attack.

First up was the bailiff, Jeff Lee, who testified that he was at the saloon from 4 to 8 p.m. and that Johnson was with him the whole time. On cross-examination, however, Lee admitted that it would have been possible for Johnson to leave the saloon for up to thirty minutes without anyone noticing.

Four other defense witnesses followed, all with similar testimony: they had seen, even spoken with, Ed Johnson at the Last Chance Saloon on January 23, during and around the time of the attack on Nevada Taylor. Under cross-examination, the witnesses stood their ground. After the fifth alibi witness testified, Judge McReynolds called it a day. Everyone was excused for the evening, the proceedings to resume at eight thirty the following morning.

During the second day of testimony, the defense produced seventeen additional witnesses. The first eight were alibi witnesses with testimony similar to that of the five who had testified the night before: Johnson was at the Last Chance Saloon throughout the evening of January 23. On cross-examination, the prosecution took issue with the clocks in the Last Chance Saloon, which the witnesses had relied upon as the basis for their testimony. Prosecutor Whitaker attempted to cast doubt upon the accuracy and function of the clocks.

With testimony from thirteen alibi witnesses on the record, the defense thought it was time to move along to other aspects of the case. They would begin by attempting to discredit the testimony of Will Hixson. The defense called Harvey McConnell, an elderly black man described locally as "a Negro given much respect" in both the white and black communities. McConnell was an amiable fellow and an honest businessman; people not only respected him but liked him as well. Shepherd began the direct examination.

SHEPHERD: Do you know or have you met Will Hixson?
MCCONNELL: Yes, Judge [the local community referred to Lewis Shepherd as "judge" out of deference to his brief stint on the bench]. I know him.

SHEPHERD: Where do you know him from?

McCONNELL: Well, Judge, the morning before Ed was arrested—

SHEPHERD: That also would be the day after the St. Elmo crime?

McCONNELL: Yes, sir, Judge. Will Hixson came to my coal yard and inquired of me concerning a man working at the "rock" church. I told him I know the men only by sight and not by name, except one. That is Ed Johnson. I know Ed pretty well. That's when Will Hixson told me that Ed was the man the sheriff wanted for the outrage the night before.

SHEPHERD: And what did you say?

McCONNELL: It can't be Johnson. He's like me. He may have enough sense to do such a thing, but he isn't brave enough.

SHEPHERD: What did Will Hixson say?

McCONNELL: He wanted to know what Ed Johnson looked like and I was describing him when Ed and another fella walked by the office headed toward town. I pointed Johnson out to Hixson.

SHEPHERD: And then what?

McCONNELL: Hixson left the office and followed behind Johnson toward the city.

McConnell's son, Cicero, was also present during the elder McConnell's conversation with Hixson. Cicero was next to take the stand. His testimony confirmed every detail of his father's story.

To the surprise of many in the courtroom, the defense team's next witness was one of their own: defense attorney W. G. M. Thomas. Thomas testified that Harvey McConnell had told the defense attorneys about his conversation with Hixson, and the story McConnell relayed to the attorneys was identical to his testimony moments ago. Thomas also testified about his interactions with Hixson.

SHEPHERD: What did you tell Will Hixson?

THOMAS: I reasoned with the young man concerning the vital part of his testimony and urged him to adhere only to the truth.

SHEPHERD: What was Will Hixson's response?

THOMAS: He denied in toto every part of Harvey McConnell's story. He even volunteered to accompany me to face Mr. McConnell. I accepted his offer, and we went to the coal yard.

SHEPHERD: What happened?

THOMAS: Mr. McConnell and Will Hixson stood face-to-face and Mr. McConnell repeated the same story we heard here today.

Thomas continued his account of what followed, describing how Hixson's head hung lower and lower as McConnell spoke. Hixson never looked McConnell in the eye during the encounter, nor did he ever deny the truth of McConnell's words.

The defense then called two employees of the Lookout Mountain Incline Railway Station, a conductor and a ticket agent. Both testified how it was unusually dark the evening of January 23: "one of the darkest nights of the year." So dark that the conductor had trouble telling if a person was white or black. The men also testified that it was already dark by six thirty, the time of the attack. This testimony called into question not only Hixson's identification of Johnson—"from a good distance away"—but also, ever so subtly, the identification of Johnson by Nevada Taylor.

And, with that last bit of testimony, Lewis Shepherd rested on behalf of the defense.

It was now the prosecution's turn to call rebuttal witnesses, to refute or nullify the testimony of those called by the defense. First, Whitaker called three witnesses, all of whom testified as to Will Hixson's good character.

Whitaker also called a representative of the Chattanooga Electric Railway. This witness testified that the ride from the Last Chance Saloon to the scene of the attack was a brief one, implying that Ed Johnson could have left the saloon, raped Nevada Taylor, and returned quickly enough that his absence would have gone unnoticed. The defense pointed out that the cars only ran every thirty minutes, and, to perpetrate the crime, Johnson would have had to have taken the trolley after Taylor's and then waited for the next trolley to return. This would have taken well over an hour, not at all the brief trip suggested by the prosecution.

Next the prosecution called the local clock salesman/repairman, and thus began the chaos of the clocks. There were so many contradictions as to when, where, and which clocks were and were not installed in the Last Chance Saloon that one of jurors actually broke down in tears.

After a brief break, one of the jurors, chosen during the recess as foreman, stood and asked Judge McReynolds if Miss Taylor could please return to the witness stand; the jury wished to reevaluate some of her answers. This was a remarkable request. Jurors—much like children—were to be seen and not heard, their role passive, not proactive. Even more unusual was Judge McReynolds's response: he granted the request. Nevada Taylor was to return to the courtroom immediately.

After reminding her that she was still under oath, McReynolds turned the proceedings over to the jurors. Juror Wrenn, the foreperson, asked that Johnson put on a black slouch hat and stand directly in front of the witness. Over the defense team's strenuous objections, McReynolds ordered Johnson to comply with the jury's wishes.

As Johnson stood there, mere inches from his accuser, juror Wrenn questioned Taylor.

> **WRENN:** Miss Taylor, tell us again—is that Negro the one that attacked you?
>
> **TAYLOR:** To the best of my knowledge and belief, he is the same man.
>
> **WRENN:** Miss Taylor, can you state positively that this Negro is the one who assaulted you?
>
> **TAYLOR:** I will not swear that he is the man, but I believe he is the Negro who assaulted me.

At that moment another juror, by the name of Beardon, jumped to his feet. Tears streaming down his face and his voice filled with emotion, he addressed Taylor.

> **BEARDON:** In God's name, Miss Taylor, tell us positively—is that the guilty Negro? Can you say it? Can you swear it?

Now Taylor was shaking, her lips trembling. She closed her eyes and raised her left hand toward heaven.

> **TAYLOR:** Listen to me. I would not take the life of an innocent man. But before God, I believe this is the guilty Negro.

Not even the defendant, with his life on the line, could hold back tears as he stood so close to the emotionally overwrought young woman. The jurors were agitated, some openly sobbing. One red-faced juror leapt from his seat and lunged toward Johnson, his fellow jurors struggling to restrain him as he pointed at Johnson yelling, "If I could get at him, I'd tear his heart out right now!"

It was clearly time for a break; the judge ordered a ninety-minute recess, telling the attorneys they were to be prepared for closing arguments upon their return.

When they reconvened later that afternoon, the defense made the unusual request that the case be given to the jury without argument. Shepherd, the seasoned trial attorney, was deeply concerned that the prosecution's closing argument would further inflame the passions of the jury—alarmingly charged as it was. However, the state refused. Judge McReynolds instructed each side that they would have one hour and forty-five minutes to present their closing argument. The time could be divided in any manner counsel saw fit. The prosecution would begin, followed by the defense, and then the prosecution would be allowed to have the final word—as they carried the burden of proof.

Assistant District Attorney E. S. Daniels, who had been assisting District Attorney Whitaker, slowly and deliberately turned to page 183 of the large bound volume he carried, the Tennessee Criminal Code. He began his closing argument by reading to the jury the definition of rape. Daniels then launched into a summary of the case, highlighting the key points of evidence for the prosecution, while instructing the jury to ignore testimony from the witnesses supporting Ed Johnson. They were, after all, men of "less than honorable character who fabricated an alibi based on a clock that did not exist."

When Daniels took a seat forty-five minutes later, Lewis Shepherd rose for the defense. Shepherd wasted no time, pouring all his outrage and frustration into an hour-long tirade against the judge, the sheriff, the prosecutors, the state's witnesses, and the Hamilton County justice system in general:

> This case wasn't about justice. This case wasn't about finding the truth. This case wasn't about preserving the rule of law. Justice and truth and the rule of law have been trampled on in this court and in this very case.
>
> I do not flatter myself that by oratory I could paint this great crime in blacker colors than it has been made by the statements of witnesses. Neither could I by oratory or rhetoric convince you of the innocence of this defendant better than can the language of the witnesses.
>
> It was an atrocious crime, and by it a good, a pure young lady has been despoiled of her virginity. But did this Negro commit the deed?

Shepherd continued, focusing directly on Judge McReynolds: "The rulings of this court have been inimical to my client and biased in favor of the state." He reeled off a lengthy list of offenses: denying a continuance (thus forcing the defense to proceed in a capital case unprepared), denying a change of venue (refusing to hold the trial in a location other than Chattanooga, where Johnson's jury pool was prejudiced), and blatant bias.

Shepherd returned to the defense table and picked up a fragile, well-worn book, written by a seventeenth-century English barrister. Shepherd often demonstrated his vast knowledge of history and love for reading by incorporating the two into his closing arguments. He read a passage from the book, mandating that all judges remain pure, then shifted focus. This time his ire was directed at the prosecution. Conviction over truth; that was the theme of Shepherd's assault on the state. After a barrage of general accusations, the closing argument took a personal turn. Shepherd lit into District Attorney Whitaker, calling him a "stooge for the lynch mob." There was no kindness reserved for Sheriff Shipp, whom Shepherd claimed had only one agenda: "Arresting Ed Johnson may not avenge this despicable crime. Convicting and condemning Ed Johnson may not achieve justice. But it does get you reelected."

Shepherd reassessed the evidence against his client, focusing specifically on Hixson's identification and the darkness on the night of the assault. Every witness testified as to how unusually dark it was; two railroad workers testified that they couldn't even tell if persons were white or black. "This evidence is without dispute." The only conclusion to be drawn, Shepherd told the jury, is that it would have been impossible for Hixson to identify Johnson from such a distance. The same was true, Shepherd said, for Taylor:

> I have no argument that Miss Taylor believes or wants to believe that the defendant was the perpetrator of this crime. But the night was so dark and she states that the crime happened so speedily that the victim of the outrage could not have been cool enough in the hour of the attack to so closely watch the assailant as later to identify him.

Shepherd accused Hixson of making up his entire story for the sole purpose of claiming the $375 reward. Shepherd reminded the jury of the McConnells' testimony and of the fact that Hixson couldn't look McConnell in the eye when confronted.

W. G. M. Thomas finished the closing arguments for the defense. The polar opposite of Shepherd, Thomas was gentle and soft-spoken. He didn't attack or condemn, rather he pled for mercy, for the life of Ed Johnson. His argument was described in the local news as "one of the most remarkable arguments ever delivered in a Tennessee Courtroom."

> This is a solemn hour. The most solemn hour that has ever met me in my professional life I feel is here now while I do the last service I can do for my poor client in this case.

Were I not convinced of the absolute innocence of the Negro sitting over there, I would be there silent in my chair or over at the other side aiding the attorney general to fasten the guilt upon him. Log chains couldn't pull me and make me stand before twelve men of my home and say a word for that man did I not believe in his innocence.

I am a lawyer and, appointed by the Honorable Court, have a sworn duty to perform, and I am determined that if that boy is convicted and sent to the gallows, his blood shall not be on my hands.

I repeat, I have done my duty in this case. I have risen from my bed at four in the morning and started out my search for the truth. Myself and Judge Shepherd have freely used our own time and money to make a trip to Nashville solely in pursuit of duty. And here I am now doing the last act that can be done in his defense.

Am I not interested in finding the right man—in finding the guilty scoundrel? For years, that old man sitting over there, his sons, and his daughters have had care of the graves where sleep my wife and little baby, the only little family I ever had, and who died a few years ago. I carried a wife and child to that cemetery tended by that old man—and now I say to him and his beautiful daughter [Thomas stands directly in front of Nevada Taylor and her father] that I am ready to do anything I can to help you find the guilty scoundrel.

If Ed Johnson is the man, then hang him. If he is not, don't let an innocent man hang for the deed of a scoundrel.

I am a firm believer in the Book of Books and in the God of the Bible. Only Ed Johnson, my God, and your God know whether Ed Johnson committed that nefarious crime. And I believe there is one other being that knows—that is the real criminal. Where he is, I do not know.

In the face of twelve good men from my own home, all of whom I know and most of whom I know intimately, I could not stand here and ask the acquittal of a man I believed to be guilty. My home is here. Every friend that has ever been a friend to me is here. My old mother lives now on McCallie Avenue and she is there while I am here talking to you. I have two sisters and three little nieces living in this city.

I could not be so false as to the womanhood dear to me and to the mothers, wives, and sisters dear to me, as to stand here and ask you to acquit this man if there were any reasonable certainty of his guilt. If I could, I'd help you find the truth in this solemn hour. That's why I'm here, I want to help you.

Thomas then turned to the evidence. He said the prosecution's case boiled down to "flimsy" circumstantial evidence that "does not hold true." Thomas specifically addressed the testimony of Nevada Taylor. With the careful and sympathetic disclaimer that no woman should ever have to suffer the ordeal that Taylor had been forced to endure, Thomas pointed out the weaknesses in her testimony. Using the court reporter's notes, Thomas read back key passages:

"I believe he is the man."

"To the best of my knowledge and belief he is the same man."

"I will not swear that he is the man, but I believe he is the Negro . . ."

Thomas was careful not to insinuate that Taylor was being untruthful. To the contrary, the testimony was meant to point out that Taylor *honestly* could not identify her attacker as Ed Johnson. Thomas commended Taylor for her inability to say that which she did not know to be the truth.

Thomas concluded the defense closing argument by discussing the testimony of the defendant. Ed Johnson had never changed his story—been confused perhaps, but never changed his story—and he had maintained his innocence throughout. And with that, Thomas sat.

District Attorney Whitaker rose and made a point of consoling Nevada Taylor before delivering the final argument. The *Chattanooga Times* summarized his closing comments:

> Nothing short of a reproduction could do justice to the great plea uttered by the District Attorney as he closed the case. It was masterly, almost cruelly denunciatory and most convincing.
>
> He pled for womanhood and girlhood of the country and rebuked the defense for asking the jury to believe the perjured testimony of a lot of "thugs, thieves and sots—the offscourings of hell"—in order to acquit a fiend guilty of despoiling the happiness and clouding the life of one of Chattanooga's fairest daughters.
>
> While he was applying some of his choicest epithets to the Negro witness, attorney Cameron arose and objected to the Attorney General's language. The objection was greeted with hisses audible in many directions.
>
> The District Attorney quickly retorted to the interruption, "You shouldn't object to the statement of truth if it's light you're after in the case"—an utterance that was approved by cheers.

Although he spoke at length, Whitaker didn't waste time rehashing facts and testimony the jury had already heard. Rather, he focused on the lost innocence of Nevada Taylor, the sinful ways of the defendant, and the grisly details of the crime itself. He finished by placing his hand on Taylor's shoulder and, looking directly at the jury, locking eyes with each individual as he said, "Send that black brute to the gallows and prove to the world that in Chattanooga and Hamilton County the law of the country does not countenance such terrible crimes, has not ceased to mete out the proper punishment for such horrible outrages."

A Foregone Conclusion

Judge McReynolds instructed the jury on the applicable law and sent them into their private deliberation room. Much to everyone's surprise, the jury would not reach a verdict that evening—four jurors were, apparently, not immediately convinced that Johnson was guilty beyond a reasonable doubt.

The jurors were not sequestered, and whatever doubts or misgivings the four holdouts harbored had vanished by nine the following morning. At 9:11, the jury foreman indicated that the jury had reached a verdict. By 9:24, all parties were waiting in the courtroom as the foreman handed the bailiff a single sheet of paper. The bailiff presented the paper to Judge McReynolds, who studied it briefly before returning it to the jury. He then asked, "Will the defendant please rise?" Ed Johnson and his attorneys stood. Judge McReynolds continued, "Mr. Jury Foreman, what is your verdict?"

"On the single count of rape, we, the jury, find the defendant, Ed Johnson, guilty."

In Tennessee, a rape conviction carried an automatic death sentence. News of the conviction quickly spread throughout the city.

McReynolds thanked the jury for their services and commended them on being "one of the finest" ever to sit in his courtroom.

It was time for the defense team to choose a course of action. The attorneys were divided, Shepherd believing it was the defense's duty to appeal the verdict. The others disagreed, saying an appeal would be useless, merely prolonging the inevitable execution. They also took issue with Shepherd's contention that it was their duty to appeal. As far as they were concerned, they had done their duty, represented Johnson to the best of their abilities, and were eager to disassociate themselves from the whole business. Thomas pointed out a third reason they shouldn't appeal the verdict: the lynch mob. The threat of a lynching had hung over the case from the beginning. There had been repeated warnings that any delay in Johnson's trial and execution would result in his lynching—and perhaps others as well. The debate continued until Shepherd, realizing his arguments were falling on deaf ears, suggested a different approach: leave the decision up to Ed Johnson.

In his letter to the public, published on February 10 by the *Chattanooga Times,* W. G. M. Thomas gave a detailed account of how a decision regarding an appeal was reached.

It was suggested that we ought to go to the jail and see the prisoner and lay the facts before him, and if he demanded an appeal, then he ought to have that right under the law. Judge Shepherd, Mr. Cameron and I went to the jail and spent a half hour with the man. We asked him if he felt that we had performed our duty in his defense, and he answered that he did not know what we could have done for him. I said: "Ed, we don't know whether you are the guilty man or not; but you and God know. The jury says you are the man."

His reply was: "Yes, they have put it on me, and I guess I have to take it, but I ain't guilty."

I then said to him: "Ed, your life has been saved up to this time, but the people believe now that the jury have acted, more than they ever did before, that you are the right man. They are outraged against you and even if you are innocent, as you say you are, we do not believe that we can save your life."

Judge Shepherd explained to him his right of appeal: that the Tennessee Supreme Court met in September next, that an appeal would stay the judgment until that time, that we did not see any reasonable grounds to suppose that the supreme court would reverse the sentence, and that we feared an appeal would cause mob violence against him.

I asked him if he had ever heard the story of "Old Dog Tray," and he said he had. I told him that old dog Tray lost his life because he was found in bad company, and I said: "Ed, the Last Chance Saloon is bad company if you are an innocent man, you, like old dog Tray, were found in bad company. Old dog Tray lost his life on that account, and it looks like you must lose your life on the same account. The jury would not believe your bad company. If you die, Ed, and you are innocent, your bad company will be the thing that kills you, because the jury refused to believe anything they said."

Without giving all that occurred at the jail, he said to us that he did not want to die by a mob; that he would do as we thought best. He said he would go over to the courthouse and tell the judge that he did not have anything more to say; that he was not the guilty man.

I want the people to know that the foregoing facts moved us to allow the law to take its course under the verdict of the jury and the judgment of Judge McReynolds.

It was just before 3 p.m. when Johnson, escorted by Chattanooga police and his attorneys, reentered the courtroom through the main doors. DA Whitaker entered the courtroom from the judge's private chambers. The prosecution was pleasantly surprised when Thomas rose on behalf of the defense and waived Johnson's right to appeal. Judge McReynolds moved to the sentencing. McReynolds would likely have sentenced Johnson to be hanged that night if it were up to him, but under Tennessee law, a person convicted of a capital offense was to be executed in no fewer than thirty days and no more than sixty days.

MCREYNOLDS: Will the defendant rise? You have been convicted of one of the most atrocious crimes known to the criminal law, and I now ask you, have you anything to say why sentence of death should not be passed upon you?

JOHNSON: No, sir. I haven't anything to say. The jury says that I am guilty, and I guess I will have to suffer for what somebody else has done.

MCREYNOLDS: Do you feel you have been given a fair trial?

JOHNSON: Everything I know of has been done for me. I guess I will be punished for another person's crime.

MCREYNOLDS: You have been ably represented and every effort has been made to find out the guilty party, and as before stated, I am satisfied that you are the guilty party. It is therefore the judgment and sentence of the law and of this court that the sheriff of Hamilton County take and safely keep you in the county jail of said county until Tuesday, March thirteenth, 1906, when, within the legal hours and in the manner prescribed by law, he shall hang you by the neck until dead. May God have mercy upon your soul.

JOHNSON: Thank you, sir.

An Unexpected Complication

Judge McReynolds and Sheriff Shipp breathed a sigh of relief; they had kept their promise to the people. The legal system had dispensed swift justice, the convicted would suffer the ultimate punishment. The protectors of Hamilton County had done their duty and reelection seemed assured—until Noah Parden stepped forward.

Parden was born in 1865 in a small Georgia farming community. His mother, a former slave, struggled to support her family, working as a cook and housekeeper. Parden had never seen his father (though rumor had it he was white). Parden's mother died when he was six, and he was shipped off to an orphanage run by missionaries. The orphanage provided the boy a stable and disciplined upbringing. When he was nineteen, Parden moved to Chattanooga and enrolled at Howard High School, working part-time as a barber to pay the bills. After five years he received his diploma and accepted an offer to study law at Central Tennessee College (CTC) in Nashville. CTC had been founded under the sponsorship of Northern Methodist Episcopal Church missionaries in 1865 as a school for newly freed slaves. While at college he met and married his wife, Mattie S. Broyles. Four years later, Parden graduated with a law degree at the top of his class and returned to Chattanooga.

African-American attorneys were allowed to practice law in Tennessee as early as 1868. The requirements for admission to the Tennessee bar were far less stringent than in many other states. To practice law in Tennessee before any justice, justice of the peace, or county court judge, an applicant need only be twenty-one years old and of good standing (as defined by the Tennessee bar). Many black attorneys met these qualifications. However, establishing and maintaining a practice in the face of the prevailing racial prejudice and economic hardship facing the black community in the turn-of-the-century South proved difficult. White clients wanted white attorneys, and because blacks were systematically excluded from juries all over Tennessee, most black clients wanted white attorneys as well. The black clients who would retain a black attorney were usually unable to pay for legal services. That Noah Parden was able to maintain a legal practice amid such social conditions was a credit to his character, determination, knowledge of the law, and, in no small part, his undisputed skills as a litigator.

Parden was an avid follower of Booker T. Washington, holding firmly to Washington's philosophy that blacks gain respect and acceptance not through confrontation but by education, hard work, and the cultivation of vocational skills.

By the time of the Johnson case, Parden had established himself as the premier black attorney in Chattanooga. However, even though he and his partner Styles Hutchins represented well over half of Chattanooga's blacks in various legal matters, the firm's success was often hampered by their clients' inability to pay. Although Parden's reputation was top-notch, it was generally conceded that white lawyers were afforded more respect by white judges and white jurors. Therefore, when black clients did have money to pay for legal services, they would often seek the services of a white attorney, leaving Parden with a vast but largely indigent clientele.

As a result, Parden became one of the earliest contingent-fee attorneys. In civil lawsuits, primarily against insurance companies renowned for taking advantage of black families, Parden adopted the following payment system: clients would pay him nothing if he lost, but if he won, the clients would pay him a portion of the judgment. Thanks to Parden's superior courtroom skills, his civil victories kept his practice afloat.

Parden was, of course, well aware of the Johnson case, having assisted in the preparation, and he watched the entire drama from a distance. He was appalled by the crime committed against Nevada Taylor and relieved when local law enforcement made an arrest. Parden, however, became more and more distraught as the case against Johnson moved forward, especially when the judge refused to consider a change in venue or give the defense adequate time to prepare. Parden was well connected and respected within the black community, and he learned that Johnson was a quiet, even-tempered man, unlikely to commit such a crime. Rumors of other suspects were rampant. Parden attempted, via Shepherd, to pass names and leads on to Sheriff Shipp, but no action was ever taken.

As the trial went on, Parden became convinced of Johnson's innocence. Skinbone Johnson, the defendant's father, came to Parden's office a few hours after Judge McReynolds sentenced the younger Johnson to die. Skinbone told Parden that he had spoken with his son before the authorities had taken him away and Ed didn't want to die. Regardless of what his attorneys said, Ed Johnson wanted to appeal and wanted Parden to represent him. Parden's initial response was to deny the request.

While Parden was a student of the nonconfrontational Booker T. Washington, Styles Hutchins, Parden's partner, was a disciple of W. E. B. Du Bois, who believed in freedom now, civil rights now, action now. Hutchins was a veteran lawyer and politician. An Atlanta native, Hutchins was one of the first black students to graduate from the University of South Carolina law program. He encountered a great deal of opposition when he returned to Atlanta to start up his legal practice. It took six months of tireless persistence, but Hutchins finally convinced an Atlanta judge to admit him to practice, making him the first black in the Georgia bar. Later in his career he moved to Chattanooga, a more racially tolerant city than Atlanta, where he soon became one of the city's most prominent and respected attorneys. In one of Tennessee's greatest political upsets, Hutchins, a black Republican, won a seat in the state legislature, ousting a popular white Democrat. After serving out his term, he returned to the full-time practice of law. By 1906, he was one of the most experienced black attorneys in Chattanooga. Hutchins was insistent: he and Parden would take Ed Johnson's appeal.

The New Defense Team

Once they took the case, Parden and Hutchins were relentless. Their first stop was at the home of Lewis Shepherd. The attorney agreed to join their effort, but he wanted the young attorney to be fully aware of what he was getting into. In Parden's own words:

> Judge Shepherd grasped my arm and held it tight. Then, he told me that Judge McReynolds and Sheriff Shipp would be very angry at any decision to appeal. He said they would fight our efforts, and he said there would be significant consequences for each involved, and he told me to be certain that I was ready before I formally filed the petition. Only then did I fully realize the difficulty that faced us.

First thing Monday morning, Parden and Hutchins arrived at the Hamilton County Courthouse and told Judge McReynolds of their intention to file a motion for a new trial and, if that motion was denied, to appeal the case to the Tennessee Supreme Court. McReynolds, shocked and dismayed, quickly looked for a way out. Local court rules required that a motion for a new trial be filed within three days of the verdict, and Monday was the third day. McReynolds told the attorneys to return the following day, when the prosecutor would be present, to formally file their motion. Parden questioned the instruction, noting the apparent violation of local court rules. Hutchins interrupted Parden, "But you're counting Sunday. The judge had never counted Sunday against a defendant." All eyes turned to McReynolds for confirmation. The judge raised his eyebrows and nodded in agreement.

Parden and Hutchins returned to the courthouse the following morning, only to be blindsided. McReynolds refused to allow the attorneys to file the motion for a new trial, citing the local rule: lawyers had three days to file the petition, and Sunday was included. McReynolds denounced the men in open court for attempting to override the local rules. "What can two Negro lawyers do that the defendant's previous three attorneys were unable to achieve? What can a Negro lawyer know that a white lawyer does not? Do you think a Negro lawyer could possibly be smarter or know the law better than a white lawyer?"

Parden maintained his composure, respectfully telling McReynolds that he understood the ruling. He also informed McReynolds that he would be filing an emergency petition with the Tennessee Supreme Court seeking a stay of execution.

Once outside the courthouse, the attorneys realized the full measure of their task. Their attempts to file an appeal would be opposed by local officials every step of the way; their efforts had not only immediately enraged whites, but also blacks, who refused to associate with them for fear of incurring the wrath of the white community. Their legal practice suffered; no one wanted an attorney who was at odds with judges, prosecutors, and law enforcement officers. Clients found new representation. Even Parden's Baptist pastor publicly denounced his efforts on behalf of Johnson:

> Now for these colored attorneys to undertake to reopen the case is calculated to stir up trouble between the races. The best element of the colored people do not approve of reopening the case and the colored lawyers who are advocating it are making a serious mistake, not only for themselves but for the community in which they live.

For Parden, a deeply religious man, this attack was especially demoralizing. There was no support from the white community, no support from the legal community, no support from the black community, no support from the religious community. Parden's only sanctuary was his home, and even that would be violated before all was said and done. Angry citizens looking to dissuade Parden from pursuing the appeal attempted to burn down his office and then attacked his home, shattering the windows with a barrage of rocks and gunshots.

Parden and Hutchins filed a writ of error with the Tennessee Supreme Court, claiming that the evidence did not warrant a conviction and that a lynch-mob mentality had permeated the entire trial, placing undue pressure on the jury to convict the defendant.

Within two weeks, the Tennessee Supreme Court declined the writ, finding no error warranting a postponement of Johnson's execution. Parden and Hutchins immediately countered by filing a petition for writ of habeas corpus in federal court. Under the Habeas Corpus Act of 1867, defendants in state criminal actions could seek relief in federal court if the state court denied the defendant due process of law or equal protection under the law. While it was easy to appeal under the act, it was nearly impossible to win relief. The due process clause was largely ineffective in affording protection for a person convicted in a state court. The U.S. Supreme Court had yet to announce which federal constitutional rights were binding on the states. In 1906, such a petition was viewed merely as a tactic to delay punishment. Parden's petition claimed that his client was denied due process, a fair and impartial trial, and equal protection of the laws in violation of the U.S. Constitution.

Parden and Hutchins knew the petition was a long shot; never before had a federal court recognized a state defendant's right to a fair and impartial trial under the U.S. Constitution. They were seeking a decision tantamount to a legal revolution. But they were convinced that the facts of the Johnson trial were so outrageous that they screamed for relief.

Federal district judge Charles Clark shocked the Tennessee legal community when, after reviewing the writ, he ordered a stay blocking Sheriff Shipp from transporting Johnson out of Knoxville, where he was being held. Shipp, other local officials, and many Chattanooga citizens were outraged that a federal judge was "interfering" with state business.

A few days later a hearing was held before Judge Clark to consider the constitutional claims raised in the writ. Clark held that the Sixth Amendment guarantee of an impartial trial did not apply to state proceedings. As such, the federal district court lacked jurisdiction over Johnson's claims, even if they were completely true. Clark reasoned that only Congress or the U.S. Supreme Court could give federal courts the power to intervene in a state criminal case, and they had as yet chosen not to do so. However, the victory celebration of the Hamilton County authorities was tempered by Clark's final remarks. Although he didn't have the authority to intervene in the matter himself, he did have the authority to stay Johnson's execution a few precious days, allowing his attorneys to prepare an appeal to the U.S. Supreme Court.

While local authorities were irked by the delay, they were confident that Johnson would be executed shortly—after all, the very idea that the U.S. Supreme Court would consider an appeal brought by two black lawyers was, in their minds, ludicrous.

Meanwhile, the pressure on Johnson's attorneys was intense. Sleeping only an hour or two a night, living out of the office, their focus was total. They quickly learned that to present an appeal to the Supreme Court, an attorney must be a member of the Supreme Court bar, formally sworn in by a justice. Neither Parden nor Hutchins was so qualified. In fact, few black attorneys were members of the Supreme Court bar, and those who were had only served as cocounsel on cases argued by white attorneys. No black attorney had ever argued before the nation's highest court. Fortunately, Hutchins was a friend of Emanuel D. M. Hewlett, a black attorney whose mastery of the law had earned him an appointment as justice of the peace by President Benjamin Harrison and reappointment to the position by Presidents Cleveland, McKinley, and Theodore Roosevelt. Hewlett had personally been involved in several cases appealed to the U.S. Supreme Court and as a result was a bona fide member of the Supreme Court bar. Once Hewlett was apprised of Ed

Johnson's plight, he agreed to meet with Parden in Washington, D.C., and assist in the appeal.

Parden had many questions and Hewlett had much to explain about the complexities of properly presenting an appeal to the U.S. Supreme Court. Under the Court's rules, an attorney who had been licensed to practice law in a state for at least five years was sworn in as a member of the Supreme Court bar only after being recommended by a current member of the bar. Hewlett agreed to make the motion that Parden be accepted.

Because this was an emergency appeal, the party seeking to be heard would present his case to one of the justices in his chambers. The justice designated to hear emergency appeals from the Sixth Circuit (the circuit encompassing Chattanooga) was Associate Justice John Marshall Harlan.

Hailing from rural, grassroots Kentucky, Justice Harlan was a middle-class American hero. The retired Union colonel loved tobacco, bourbon, and baseball. A man known both for his liberal fashion—Justice Harlan often wore bright, colorful clothing not associated with that of a Supreme Court justice—and liberal ideas, he was a rebel in his own right. Harlan was the only justice of his time comfortable associating with Hispanics, blacks, and Asians. Justice Harlan was perhaps best known for his powerful dissent in *Plessy v. Ferguson,* where he denounced the majority's endorsement of the "separate but equal" doctrine, calling the social principle nothing more than a "badge of slavery." According to Harlan, constitutional rights belonged to each individual: "Our Constitution is color blind and neither knows nor tolerates classes among citizens." Justice Harlan was also alone among his brethren on the Court in his belief that the Bill of Rights applied to the states as well as the federal government. Hewlett assured Parden, if there was a justice on the bench who would be sympathetic to their position, it was Harlan.

On the morning of March 15, 1906, just three days short of Johnson's scheduled execution, Noah Parden and Emanuel Hewlett climbed the steps of the U.S. Capitol Building. They checked in with the Supreme Court receptionist and took a seat, waiting to be called into Harlan's chambers. The wait was long and excruciating. Parden's hands shook as he read and reread his brief. He was about to do something no black attorney had ever done in the history of the United States—argue a case before a justice of the Supreme Court.

"Mr. Hewlett. Mr. Parden. He will see you now."

The two men entered the Supreme Court Conference Room. Tall oak bookshelves overflowing with legal texts lined each wall of the huge room, stretching floor to ceiling; a massive oak table surrounded by nine chairs sat in the center. Eight were empty. At the far end, behind a mess of papers and books, sat a single man. The oldest and longest-serving member of the nation's highest tribunal addressed the men before him: "Mr. Parden, Mr. Hewlett, tell me why the United States Supreme Court should care about this case."

Parden took his cue: "Your Honor, never has there been a more obvious injustice than in this case. Here we have a defendant who is certainly innocent, but who has never been afforded the presumption of innocence." With that, Parden launched into every detail of Ed Johnson's ordeal: the lack of evidence, the inappropriate venue, the continual mob threat, the all-white jury, the inexperienced civil attorneys, the outrageous actions of the jurors during the trial, and the decision on the part of Johnson's counsel to waive his right to appeal. In one sense, Parden was arguing for Johnson's life, but in a broader sense he was arguing for a landmark decision. He was asking the Supreme Court to directly intervene in a state court criminal trial for the first time in the nation's history, to make the right to a fair trial, guaranteed by the Sixth Amendment, binding on state courts, to forever change how state courts treated their prisoners.

With much left to say, Parden's time was up. He laid a copy of his brief before Justice Harlan. "Sir, there's not much time. They are going to hang him in seventy-two hours. I beg of Your Honor to give him this review." The elderly justice said nothing, just nodded.

A Reprieve

Parden boarded a train back to Chattanooga and found Hutchins waiting for him on the platform. Grinning from ear to ear and waving a piece of paper, Hutchins ran to Parden and threw his arms around him. Parden read the message in disbelief, then read it again.

Washington D.C.—March 18
To Honorable C.D. Clark, U.S. Circuit Judge, Chattanooga, Tennessee

Have allowed appeal to accused in habeas corpus case of Ed Johnson. Transcript will be filed tomorrow and motion also made by Johnson's counsel for formal allowance of appeal of court.

Signed: JOHN M. HARLAN, Associate Justice

The Supreme Court had done the unimaginable. Ed Johnson's execution would be stayed pending a hearing in Washington, D.C. Similar telegrams were sent to Sheriff Shipp, Judge McReynolds, and District Attorney Whitaker, informing them of the Court's decision. Just to make doubly sure that the Chattanooga authorities understood that the Supreme Court was staying Ed Johnson's execution, Harlan had the Court clerk send an additional telegram to Shipp and McReynolds making clear the Court's order.

> All further proceedings be stayed and the custody of the accused retained pending an appeal in Washington.

> JAMES H. McKENNEY,
> Clerk of the United States Supreme Court

Not everyone shared Parden's relief and excitement. An article in the *Chattanooga Times* following the Supreme Court's stay presented an accurate depiction of local sentiment in Hamilton County, taking serious offense to the Court's ruling. This intervention was unacceptable. People in Washington, D.C., couldn't tell them when and how to deal with their criminals.

> The gallows in the Hamilton County Jail has again been disappointed in the case of Ed Johnson, convicted by the state courts of rape and sentenced to death.
> All of this delay is aggravating to the community. The people of Chattanooga believe that Johnson is guilty and that he ought to suffer the penalty of the law as speedily as possible.

Monday evening, March 19, was filled with an ironic mix of celebration and tragedy. On the Georgia side of Lookout Mountain, Parden and Hutchins joined Lewis Shepherd at his weekend home for a much needed retreat. The men spent the evening reveling in the success of Parden's presentation to Justice Harlan and planning the next steps in their mission to save Ed Johnson. There were laughs and cheers as they toasted, "To justice!"

Meanwhile, on the other side of Lookout Mountain, Sheriff Shipp was reeling. Reelection was no more than a week away and the people were angry. Many voiced their displeasure with Shipp's efforts to protect Johnson. Talk circulated through the town, and a common theme was emerging: "Tonight would be a good time to set things right." And yet despite the talk, despite the public outrage, and despite the previous lynching attempt, Shipp, instead of posting extra deputies at the jail, decided to give all his deputies, save one, the night off. They had been working too hard, he insisted. He expressed his confidence that Deputy Jeremiah Gibson, the most elderly of his deputies, could handle matters at the jail. Shipp also declined to seek help from the city police or the state National Guard.

By 7 p.m., Deputy Gibson sat alone in the office of the Hamilton County Jail, with only Shipp's assurances that the night would be calm and uneventful.

Mob Rule

It began with a small group of armed men outside the jail. Within minutes their number had doubled, and they made their way onto the first floor. Talk escalated in volume and hostility. More people arrived. Excitement mounted. And at some indefinable moment, the crowd became a mob. The first barrier between the mob and the man they wanted was a large steel door with rods extending into the stone and cement foundation of the building, fastened by a sturdy metal lock. The pounding of a sledgehammer reverberated throughout the jail.

Ed Johnson was awakened in his third-floor cell by the panicked shouts of fellow inmates housed on the floor below. The only other prisoner on the third floor was a white woman, Ellen Baker. For reasons unbeknownst to Johnson, deputies had moved all the other inmates to the second floor earlier that day. Johnson peered out his window between the steel bars and saw about two dozen armed men, several wearing handkerchiefs over their faces to disguise their identities. Johnson asked Baker what was happening; she replied, "You stupid nigger, they're here to kill you!"

Meanwhile the mob had successfully forced open the steel door below and surged up the spiral staircase to the third floor. At the top of the stairs they faced three more doors—all locked. The first steel-plated door was quickly removed. The second door proved more of a challenge; despite the use of multiple sledgehammers and an ax, the rivets held. The men realized they needed a key. They seized Deputy Gibson's key ring and weapon. Although he verbally rebuked the mob, Gibson made no effort to resist or call for help. The key proved useless, as the pounding had destroyed the lock mechanism. The mob resorted to the sledgehammers, and the pounding resumed with new fury and determination.

The now-panicked Johnson peered out his third-floor window. The number of people gathered in the courtyard below had increased to more than 250, and more were joining by the minute. The growing crowd was a frenzied mass of screaming, chanting, and dancing figures. Voices hurled curses, intermingled with scriptures and gunshots. Johnson retreated to his bunk, drew the covers over his face, and slowly recited the Twenty-third Psalm.

Sheriff Shipp received word of the mob and walked the half mile to the jail. He demanded that the mob disperse but was ignored. The sheriff offered no physical resistance. He didn't draw his weapon; he was a passive witness to the unfurling tragedy.

An hour later, the final rivet on the second door fell amid cheers: "We're coming to get you, Negro. No damn Supreme Court will save you tonight, Negro." The men used Deputy Gibson's keys to open the third and final door and then the lock on Johnson's cell. Johnson did not struggle as his hands were bound behind his back and he was dragged from his cell.

Johnson was paraded out the front door of the jail for the crowd to see. He looked up for a moment and his eyes widened—perhaps there was hope—several uniformed police officers were in the crowd. Could they be here to scatter the mob, to rescue him? Then Johnson saw the policemen laugh and joke with the crowd; they were part of the mob. Johnson was spat upon, beaten with fists, feet, stones, and rifle butts. Bruised and bloodied, he was dragged six blocks to the county bridge in what a reporter later described as "a strange funeral procession." During the march, one of the mob tied a rope in a hangman's noose. Most of the mob stood at a distance, content with the role of spectator. Two men climbed up the side of the bridge and threw the rope over the steel girder, dropping the noose down to their accomplices below, who placed it around Johnson's neck. The mob demanded a confession, but Johnson continued to protest his innocence, further infuriating them. After another barrage of insults and threats, they again demanded a confession and Ed Johnson uttered his final words: "God bless you all, I am innocent." With that Johnson was hauled up into the air by his neck, to swing from the support beams above the bridge. For nearly two minutes his body jerked, his legs kicked. Impatient, some in the crowd opened fire. Bullets ripped through Johnson's body. One bullet severed the rope and the tattered body dropped to the ground. Not yet satisfied that Johnson was dead, another round was blasted into Johnson's torso. A man then stepped forward, methodically reloading his revolver; he placed the barrel against Johnson's head and fired five times. Another member of the mob stepped forward and pinned a note to Johnson's body. "To Justice Harlan. Come get your nigger now."

The Supreme Court Steps In

Up until the mob took Ed Johnson, lynching had been a local matter, dealt with in the community in which it occurred. Often dismissed as soon as it happened, a lynching quickly became history not to be revisited, the community moving on. But this time was different. The lynching of Ed Johnson would not quickly and quietly fade into Chattanooga history. There would be no moving on for the locals in Hamilton County, Tennessee. In a matter of hours, the national spotlight would be upon them, and their local lynching would become a national affair.

There were mixed reactions the following morning. While portions of the white community felt justice had been served, the black community was outraged, staging a one-day walkout in manufacturing and textile plants across Chattanooga. White leaders and businessmen publicly denounced lynch law; lynching was bad for business. These men were trying to preserve the image of Chattanooga as a progressive, economically flourishing metropolis with few of the racial tensions found in other Southern cities. However, according to many, it wasn't the lynch mob at fault for the death of Ed Johnson, but the U.S. Supreme Court. Judge McReynolds, Sheriff Shipp, DA Whitaker, and others made similar statements with a common theme: if the federal courts had minded their own business, the mob would never have reared its ugly head. Local news further fanned the flames of hatred. On Tuesday afternoon, March 20, the *Chattanooga News* wrote:

> The lynching was the direct result of the ill-advised effort to save the Negro from the just penalty of the laws of Tennessee. Had not that effort been made, the Negro would have been legally executed today at the county jail. There was not a scintilla of doubt in the minds of the jury that he was guilty.
>
> The *News* deems it timely to mention that this community was content to let the law take its course provided there was no unnecessary delay. It was the appeal to the federal courts that revived the mob spirit and resulted in the lynching. This fact should be a lesson in the future.
>
> There is no community south or north which will submit to delay in punishment for this particular crime. The Supreme Court of the United States ought in its wisdom to take cognizance of this fact.

When news of the lynching reached Washington, the justices of the Supreme Court were shocked; never had there been such complete and total disregard for the authority of the Court. Although the Supreme Court was officially recessed for the spring, they met unofficially in the home of Chief Justice Melville W. Fuller. The justices emerged from the meeting resolute that action be taken. Justice Harlan expressed his anger in an interview with the *Washington Post.*

> The fact was that Johnson was tried by little better than mob law before the state court. . . . There was reason to believe that the man was innocent. But be that as it may, whether guilty or innocent, he had the right to a fair trial, and the mandate of the Supreme Court has for the first time in the history of the country been openly defied by a community.

Justice Oliver Wendell Holmes was equally enraged, describing Johnson's state court trial as "a shameful attempt at justice. . . . In all likelihood, this was a case of an innocent man improperly branded a guilty brute and condemned to die from the start."

The outrage in Washington extended beyond the bench. President Theodore Roosevelt condemned the lynching, calling it "contemptuous of the Court. It is an affront to the highest tribunal in the land that cannot go by without proper action being taken."

But what was the proper action? The Court was in unfamiliar territory; there was no precedent, no historical guidance. While the Court was discussing what action they should take, U.S. Attorney General William Moody was meeting with President Roosevelt to discuss a federal course of action. Both men agreed that those responsible for the lynching must be punished, and both harbored serious doubts as to the ability and willingness of local authorities to effectuate such punishment. They decided that the most logical course of action was to conduct a federal investigation and support the Supreme Court in whatever action it undertook. The Justice Department always had the option of instituting criminal charges at a later date if it appeared necessary to do so.

President Roosevelt ordered the plan into action, and two Secret Service agents were immediately sent to Chattanooga to compile as much information as possible on the events surrounding Johnson's lynching.

On the afternoon of March 23, senior Secret Service agents McAdams and Dickey arrived at the local train station in Knoxville, Tennessee. They met immediately with J. R. Penland, the U.S. attorney for the Eastern District of Tennessee. Penland provided the federal agents with a brief factual overview, supplemented by various newspaper clippings, background information, anonymous tips received by mail, and a list of potential contacts in Chattanooga. Two names were highlighted: Noah Parden and Styles Hutchins.

While U.S. Attorney Penland had embraced the Secret Service agents as colleagues, their reception in Chattanooga was hostile. Though the agents tried to keep their identities a secret, the two strangers stood out and word traveled. No one was talking. The white community refused to betray their own, and the black community, with the lynching of Ed Johnson fresh in their minds, was too frightened to speak.

With a town full of uncooperative witnesses, progress was slow. During their first week the agents elicited some useful information from the Chattanooga telegram office. Messages had indeed arrived announcing that the U.S. Supreme Court had agreed to hear Johnson's appeal, and these telegrams were delivered immediately to Judge Clark, Judge McReynolds, and Sheriff Shipp.

Far more productive was the discussion the agents had with Dr. Howard Jones, the Baptist preacher at the downtown church near the jail where Johnson had been held. He told Dickey and McAdams that he had heard about the planned lynching a good ten hours before Johnson was dragged from his cell. Dr. Jones said he had relayed the information to the sheriff's deputies at that time. He also told the agents that he had immediately called the city police when he realized a mob was gathering. The police told Dr. Jones that the mob was not their concern. The Secret Service investigators had their first evidence that local authorities had known about the lynch mob and did nothing to stop it.

Noah Parden turned out to be the key to the investigation. Although he could offer no firsthand account of what had gone on, witnesses were far more comfortable confiding in Parden than they were telling their stories to strangers. With Parden acting as mediator, the federal agents were able to gather witness statements from inmates in the Hamilton County Jail, several black police officers who had been on duty that night, and a number of other black citizens who either directly witnessed the mob attack or were made aware of the threat earlier that day.

A month after Johnson was lynched the Secret Service agents filed a report detailing the events of the days including and immediately surrounding the lynching:

> We have secured evidence against twenty-one members of the mob and are still gathering evidence.
>
> The truth is, Johnson's death at the hands of the mob was to Sheriff Shipp, who stands for re-election, a political necessity. Shipp doubtless observing this instead of taking measures to repel the mob rather invited it, at least, did not suppress it.
>
> We have had great difficulty in obtaining evidence, some witnesses, who could give valuable and convicting evidence are afraid to disclose anything. All are afraid for their personal safety.

In view of this condition, we believe it folly to think for a moment of local prosecutions, it would be simply impossible to convict in the local United States court, relying on jurors who would be impressed by the very atmosphere around them and would be subject to local manipulation.

The report listed the names of witnesses and the names of those implicated in the lynching, including Sheriff Shipp. Meanwhile, Shipp was reelected by a landslide, thanks in part to the efforts of the *Chattanooga News*.

We repeat that we do not understand how a white man can withhold support from Sheriff Shipp under all the circumstances.

That he will be elected the *News* has no doubt, but his majority should be large enough to forever bury the crowd that has sought to make capital out of the Johnson case. It should be large enough to show the whole country that this county proposes to stand by a sheriff who believes in protecting the womanhood of the South.

Local citizens reelected Shipp by the largest margin of victory in Hamilton County history. They wanted to send a message to Washington: federal interference was not welcome; they supported their man.

While life was good for Shipp, it had taken a mean turn for Parden and Hutchins. They were ostracized at home. Their practice fell apart and their personal lives had descended into a morass of threats of violence.

On May 17, 1906, the Supreme Court and the Justice Department agreed on an appropriate federal course of action. Attorney General Moody agreed to charge those involved in the lynching with criminal contempt of the Supreme Court under Section 725 of the U.S. Code, in which Congress defined the power of the federal courts to punish for contempt, a charge never before brought in the history of the United States. In return the Court agreed to cease its own pursuit of the mob and allow the Justice Department to spearhead the prosecution. Papers were officially filed at the Supreme Court on May 28, 1906, charging Sheriff Joseph Shipp, some of his deputies, and identified members of the mob with criminal contempt of the U.S. Supreme Court.

The Trial of Sheriff Shipp and the Mob

News of the federal charges sent shock waves through Chattanooga. Shipp had been so sure that the threat of federal action would blow over that the charges caught him completely off guard. He issued a statement to the press:

I have no desire to be considered in defiance of the Supreme Court. But in my judgment, the Supreme Court of the United States was responsible for this lynching. I had given that Negro every protection I could. Nevertheless, I must be frank in saying that I did not attempt to hurt any of the mob and would not have made such an attempt if I could.

Had not the Supreme Court of the United States interfered, we would have been able to set an example for the maintenance of law and order and a speedy trial in cases of this kind that would have been of great value throughout this country.

I regard it as very unfortunate that this case had not been left to the state authorities where it originated.

It was not until it was known that the Supreme Court had granted a hearing in this case and it had been stated it would probably be from two to five years before the case would be disposed of that the public showed any disposition to interfere in the matter.

I am thoroughly conscious of having discharged my duty in this case and under most trying circumstances and shall wait the result with confidence of a complete vindication.

Shipp's statement was published and circulated nationwide. While it raised eyebrows in Washington, the sheriff's popularity skyrocketed at home. A legal defense fund was created to help all those brought up on the federal contempt charge. Literally dozens of attorneys volunteered to represent the hometown hero. Shipp selected Robert Pritchard, one of Tennessee's most prominent criminal defense attorneys and a longtime friend. At the suggestion of Pritchard, Shipp also hired Cincinnati lawyer Judson Harmon, who had served as U.S. attorney general under President Grover Cleveland and was an experienced federal litigator.

On October 15, 1906, all parties were gathered in Washington. Attorneys for each of the twenty-six defendants stood one by one and entered their pleas of not guilty. Attorney Harmon spoke for Shipp, submitting a detailed brief enumerating Shipp's main defense: the Supreme Court lacked jurisdiction. Once all of the pleas were on the record, the Court set December 4 to hear oral arguments, not on the merits of the case; rather, the Court wanted to conduct a hearing to decide whether it had jurisdiction.

On December 4, the twenty-six defendants, flanked by their attorneys and backed by a group of Chattanooga citizens who had made the journey to show their support, entered the federal courthouse. On the other side of the courtroom sat Solicitor General Henry M. Hoyt, joined by three other veteran prosecutors. Seated directly behind Hoyt were Secret Service agents Dickey and McAdams, and Noah Parden.

Hoyt was the first to speak. He began by maintaining that the trial of Ed Johnson lacked any notion of justice or fairness. He then cited Supreme Court decisions justifying federal intervention. While he noted the Court's own words that federal judges should rarely interfere in state-court affairs, he argued that never had there been a case that so "imperatively demanded federal intervention."

This is the first time in the history of this country and of the Court that an order of the Court has been disobeyed and its authority condemned. This Court pre-eminently represents and effectuates the judicial branch of power under our government, and it is more important to sustain its paramount authority and dignity than that of any other judicial authority.

It is to be certainly assumed, then, that the Court will apply in the vindication of its own authority the doctrines which it has laid down in cases coming within its appellate jurisdiction as to the authority of the lower federal courts over contempts.

Flagrant contempt.

Of course this shocking occurrence, conceived in lawlessness and revenge, carried on by violence and ending with murder at the hands of the mob, was an offense against the state as well as against the United States and this Court.

This Court may and should inflict due punishment for that disobedience.

Hoyt recognized the true implications of this case, later telling a reporter from the *Washington Star*: "This proceeding is about nothing less than establishing and protecting the rule of law."

Judson Harmon, Shipp's Cincinnati attorney, was given his opportunity to respond. Harmon attempted to take the focus from his client's actions and highlight the issue of states' rights. He attacked Johnson's appeal, arguing that it contained no evidence whatsoever that the Constitution had been violated. No violation of Johnson's federal constitutional rights meant no jurisdiction for the U.S. Supreme Court to hear the appeal: "If an order be made without jurisdiction, there can be no punishment for contempt."

Harmon, like Hoyt, cited numerous Supreme Court decisions that in his opinion supported his position. Justice Harlan asked Harmon, "What about this situation where a juror made threatening moves and statements during the trial against the defendant? Doesn't that demonstrate the clear prejudice of the very people who swore to be impartial?"

Harmon responded that the juror's behavior was inappropriate but harmless, as the trial was nearly over and the juror apologized.

Harmon then argued that the Bill of Rights only applied to federal courts and federal actions, and he was again challenged by Justice Harlan: "What of the argument that the Fourteenth Amendment [incorporates] the Bill of Rights on state courts? If we determined that it did, would that make a difference?"

"Well . . . that is not the law . . . " Harmon responded.

At that point Justice Holmes interrupted, "But you would agree that this Court had the authority to determine that the Sixth Amendment is binding on the state courts, do you not?"

Harmon was stunned. He would expect such a question from Justice Harlan, the Court's liberal wild card, but Justice Holmes? Harmon said he was unsure how to answer and quickly moved on. The justices continued to hammer Harmon throughout the remainder of his argument. By the conclusion of the hearing it was obvious the justices were outraged by the blatant disregard for the Court's authority.

Three weeks later, Pritchard showed up on the sheriff's doorstep. Pritchard made no effort to hide his glum mood. He handed Shipp a document and directed the sheriff's attention to the highlighted portions. The Supreme Court's decision was unanimous:

> When a claim under the Constitution of the United States is properly alleged, however unfounded it may turn out to be, this Court deliberately considers the claim and retains the case in its grasp and under its power in all respects and for all purposes until final judgment dismissing, affirming, or reversing has been rendered and the mandate thereupon executed. If an appeal is technically frivolous, it is for this court to say so. The power and dignity of this Court are paramount. The trial of this case will proceed.

The Supreme Court was sending a clear message to every state and local official in the nation: their authority was supreme. Disregard for this authority would not be tolerated—the rule of law must be upheld. It was time to prepare for trial.

Edward Terry Sanford, an experienced and highly successful litigator within the Justice Department, was selected to head up the prosecution. A Southerner with a Harvard education, Sanford was a firm believer in equal rights, who pointed to Justice Harlan as the justice he admired most. While he understood the Southern mentality, he aligned himself with the liberal North. Sanford was the perfect choice to take on Chattanooga's good ol' boys.

Procedurally the Supreme Court approved a plan under which they would appoint a commissioner to preside over evidentiary hearings, listen to witnesses, and compile an official record. The completed record would be reviewed individually by each justice. The justices would then meet together and issue a ruling.

To the satisfaction of both sides, the Court appointed James D. Maher, deputy clerk of the U.S. Supreme Court, to preside as commissioner. However, against the advice of federal investigators, the Court ruled that the evidentiary hearing would take place in Chattanooga—with the caveat that Commissioner Maher could move the proceedings to Washington if there was any hint of witness intimidation or other inappropriate behavior.

Sheriff in the Docket

On February 12, 1907, the actual trial of Sheriff Joseph Shipp and the numerous codefendants for contempt of the Supreme Court began. Between the twenty-six defendants, their families, friends, foes, and a slew of spectators, there wasn't an empty seat in the courtroom. The government's first witness was J. L. Chivington, a reporter for the *Chattanooga Times,* who had covered the Johnson case. He was present the night of the lynching and reported every detail. In his nearly three hours on the stand, Chivington made two key points for the prosecution. First, Shipp usually had six or seven deputies on duty during the late-evening hours, as opposed to the lone deputy on duty the night of the lynching. Second, Chivington testified that "feelings was high at about the time of the lynching." The community was emotionally charged following news of the appeal, and talk of a lynching was common. This supported the prosecution's argument that local officials should have been aware of and prepared for the possibility of a lynch mob.

The prosecution's next witness was A. W. Brazelton, secretary to circuit judge C. D. Clark. Brazelton testified that, upon receiving the telegram from the Supreme Court on March 18, he immediately called Shipp and relayed the information.

Edward Chaddick, manager of the Western Union telegram office in Chattanooga, was the third witness to take the stand. He testified that, according to his records, his office received the telegram from the Supreme Court on the afternoon of March 19, the day of the lynching, and the telegram was hand-delivered to Sheriff Shipp the same afternoon. Chaddick's testimony was confirmed by a delivery slip signed by Shipp.

Next to take the stand was Ellen Baker, the only other inmate who was on the third floor with Johnson the night of the lynching. While Baker was illiterate and far from sophisticated, her testimony was nonetheless compelling and her story unwavering. Sanford questioned her about the afternoon of the lynching when all of the other prisoners were removed from the third floor.

BAKER: I asked Mr. Gibson [the lone deputy at the jail] about it and he said that a mob was coming at night.

SANFORD: Did you say anything to [Deputy Gibson] about whether you would be hurt? Were you scared or not?

BAKER: Well, he said they wouldn't hurt me; for me to go on back up there and go to bed. He said there was going to be a mob that night.

SANFORD: Was there any unusual disturbances going on at that time, that you could tell?

BAKER: No, sir.

SANFORD: What did you do then?

BAKER: I went back upstairs and went to bed as directed.

SANFORD: When did you see or speak to Jailor Gibson next?

BAKER: It was after dark. Mr. Gibson told me that a mob was coming.

SANFORD: What did Mr. Gibson say to you?

BAKER: Why, he told me to hush hollering, there wasn't nobody going to hurt me.

Baker's testimony supported the prosecution's argument that local authorities had known of the impending mob and yet did nothing to prevent it.

On the second day of the trial, Sanford called Julia Woffard. The surprise witness drew stares and whispers from the defense. Woffard was a young black woman who had worked as Shipp's cook for nearly two years and had been working for the sheriff at the time of the lynching. Shipp gave the woman a puzzled stare as Sanford began his examination.

SANFORD: Did you ever hear Captain Shipp say anything in reference to any delay in the proceedings in the Ed Johnson case? If you did, just state what you heard.

WOFFARD: I heard him say one day at the dinner table that if the execution would be stayed, Ed Johnson would be mobbed.

SANFORD: Did you hear Captain Shipp, on the day that Ed Johnson was lynched, say anything in reference to whether the Supreme Court had taken any action or not? If so, state what he said, and the time.

WOFFARD: I heard him tell his wife that afternoon that he was going to get a hearing—he would get a trial, or something like that. I don't know exactly the words.

SANFORD: That who was going to get a hearing?

WOFFARD: That Ed Johnson was.

SANFORD: That was in the afternoon?

WOFFARD: That was Monday, and Ed Johnson was mobbed that night.

Central to the defense was the contention that Shipp was never properly informed of the Supreme Court's decision to stay Johnson's execution. Woffard's testimony directly contradicted this argument. Woffard's testimony also called into doubt the sheriff's claim that he had no idea there would be a lynch mob on March 19.

On day three of the trial the government called John Stonecipher, a contractor originally from Georgia. Stonecipher implicated a number of men from the mob, including Padgett, Mayes, Ward, and Handman. He testified about his conversations with the men on the day of the lynching.

SANFORD: Did you have any conversation with them that related to a lynching in any manner? If so, state what it was.

STONECIPHER: Mr. Padgett asked me if I had heard what the Supreme Court had done in the Johnson case. I told him I had understood that they had stayed the execution. He said yes, that is what he had understood, and it was a damned outrage.

SANFORD: Go ahead. Keep right on. Just tell the conversation.

STONECIPHER: Then Mayes said, "We'll see to that ourselves."

SANFORD: Was that in Padgett's presence?

STONECIPHER: Yes, sir. They were both together.

SANFORD: Did you see Ward that evening?

STONECIPHER: Yes, sir. I saw Ward that same evening.

SANFORD: Where did you see Ward?

STONECIPHER: I saw him in front of Muellery's saloon, on Market Street.

SANFORD: What was said? Did you have any conversation with him?

STONECIPHER: I stopped on the curb, waiting for a car to go home, and Ward called to me. He says, "Ain't you from Georgia?" I says, "I used to live there." He says, "We want you to help us lynch that damn nigger tonight."

SANFORD: What was that?

STONECIPHER: He says, "We want you to help us to lynch that damn nigger tonight."

SANFORD: What did you say?

STONECIPHER: I says, "I don't believe it would pay. I believe Sheriff Shipp would shoot the red-hot stuff out of you."

SANFORD: What did he say?

STONECIPHER: He say, "No, it is all agreed. There won't be a sheriff nor deputy there."

Stonecipher, who had seen defendant William Mayes hours after the lynching, testified that Mayes's face was "skinned up pretty bad."

STONECIPHER: I says, "Hello, Bill, what is the matter with your nose?" He says, "I skinned it last night breaking that damned jail door down and getting that nigger out."

Sanford went on to question Stonecipher about his interactions with the defendants after the night of the lynching. Stonecipher testified regarding a conversation with defendants Padgett and Handman in a local café the day after the lynching.

STONECIPHER: I went in and Padgett had the *Morning Times,* and the first word he said, he said, "This damn paper has printed a lie about this lynching." I said, "How do you know it is a lie, Henry?"

SANFORD: What did he answer?

STONECIPHER: He told me he was there. And just as he said that Alf Handman come in. . . .

SANFORD: Was anything further said between you at that time?

STONECIPHER: And Henry says, "We did the nigger up all right, didn't we?" Alf says, "You bet we did." That was all that was said.

The next witness was the jailhouse cook, Press Walker. Walker testified that on the day of the lynching he had heard several deputies discussing the Supreme Court telegram over sandwiches and beer. Soon thereafter, Walker testified, all the deputies save Gibson left the jail and went home for the evening.

The final witness of the day was Howard Jones, the Baptist minister from Chattanooga. Jones testified that on the evening of March 19 he notified police that a lynching was in progress, only to be told by the officer on duty that the police were aware of the lynch mob but refused to take any action. Jones testified that he then ran to the jail himself to see if he could dissuade the mob. However, when he arrived, the mob was already headed toward the bridge. According to Jones, Shipp was still at the jail and was not restrained in any way, nor was there anyone guarding the sheriff or preventing him from going after the mob.

> **JONES:** I suggested to him that we go and try to identify some of the members of the mob. [Shipp] said that would be a very dangerous thing to do, that they were very desperate men. While we were talking, a fusillade of shots were heard from the bridge.

The defense declined to cross-examine Jones, and the minister was excused from the stand. The remainder of the government witnesses identified various defendants as participating members of the mob or corroborated the testimony of previous witnesses. Over five days the government called thirty-one witnesses. It became readily apparent that this trial was going to require far more time than was initially anticipated. Because of other pressing duties in Washington, Commissioner Maher announced that they would recess until June—four months later.

The parties reconvened on June 10, 1907. The courtroom in Chattanooga was once again packed, emotions still ran high. Sanford was back in action, the government having spent the last four months shoring up their case.

The government called A. J. Ware, a justice of the peace in Chattanooga. Ware testified that on the night of the lynching he got off duty around 10 p.m. Told that a lynching was in progress, he hurried to the jail, only to find he was too late to help protect Johnson. Ware chased the mob to the bridge, arriving in time to witness the gruesome finale from a few feet away. Ware was able to identify defendants Williams and Nolan as being directly involved in the lynching.

Confident in their case against Sheriff Shipp and a number of the defendants, Sanford rested the government's case.

For the next two weeks the defense called a host of alibi witnesses. Family, friends, colleagues, all vouched not only for each defendant's whereabouts but also their sterling credibility and high moral character. The defense witnesses also attempted to demean the character and credibility of the prosecution's witnesses.

The various defendants took the stand and gave their alibis; each had a story for where he was and a slew of friends and family to back him up. Only one defendant admitted to being present at the lynching, although he claimed he was only there as a spectator, nothing more.

Each of Shipp's deputies took the stand and testified that they had no idea there would be a lynching the night of March 19. Deputy Gibson also denied any foreknowledge of the lynching, adamantly denying he had told inmate Ellen Baker that a mob was coming that night. On cross-examination, Gibson admitted that he sought no help the night of the attack on the jail, and the elderly deputy could offer no explanation as to why he never drew his weapon during the attack.

The final witness for the defense was none other than the hometown hero, Sheriff Joseph Shipp. Shipp's friend Pritchard conducted the direct examination.

PRITCHARD: I will ask you to state whether or not you conspired with your deputies, or any one of them, or anyone else, looking towards the lynching of Ed Johnson?

SHIPP: I never conspired with any living man, my deputies or anyone else; and I had no knowledge, not the slightest, that there would be any effort on my part or anybody to interfere with Johnson.

PRITCHARD: I will ask you, Captain, if you remember Julia Woffard and her testimony here in regard to the conversation she says she heard at your dinner table, and whether any such conversation as that took place?

SHIPP: Yes, I heard her testimony. I know Julia Woffard. She was a domestic in my family. But there was no such conversation. The truth was that, on account of the fact that my wife was very much worried and in constant dread of all this trouble and excitement that we had passed through, I scrupulously avoid talking of it and speaking of it in my family.

PRITCHARD: I will ask you when you first heard or knew that there was a mob at the jail the night this lynching took place.

SHIPP: Well, I had gone home that night, I think, about half past six. My office work had been greatly interfered with; the criminal court was in session; I was making preparations to hang this man the next day, and I had a campaign on at the same time. I was seated at a table when the telephone bell rang. I went to the phone and I recognized Attorney General Whitaker's voice. He wanted to know if I knew what was going on at the jail. I told him I did not. "Well," he said, "you had better get down there."

PRITCHARD: Then what did you do?

SHIPP: I hung up the telephone just as quickly as I could, so that I might get another connection. I wanted to call the jail. I then tried to get the jail immediately after disconnecting with him, and I could not get the jail. I at once anticipated what was the matter as soon as I did not get an answer. I anticipated that if there was a mob there, the telephone had been torn out. I hung the telephone receiver up at once, rushed around the room, and got my hat and coat, started for the jail, running most of the way and walking rapidly the balance of the way. . . . Just as I got opposite the jail and just before turning into the walk leading up to the office, I saw five or six men standing out in the middle of the street; and without stopping, going rapidly, I made the remark "What is the matter?" No one answered at all, and then I went up the walk and found quite a number of men in the walk and up the steps leading to the office. I made my way through the crowd, shoving them to one side, and got into the office. As soon as I got in, I saw that the iron door, the outside door, was open. I entered rapidly, and just as I reached the inside of the door, I saw Mr. Gibson sitting back against the wall with three or four men standing around him. I had started over to make some inquiry of him, and just at that time I was seized from behind by several men—I do not know how many. When they seized me, I did not know but what they were going to do me some violence, and I reached back for my gun, which I had in my pocket. They assured me that they did not intend to hurt me. I was somewhat indignant and stated to them that I was not afraid of them hurting me. They rushed me up the steps and carried me into the hallway that is above the level of the floor that Johnson was on . . . and stood over me there with a guard during the progress of the work.

PRITCHARD: State whether or not you were kept a prisoner there by these people till after they had got Johnson and left the jail with him.

SHIPP: Yes, sir; I was.

Shipp was a confident witness. He felt sure that he had both the law and the facts behind him, not to mention the support of the Chattanooga populace. But in the courtroom Terry Sanford proved to be a formidable foe, ready for the sheriff.

SANFORD: There was a great deal of race feeling in this community at the time that all these matters engendered, was there not?

SHIPP: Well, yes, sir; I would say that there was some race feeling.

SANFORD: Did you make any special effort to get your deputies, or to have any special guard at the jail that night [night of the lynching] for Ed Johnson?

SHIPP: I did not.

SANFORD: Captain, did you recognize any of those men who were surrounding Mr. Gibson?

SHIPP: No, sir, I did not.

SANFORD: Did you recognize anybody in there that night . . . and if so, whom did you recognize?

SHIPP: I did not recognize anybody that was breaking into the jail.

SANFORD: How long were they with you?

SHIPP: Well, I think I was there about thirty minutes.

SANFORD: And did you recognize a single man?

SHIPP: No, sir.

SANFORD: Did you ask them their names?

SHIPP: No, sir; I did not.

SANFORD: Were they calling each other by name?

SHIPP: I did not hear any names called among them.

SANFORD: Did you call a posse there to relieve you or help you protect the prisoner?

SHIPP: No, I did not. I did not think there was anybody there that would have responded to my call if they had been called upon.

SANFORD: You did not make any effort at all?

SHIPP: No, sir; I did not. I made no effort except that I remonstrated the mob.

SANFORD: You used no force?

SHIPP: No sir.

SANFORD: You did not pull your gun?

SHIPP: I had no adequate force, and knew that the pulling of a gun would be useless.

SANFORD: Were you sheriff of the county?

SHIPP: Yes, sir.

SANFORD: And you did not pull your gun?

SHIPP: No.

SANFORD: You had strength enough to pull the trigger, I suppose?

SHIPP: Oh, I guess I could have pulled the trigger.

On June 29, 1907, the defense rested their case, and the record was complete, the proceedings adjourned. The transcripts would be passed on and scrutinized by the Supreme Court.

It would be more than a year before the Supreme Court would make its next move. In the fall of 1908, the Court dismissed the charges against seventeen of the defendants, after the government conceded that it lacked sufficient evidence to proceed against these individuals. However, the Court wished to hear oral arguments before ruling in the nine remaining cases.

On March 2, 1909, the lawyers for both sides met in Washington to make their final arguments before the nation's highest tribunal. Because Sanford had stepped down from his position with the Justice Department to serve as a federal judge in his hometown, Attorney General Bonaparte delivered the closing argument for the prosecution.

Thank you, Mr. Chief Justice.

This proceeding is unique in the history of courts. Its importance cannot be overestimated. Lynchings have occurred in defiance of state laws and state courts without attempt, or at most with only desultory attempt, to punish the lynchers. Perpetrators of such crimes have heretofore been censured only by public opinion; courts have remained silent. Powerful as such opinion always is, severe as it has been in its rebuke of such deeds, it has been inadequate to check these outbreaks of lawlessness.

Only recently have lynchings become so numerous that the whole country was aroused to earnest discussion of mob violence and a remedy for it. It is indeed useless to seek relief unless the judiciary can punish those who snatch and kill the men it has imprisoned. The arm of justice fetters men for years. It strikes death to the murderer. It can take property and life. Must it confess too weak to protect those whom it has confined?

The arm can destroy. Can it not protect? If the life of one whom the law has taken into its custody is at the mercy of a mob, the administration of justice becomes a mockery.

Bonaparte spent hours taking the Court through a detailed account of Johnson's trial, his "waiver" of appeal, and the appellate efforts of Noah Parden and Styles Hutchins. Bonaparte honed in on disregard for the rule of law not only in Chattanooga but throughout the South.

When this Court granted a stay of execution upon application of Johnson, it became its duty to protect him until his case should be disposed of.

It matters not with what crime he was charged. It is immaterial what the evidence was at trial. Sentenced to death, Johnson came into this Court alleging that his constitutional rights had been invaded in the trial of his case, and upon this, the Supreme Court said he had a right to be, and would be, heard.

From that moment until his case should be decided, he was under the protection of this Court. And when its mandate, issued for his protection, is defied, punishment of those guilty of such contempt must be certain and severe.

Bonaparte then walked the Court through every gruesome detail of the lynching, then focusing on the actions (or lack thereof) of the defendants.

Never before in its history has an order of this Court been disobeyed with such impunity.

It is not surprising that in the early history of this country, when the jurisdictions of the federal and the state governments were not clearly defined or well understood, states should have resisted the orders of this Court.

But it is remarkable that individuals should now undertake to defy the mandate of this great tribunal.

Justice is at an end when orders of the highest and most powerful court in the land are set at naught. Obedience to its mandates is essential to our institutions.

Contempts such as this strike down the supremacy of law and order and undermine the foundations of our government. Recurrence of such acts must be prevented. The commission of the offense has been established, and punishment should be imposed in accordance with its gravity.

Where a riot and the lawless acts of those engaged therein are the direct result of opposition to the administration of the law by this Court, those who defy its mandate and participate in, or who knowingly fail to take the proper means within their official power and duty to prevent, acts of violence having for their object to, and which do, defeat the action of this Court are guilty of, and must be punished for, contempt.

Six hours after he stepped to the podium, Bonaparte had finished. Early the next morning, attorney Harmon, lead counsel for Sheriff Shipp, began his final argument.

The testimony shows that Sheriff Shipp did not conspire, aid, or abet the lynchers and did not fail in his duty to take proper precautions to guard him.

It is alleged that the prisoner had been heavily guarded until the night of the lynching and that the guards were purposely withdrawn in order to permit the lynching. The record shows that the jail had not been guarded with extra guards after Johnson's conviction on February ninth.

The government seems to bring a wholesale indictment against the whole citizenship of Chattanooga and Hamilton County. The undisputed testimony of dozens of witnesses is swept aside by the simple announcement that it is absurd and ridiculous. The testimony of gray-haired ministers, of veteran physicians, of merchants, manufacturers, and officials, is all treated in the same manner. To all of these, counsel for the government say:

"It is absurd for the defendants and their witnesses to say that the community was in a state of peaceful repose on March nineteenth or preceding days. It is idle for them to say that they did not apprehend mob violence to Johnson."

It is possible that Captain Shipp acted with poor judgment on the night of the lynching. It is easy to see now that he should have had the jail guarded and should have been prepared for a mob. But if he had done so, he would have been wiser and would have shown more foresight than any other citizen of Chattanooga.

It is easy to see now, looking back over events as they occurred on that night, that Captain Shipp, instead of going to the jail, should have gone to police headquarters or the armory, where the militia were drilling, and organized a posse.

It must be remembered, however, that Captain Shipp did not have time to carefully consider the situation and coolly decide the best course to pursue. He was called upon in the night and told by the prosecuting attorney that he should go at once to the jail.

Certainly Captain Shipp cannot be convicted for contempt of this Court simply because, in the performance of his duties, he exercised bad judgment. He says himself that if he had the thing to do over again, he, perhaps, would know better what to do and would act differently, but at the time he acted on the spur of the moment and had gone to the jail for the purpose of seeing what the trouble was and to do what he could to protect the prisoner.

Captain Shipp denied, in his testimony, all the charges in the information with reference to a conspiracy with those engaged in the lynching.

He denied any intention to aid or abet, in any way, those engaged in the killing of Johnson. He denied that he anticipated or had reason to anticipate or expect a mob on the night of March nineteenth.

He insisted that he had the very greatest respect for this honorable Court and had done no act, and omitted no duty, from which a contrary conclusion could be drawn.

Captain Shipp has lived in Chattanooga since 1874. He was a Confederate soldier and has, for many years, been a member of the Confederate Veterans' organization and is quartermaster general of the entire organization. He was on the staff of the late General John B. Gordon and the late General Stephen D. Lee. He has been a Mason for over forty years and a member of numerous other secret societies.

His splendid character is testified to by every witness whose testimony has been referred to in this brief. Old men and young men, political friends and political adversaries, ministers of all denominations, veterans of the Civil War who wore the blue and who wore the gray, men of all classes and all persuasions who have known Captain Shipp during his long life in Chattanooga, all, in one voice, say to this Court that he is a truthful, law-abiding, honorable gentleman.

Can this Court say that a man with such a character and such a record would suddenly, without any motive whatever, betray his trust, sacrifice the life of a prisoner in his keeping, become a perjurer and a murderer, in order to show his contempt and disregard for the orders of this, the highest and greatest court in the world?

Harmon spoke for nearly two hours and then returned to his seat. His summation was followed by brief arguments from attorneys representing the other defendants. The justices listened in silence, never once interrupting the attorneys during their statements.

For three weeks the individual justices reviewed more than two thousand pages of testimony from the hearing in Chattanooga, meeting during the third week of April to discuss their findings. While the justices were unanimous in their ruling that the Supreme Court did indeed have jurisdiction to oversee contempt charges against Shipp and the other defendants, they were sharply divided as to whether Shipp and the other defendants were responsible for the lynching of Ed Johnson.

A break came with the arrival of a telegram from Mississippi, telling of a lynch mob that had murdered a black man accused of killing a white woman. The leader of the mob was U.S. senator W. V. Sullivan, who said, "I led the mob which lynched Nelse Patton and I'm proud of it." Accord-

ing to the telegram, no charges were being brought against any participant. The details of the lynching were enough to shift several members
of the Court, creating the bare majority needed to render a ruling.

Chief Justice Fuller decided it would be best for him to write the
majority opinion, given the controversial nature of the case. On Monday,
May 24, 1909, the Court met in open session and announced that it had
reached a final decision in the matter of *United States v. Shipp*. Chief Justice Fuller, with the eyes of the nation upon him, read aloud the highly
anticipated decision.

> It is apparent that a dangerous portion of the community was
> seized with the awful thirst for blood which only killing can quench,
> and that considerations of law and order were swept away in the
> overwhelming flood. The mob was, however, willing at the first
> attempt to accept prompt administration of the death penalty
> adjudged at a trial conducted according to judicial forms, in lieu of
> execution by lawless violence, but delay by appeal, or writ of error,
> or habeas corpus was not to be tolerated. . . .
>
> In this instance an appeal was granted by this Court, and proceed-
> ings specifically ordered to be stayed. The persons who hung and
> shot this man were so impatient for his blood that they utterly disre-
> garded the act of Congress as well as the order of this Court.
>
> The assertions that mob violence was not expected and that there
> was no occasion for providing more that the usual guard of one man
> for the jail in Chattanooga are quite unreasonable and inconsistent
> with statements made by Sheriff Shipp and his deputies, that they
> were looking for a mob on the next day. Officers and others were
> heard to say that they expected a mob would attempt to lynch John-
> son on the twentieth. There does not seem to be any foundation for
> the belief that the mob would be considerate enough to wait for the
> twentieth.

Fuller took great care to emphasize Shipp's own statement to the
media following Johnson's lynching.

> ". . . I am frank to say that I did not attempt to hurt any of them,
> and would not have made such an attempt if I could. . . . The
> Supreme Court of the United States was responsible for this lynch-
> ing. . . . In my opinion the act of the Supreme Court of the United
> States in not allowing the case to remain in our courts was the most
> unfortunate thing in the history of Tennessee. . . . The people of

Hamilton County were willing to let the law take its course until it became known that the case would not probably be disposed of for four or five years by the Supreme Court of the United States. The people would not submit to this, and I do not wonder at it."

[Shipp] evidently resented the necessary order of this Court as an alien intrusion, and declared that the Court was responsible for the lynching. . . . In other words, his view was that because this Court, in the discharge of its duty, entered the order which it did, that therefore the people of Hamilton County would not submit to its mandate, and hence the Court became responsible for the mob. He took the view expressed by several members of the mob on the afternoon of the nineteenth and before the lynching, when they said, referring to the Supreme Court, that "they had no business interfering with our business at all." His reference to the "people" was significant, for he was a candidate for reelection and had been told that his saving the prisoner from the first attempt to mob him would cost him his place, and he had answered that he wished the mob had got him before he did.

It seems to us that to say that the sheriff and his deputies did not anticipate that the mob would attempt to lynch Johnson on the night of the nineteenth is to charge them with gross neglect of duty and with ignorance of conditions in a matter which vitally concerned them all as officers, and is directly contrary to their own testimony. It is absurd to contend that officers of the law who have been through the experiences these defendants had passed through two months prior to the actual lynching did not know that a lynching probably would be attempted on the nineteenth. . . .

In view of this, Shipp's failure to make the slightest preparation to resist the mob; the absence of all of the deputies, except Gibson, from the jail during the mob's proceedings, occupying a period of some hours in the early evening, the action of Shipp in not resisting the mob and his failure to make any reasonable effort to save Johnson or identify the members of the mob, justify the inference of a disposition upon his part to render it easy for the mob to lynch Johnson, and to acquiesce in the lynching. After Shipp was informed that a mob was at the jail, and he could not do otherwise than go there, he did not and in fact at no time hindered the mob or caused it to be interfered with, or helped in the slightest degree to protect Johnson. And this in utter disregard of this Court's mandate and in defiance of this Court's orders. . . .

Although Shipp was in the midst or near the members of the mob for about an hour when they were in the jail, he did not seek to obtain information so that he could identify any of them, and he testifies that he does not know any member of the mob.

Only one conclusion can be drawn from these facts, all of which are clearly established by the evidence—Shipp not only made the work of the mob easy, but in effect aided and abetted it. . . .

In our opinion . . . this lamentable riot was the direct result of opposition to the administration of the law by this Court. It was not only in defiance of our mandate, but was understood to be such. The Supreme Court of the United States was called upon to abdicate its function and decline to enter such orders as the occasion, in its judgment, demanded, because of the danger of their defeat by an outbreak of lawless violence. It is plain that what created this mob and led to this lynching was the unwillingness of its members to submit to the delay required for the appeal. The intent to prevent that delay by defeating the hearing of the appeal necessarily follows from the defendants' acts, and if the life of anyone in the custody of the law is at the mercy of a mob, the administration of justice becomes a mockery.

Sheriff Shipp, Deputy Gibson, Nick Nolan, Henry Padgett, William Mayes, and Luther Williams were found guilty of contempt. However, due to insufficient evidence, the charges against defendants Galloway, Justice, and Ward were dismissed.

Five months later, on November 15, the justices met again to sentence the defendants convicted in *United States v. Shipp*.

You, Joseph F. Shipp, Jeremiah Gibson, Luther Williams, Nick Nolan, Henry Padgett, and William Mayes, are before this Court on an attachment for contempt. You have been found guilty.

Sheriff Shipp, Luther Williams, and Nick Nolan are hereby sentenced to ninety days imprisonment. Jeremiah Gibson, Henry Padgett, and William Mayes are hereby sentenced to sixty days imprisonment. All sentences are to be served at the United States Jail in the District of Columbia.

This Court is adjourned.

With that, the landmark case of *United States v. Shipp* came to a close. The impact of the decision reverberated around the country. In 1909, the year of the decision, the number of lynchings in the United States dropped from 97 to 82, and the numbers would continue to steadily decline in the years to come. The number of lynching attempts prevented by local law enforcement officers was on the rise—police officers and sheriff's deputies nationwide took the *Shipp* decision to heart. Their jobs as guardians of the accused were not to be taken lightly; if they neglected their duties, there would be consequences.

While the sentences for Shipp and his colleagues were short and the prisoners served their time in a private room shared only by the six of them with a view of the city and their own bathroom, the Supreme Court accomplished its mission—it sent a message to each individual in the United States: the rule of law is supreme and the sanctuary of the justice system must be adhered to.

Epilogue

Sheriff Joseph Shipp returned to Chattanooga on January 30, 1910 (he was released early for good behavior). Shipp was greeted by the cheers of more than ten thousand supporters and a band playing "Dixie." It was a hero's welcome. A monument was erected in his honor.

There was no welcome-home extravaganza for Noah Parden and Styles Hutchins. Neither attorney ever returned to Chattanooga. They had received word from friends and family that violence and death awaited them in Tennessee. The men headed north—lecturing and writing about the events surrounding the Johnson case. Both eventually settled in Oklahoma. Neither Parden nor Hutchins would ever practice law again.

Nevada Taylor never recovered, passing away on May 14, 1907, only twenty-three years old. According to local reports, "Death was ascribed to nervous prostration incidental to the crime committed under the very shadow of the historic Lookout Mountain."

Ed Johnson was buried in 1906, his case forgotten for nearly a century. In the 1980s, LeRoy Phillips Jr., born, raised, and educated in Chattanooga, had been practicing law for nine years when, in the course of some legal research, he stumbled across the Johnson case. Intrigued and appalled, he became engrossed. The more time he invested in researching the tragic events, the more it haunted him. In 1988, he joined forces with journalist Mark Curriden to write a book detailing the history and impact of the Johnson case, *Contempt of Court: The Turn-of-the-Century Lynching That Launched 100 Years of Federalism.*

But writing the book wasn't enough for LeRoy Phillips—he filed a state court petition to set aside the rape conviction of Ed Johnson on the grounds that the appeal was prevented by agents of the state: Sheriff Shipp and his deputies. The state of Tennessee offered no opposition.

On February 25, 2000, the presiding judge in the Hamilton County Criminal Court—the very court in which Johnson was convicted ninety-four years earlier—overturned the conviction of Ed Johnson.

Along the eastern slope of Chattanooga's historic Missionary Ridge lies a small cemetery. A rusty sign identifies the site as Pleasant Garden, a "resting place for Negroes." Neglected for decades, Pleasant Garden is a mess of overgrowth and sunken graves. Amid the disarray, an unassuming tombstone bears the faded inscription:

God Bless you all. I AM A Innocent Man.
ED JOHNSON
BORN 1882
DIED MARCH 19, 1906

CHAPTER TWO

When the Constable Blunders

The fruit of the poisonous tree sets the guilty free

The criminal is to go free because the constable has blundered.

—Justice Benjamin Cardozo

The criminal goes free, if he must, but it is the law that sets him free.

—Justice Tom C. Clark

Police officers patrolling on West 176th Street in New York City watched as four men quickly loaded two large duffel bags into a double-parked car. As the officers approached, one of the men slammed the trunk closed and another man ran away. The police—without a search warrant—forced open the trunk and found eighty pounds of cocaine and heroin in the bags. The trial judge ruled the drugs inadmissible because the officers had improperly searched the trunk. Case dismissed; dope dealers released.

Most Americans take great exception to this idea that criminals go free because of some police error. Such an outcome strikes us as fundamentally unfair; a windfall for criminals and a body blow to public safety. How can a misstep by the police lead to a complete exoneration? How can we let criminals go free?

The American exclusionary rule exacts a high cost. The incriminatory evidence (the drugs, the blood, the knife) that is on display for the world to see is now rendered unusable against the very criminal that produced it; a legal loophole that allows dope dealers, rapists, and even murderers back onto the streets. Jurors are prevented from considering evidence that often shows beyond all doubt that the defendant is guilty of the crime. It is understandable—expected—that this perception serves to undermine public confidence in our system of justice.

And yet, despite the hostility—not just from the public, but from members of the judiciary, too—the forty-year-old exclusionary rule remains the law of the land. And in many respects, it is the single most significant concept in the American criminal justice system: it is the mechanism that puts teeth into the Fourth Amendment.

Interestingly enough, however, the exclusion of evidence proving guilt was not a concept envisioned by the Founding Fathers. When the Fourth Amendment to the Constitution was drafted, prohibiting unreasonable searches and seizures, it provided no means to enforce the prohibition: the "guarantees" of the Fourth Amendment existed only on paper. For nearly two centuries, police could conduct unreasonable searches and seizures—and the fruits of those endeavors were *admissible* against the suspect.

Critics sought some remedy, asking if there was nothing to prevent the government—the police—from acting with impunity even when there was insufficient cause or no warrant? Some legal reformers suggested that, should the police illegally enter someone's house, they could be criminally prosecuted for trespass. Others have suggested that the police could be sued civilly for illegal conduct, the threat of monetary damages against the officer serving as a deterrent. In the mid-twentieth century, neither "remedy" was seen as a realistic means of ensuring against unreasonable searches and seizures. What jury would convict a cop for entering a home and seizing contraband? What jury would award a judgment to a person caught with contraband by an officer who illegally entered? Not until 1961 did the U.S. Supreme Court act to provide an answer.

Since its inception, the exclusionary rule has been the subject of intense debate. While Chief Justice Earl Warren held that the purpose of the rule was to deter illegal police behavior, a later chief justice found "no empirical evidence to support the claim that the rule actually [works]."

The debate rages today. Recently, several cases and scholarly writings have given new life to the vehement criticism of the "exoneration rule." In 1995, several congressional leaders proposed legislation that would essentially abolish the exclusionary rule; this bold proposal drew fervent opposition from all political walks of life. Ten years later, the battle over the efficacy of the exclusionary rule continues, no resolution in sight. Who would have thought that the catalyst for this intense and high-level debate would stem from a box full of dirty pictures found in the home of a single mother?

What led the Supreme Court to craft such a drastic remedy? Frustration with police officers who often disregarded basic Fourth Amendment protections. And the surprising catalyst was the 1957 police search of the home of Dollree Mapp.

The Constable's Blunder

May 22, 1957, 3 a.m. An explosion rocks a poor, crime-ridden borough of Cleveland, the residents waking with a start. Someone had planted a bomb on the front porch of the neighborhood's soon-to-be-infamous resident: boxing promoter Don King.

As the first major black boxing promoter, King would go on to dominate the world of heavyweight title fights, promoting boxing greats Muhammad Ali, Evander Holyfield, and Mike Tyson. However, before his rise to fame and power, King ran an illegal gambling enterprise and served four years in prison for manslaughter.

Although the blast at King's house was confined to the porch and no one was injured, it was apparent that someone had a score to settle. Despite his being a major league bookie, "The Kid" King had made a surprising move: he had cooperated with the police. Three days before his front porch went up in flames, King had sat down with police sergeant Carl J. Delau and ratted out a notorious gang of numbers runners. King alleged that a man named Shondor Birns had been the brains behind a shakedown of five local racketeers—including King. Birns then forced each racketeer to pay him $200 a week and hired two henchmen to ensure that the payments were made. As Sergeant Delau listened intently, King told him how he had first cut his payments to Birns in half and eventually stopped paying him altogether.

King's house was bombed three days after his meeting with Sergeant Delau. Only hours after the explosion, Delau and the Cleveland Police Department brought four men in for questioning, including Shondor Birns. And while Birns, the primary suspect in the bombing, was safely in custody, the police received an anonymous tip. The caller told Delau that evidence related to the bombing could be found at a two-family home located at 14705 Milverton Road. Further, the caller alleged that the suburban home was a clearinghouse for illegal gambling.

Milverton Road slices through a middle-class Cleveland suburb adjacent to Shaker Heights, an area featuring a line of colonial-style shops and eateries scattered throughout a picturesque garden landscape. The two-story home at 14705 Milverton Road was a well-kept brick building with white shutters and striped, vinyl awnings surrounding its many windows. A walkway led to the front door, ending in three decorative steps, the sides closed in by cast-iron railing. Minerva Tate and her long-time houseguest, Virgil Ogletree, lived on the first floor. The building's owner, Dollree Mapp, a thirty-two-year-old black divorcée, lived on the second floor.

Mapp had a curvaceous figure, along with prominent cheekbones and a killer smile. Her good looks had caught the eye of several professional boxers; she had previously been married to heavyweight Hall of Famer Jimmy Bivens. Although the union was brief, it produced her now eleven-year-old daughter, Barbara, who lived with Mapp. After the marriage's dissolution, Mapp began dating Archie Moore, the onetime light heavyweight champion of the world. This more recent boyfriend had met Mapp's ex-husband in the ring—a matchup that resulted in Biven's victory by decision.

When the officers arrived at 14705 Milverton Road and rang the doorbell, Mapp stuck her head out of the second-floor window and asked the officers what they wanted. One of the officers told her that they wanted to come in and ask her questions, though he did not say why. The officers then asked Mapp if they could search her home. She told them she would call her lawyer and seek his advice.

Mapp called Alexander L. Kearns, an attorney she had just hired to file a lawsuit against former boyfriend Archie Moore. At sixty-two, Kearns was a prominent attorney who had practiced in Ohio for more than forty years. But Kearns was in court and Mapp's call was directed to a young associate, Walter Greene. Greene advised Mapp to withhold consent unless the officers produced a search warrant. Mapp told the cops she would not let them in; they retreated from the front steps and waited at the curb.

Delau contacted the station and told his boss that Mapp would not let him into the house without a search warrant. Three hours passed. Then Lieutenant White and at least three other officers arrived. The police headed back to the front door, but Mapp did not immediately respond to their knocking. Just as attorney Walter Greene arrived on the scene, the police tried to kick down Mapp's front door, then smashed the glass panes at the top half of the door and reached through and unlocked the door.

As the police rushed into the home, they were met halfway up the staircase by Mapp, demanding to see a search warrant. Lieutenant White held up a piece of paper and said, "Here is the search warrant." When Mapp asked to inspect the document, White refused. She snatched the paper from the officer and stuffed it down her dress; White grabbed Mapp, reached down her dress, and seized the paper. Mapp was never allowed to read the "warrant"; if she had, she would have found nothing but a blank piece of paper. The police had entered her home without a warrant.

Lieutenant White grabbed Mapp, twisted her hand behind her back, and handcuffed her. She yelled that the handcuffs hurt and was taken upstairs to her home while the police searched.

Meanwhile, Walter Greene attempted to follow the police inside, but was denied entry. Over the course of both Mapp's arrest and the subsequent search, Greene heard Mapp scream several times. With each cry, the attorney made a new attempt to enter the home, only to be denied again and again.

To recap, the officers had no warrant; Mapp was handcuffed and had been locked in her bedroom; and her attorney was confined to the outside steps. It seemed that the officers now had carte blanche to rifle through any—and all—of Mapp's personal possessions. And they did. The officers began a systematic search for both gambling paraphernalia and a person "wanted for questioning" for the bombing of Don King's home. Given that "gambling paraphernalia" could range from a ledger book to a scrap of paper, the officers' search was thorough. They began their hunt in Mapp's bedroom; as the thirty-two-year-old woman looked on, several officers began opening her dresser, her chest of drawers, and a few suitcases. The search then moved to Mapp's kitchen, dinette, living room, and the bedroom of her eleven-year-old daughter. The police rummaged though a photo album and personal papers. When finished, the search allegedly netted a handgun and a number of lottery slips.

According to Mapp, when the police were done in her home, they entered the building's basement, where they found a slew of "obscene" books in an old box—works with the memorable titles *The Affairs of the Troubadour, Little Darlings, London Stage Affairs,* and *Memories of a Hotel Man.* The officers also found several "obscene" drawings and photographs of people engaging in various sex acts. Where these objects were discovered would later become a point of dispute. Delau would testify that he found these "pornographic" materials in Mapp's bedroom—not in the basement.

While one team of police was searching Mapp's home and the basement, the other entered Minerva Tate's first-floor unit and arrested Virgil Ogletree, a man who had been identified earlier as a suspect in the King bombing. But Virgil Ogletree would never be prosecuted. Although he was temporarily detained and questioned, he was eventually released, free from any charges.

Dollree Mapp was not so lucky. Based on the lottery slips found in her home, she was initially charged with possession of gambling paraphernalia, though the charge was dropped because of insufficient evidence. However, almost a year later, Mapp was rearrested and this time charged with possession of the "lewd and lascivious" materials found in the box a year earlier. This was a felony, and if convicted, Mapp could be sentenced to seven years in prison.

In the days following her indictment, Mapp stayed busy to keep her mind off her upcoming trial. She and her daughter remained in the brick home on Milverton Road. Mapp continued her adult education courses and began working at an interior decorating shop. Unfortunately, this part-time position was not enough to pay Kearns's attorney's fees. However, a white businessman who was sympathetic to the plight of black Americans came to her assistance and paid all her legal bills.

The Criminal's Day in Court

On a crisp September morning at the Cuyahoga County Courthouse in downtown Cleveland, Dollree Mapp took her seat beside attorneys Kearns and Greene. The Honorable Donald Lybarger announced, "*The State of Ohio v. Dollree Mapp.*"

Unlike their contemporary successors, trials in 1958 were typically not preceded by a flurry of in limine (pretrial) motions to suppress illegally seized evidence. Although Kearns brought a Fourth Amendment claim that the materials were the product of an illegal search, it was dismissed out of hand. It wasn't the court's concern how the evidence was gathered. The judge reasoned that all relevant evidence was admissible, regardless of how it had been obtained. The judge was not acting capriciously—that was the norm. All the allegedly obscene materials would be presented to the jury.

But even the titillating introduction of "pornography" could not spice up an otherwise routine trial, lacking the sort of passion representative of a proceeding that would generate a sweeping Supreme Court decision. The points of contention focused on whether the seized books, drawings, and photographs fell under the legal definition of *obscene* and where the materials had been found. The prosecution introduced thirteen exhibits, encompassing everything from *Memories of a Hotel Man* to several "lewd" photographs. Delau and Officer Michael Haney testified that they were in the bureau drawers and suitcases in Mapp's bedroom. Mapp claimed they were seized from the basement—two floors down from her actual living quarters.

Kearns began the defense case-in-chief by calling his associate Walter Greene. Earlier in the trial, an officer had testified that the police had gained entrance into Mapp's home by prying the screen door open. However, Greene testified that Delau broke the glass in the door, reached in, and unlocked the door. Further, Greene declared that when he asked Delau if he had procured a search warrant, the sergeant insisted that he had. But the document was never produced; if Greene was correct, Delau had lied.

Kearns then called his second witness, Dolores Clark, Mapp's friend who occasionally worked with her at the Milverton home. Clark testified that a former tenant in Mapp's complex named Jones had left one day with some of his belongings but without telling anyone when or even whether he would return. According to Clark, after the man had not returned for some time, she and Mapp went through Jones's bedroom, boxed up his belongings, and put them in the basement.

Clark claimed that the items in the box included men's clothing, letters, shoes, and other "junk." Further, she stated that while she and Mapp were cleaning out the man's room, Mapp found a brown paper bag in his dresser that contained the allegedly obscene materials. The women sealed the bag and placed it in the box with the rest of his belongings. When Clark was shown the books and drawings presented by the prosecution, she testified that the books may have been included in the box.

As for whether a search warrant ever existed, there were various accounts. Officer Haney claimed that Lieutenant White had procured a search warrant before the officers entered Mapp's home. But at trial, Lieutenant White was not called to testify by either side. Seeing an opening, Alexander Kearns grilled Officer Haney on the warrant's existence.

KEARNS: Where is the search warrant?
HANEY: I don't know.
KEARNS: Do you have it here?
HANEY: I don't have it.
KEARNS: Would you tell the jury who has it?
HANEY: I can't tell the jury who has it, no, sir.
KEARNS: And you were one of the investigating officers in the investigation by the police department?
HANEY: Yes.
KEARNS: But you can't tell us where the search warrant is?
HANEY: No, I cannot.
KEARNS: Or what it recites?
HANEY: No.

Officer Haney had no evidence to support his assertion that a search warrant existed. Nonetheless, in terms of its impact on the trial, the issue was not terribly significant. The evidence was not going to be excluded either way. Any contention concerning the existence of a warrant only went to the question of witness credibility.

Then it was Mapp's turn, and she told a strikingly different story from the one offered by the police. With the jury watching, she described the police entry into her home:

> When they came in, I said, "Inspector, I want to see the search warrant." And I was standing on the top landing of the stairs, and I didn't know who the inspector was when he was in plain clothes. He said, "Here is my search warrant." He held it back from me, and I remember Mr. Greene told me I should see it and read it, and I told him I wanted to see it. He said, "You can't see it. At that I reached over, took the search warrant from his hand, and put it down in my bosom. One of them said, "What are we going to do now?" The one that grabbed me said, "I'm going down after it." I said, "No, you are not." He went down anyway.

Next, Mapp said that while she was sitting handcuffed in the bedroom, Officer Haney walked into the room with the brown paper bag containing the books and drawings that she and Clark had packed away in the basement. However, under cross-examination she admitted that some of the "obscene" pencil sketches were actually found in a suitcase in her room. It appeared that Mapp may have lied about some key details.

The closing arguments were brief. The two sides offered their interpretations of the witnesses' testimonies, and the prosecution waved around the collection of "obscene" materials. Judge Lybarger admonished the jury not to consider the validity of the officers' alleged search warrant—even though the prosecution never produced a copy of a warrant or a witness who could confirm its existence. The jurors were charged with only two questions: Were the materials obscene and did Dollree Mapp possess them? The jury took twenty minutes to convict.

Mapp faced the maximum sentence under Ohio law: seven years in prison. She was to be shipped to the Ohio Reformatory for Women at Marysville, but Kearns convinced the judge to allow Mapp to post $2,500 bail and remain free until her appeal could be heard. Mapp returned to her house on Milverton Road. She continued to receive the checks from her anonymous benefactor; though her freedom remained tenuous, at least her legal fees would continue to be paid.

Building the Bomb

The foundation for Mapp's appeal lay in the past. Nearly four years after the ratification of the U.S. Constitution, the American people wanted assurances that their new government would not repeat the mistakes of the English Parliament. But the Constitution gave no such guarantees; while it stated specifically what the government could do, it did not say what the government could not do. And so, after four years of Federalist and anti-Federalist papers, town hall debates, and public outcry, the new government heeded Thomas Jefferson's words: "A Bill of Rights is what the people are entitled to against every government on Earth, general or particular, and what no just government should refuse, or rest on inference."

Although twelve amendments to the Constitution were proposed, only ten were ratified. The Fourth protected citizens against "unreasonable searches and seizures." As people who had been subjected to the oppressive tactics used by the British Crown to ensure colonial loyalty, members of the First American Congress believed that two devices in particular compromised the liberty of every citizen: the general warrant and the writ of assistance.

The English general warrant bestowed upon its beholder the power to "seize, take hold and burn books, and things offensive to the state." These warrants did not need to be based on probable cause. In fact, they could be issued without even the slightest suspicion of wrongdoing. Further, the warrants were not specific to the individual—the warrant's holder was essentially issued a blank check that lasted for the lifetime of the issuing monarch. When these characteristics were brought together, a general warrant meant that once the document was issued, its holder could search anyone, at any time, for any reason. The "general warrant" was no warrant at all—but merely a formality for the granting of a carte blanche.

But not until 1763 did vocal opposition to the general warrant begin to mount. This opposition was largely attributed to the work of John Wilkes, a popular member of the English Parliament, who published a widely circulated newspaper that disseminated his anti-Crown messages. In one of these newspapers, he attacked the very idea of a general warrant. Almost immediately after publication, Secretary of State Lord Halifax issued a general warrant that allowed the state to search for and seize the authors, printers, and publishers of the critical article. But Wilkes scoffed at the order, declaring the document "a ridiculous warrant against the whole English nation."

Soon after his act of defiance, Wilkes challenged the legality of the general warrant and—in a surprising decision—won. Lord Chief Justice Pratt, in a vehement opinion that abolished the general warrant, wrote:

> If such a power is truly invested in a secretary of state, and he can
> delegate his power, it certainly may affect the person and property of

every man in this kingdom, and is totally subversive of the liberty of the subject.

However, there still remained another insidious instrument of the British Crown: the writ of assistance. In the eighteenth century, the British imposed exorbitant taxes on all goods headed for the colonial seaboard. To avoid these duties, the colonists attempted to smuggle in various goods. When the British became aware of these tactics, they modified the general warrant to aid customs officials in their efforts to prevent the smuggling. The resulting "writ of assistance" gave its holder unlimited discretion to search any "suspected" premises. And like the general warrant, the writ of assistance also expired only with the death of the issuing monarch—another carte blanche.

Opposition to writs of assistance was fueled by the death of King George II in 1760. Upon his death, all present warrants were invalidated. Seeing an opportunity, the colonists rose up against the issuance of any new writs. In particular, a group of Boston merchants hired an eloquent attorney, James Otis, to challenge the writs' legality in the Massachusetts courts.

Otis gave the case his all—including a passionate five-hour oration. Future American president John Adams, who listened intently to Otis's words, commented on the colonists' response to the famous speech: "Every man of a crowded audience appeared to me to go away, as I did, ready to take arms against writs of assistance . . . then and there the Child Independence was born." Nonetheless, Otis lost. Although his words did not resonate with the court, his powerful speech inspired others. The opposition against the writs of assistance was gaining momentum. As a result, American courts began to refuse to issue the writs.

When the colonists' disdain for the writ of assistance is combined with their hostility toward the general warrant, their anger over the omission of a provision in the new Constitution to protect them against these intrusive devices is easily understood. The Constitution would not be complete without the inclusion of protections that prohibited the new federal government from usurping its citizens' liberties; the old abuses of the Crown would not be acceptable in the fledgling republic.

And so the Fourth Amendment was born. But although the First Congress of the United States added this fundamental right to be free from unreasonable searches and seizures, they did not provide a means to enforce it.

Indeed, for nearly two centuries, the protection existed only on paper. Not until Dollree Mapp's case was decided by the U.S. Supreme Court in 1961 were Americans secure in the protection guaranteed by the Fourth Amendment. But in the line of cases leading up to the revolutionary decision in *Mapp v. Ohio,* the Court's obvious uneasiness in this area of the law left many scholars wondering if a reasonable method of enforcement would ever be crafted.

Often regarded as the first precedential step toward the development of the exclusionary rule, *Boyd v. United States* was an 1886 civil case filed by two New York businessmen. These entrepreneurs faced governmental charges of forfeiture for their importation of thirty-five cases of plate glass—an act that violated both import and revenue laws. To prove the quantity and value of the plate glass, prosecutors sought to discover the invoices for these goods. As a result, they served a subpoena on the defendants, which mandated that if the businessmen did not produce the requested documents, "the allegations which it is affirmed they will prove, shall be taken as confessed." In response, the defendants produced the invoices and were duly convicted.

On appeal to the U.S. Supreme Court, the defendants argued that the compelled production of the invoices violated their rights under both the Fourth and Fifth Amendments. According to the Supreme Court, the defendants got it half right. The Court held that if a defendant was forced to produce certain books or papers against himself, the Fifth Amendment prohibition against self-incrimination demanded exclusion of those documents at trial. And with this ruling, the evolution of the exclusionary rule had begun. Even though the vehicle was the Fifth Amendment—rather than the Fourth Amendment—evidence was indeed barred from use at trial.

But as the nineteenth century faded into the twentieth, the Supreme Court of the United States continued to strictly adhere to the common-law rule that the progress of a trial should not be interrupted to banter over the legality of the method employed to obtain the evidence; the one exception, of course, being the new rule articulated in *Boyd.* If the evidence was relevant, it was admissible. And the means by which it came to light were inconsequential.

Lighting the Fuse

The slow evolution of the exclusionary rule reached a milestone in 1911 when Fremont Weeks, an employee of an express company in Kansas City, was suspected of using the mail to send illegal lottery tickets to various gambling customers. Missouri officials barged into Weeks's place of employment without a warrant and arrested him. At this same time, another team of officers, also without benefit of a warrant, forced their way into Weeks's home and began searching. They found papers and other articles they suspected were related to gambling. Later that same day, the officers returned once more—this time with a federal marshal. Once again, neither the officers nor the marshal had a search warrant. The police were let in by a boarder. And during this second search, the officers seized additional items of incriminating evidence.

During trial, Weeks's attorney objected to the admissibility of the items seized, citing the Fourth and Fifth Amendments. The objection was overruled, the items came into evidence, and Weeks was convicted on the gambling charges.

On appeal to the U.S. Supreme Court, Weeks's attorneys once again argued that since the search of Weeks's home was unreasonable because the police had failed to obtain a warrant, everything seized should be excluded from evidence.

In a wholly unexpected opinion, the Supreme Court unanimously reversed the conviction, ruling that because the search was unreasonable, the fruits of the search should have been excluded from trial.

In support of this newly crafted rule, Justice Day's opinion stated:

> If letters and private documents can thus be seized and held and used in evidence against a citizen accused of an offense, the protection of the Fourth Amendment, declaring his right to be secure against such searches and seizures, is of no value, and, so far as those thus placed are concerned, might as well be stricken from the Constitution. The efforts of the courts and their officials to bring the guilty to punishment, praiseworthy as they are, are not to be aided by the sacrifice of those great principles established by years of endeavor and suffering which have resulted in their embodiment in the fundamental law of the land. . . .
>
> To sanction such proceedings would be to affirm by judicial decision a manifest neglect, if not an open defiance, of the prohibitions of the Constitution, intended for the protection of the people against such unauthorized action.

This was a stunning reversal. However, it had little real impact. *Weeks* was a federal case, and its holding only limited illegally seized items from federal prosecutions; the vast majority of all prosecutions were of state origin, and *Weeks* did not speak to those cases. Nonetheless, the Fourth Amendment exclusionary rule was born.

Indeed, though previous Court decisions had tinkered around with the concept of the rule, *Weeks* marked the first time the Court actually utilized it. And although it had a limited application, this revolutionary holding would serve as the foundation for a dramatic series of cases to come.

A Knot in the Fuse

April 25, 1944. The phone rang in the district attorney's office in Denver, and investigator Ray Humphries answered. On the other end of the line, the anonymous caller told the officer the story of a distressed woman in room 602 of the downtown Cosmopolitan Hotel. After recently having had an illegal abortion, the woman was now in dire need of medical assistance. Joined by his assistant, investigator Humphries rushed to the scene. The two men entered room 602 and found Gertrude Martin, who told the officers that her abortion had been conducted by Dr. A. H. Montgomery and that she had been examined before and after the abortion by Dr. Julius A. Wolf.

In 1944, Colorado law held that performing or assisting in an abortion was a felony, the exception being for certain extenuating medical circumstances. The investigation into Gertrude Martin's abortion continued for another two days and the district attorney's office decided to arrest Dr. Wolf.

Proceeding without a warrant, the officers went to Wolf's office, where they found the physician sitting at his desk, and arrested him. On their way out, an appointment book caught the eye of one of the investigators. The cop picked up the record and began to look through it. The book turned out to be a ledger containing both a roster of Wolf's patients and the amount that each had paid for his services. The officers noted that several of the female clients had paid extremely high fees—an indication that they may have received abortions.

With this lead, the officers contacted the listed women and learned that Wolf had indeed performed illegal abortions. Wolf was subsequently charged with conspiracy to commit abortions—a violation of state law. He was found guilty and sentenced to the Colorado State Penitentiary for up to five years. After a failed appeal, Wolf sought review from the U.S. Supreme Court.

It had been thirty-one years since the *Weeks* decision, and when the Supreme Court granted certiorari (review) to Wolf's case, many legal scholars predicted that the case would serve as the vehicle for the Court to apply the exclusionary rule to the states.

They were wrong. Writing for the majority, Justice Felix Frankfurter outlined the gravity of the issue presented in his first paragraph:

The precise question for consideration is this: Does a conviction by a state court for a state offense deny the "due process of law" required by the Fourteenth Amendment, solely because evidence that was admitted at the trial was obtained under circumstances which would have rendered it inadmissible in a prosecution for violation of a federal law in a court of the United States because there deemed to be an infraction of the Fourth Amendment as applied in *Weeks v. United States*?

Frankfurter in his opinion noted that since the *Weeks* opinion some thirty-one years earlier, thirty states had rejected the exclusionary doctrine outright, while only seventeen states actually applied it. Frankfurter further noted that many states were employing other methods to protect their citizens' Fourth Amendment rights. In particular, Frankfurter suggested internal police discipline "under the eyes of an alert public opinion." And with these various states' approaches in mind, Justice Frankfurter stated, "In a prosecution in a state court for a state crime, the Fourteenth Amendment does not forbid the admission of evidence obtained by an unreasonable search and seizure." Even though the individual states were bound by the Fourth Amendment, the Supreme Court would not dictate how the states should accomplish that goal.

But the Court was far from unified in this monumental decision. Indeed, Justice Murphy's fervent dissent demonstrated that the *Wolf* decision engendered significant opposition. In his opinion, Murphy commented on Frankfurter's assertion that other alternatives were available to the states to enforce the guaranteed rights of the Fourth Amendment:

> Alternatives are deceptive. [The majority's] very statement conveys the impression that one possibility is as effective as the next. In this case their statement is binding. For there is but one alternative to the rule of exclusion. That is no sanction at all.

With this simple line, it seemed that the Supreme Court had framed the battle to come: the exclusionary rule or no rule at all. And as the twentieth century reached the halfway mark, the Court had thus far opted for the latter. But the conflict was not over. Though the issue had its roots in seventeenth-century England and had engendered debate for nearly three hundred years, the *Wolf* decision did not put an end to the question of how to protect American citizens from state action that invaded their privacy.

The Criminal Appeals

As Alexander Kearns began preparation for his appeal of Mapp's conviction to the Eighth District Court in Ohio, he had two main arguments. There was the First Amendment issue, challenging the Ohio obscenity statute as vague and overbroad. And there was the Fourth Amendment argument: the dual contention that the police had acted unreasonably and that the best remedy was to exclude the evidence.

Realistically, given the *Wolf* doctrine and the recent Ohio decision of *State v. Lindway*—which reaffirmed that evidence obtained by an unlawful search and seizure is nonetheless admissible in a state criminal prosecution—the Fourth Amendment argument was a long shot.

In his long and highly detailed brief, Kearns raised both issues, only to have the district court reject each and affirm Mapp's conviction. It seemed Dollree Mapp was headed to the Ohio Reformatory for Women.

But Kearns refused to give up, and with the assistance of Greene—and the financial backing of Mapp's anonymous benefactor—he filed a brief with the Ohio Supreme Court. By this time, Mapp's case had caught the attention of the American Civil Liberties Union, and Bernard Berkman of its Ohio office filed an amicus curiae (friend of the court) brief on Mapp's behalf. Much like Kearns's brief, Berkman's submission focused primarily on the constitutionality of Ohio's obscenity statute.

Another Defeat

The Ohio Supreme Court, citing its recent decision in *Lindway,* rejected the exclusionary remedy out of hand. However, the First Amendment argument nearly prevailed. Four of the seven justices found the Ohio obscenity statute to be unconstitutional. But, according to Ohio's constitution, six of the seven justices had to concur for the court to find a state statute unconstitutional.

> I cannot agree that mere private possession of such [obscene] literature by an adult should constitute a crime. The right of the individual to read, to believe or disbelieve, and to think without governmental supervision is one of our basic liberties, but to dictate to the mature adult what books he may have in his own private library seems to be a clear infringement of his constitutional rights as an individual.

The court's First Amendment opinion had framed an issue that became the center of speculation as Kearns set his sights on the U.S.

Supreme Court: Would the Court review the constitutionality of the Ohio statute under a First Amendment analysis, or would it revisit the exclusionary rule's application to the states? And if they did the latter, would *Mapp v. Ohio* become the vehicle for nothing short of a revolutionary change in American criminal procedure?

The Bomb Squad

"Impeach Earl Warren." In the 1960s, this phrase reflected a nation unsettled by an unusually active Supreme Court. The Warren Court, named after Chief Justice Earl Warren, brought the "least dangerous branch of government" to the forefront of political discourse. During the sixteen years of Warren's reign, the nine justices handed down a series of cases aimed at protecting and expanding constitutional rights. Consequently, these decisions altered traditional power structures in radical ways: They desegregated the school system. They reapportioned voting districts. They forbade prayer in public schools. The culmination of these holdings—and a series of others—polarized a nation, enraged large numbers of voters, and usurped congressional power.

Nevertheless, whether one was for or against the judicial revolution of the 1960s, the Warren Court left an indelible legacy, changing America forever. And although the protests and threats of the Court's opponents did not go unnoticed, at times their concerns seemed overshadowed by the era in which they were voiced. Indeed, the 1960s was perhaps the most turbulent decade in our nation's recent history: The Bay of Pigs. JFK's assassination. Vietnam. The Great Society. Martin Luther King's assassination. Neil Armstrong. The civil rights movement. From politics to pop culture, the 1960s dramatically transformed nearly every facet of American life.

On the world stage, the insecurity of a nation deeply embroiled in the Cold War manifested itself in gripping world events like the building of the Berlin Wall, the Cuban missile crisis and the threat of a nuclear war, and the shock of the Tet offensive. A country that had defeated two of the world's great military powers only twenty years before was now faced with the possibility of a Soviet invasion, nuclear destruction, and a seemingly unwinnable war in Southeast Asia.

Domestically, America was at war with itself. The civil rights movement brought the nation's citizens out to the streets. There were the hippies, the Black Panthers, the Ku Klux Klan, the NAACP. People who had never bothered with the complexities of politics now felt passionately enough about issues to take their positions and emotions to town meetings and protest marches.

Cultural icons such as the Beatles, Elvis, Bob Dylan, and Marilyn Monroe changed not only the way we thought but also the way we viewed ourselves. Audiences flocked to see provocative movies such as *Dr. Strangelove, Easy Rider,* and *The Graduate.* Television had become the dominant means of mass communication. In the afternoons, teenagers would dance in their living rooms to the sights and sounds of *American Bandstand.* At night, families would join together for the weekly install-ment of *The Flintstones, Bewitched,* and *The Andy Griffith Show.* As the new American culture infiltrated every aspect of daily life, taboos about sex, violence, and language began to diminish. This shift in societal norms resulted in the "liberation" of America's youth.

Change was in the air. And in the middle of the highly publicized rev-olution taking place on college campuses, in Congress, and on the streets, sat nine men in the U.S. Supreme Court. Though secluded by walls of granite and marble, these justices engaged in a legal revolution that served as a primary catalyst for the dramatic changes taking place outside of Washington.

In only thirteen years, the Warren Court handed down decisions that transformed everything from elections to police conduct. The Court's rul-ings and political makeup have been a topic of heated debate since Earl War-ren's appointment in 1953. Though countless explanations have been given for the series of revolutionary decisions, most historians attribute the extraordinary changes in the law to the Warren Court's namesake.

Born and raised in Los Angeles, California, Earl Warren dedicated the majority of his adult life to the justice system. Upon law school gradua-tion from the University of California at Berkeley, he served as an army officer during World War I. When he returned from active duty at Camp McArthur in Waco, Texas, Warren received a position clerking for the California Assembly Judicial Committee and served as an aide to the Oakland city attorney. At thirty-one, he was appointed assistant district attorney of Alameda County. Five years later, his boss resigned and Earl Warren took over the head position. He was elected to the office the fol-lowing year and served three consecutive terms.

His time as a district attorney did little to foreshadow his liberal legacy. Although the majority of his colleagues described his prosecution tactics as fair, he was thorough, vigorous, and efficient in bringing criminals to justice. Little deference was given to a suspect's constitutional rights.

Though these practices stood in stark contrast to the principles expounded by the future chief justice, it was in this office that he started his first crusade: he waged a successful campaign against the rampant organized crime that plagued his district.

Warren's successes in Alameda sparked aspirations beyond the confines of the San Francisco area. He quickly became active in several statewide law enforcement organizations, including the Peace Officers Association, the State Bureau of Criminal Investigation, and the District Attorneys Association. His participation in these groups garnered key support for his later initiatives. Among them, District Attorney Warren proposed a series of state constitutional amendments: The first made California judicial appointments subject to electorate approval. Another created the position of a state attorney general. And the final amendment proposed that a defendant's choice to remain silent at trial could be used against him by the prosecution.

All the amendments passed with ease. However, thirty years later—and in a stroke of irony—Earl Warren's own Supreme Court in *Miranda v. Arizona,* nullified the Warren-drafted amendment concerning the use of a defendant's silence.

Warren's creation of the Office of the Attorney General was a strategic reflection of his own ambition. When the state office became an established and respected position, he would run as soon as the current Republican incumbent retired. And in 1938, when the current attorney general declared his intention to retire, Warren ran and won.

His four years as attorney general seemed to further contradict the stances that he would later take as chief justice: Warren withheld the judicial appointment of a supporter of organized labor and criminal defendants; he snubbed a U.S. Senate committee investigating possible violations of the civil liberties of California farm laborers; and—perhaps most surprising—he was actively involved in the forced evacuation and internment of over 110,000 Japanese-Americans from the West Coast after the 1941 bombing of Pearl Harbor.

After serving a term as attorney general, Warren was elected governor of California. His time in the executive office proved to be a turning point in his political ideology. Perhaps the burden of the responsibilities that come with the executive position gave him a new insight into the impact government has on people's lives. Whatever the reason, Governor Warren began to take a deep interest in promoting social programs. He also became an integral part of the liberal establishment of the Republican Party. And in 1948, Governor Warren was chosen by his party as the vice presidential candidate on the Thomas Dewey ticket. Although the Republicans lost to the incumbent, President Truman, Warren had received his first taste of the national arena.

Defeated—but far from disheartened—Warren returned to Sacramento to implement revolutionary social programs such as unemployment benefits and old-age pensions. During his third term in the governor's office, Warren's popularity reached its zenith. The combination of his close bid for the vice presidency and his progressive programming made him a respected national figure. This newly acquired fame gave Warren the momentum to make a bid for the 1952 Republican presidential nomination. However, shortly after his declaration of candidacy, he became extremely ill. During his sickness, surgeons were forced to remove a large section of his intestines. Rumors began circling—perhaps at the hands of opponent Robert A. Taft—that Warren was dying of cancer. Party officials began looking for a new candidate, settling on World War II hero Dwight D. Eisenhower. As the slogan went, everybody liked Ike—including Warren. Therefore, when the Republicans nominated Eisenhower in 1952, Warren immediately threw his support to the nominee and actively campaigned on his behalf.

After defeating Stevenson in the general election, Eisenhower intended to offer Warren the position of solicitor general, with the promise that he'd consider him for the U.S. Supreme Court should one of the justices retire. Shortly after Warren's appointment, Eisenhower received word of Chief Justice Frederick Vinson's sudden and unexpected death.

Chief Justice Vinson had been brought on board by President Harry Truman in an effort to bring harmony to a deeply divided Court. But in seven years on the bench, Vinson did little to bridge the chasm. Now Eisenhower needed a politically moderate leader to do the job.

Some said that Warren was too liberal. Some said he was too conservative. The conflicting accounts regarding Warren's ideology gave Eisenhower the impression that Warren would come out somewhere in the middle. Based upon this perception, Earl Warren was named the fourteenth chief justice of the U.S. Supreme Court. The decision would perhaps be Eisenhower's most significant legacy—though he later stated that it was "the biggest damn fool thing [he] ever did."

When Warren joined the bench on October 5, 1953, he walked into an ideological war zone. Justices Jackson and Black had been engaged in open combat for years. Justices Douglas and Frankfurter were barely speaking to each other. Philosophical factions were in evidence at every turn. Consensus was a rarity.

Aside from the internal struggle, the Vinson Court had been plagued with prolonged absences. Many historians attribute this—as well as other problems—to Vinson's poor leadership; Justice Frankfurter had even been heard referring to the chief justice as a "damn fool!" The combination of the dramatic ideological differences and a lack of control left Warren stepping into a Supreme Court in disarray.

The Court's internal battles were highlighted by the historical differences in the justices' political affiliations. On the right sat Justices Stanley Reed, Harold H. Burton, and Felix Frankfurter. Justice Reed was a former solicitor general and proponent of the New Deal who had made a dramatic move to the right during his tenure on the bench. Justice Burton was a Republican stalwart who had represented the state of Ohio as a U.S. senator after serving as mayor of Cleveland. Justice Frankfurter was a Harvard law professor and founder of the ACLU, who had also grown increasingly conservative during his time as a federal jurist.

The liberal faction of the Court consisted of Justices Hugo Black and William O. Douglas. Justice Black, the former U.S. senator and ex-Klansman, was the first nominee of the New Deal era. Justice Douglas, the former chairman of the Securities and Exchange Commission, had been a popular professor at Yale Law School prior to his assignment to the bench. These jurists were reliable liberal votes when issues of constitutional rights were brought before the Court.

Somewhere in the middle of the political spectrum were former attorney generals Robert H. Jackson and Tom C. Clark and former Seventh Circuit justice Sherman Minton. These justices carried a centrist ideology that would produce the crucial swing votes in many of the Court's decisions.

When put together, these eight justices represented a vast array of political views, and the dramatic philosophical differences eroded the cohesiveness necessary to build a functioning judicial body. Chief Justice Vinson had failed to bring the jurists together. In fact, many would argue that his passive style had made the situation worse. In the 1952 session alone, the Court filed 201 dissenting opinions. Eighteen of these were filed by Vinson himself. Relations among the jurists were at an all-time low. The Court was in need of a unifying leader.

Between his proven leadership skills and apparent centrist ideology, the neophyte chief justice seemed to provide the perfect remedy. But in Warren's first months as head of the world's most powerful judicial body, many—including Warren himself—were uneasy about his capabilities. In these early days, the chief justice complained to fellow justice Robert Jackson that his lack of legal experience had not prepared him for his new role, and that he was having a difficult time finding the significance of some of the cases before the Court.

Then, in 1954, the Court granted certiorari for five segregation cases. Under the name *Brown v. Board of Education,* the developing Warren Court made one of its most important decisions, both in terms of public policy and the Court's dynamics.

Warren had never been either a vocal advocate or a zealous opponent of segregation during his time as a California politician. Nonetheless, he believed that a "separate but equal" educational system—as mandated by *Plessy v. Ferguson*—did not result in comparable education between whites and blacks. As opposed to Vinson, whose main concern was congressional reaction to the overruling of the *Plessy* principle, Warren seemed apprehensive only about the effective implementation of such a decision. For him, the question was never *why* the Court should eradicate segregation, but *how*.

With a sense of urgency, the rookie chief justice seized this crucial opportunity to establish his presence on the Court. In a series of maneuvers, Warren managed to change the minds of the Court's most stalwart segregation proponents. He remained relatively silent during *Brown*'s oral arguments, and his strategic maneuvers took place behind closed doors. Using his power of judicial conference scheduling, Warren slated the Court's debate on *Brown* a full two months after oral arguments. Breaking precedent—and to the associate justices' surprise—Warren did not confine debate to the formalized conditions of the judicial conferences. Instead, he took an informal approach, stating that the segregation cases would be talked over "from week to week . . . in groups, over lunches."

And over time, Warren brought four other justices into his corner. Armed with the knowledge that these jurists would be enough to overturn *Plessy,* he continued the informal discussions with confidence. At these meetings, Warren made the assertion that they could not sustain *Plessy* unless they granted the premise that blacks were inferior to whites. Warren had definitively framed the issue as a question of polarized morality. The four justices who had previously been ardent supporters of the "separate but equal" doctrine ultimately joined their colleagues to hand down a unanimous decision. Warren's informal approach, scheduling maneuvers, and infusion of morality had brought the divided Court to an astonishing consensus. *Brown v. Board of Education* did not merely desegregate the public school system, it established Earl Warren as a force to be reckoned with.

Brown caused an uproar. There were riots. There were protests. There were angry letters. President Eisenhower refused to comment on the decision for nine years. Senator Joseph McCarthy labeled the *Brown* decision a product of Communist infiltration. And an enraged South began an all-out public relations war against the nation's highest judicial body.

Perhaps as a result of the public outcry, the Warren Court essentially laid low for several years. And in those years, the Court's composition underwent significant changes. The politically moderate Jackson died shortly after *Brown* and was replaced by conservative John Marshall Harlan. In 1956, another moderate jurist—Sherman Minton—resigned. His position was filled by former New Jersey Supreme Court justice William J. Brennan. Brennan and Warren soon became close friends, and—as history would show—a powerful ideological team. In addition, Felix Frankfurter's two conservative allies—Justices Burton and Reed—were replaced by Eisenhower appointees Charles E. Whittaker and Potter Stewart. Justice Whittaker, a former Eighth Circuit justice, was a stalwart Midwestern Republican who left the Supreme Court after only five years due to a nervous breakdown. Like Justice Whittaker, Justice Stewart was also a federal circuit jurist; however, his conservative roots eventually shifted toward the center during his tenure as a Supreme Court justice.

With this shake-up, the Court was now divided into two ideological camps. Led by Warren, the liberals included Black, Douglas, and Brennan. Led by Frankfurter, the conservatives included Harlan and Whittaker. And the all-too-crucial swing votes were in the hands of Stewart and Clark.

Again, the Court represented a deep ideological divide. Nevertheless, the leadership established by Warren played a vital role in the Court's dynamics. Though the unanimity of *Brown* might have been impossible in the same Court that would decide Dollree Mapp's appeal, the relationships among the justices were more congenial than in the time of Chief Justice Vinson.

In contrast to most of the Court's major decisions, the *Mapp* opinion would not be written by Chief Justice Warren. That duty was delegated to moderate jurist Tom C. Clark.

Born in Dallas, Texas, Justice Clark had a personal résumé that was indicative of both a respected soldier and a successful lawyer. As a teenager, Clark served as an infantryman for the Texas National Guard during World War I; his time in the military also garnered him an undergraduate education at Virginia Military Institute. Upon his return from the Great War, Clark enrolled in law school at the University of Texas at Austin. He then opened a private practice in Dallas and, after several years, served as a civil district attorney for the city. His first taste of a public career appealed to him. Upon a brief return to private practice, Clark joined the Justice Department and served as a civilian coordinator for the Japanese internment camps in California during World War II. He would later be promoted at the Justice Department to serve as head of the antitrust and criminal division.

Near the end of World War II, Clark was appointed U.S. attorney general by President Harry S. Truman. And with the death of U.S. Supreme Court justice Frank Murphy, President Truman nominated the attorney general to fill the vacancy.

A Democrat, Clark often sided with the liberal majority, though his surprising alliance with the Court's conservative element in several cases made him the sought-after swing vote. And although he played a key role in many of the Court's important decisions, *Mapp v. Ohio* would prove to be Clark's most significant contribution to the American legal system. Indeed, it would be this Texas native who would author what future Supreme Court justice Abe Fortas described as "the most radical decision in recent times."

The Criminal's Last Chance

More than three years after the raid on the home on Milverton Road, Alexander Kearns and Walter Greene filed a notice of appeal to the U.S. Supreme Court. It was a long shot to even be granted a hearing, and they knew it. But it was their last chance to overturn Mapp's conviction. Every year, the Supreme Court receives thousands of these petitions. Many posit legitimate constitutional issues. However, the Supreme Court is only able to grant review to about eighty cases per session. Generally, the only cases to make it onto the Court's docket are those presenting a novel question of law, demonstrating a dispute between one or more states, or pertaining to treaties made with other countries.

Working in Mapp's favor was that one of the issues presented in her case had been receiving some notice. Police abuses like those listed in *Boyd, Weeks,* and *Wolf* showed no sign of slowing. And as of 1961, the Supreme Court had yet to proffer any remedy to safeguard Fourth Amendment rights against violations by law enforcement. Against this backdrop, the Court granted certiorari and requested briefs.

Dollree Mapp would get yet another day in court. Mapp's lawyers focused their brief on the First Amendment argument that the Ohio obscenity statute was unconstitutional. The Fourth Amendment search-and-seizure issue was referenced only briefly. While Clark would spend a great deal of the *Mapp* opinion on the implications of the *Wolf* decision, Kearns did not even cite *Wolf* in his brief. Kearns did, at least, assert that the unlawful search of Mapp's home "portrayed a shocking disregard of human rights." This memorable sound bite referenced the Court's decision in *Rochin v. California.*

In *Rochin,* police barged into the defendant's home and found two capsules lying on his nightstand. When the defendant saw the police, he grabbed the pills and swallowed them. A struggle ensued, with three offi-cers jumping on the defendant, trying to get the capsules; one officer went so far as to grab Rochin by the neck to prevent him from swallow-ing the pills. Rochin fought them off and was eventually handcuffed and taken to a hospital, where doctors pumped his stomach and extracted the capsules, which were found to contain morphine. Based almost exclu-sively on the extracted capsules, Rochin was charged and convicted of drug possession. Citing the "shocking disregard of human rights," the nine justices of the Supreme Court excluded the evidence, although they did not exclude the evidence based upon the Fourth Amendment—they excluded it because of the "shocking" conduct of the police.

By analogizing *Rochin* to *Mapp,* Kearns briefly argued that the fla-grantly illegal search of Mapp's house constituted an unreasonable viola-tion of her constitutional rights. Even so, this argument seemed to be an afterthought in a brief that focused primarily on First Amendment issues.

As he did in Ohio, ACLU attorney Bernard Berkman filed an amicus curiae brief in support of Kearns's efforts. Berkman's brief also primarily focused on the First Amendment theories. Only three sentences in the ACLU brief were dedicated to the search-and-seizure issue. In these few lines, Berkman requested that the Court reconsider the *Wolf* decision and "conclude that the ordered liberty concept guaranteed to persons by the due process clause of the Fourteenth Amendment necessarily requires that evidence illegally obtained in violation thereof, not be admissible in state criminal proceedings." And that was it. Neither Berkman nor Kearns expected Dollree Mapp's case to be the instrument that would turn the American criminal justice system on its head.

The state of Ohio countered with Cuyahoga County assistant prose-cutor Gertrude Bauer Mahon to argue the government's position. At fifty-seven, Mahon might have been considered an unusual choice. The Ohio attorney had attended Mary Manse College in Toledo and then John Marshall Law School. Mahon was one of only a handful of women to attend law school in the 1940s. Upon graduation, she got a job as an assistant prosecutor in Cuyahoga County. Mahon had been the prose-cuting attorney at Mapp's trial and had represented the county through-out Mapp's entire appellate process. Because of her experience and knowledge of the case, she would now be sent to the Supreme Court to battle Kearns and Greene for the fourth—and final—time.

Like those of her adversaries, Mahon's brief primarily focused on the constitutionality of the Ohio obscenity statute. However, she did respond to Kearns and Berkman's secondary contention regarding the "unlawful" search-and-seizure issue:

The constitutional guarantee against unreasonable searches and seizures was never meant to prevent the administration of criminal justice. It speaks of the right of the people to be secure in their persons, house, papers, and effects. Nothing is said in that provision guaranteeing security and immunity in the commission of crimes.

In merely a paragraph from Kearns and another from Mahon, the arguments encompassing centuries of debate came before Earl Warren and his eight associates.

The Attempt to Defuse

March 29, 1961, 12 p.m.

CLERK OF THE SUPREME COURT: All rise! Oyez, oyez, oyez. The honorable chief justice and the associate justices of the Supreme Court of the United States. All persons having business before the Honorable Court are admonished to draw nigh and give their attention, for the Court is now sitting. God save the United States and this Honorable Court.

JUSTICE WARREN: *Dollree Mapp, et cetera, appellant, versus Ohio.*

THE CLERK: Counsel are present.

WARREN: Mr. Kearns?

KEARNS: Mr. Chief Justice, this Honorable Court, if the Court please:

We have a situation here arising in Cuyahoga County, Ohio. The defendant-appellant in this case was living in a residential neighborhood, owned her own home, and living there in a two-family house on the second floor, having rented the first floor to a tenant. One day these police officers of the city of Cleveland, three in number, came to the house and wanted to be admitted for the purpose of making a search. When they rapped at the door or rang the bell, she looked out the window and asked them what they wanted. And they said that they wanted to search the house.

THE COURT: What time of the day was this, day or night? [In older Supreme Court transcripts, the chief justice is the only member of the Court to be singled out by name.]

KEARNS: In the daytime.

THE COURT: On a weekday? On a weekday in the daytime?

KEARNS: Weekday, yes. And she said that she would call her lawyer and see what he said. She called her lawyer, Mr. Greene, who is my associate; and he said to her, if they have a search warrant, you permit them into the house. So she told them that they'd have to have a search warrant. Neither one of them did. But they testified that a search warrant was procured by a Lieutenant White. When they came to the house with the search warrant— or supposed search warrant—by the time they arrived, Mr. Greene was also there.

THE COURT: You say "supposed search warrant"?

KEARNS: There was no search warrant, Your Honor. I intend to go to that from the evidence as we proceed.

This Lieutenant White came and showed a piece of paper and Mrs. Mapp demanded to see the paper and to read it, see what it was, which they refused to do, so she grabbed it out of his hand to look at it. And then a scuffle started, and she put his piece of paper into her bosom. And, very readily the police officer put his hands into her bosom and removed the paper and thereafter, thereafter handcuffed her while the police officers started to search the house.

Now the evidence discloses that no search warrant existed, although they claimed there was a search warrant. There is absolutely no evidence of any magistrate that had been asked for a search warrant; there was no record of a search warrant. We asked during the trial of the case that the search warrant be produced and it was not. The fact of the matter is that our own [Ohio] Supreme Court found that it was very questionable as to whether there was a search warrant in this case.

THE COURT: What was the piece of paper? Did that get identified?

KEARNS: We don't know what it was. She was not given an opportunity to read it. She doesn't know what it was. It was a piece of white paper. But the police officers never produced it, because, as a matter of fact, if it please Your Honors, I waited in the trial of the case for Lieutenant White, who was supposed to be the man who procured the search warrant, to take the stand so that at least I could cross-examine him as to where, when, and how he procured the search warrant and what the search warrant contained. But the state was clever enough not to put him on the stand; and no other police officer knew anything about it.

THE COURT: You couldn't have called him?

KEARNS: If I called him, Your Honor, it would have made him my witness.

THE COURT: I know, but hostile witnesses—one has freedom with a hostile witness.

KEARNS: I agree, we have freedom with hostile witnesses. But I've been practicing criminal law for a number of years, and I know what a police officer of experience can do to you if you're not careful, as far as a jury is concerned.

THE COURT: Anyhow, you didn't call him.

KEARNS: I did not. I did not. But the prosecutor promised—and we have the prosecutor here—that the search warrant would be produced, and it never was. So the situation is that the home was entered, the place was searched from cellar to roof by all these police officers. They found some paraphernalia in the basement pertaining to some lottery, belonging—later it developed—to someone else. She was then arrested and tried for having in her possession obscene literature.

THE COURT: May I trouble you to tell us what you deem to be the questions that are open before this Court? And I'll tell you why I ask that question: Unless you correct me, I assume it is still the law of Ohio that the decision of your Supreme Court is what is contained in the syllabus. I find that the court hasn't decided questions of evidence or the charge, et cetera, et cetera. It decided only questions of the constitutionality of the statute.

KEARNS: That's what they decided. That's what the—

THE COURT: So far as I read the syllabi, I can't tell that any of these questions about search and seizure—no—

KEARNS: Unlawful search and seizure.

THE COURT: Are you asking us to overrule the *Wolf* case in this Court? I notice it isn't even cited in your brief. I just want to know what's before us, Mr. Kearns.

KEARNS: That's one of the questions I'm trying to—Judge Frankfurter, I thought I would start giving you the factual situation, and now I'll come to the questions. Two questions, as we see it. Very respectfully submitted is the question of, is the statute constitutional under which she was convicted? And the search-and-seizure proposition in this case.

THE COURT: Well, that means you're asking us to overrule *Wolf against Colorado.*

KEARNS: No, I don't believe we are. All that we're asking is that we have this *Lindway* case that I'm setting forth in our brief that is controlling the entire state of Ohio.

THE COURT: And that holds that, although evidence is illegally procured, it is admissible; right?

KEARNS: That's right.

THE COURT: And that the familiar doctrine in so many states in this Union, and which we dealt with in the *Wolf* case. You don't even refer to it in your brief.

KEARNS: Well, we went through the *Wolf* case, but we don't refer to it here. I think maybe the state got it. But the fact of the matter is that we are, as citizens of Ohio, deprived of our constitutional rights against unlawful search and seizure.

THE COURT: Mr. Kearns, does the state contend that there was a valid search warrant here?

KEARNS: I don't believe they do, Your Honor, although they speak of it, and they've spoken of it in the Court of Appeals and before the Ohio Supreme Court. But they don't contend that there was.

THE COURT: Is the question of no search warrant in the trial court?

KEARNS: There was an unlawful search.

THE COURT: Did you raise the question of no search warrant in the trial court?

KEARNS: I did. I even filed a motion to suppress the evidence in the trial court, which motion was overruled.

THE COURT: What was the response of the prosecution to that?

KEARNS: There is nothing in the record of any response, nothing. The record shows a motion to suppress the evidence was filed, was argued for the court, and the court overruled it. And I'll say to this Court very honestly that the court overruled that because of the *Lindway* case. It is the *Lindway* case that controls them, because time and time again we've had the same question in our courts, in which the court would turn to me and say, Well, Mr. Kearns, can we say anything about this, since the *Lindway* case is still on the books?

THE COURT: And the *Lindway* case conceded that if there was an unlawful search, the fruits of it may nevertheless, if relevant, be introduced into evidence in trials in your state. Is that it?

KEARNS: That is right, and if they do not find contraband, then they are liable to a suit for being trespassers. But let us look at this other question: Here is a woman who is lawfully in her own home. She's not exhibiting anything like this. She's not trying to sell it. She's not doing anything assuming that they did find it in her home. The sentence, the sentence imposed upon her is one to seven years, for having—exercising, let us say—her right to look at a book that she shouldn't look at, to have in her possession a book that she shouldn't have. Not that she's a criminal, not that she has a former record, but one to seven years imposed upon her for daring to have a book of this sort in her home.

THE COURT: What can we do about the length of the sentence, if you're criticizing the length of the sentence?

KEARNS: Well, constitutionally, haven't her constitutional rights been violated?

THE COURT: On the length of the sentence?

KEARNS: Yes, by the severity of it.

THE COURT: And you think that's cruel and unusual punishment?

KEARNS: Cruel and unusual punishment, yes. And we cite it in our brief with the constitutional provision. Isn't it cruel and unusual, in a matter of this sort?

THE COURT: I may be wrong about it; you correct me on it. I thought that the phrase *cruel and unusual* related to the character and the type of the punishment, and not the length of it. Am I wrong about that?

KEARNS: Your Honor, the character and type, you're right. But in this case the court had the right to give her a money fine under the same statute, had he seen fit to do so. Now, where we have a person who commits crime, where we have a person who's a criminal and the record so shows, that's one thing. But here we have an honest-to-goodness mother of an eleven-year-old child, living in her own home, not bothering anybody; and she is not given a fine under this statute. She is sentenced to seven years in the penitentiary for daring to have this in her possession.

THE COURT: I thought your real argument was that that conduct just couldn't be a crime, and that therefore this statute's an unconstitutional one.

KEARNS: That is true. But I'm assuming for the purpose of the discussion that the books were there and that this Court may feel that it was a crime. But we do say that this is not a crime under the factual situation in this case that she did not intend to commit a crime; that she did not intend to injure any of the other citizenry of the state of Ohio.

THE COURT: Assume for the moment that she was constitutionally convicted, do you still contend that the punishment is cruel and inhumane?

KEARNS: I do. I do, for the sake of this discussion, if she was con-

stitutionally convicted. But I say, of course, that she was not constitutionally convicted.

THE COURT: I understand that.

KEARNS: And, as I'll explain, four judges of the seven found that
she was not constitutionally convicted. But under our particular
procedure we need six of the seven jurists to hold this unconstitutional, and we only had four of the seven. That's the situation that we're asking that this Court look into and correct the
rights of this particular individual, this plaintiff—defendant-
appellant.

At this point Kearns yielded a few minutes of his time to Berkman,
the ACLU attorney, to discuss the First Amendment issue. Berkman
referenced the search-and-seizure issue, but only briefly. The Court
then allowed prosecutor Mahon to respond. Mahon spent a considerable amount of time arguing the constitutionality of Ohio's obscenity
statute before turning to the Fourth Amendment and the exclusionary
rule.

MAHON: On the other issue, I think, that is before this Court, on
this search and seizure, on the trial of this case the two officers
that testified were already on the scene when this Lieutenant
White came out there, ostensibly with a search warrant. The
record doesn't show, and we have admitted, and as the [Ohio]
Supreme Court held, this was an unlawful search insofar as this
particular evidence was concerned, at least. There was no search
warrant to cover it.

But on the motion to suppress this evidence at the time of the
trial, the court relied upon the *Lindway* case in overruling the
motion to suppress. And, of course, the constitutional provision
against an unreasonable search and seizure, this Court has held
in the *Wolf* case, does not prevent a state from offering into evidence, it doesn't affect the competency of evidence tending to
establish the commission of a crime.

Now, we're relying on the *Wolf* case, too, with this Court. And
if this is a settled proposition insofar as the states are—rules of
evidence are concerned. It really is a judicial rule of evidence, and
Ohio does not follow the exclusionary rule. And this Court has
held that the state has a right to, and it is not in violation of the
Fourteenth Amendment to so admit evidence, even though
obtaining without a search warrant.

I have never been able to reconcile in the Constitution against an unreasonable search and seizure and the competency of evidence establishing the commission of a crime are not directly related in this respect: That the evidence establishes a crime, what defense is there in the absence of a search warrant? It's a collateral matter. It provides for a civil suit for trespass if a constitutional right is violated. Police officers are amenable to—as held in the *Lindway* case, and I'm reading from the *Lindway* case right now:

"An officer of the law who makes a search and seizure in a dwelling or other premises without a warrant or with an illegal warrant in contravention of Section Fourteen, Article I, of the constitution of Ohio is a trespasser and amenable to an action for such trespass."

There are many constitutional and statutory safeguards provided in the Ohio constitution and the Ohio statutes to ensure that persons accused of crimes shall have a fair and impartial trial, and those safeguards apply to matters of form as well as substance. But neither the laws of Ohio nor the Ohio courts are solicitous to a person accused of a crime in concealing the evidence of their guilt; and under Ohio laws many presumptions are indulged in favor of accused persons, and a strong measure of proof is required as to every material fact necessary to establish the guilt of the accused. But such indulgence does not reach to the extent of rejecting competent evidence because of the method by which it was procured.

And so, in the Ohio constitution and under the Ohio laws, the fact that there was a search warrant would not make the evidence any the more competent or the fact that there was no search warrant would not make it any the less competent. It has no bearing whatsoever on the evidence itself proving the corpus delicti of the crime. Your Honors, we, the state of Ohio, believe that we have a right to rely on your decision in the *Wolf* case, if there is anything to the doctrine of stare decisis. And we respectfully submit that there has been no violation of any constitutional right of the defendant in this case on trial, by reason of there having been no proper search warrant. We feel that that constitutional provision does not cancel out evidence of a criminal offense, nor does it constitute a defense to the commission of a crime.

WARREN: Is the search warrant in existence?

MAHON: Insofar as the record is concerned, it doesn't show any.

WARREN: Is there any record of it in the records as to whether—

MAHON: There's no record that there was a search warrant. The two officers who testified, who were the only ones, Mr. Chief Justice, you find in the record who made this particular search and found this evidence—they talk about twelve police officers being there and surrounding the place and making this search. But the only officers who turned up with evidence were Sergeant Delau and the patrolman who testified in this case. They had nothing to do with obtaining a search warrant. When the defendant requested, told them to get one, the officers said they waited and then Lieutenant White came out there. They thought he had a search warrant. Now, that's what the record shows.

WARREN: All right, thank you.

KEARNS: Do I have—

WARREN: Yes, you have some time left, I think, Mr. Kearns.

KEARNS: Now, I just want to say a word about the reading from the second opinion of our Judge Herbert of the [Ohio] Supreme Court and he said:

Section Fourteen, Article One, of the Ohio constitution, provides:

"'The right of the people to be secure in their persons, houses, papers, and possessions shall not be violated; and no warrant shall issue, but upon causes, supported by oath or affirmation, particularly describing the place to be searched and the person and things to be seized.'"

The judgment in the *Lindway* case is not in conflict with this constitutional provision. Had I been a member of this court at that time, I would have joined in the judgment as all the members of the court then did because the evidence there clearly established that the defendant was operating a bomb manufacturing shop in the basement of that house. As stated by [Judge] Jones . . . in the concurring opinion in that case—

THE COURT: May I ask you what relevance that has to your point?

KEARNS: The relevance that it has to our point—

THE COURT: The state constitutional provision?

KEARNS: The state constitutional provision, as well as the federal constitutional provision—

THE COURT: You were reading from, I thought, the state—

KEARNS: I was reading from the state constitutional provision—

THE COURT: Pardon me, I'm sorry.

KEARNS: —but it's practically a copy of our own federal constitutional provision, which is the same, that the people be secure in their homes against unlawful search and seizure.

THE COURT: Yes, but you were reading what the [Ohio] Supreme Court held with reference to its own state constitutional provision.

KEARNS: Not that they held. This is the dissenting opinion, Your Honor. Judge Herbert, reading the state constitutional provision, which is identical with the federal constitutional provision as to unlawful search and seizure.

But I just want to show this Court—

THE COURT: That doesn't reach the question that you were asked about several times, and that is: Assume what is asserted, that it would be illegal under the federal Constitution, what do you do with the *Wolf* case—because that did justify holding it unconstitutional to admit evidence of the results of the search as it was made.

KEARNS: Well, we feel that in the *Wolf* case this Court did not intend to make it a general matter or proposition of that sort, because of the fact that there are such exceptions where, as in the *Lindway* case, where there is real criminality, where there is violation of law knowingly, intentionally, and profitably, as in the case. In this case, shall we have our constitutional rights denied when we do not violate a law except, probably looking at or reading for the mental state, the wrong type of literature?

THE COURT: Do you think this comes within the doctrine of *Rochin*?

KEARNS: I think it does. I think it does. I think it does. Here we have a situation, if it please the Court, where there was absolutely no intent to violate the law, the public could not be injured. We were speaking of the damage that narcotics may cause by being in possession. That's a matter of health, that's a matter of the body. Here we are trying to control the American mind as to what they shall read and as to what they shall not look at.

THE COURT: What particular acts bring it within the *Rochin* case?

KEARNS: I can't say definitely, Your Honor. I'm very sorry, but I don't have all of the facts in the case, just the conclusion that I came to on that. I want to thank the Court very, very much for the opportunity of appearing before you.

Battered and Bloodied

It was over. Kearns's oral defense of Dollree Mapp had been a train wreck. Three years of petitions, briefs, and oral arguments appeared to have been for naught. He had thought all along, and with some cause, that Mapp's best chance was rooted in the First Amendment challenge to the Ohio obscenity statute; Justices Frankfurter, Warren, and at least some of their colleagues thought otherwise. Prodded by the contentious justices, Kearns seemed unprepared to participate in a Fourth Amendment discussion. When Justice Frankfurter inquired about his stance on *Wolf,* Kearns dodged the question and turned to the jury instructions issued at Mapp's trial. When Kearns was asked about *Rochin*—one of the few search-and-seizure cases he listed in his brief—he could not recount the facts.

In fact, not only did he fail to articulate an effective Fourth Amendment argument, he was only able to briefly mention his primary First Amendment assertion. Consequently, when Kearns yielded his time to Bernard Berkman, the ACLU attorney was saddled with engaging the justices on the topic in which they were most interested.

Although the majority of Berkman's brief had focused on the First Amendment issue, he astutely picked up on the direction in which the justices wanted to proceed during oral argument and stated:

> The American Civil Liberties Union and its Ohio affiliate [are] very clear as to the question directed toward the appellant, that we are asking this court to reconsider *Wolf v. Colorado* and to find that evidence that is unlawfully and illegally obtained should not be permitted into a state proceeding and its production is a violation of the federal Constitution's Fourth and Fourteenth Amendment. We have no hesitancy in asking the Court to reconsider it because we think that it is a necessary part of due process.

Berkman had directly requested that the Court reconsider the *Wolf* doctrine. Even so, Gertrude Mahon would not budge. Indeed, she was the only advocate to stick to the primary issues presented in the briefs. Nevertheless, Mahon saw the unexpected detour the arguments had taken and realized she had to address the Court's Fourth Amendment concerns.

For the first time, Mahon publicly admitted that the officers entered Dollree Mapp's house without a search warrant; however, she maintained that the Court should nevertheless uphold the search on two grounds: First, she noted that *Lindway* explicitly stated that Ohio did not follow the exclusionary rule. Second, Mahon stated that applying the exclusionary rule to the case at hand would essentially free countless criminals. In her own words: "We feel that that constitutional provision does not cancel out evidence of a criminal offense, nor does it constitute a defense to the commission of a crime."

The issue was now before the Court. Though awkwardly and largely without support in the briefs submitted by the parties, the Warren Court had been asked to reconsider the nearly twenty-year-old *Wolf* holding.

Shifting the Debate

Following the Court's first formal discussion of *Mapp,* several justices were riding in the elevator together. Clark remarked to William Brennan and Hugo Black, "Wouldn't this be a good case to apply the exclusionary rule, and do what *Wolf* didn't do?" Though such "out of conference" discussions had become standard practice since the early days of the Warren Court, that the comment had come from Clark was surprising. In the years following *Wolf,* it appeared that Clark supported keeping the doctrine intact. In fact, two post-*Wolf* cases had presented opportunities for the moderate jurist to actively support overruling the precedent, but in both cases, Clark refused to modify his earlier position.

However, nearly seven years before *Mapp,* Clark began demonstrating a shift in his thinking about *Wolf* and the exclusionary rule. In *Irvine v. California,* while Clark voted to uphold a state conviction based upon illegally seized evidence, he displayed some reluctance:

> Had I been here in 1949 when *Wolf* was decided, I would have applied the *Weeks* doctrine to the states. But the Court refused to do so then, and it still refuses today. Thus, *Wolf* remains the law and, as such, is entitled to the respect of this Court's membership.

Indeed, as the time drew near for a ruling on *Irvine,* the Court was evenly split—four to four. Clark was the tiebreaker. Before him lay the possibility of doing what *Wolf* had failed to do. And although he seemed to waver, his reverence for stare decisis would not allow him to use *Irvine* as the vehicle to overturn *Wolf.*

Now seven years had passed, and once again—as in *Irvine*—the Court appeared to be heading for a split. Chief Justice Warren picked Clark to write the majority opinion. With his respect for stare decisis in mind, Clark sent a first draft of his opinion to his fellow justices to elicit feedback. The responses indicated a division that would not merely separate a Court, but would fuel bitter debate into a new century.

Justice Stewart wrote:

As I am sure you anticipated, your proposed opinion in this case came as quite a surprise. The idea of overruling *Wolf* was not even discussed at the conference where we all agreed, as I recollect it, that the judgment should be reversed on First Amendment grounds.

Justice Brennan replied:

Of course you know I think this is just magnificent and wonderful. I have not joined anything since I came with greater pleasure.

Chief Justice Warren stated simply:

Dear Tom . . . I agree.

Justice Douglas declared:

That is a mighty fine opinion you have written. Please join me in it.

Justice Harlan, however, was not impressed:

The upshot of all this is that I earnestly ask you to reconsider the advisability facing the Court, in a case which otherwise should find a ready, and non-controversial solution, with the controversial issues that your proposed opinion tenders. Perhaps you will have gathered from the foregoing that I would not be able to join you in your present opinion!

Additionally it seemed as if Frankfurter, who had authored the *Wolf* opinion, would be opposed. And the response received from Stewart indicated that he would likely join Justices Frankfurter, Harlan, and Whittaker in a dissenting opinion. The crucial swing vote would fall into the hands of an ex-Klansman and former U.S. senator—Justice Hugo Black. Though Black's liberal persuasion indicated that he would be willing to join with Clark, the senior justice was unswayed by the assertion made in Clark's first draft that the exclusionary rule was somehow inferred from the Fourth Amendment. Rather, Black believed that the application of the exclusionary rule to the states could only be achieved by "bringing the Fifth Amendment to the aid of the Fourth." Realizing that he needed Black's vote, Clark began work on his second draft.

The Criminal Goes Free

On a humid summer day, Justice Clark handed down one of the most influential rulings in American criminal procedure. In a five-to-four vote, Clark had convinced Black. And with that bare majority, Clark declared:

> That the exclusionary rule is an essential part of both the Fourth and Fourteenth Amendments is not only the logical dictate of prior cases, but it also makes very good sense. There is no war between the Constitution and common sense. Presently, a federal prosecutor may make no use of evidence illegally seized, but a State's attorney across the street may, although he supposedly is operating under the enforceable prohibitions of the same Amendment. Thus, the State, by admitting evidence unlawfully seized, serves to encourage disobedience to the Federal Constitution which it is bound to uphold.

In supporting his assertion that precedent dictated the extension of the exclusionary rule, Clark wrote, "The Court clearly stated that use of the seized evidence involved 'a denial of the constitutional rights of the accused.'" In stern and uncompromising language, Justice Clark chastised his own Court for taking so long to reach the present decision. He then turned his focus toward the future:

> Having once recognized that the right to privacy embodied in the Fourth Amendment is enforceable against the States, and that the right to be secure against rude intrusions of privacy by state officers is, therefore, constitutional in origin, we can no longer permit that right to remain an empty promise. Because it is enforceable in the same manner and to like effect as other basic rights secured by the Due Process Clause, we can no longer permit it to be revocable at the whim of any police officer who, in the name of law enforcement itself, chooses to suspend its enjoyment. Our decision, founded on reason and truth, gives to the individual no more than that which the Constitution guarantees him, to the police officer no less than that to which honest law enforcement is entitled, and, to the courts, that judicial integrity so necessary in the true administration of justice.

The government was now forced to obey its own laws. If the police violated a defendant's Fourth Amendment rights, then the evidence that flowed from that breach could no longer be used against the suspect. Simply, if the constable blundered—the suspect could go free.

The premise of the exclusionary rule is that by excluding the illegally seized evidence the police will be sufficiently chastised by the exclusion and thus motivated to follow the law the next time they are confronted with a search-and-seizure situation. Clark, writing for the Court, recognized that the Fourth Amendment harm cannot be undone by excluding the "bad" evidence, but that exclusion will act as a deterrent to future illegal conduct.

Perhaps anticipating this harsh effect of his extension of the exclusionary rule, Clark then went on the defensive:

> The criminal goes free, if he must, but it is the law that sets him free. Nothing can destroy a government more quickly than its failure to observe its own laws, or worse, its disregard of the charter of its own existence. As Mr. Justice Brandeis, dissenting, said in *Olmstead v. United States*: "Our government is the potent, the omnipresent teacher. For good or for ill, it teaches the whole people by its example. . . . If the government becomes a lawbreaker, it breeds contempt for law; it invites anarchy."

But Clark's eloquent words would prove ineffective at pacifying the outraged conservatives of the Court. Joined by Frankfurter and Whittaker, Harlan drafted a vehement dissent. Harlan argued that not only should the exclusionary rule not be applied to the states, but that *Mapp* was the improper vehicle to make such a ruling. Beginning with the latter argument, Harlan recalled that the Fourth Amendment issue was barely broached in any of the briefs. Further, the parties had posed a legitimate constitutional question with regard to the Ohio obscenity statute. Noting the awkward way in which the Fourth Amendment issue had come before the Court, Harlan wrote:

> The unwisdom of overruling *Wolf* without full-dress argument is aggravated by the circumstance that that [*Wolf*] decision is a comparatively recent one to which three members of the present majority have at one time or other expressly subscribed, one to be sure with explicit misgivings. I would think that our obligation to the States, on whom we impose this new rule, as well as the obligation of orderly adherence to our own processes would demand that we seek

that aid which adequate briefing and argument lends to the determination of an important issue.

Citing both the inadequacy of the arguments presented and the principle of adhering to precedent, Harlan admonished the majority for its surprising holding. And after declaring his displeasure for the majority's decision to use *Mapp* to lay down the exclusionary rule, Harlan turned to the rule itself:

> I would not impose upon the States this federal exclusionary remedy. The reasons given by the majority for now suddenly turning its back on *Wolf* seem to me notably unconvincing. For us the question remains, as it has always been, one of state power, not one of passing judgment on the wisdom of one state course or another. In my view this Court should continue to forbear from fettering the States with an adamant rule which may embarrass them in coping with their own peculiar problems in criminal law enforcement.

Appealing to federalism, the dissenters pronounced their desire to allow the states significant leverage in their method of enforcing the Fourth Amendment. After briefly citing a few examples of other constitutional safeguards employed by the several states, Harlan attacked the majority's motivation for expanding the exclusionary rule:

> I regret that I find so unwise in principle and so inexpedient in policy a decision motivated by the high purpose of increasing respect for Constitutional rights. But in the last analysis I think this Court can increase respect for the Constitution only if it rigidly respects the limitations which the Constitution places upon it, and respects as well the principles inherent in its own processes. In the present case I think we exceed both, and that our voice becomes only a voice of power, not of reason.

Although Harlan had raised a detailed opposition to the majority opinion, his words would have no impact. By a five-to-four vote, Clark's opinion was now law.

Legal Explosion

Like the bomb that had awakened the residents of that Cleveland borough four years earlier, the exclusionary rule exploded onto the American scene.

Cries damning the "activist" Warren Court rang from every corner. Just as *Brown v. Board of Education* had sparked heated national debate and vehement criticism, so, too, did *Mapp v. Ohio.* Earl Warren's legacy would rest on these two landmark decisions (and on *Miranda,* still five years in the future).

Indeed, *Mapp v. Ohio* changed the law in nearly half of the states and created a national debate. On one side stood those who felt that the exclusionary rule was the only way to protect the rights guaranteed by the Fourth Amendment. On the other—and much larger—side stood those who felt that the "exoneration rule" was merely a way of protecting criminals by not admitting potentially reliable evidence at trial. The debate that had encompassed three centuries of judicial wrangling had now made its way into the public discourse.

Despite the harsh public criticism of *Mapp,* the Court did not back down and, over the next two years, expanded the scope of the exclusionary rule. The Court held that all evidence flowing from an initial Fourth or Fifth Amendment violation was the "fruit of the poisonous tree" and was therefore inadmissible against the defendant. For instance, if during an illegal entry into a house the police find a key to a safe-deposit box and they then use to find contraband in the box, that contraband, as well as the initial key, is forbidden fruit and likewise inadmissible.

The Court, however, also placed some limitations on the rule: if the circumstances were sufficient to show that there was an "attenuation of the taint" from the initial violation, the evidence *would* be admissible. Going back to the safe-deposit-box-key analogy, if the police also found a document in the box that incriminated yet another individual, and that individual was subsequently arrested and confessed, that confession would be sufficiently removed from the initial illegal entry to be free of the taint and therefore admissible.

With Chief Justice Earl Warren's retirement in 1969 came the appointment of the decidedly more conservative Warren Burger. A staunch Republican, Chief Justice Burger was highly critical of many of the Warren Court's rulings—in particular, *Mapp v. Ohio.* With Burger's appointment, speculation concerning the vitality of *Mapp* grew; with three other new Nixon appointees, the liberal era of the Warren Court had officially come to an end.

Important exceptions to the exclusionary rule also began to have widespread application during the Burger Court's reign. Under the "inevitable discovery" and "independent source" doctrines, even if an initial constitutional violation would have led to the discovery of incriminating evidence, if the prosecution can prove that the evidence would inevitably have been discovered—through an independent source—it will be admissible. For instance, in a murder case where the defendant gave a confession induced by unlawful means, telling the location of his victim's body, the body would nonetheless be admissible if the state was able to prove it would have been discovered even without the illegal confession. With these major exceptions, the exclusionary rule was no longer an automatic block to evidence.

A second significant limitation was the "good faith" exception. This exception precludes application of the exclusionary rule in cases when the police acting with a warrant—even a defective warrant—have a good-faith belief that it is valid. The Court reasoned that the police had done all that could reasonably be expected of them.

The Burger Court, followed by the Rehnquist Court, narrowed the scope of the rule. From special rules for searching a motor vehicle to fastidious principles for extracting items from a suspect's body, the laws of search and seizure have metastasized into a complicated tangle of exceptions and specialized rules.

Even so, the Supreme Court's efforts to limit the scope of the exclusionary rule did little to calm critics. Twenty-five years after Justice Clark's revolutionary opinion, the American public was as disenchanted with its criminal justice system as it had been in the 1960s. And although the transition to the exclusionary rule was met with fervent opposition from the nation's citizenry, it was the American system of law enforcement that was most affected by the dramatic changes that *Mapp* commanded. As one former New York City deputy police commissioner said:

> The *Mapp* case was a shock to us. We had to reorganize our thinking, frankly. Before this, nobody bothered to take out search warrants. . . . Well, once that rule was changed, we knew we had better start teaching our men about it.

Across the nation, police departments began implementing programs to better teach their officers the legal requirements of the Fourth Amendment. These efforts were not met with universal acceptance. One police instructor described his students as being "unreceptive to the changes in criminal law that [were] rapidly expanding individual rights." Some officers said, "They're handcuffing us," and, "The pendulum has swung too far." In response, the instructor replied, "Don't throw rocks at me. I didn't make the rules. But we all have to live with them. Who needs judges beating our brains out?"

Proponents of the exclusionary rule insist that when police officers lose evidence against a suspect, it deters them from violating the Fourth Amendment in the future. But this argument is based on two assumptions. First, it assumes that officers are informed when the evidence they have illegally seized has been excluded at trial. However, most police departments lack any formal procedure for notifying officers of such exclusions. How can the rule deter illegal police conduct if the offending officers never learn that their mistakes are putting criminals back on the streets? Second, the argument assumes that when the officers are actually informed of the exclusion, they understand the nature of their error. The inference is that once the officers learn of the successful suppression hearing, they generally attempt to obtain a better understanding of the laws of search and seizure. However, studies show that offending officers actually perform worse on search-and-seizure tests than officers who have never had any evidence excluded.

Though disheartening, these studies do not address *Mapp*'s most disturbing effect: What if the police recognize their error, but will nonetheless do anything to bring the criminal to justice? Is it acceptable for officers to perjure themselves to convict a criminal?

In 1994, a specially appointed commission found that police perjury was one of the most common forms of corruption facing the criminal justice system. Further, the commission stated that the most widespread form of officer perjury occurred during pretrial suppression hearings— those proceedings that determine if illegally seized evidence will be excluded from trial. During these hearing, many officers engage in what is known as dropsy testimony. In dropsy testimony, an officer falsely testifies that he witnessed the defendant drop evidence (usually narcotics) in the middle of a chase. Because this gives the officer probable cause to both arrest and search the defendant, the evidence is deemed admissible. However, studies have shown that in many of these instances, the officer probably stopped the defendant without probable cause and conducted an illegal search: the defendant had not dropped the evidence, but rather retained it on his person.

Commenting on dropsy testimony, Judge Irving Younger said:

> Before *Mapp,* the policeman typically testified that he stopped the defendant for little or no reason, searched him, and found narcotics on his person. This had the ring of truth. It was an illegal search. . . . But the evidence was admissible . . . since it made no difference, the policeman testified truthfully. After the decision in *Mapp,* it made a great deal of difference. For the first few months, New York policemen continued to tell the truth about the circumstances of their searches,

with the result that the evidence was suppressed. Then, the police made the discovery that if the defendant drops the narcotics on the ground, after which the policeman arrests him, then the search is reasonable and the evidence is admissible. Spend a few hours in New York City Criminal Court nowadays, and you will hear case after case in which a policeman testifies that the defendant dropped the narcotics on the ground, whereupon the policeman arrested him. Usually the very language of the testimony is identical from one case to another.

Since the implementation of the exclusionary rule in 1961, there has been a significant increase in police perjury. But the problem gets worse: it appears that the officers may have judicial accomplices. Several reports indicate that some judges will knowingly accept police perjury in order to circumvent the harsh effects of the exclusionary rule. In "The Dirty Little Secret," author Morgan Cloud lists five main reasons judges may accept such testimony. First, the judges claim that it is difficult to determine when a witness is lying. Second, they do not want to suppress probative evidence if they know that a guilty defendant will go free. Third, some judges operate under the belief that most criminal defendants are guilty. Fourth, many judges assume that criminal defendants are inclined to commit perjury themselves—therefore, many jurists choose to accept the testimony of an officer over that of a criminal defendant. Finally, judges do not like to label government officials liars—especially since these same officials frequently appear in court. Commenting on this final point, Chief Justice Warren Burger stated, "It would be a dismal reflection on society to say that [when] the guardians of its security are called to testify in court under oath, their testimony must be viewed with suspicion."

Looking back, many people still wonder why the Warren Court chose *Mapp* as the vehicle to lay down the exclusionary rule. One reporter claimed:

> It was Mr. Warren's tendency to interpret the Constitution in terms of the result he found desirable that drew the most criticism. The result, critics say, was to transform the Supreme Court into a perpetual constitutional convention, updating the Constitution to be square with the liberal majority's concept of what the law ought to be.

Was this assertion correct? In *Mapp,* a police officer forced his way into a private home without good cause and without a search warrant. Dollree Mapp was a sympathetic defendant, one who would not anger the public if she went free as a result of the constable's blunder; one who might have been undeserving of seven years in prison.

Would the exclusionary rule be in effect today if the Court had chosen a different case with a less sympathetic defendant? Take for example the 1997 New York case of *People v. Turriago*. In a wooded area of upstate New York, the police stopped a speeding U-Haul van around 2 a.m. Because it was hunting season, the officers were concerned about people carrying loaded weapons and hunting at night. Therefore, when the officers pulled over Leonardo Turriago, they asked him to consent to a search of the U-Haul for weapons. According to the officers, Turriago agreed; to their surprise, they found a body in a steamer trunk in the rear of the van. As a result of this discovery, Turriago was convicted of second-degree murder.

On appeal, Turriago argued to exclude the body from evidence because the officers did not have cause to make the initial stop. If upheld, Turriago's contentions would constitute a violation of his Fourth Amendment rights—and the exclusionary rule would apply. But the New York Court of Appeals would not let another criminal—a mur-derer—go free. Although the appellate court held that the officers did not have sufficient cause to stop the car, the court, in a strained effort, cited "inevitable discovery" and the body was deemed admissible. Turriago did not go free.

With facts like these, one has to wonder what the result might have been if a cold-blooded killer had come before the Warren Court instead of Dollree Mapp. Would the Court have freed the defendant in a case like this in order to expand constitutional protections? If not for an attractive single mother and her collection of "obscene" materials, the criminal jus-tice system might be dramatically different today.

More than forty years after the exclusionary rule was applied to the states, the same questions are asked and the same arguments made. Why did the Court decide to impose the exclusionary rule upon the states in *Mapp* without being prompted by either attorney? Does the rule really deter illegal police behavior? Should the criminal go free because the constable has blundered? Is there a viable alternative that would be as effective in protecting the Fourth Amendment?

With the rise of a more conservative court, many commentators expected new answers to these lingering questions—some even pre-dicted that the Court would reverse the *Mapp* decision. But so far, the Supreme Court has barely broached the issue.

Aftermath

Mapp marked the beginning of what would later be known as the "judicial revolution of the 1960s." In a dramatic series of cases, Earl Warren and his eight brethren changed the face of the American legal system. In *Baker v. Carr,* the Court reapportioned electoral districts. In *Engel v. Vitale,* the Court declared prayer in public schools to be unconstitutional. In *Gideon v. Wainwright,* they held that if a defendant could not afford an attorney, the state had a constitutional obligation to provide one. In *Miranda v. Arizona,* the Court mandated that all officers inform every suspect they take into custody of both their right to remain silent and their right to an attorney before they elicit a confession.

Three years after the Warren Court handed down *Miranda,* Chief Justice Earl Warren retired at age seventy-nine. He spent the majority of his time on his memoirs. Only five years after leaving the bench, Earl Warren died of heart attack. He was buried with military honors at Arlington National Cemetery in Washington, D.C.

Today, Earl Warren is remembered as one of the most influential figures in American legal history. Years after his retirement from the Court, his revolutionary precedents remain mostly intact. He's both loved and hated, but it's difficult to converse about modern American law without mentioning his name and his influence. Although his career has been the subject of countless literary works, it is perhaps best encompassed by Warren's own simple admission:

"Everything I did in my life that was worthwhile, I caught hell for."

After serving as a Supreme Court justice for more than seventeen years, Justice Clark retired in 1967 to avoid a conflict of interest when his son, Ramsey, was appointed U.S. attorney general. Clark's successor was the first black Supreme Court justice, Thurgood Marshall.

Clark kept active during the years following his retirement. He served as the first chairman of the Federal Judicial Center, a congressionally created organization that focused on improving federal court administration. Clark also sat by designation on several United States Courts of Appeals, where he remained a jurist until his death at age seventy-seven. But it would be his opinion in *Mapp* that would preserve his legacy.

Following the landmark decision that bore her namesake, Dollree Mapp continued to live in the brick home on Milverton Road. Seven years after the Supreme Court reversed her conviction, Mapp moved from the Cleveland suburbs to Queens, New York. Two years later, police officers suspecting her of selling drugs made the effort to obtain a search warrant; they found fifty thousand envelopes of heroin and assorted stolen property in her home.

Mapp's attorney challenged the legality of the search warrant at trial and lost; the court ruled that the evidence against his client was admissible. Mapp was convicted and sentenced to twenty years to life at the New York State Correctional Institution for Women. The constable did not blunder; the criminal did not go free.

CHAPTER THREE

Rules of Engagement

Randy Weaver and the Ruby Ridge killings

Government is not reason, it is not eloquence; it is force. Like fire, it is a dangerous servant and a fearful master.

—George Washington

The twentieth century saw the deaths of untold millions at the hands of governments and the armies they fielded—citizens murdered by both foreign invaders and fellow countrymen. For all the progress in science and technology, more people died at the hands of their fellow men in this bloodiest of centuries than in all previously recorded history. Americans watched from afar at the slaughter taking place on far-flung foreign shores: the machine-gun extermination of an entire generation of men during World War I; the Turkish-inflicted genocide of the Armenians; the Japanese rape of Nanking in the 1930s; the Nazi campaign of extermination of Europe's Jews; six years of World War II; the Communist purges and man-made famine that killed more Soviets than did Hitler's armies; the Khmer Rouge's killing fields; the famine during Mao's Great Leap Forward; the charnel houses of Rwanda and Yugoslavia in the 1990s.

America's modern-era abuses of power—the internment of Japanese-Americans during World War II, the My Lai massacre, the National Guard troops firing on students at Kent State—were relatively benign when compared to the foreign human rights catastrophes of the last hundred years. The U.S. government has not engaged in a policy of mass murder of noncombatants, nor has it sought to slaughter, starve, or bludgeon its own citizens.

But the growth of the federal government in the years since the end of the Second World War fed into the paranoia of a segment of the American public: the militias. In the 1980s, the militia movement grew significantly, with thousands of members organizing against the perceived threat of an arrogant and hostile federal government, intent on oppressing Americans unwilling to swear allegiance.

The 1992 shoot-out at a place called Ruby Ridge in northern Idaho and the subsequent trial of Randy Weaver exposed media-hyped fear of the militias, married to the government's desire for power. Above all, it revealed the hypocrisy of those citizens—and the government that does their bidding—who claimed that all Americans have basic liberties, including the right to be left alone. The government reacted all too quickly, with lethal force, when one family tried to exercise that right.

When news reports of the siege first started trickling in from the Idaho panhandle, many Americans wrote off the incident as the antics of some gun-toting, antigovernment nut who had gone over the edge, resulting regrettably in some people being killed. But as more of the story came to light, it was clear that one family's search for solitude, freedom, and religious enlightenment had led to the standoff. It took the lives of three people, cost two men their freedom, and exposed the U.S. government's intolerance and ruthlessness toward those who chose a life apart from "normal" Americans.

The watchful militias saw violence erupt again just eight months later at the Branch Davidian compound in Waco, Texas. After a fifty-one-day siege, government forces moved in, ostensibly out of concern for the children being held by David Koresh and his followers; the compound was soon engulfed in flames. The fire killed seventy-six, among them twenty-five children. Adding to the death toll were four federal agents and six Davidians—including one child—killed after the Bureau of Alcohol, Tobacco, and Firearms attempted to serve an arrest warrant.

In the aftermath of Ruby Ridge and Waco, the fear of and loathing for the federal government grew among the members of the militias, culminating in the single greatest act of terrorism committed on American soil before 9/11.

On April 19, 1995—the second anniversary of the Waco fire—Timothy McVeigh detonated a two-and-a-half-ton bomb outside the Murrah Federal Building in Oklahoma City. The massive blast tore through the building, killing 168 and wounding more than 500. The killings at Ruby Ridge and Waco were McVeigh's motivation; *The Turner Diaries,* a novel outlining a plan for the radical right's violent overthrow of the American government, was his blueprint.

The Seeds of Racial Hatred

It is impossible to understand why events unfolded as they did at Ruby Ridge without first understanding Randy Weaver. He and his family did lead an unconventional life; they were separatists who simply did not want to be bothered by anyone. Weaver was also a religious extremist whose primary goal was to stay with his family and await what he thought was the imminent end of the world. Had Weaver's life taken a different path, he might have been seen as a modern Henry David Thoreau, communing and at peace in nature. Properly understood, Randy Weaver was a threat to no one. Unfortunately, Weaver was pigeonholed by government agents with dangerous right-wing extremist groups such as the Aryan Nation and the Ku Klux Klan.

On the far end of the spectrum lay the Ku Klux Klan and neo-Nazi groups; threats and intimidation were their means of "persuasion." Then there were the less dangerous and nonviolent separatist and survivalist groups. Whereas white supremacist groups were proactive, the separatist and survivalist groups tended to be passive, choosing isolation as an alternative to violence.

Unfortunately, categorization and grouping of the individuals in this spectrum is far from a precise business. There are enough similarities between the groups that making generalizations such as "dangerous" or "benign" can be difficult. The groups are predominately white and have a strong religious component, but the separatists and survivalists tend to believe in a Christian God, while the supremacists generally do not, instead practicing a form of paganism.

Both groups oppose restrictive gun laws and view the right to bear weapons as sacrosanct. But a crucial distinction remains: the racists use guns to terrorize and kill, whereas the survivalists use them only in self-defense. This difference is easily lost on the many who are inclined to view them all as gun-toting radicals with extreme beliefs.

At the time of Ruby Ridge, the Ku Klux Klan and the neo-Nazis were the primary racist groups in America. The history of the Klan can be traced back to the end of the Civil War, when groups of former Confederate soldiers targeted newly freed slaves. Their actions quickly escalated from taunts and pranks to intimidation, violence, and murder. By 1868, these white Southerners, led by former Confederate general Nathan Bedford Forrest, formed the Ku Klux Klan. Klan members, their identities cloaked by white masks and robes, terrorized and murdered blacks with virtual impunity.

Congress reacted to the growing violence by outlawing "night riding" and even suspended habeas corpus for a time. But with the end of Reconstruction and the withdrawal of Northern troops, Klan activity subsided and the organization became dormant, while Southern states enacted Jim Crow laws to control and keep the newly freed slaves "in their place."

Following World War I, the Klan reemerged as a national organization, and by the 1920s its membership had grown to nearly 4 million. This surge is attributed to an anti-urbanization sentiment in rural America and to D. W. Griffith's movie *Birth of a Nation,* which portrayed Klansmen as patriots courageously fighting for their way of life. The Klan had expanded and was now antiblack, anti-Semitic, and anti-Catholic; people were reacting to an alleged "Catholic menace," fueled in part by rumors of the pope's agents trying to infiltrate the U.S. government. The Klan of the 1960s was responsible for murders and bombings throughout the South, including one that destroyed a church and killed four young black girls in Birmingham, Alabama.

During the resurgence of the Klan in the 1920s, a theory of an international Jewish conspiracy to rule the world gained prominence in America. Discussed in the *Protocols of the Elders of Zion,* a political forgery created by the Russian Okhrana, or Czarist secret police, around the turn of the century, the book falsely claimed that Jews were responsible for the sluggish economy, the country's urban growth, and many other national ills. The book also foreshadowed the end of the world. American automobile tycoon Henry Ford helped to spread the lie, publishing the *Protocols* in his weekly Michigan newspaper. From essays in this newspaper came *The International Jew,* a book that sold nearly half a million copies in the United States, was translated into sixteen languages, and became a staple in Klan and Nazi propaganda. Ford later denied responsibility for and retracted publication of the book, closing his newspaper as well. Nonetheless, the book remained popular at right-wing gatherings as late as the 1980s.

It was William Pierce who popularized the modern paranoia about Jewish control of America, or the "Zionist Occupied Government." In 1978, Pierce wrote *The Turner Diaries,* a novel describing a future in which white revolutionaries fought against a corrupt government run by Jews, liberals, and blacks. His book encouraged racist organizations, depicting ethnic cleansing reminiscent of Nazi Germany as a way to "successfully" achieve global domination by whites. Timothy McVeigh apparently copied an event in this book when he bombed the Murrah building in Oklahoma City in 1995. In Pierce's story, an FBI office was bombed, and the loss of innocent lives was an unfortunate consequence meant to teach the government a lesson.

The neo-Nazis, a group spawned through claims of the "vast Jewish conspiracy," began as a German underground movement and migrated to Great Britain in the early 1960s. Neo-Nazism appears to have started as a response to the Communist threat arising from the 1950s Cold War, with Hitler's model of destroying the Soviet Union as the blueprint to be emulated. As neo-Nazism migrated to the United States, the unifying fear was not Communism but racial desegregation and the civil rights movement.

The founder of the American Nazi movement was George Lincoln Rockwell. Rockwell's involvement in the Korean War—he was a naval aviator during World War II and returned to active duty when the North Koreans invaded—solidified his paranoia that the blacks, Jews, and other minorities were instruments for the Communist takeover of the United States. He envisioned an all-white Protestant America. Rockwell and his neo-Nazis believed the U.S. government was controlled by a Jewish-controlled media and a Jewish-controlled government, called ZOG (the Zionist Occupied Government). They believed the only way to achieve their goal of a "pure" America was through violence. Thus, these Nazis, or skinheads as they became known, took their "idealized" version of America to the streets, where they committed acts of violence against blacks, Jews, homosexuals, and interracial couples.

Another violent, racist group is the Christian Identity movement. This group uses the Bible to justify anti-Semitism and racism, referring to Jews, blacks, and Latinos as "mud people" who conspire against whites all over the world in an effort to take control. Christian Identity pastor Richard Butler recruited American Nazi leader George Lincoln Rockwell, in the early 1960s, when Rockwell expressed a desire to recruit more members through a Christian focus. Butler founded the Aryan Nation in the 1970s. He greatly admired and respected Hitler because of the dictator's efforts to eliminate Communism. The group's focus on Communism made the Aryan Nation increasingly influential in the late 1970s and early 1980s, when the tensions between the United States and the Soviet Union were high. Since then, the Aryan Nation has partnered with the neo-Nazi movement. The Aryan Nation is known for its violence against all people who do not meet their definition of "true Americans."

A Breed Apart

Separatists, unlike the supremacists, do not necessarily believe that whites are better than other races; separatists believe that each race should live separately among its own people, not commingling with others. They are not known for race-related violence, nor are they prone to hate crimes or hate literature. Many separatists, like the Weavers, are highly religious and believe biblical prophecies will occur, as described.

The separatists, like the militia movement, are composed of people fearful of government interference. Although the movement is a relative newcomer, emerging in the 1980s, it grew quickly after the incidents at Ruby Ridge and Waco. Separatists are not known for aggressively seeking violence, but rather for protecting their "God-given rights." The separatists, like the other militia groups, are characterized by their stockpiling of weapons to fight the government, should its oppression become too onerous.

President George Bush's statements during Operation Desert Storm in 1991 inflamed these groups. He said cooperation with the United Nations was necessary for peace and spoke of a "New World Order." Many in the militia movement understood this to be an endorsement of a one-world government, something they feared because of their interpretation of Revelation, the last book of the Bible. Revelation speaks of the Antichrist, who arises to unite the world under one government, bringing plagues and torment upon the world, demanding allegiance by forcing people to put the "mark of the beast" on their right hand or forehead. Anyone refusing to take the mark of the beast will have his or her head cut off, yet anyone who takes the mark of the beast will have heaven's gates forever closed.

Following President Bush's comments, some members of the various militia groups began buying military-style weapons and undergoing military training. Although these groups have a "paranoid" ideology, they are not known for acts of terrorism; contrary to press reports, Timothy McVeigh was not part of any militia. Despite the absence of violent behavior, many militia members frequently violate federal firearms laws. A literal interpretation of the Second Amendment, coupled with a belief that they are in fact the "militia" referred to in that text—"A well regulated militia, being necessary to the security of a free state, the right of the people to keep and bear arms, shall not be infringed"—has led many militia members to believe that all gun-control laws are unconstitutional.

A third group that tends to get pigeonholed with the neo-Nazis and the Klan are the survivalists. Survivalists believe that government tyranny is imminent and that the end of the world is near. They stockpile guns, ammunition, food, water, medicine, and generators to prepare for the chaotic world they believe will result from the government's lawless actions. The survivalist movement has existed in one form or another since the late 1950s, when some Americans took preparations for nuclear war to new levels. Biblical scripture forecasts the world engulfed in fire, with snow in times of heat. In the aftermath of a nuclear war, "nuclear ash" would fall to the ground like snow. These survivalists interpreted these biblical prophecies as a description of nuclear war, and many sought the shelter of remote forest areas. As the Cold War came to a close and the fear of an impending nuclear war waned, so, too, did the number of survivalists. Later, the movement reemerged during Operation Desert Storm. Saddam Hussein was viewed as a preacher of Babylon (another biblical prophecy), and many believed a full-scale World War III was about to begin.

Although survivalists share some similarities with both separatists and the militias, they are a distinct group. Survivalists accumulate guns and ammunition, as do militias, but survivalists are generally viewed as innocuous. Fearing for their safety, many survivalists hide out in rural sections of Montana, the Dakotas, and Idaho. Northern Idaho has been particularly popular with many survivalists, including Randy Weaver and his family. The Weavers stockpiled guns and supplies at their twenty-acre home, preparing for the end of the world, which they believed was imminent. Weaver was not a member of any militia; he and his family were survivalists, who wanted nothing more than to be left alone.

Survivalist, militia, and racist groups were all founded on fear—fear of the end times, fear of a tyrannical government, fear of losing power to other races and religions. Among each of these groups, these fears fueled a desire for a means of self-defense. For Randy Weaver, those means were isolation from others. Many Americans had difficulty distinguishing the Weavers' peaceful existence from the violent actions of the neo-Nazis and the Klan, confusing survivalists, like the Weavers, with those violent and dangerous racist groups. The fear of this extra-mainstream conglomeration would eventually become hatred, and the government's response to this hatred would have devastating results for Randy Weaver and his family.

The Man in the Middle

Randy Weaver was born in the small farming community of Villisca, Iowa, in 1948. Weaver inherited a rebellious streak from his father, who, although deeply religious, did not practice any organized religion. Randy Weaver defined his faith through his own interpretation of the Bible; no denomination seemed to take the Bible seriously enough for him.

Weaver graduated from high school in 1966, enrolled in community college, and met his future wife, Vicki Jordison. Vicki and Randy had a lot in common: both came from rural Iowa communities and close-knit families who defined religion on their own terms. Vicki joined Randy at Iowa Central Community College in 1967, but Weaver soon dropped out to enlist in the army with hopes of fighting in Vietnam. Meanwhile, Vicki was finishing up her studies in a program that would earn her an associate degree in business management.

Weaver successfully completed Green Beret training, but he never made it to Vietnam. Despite his special training, he was stationed at Fort Bragg, North Carolina. Weaver's friends said he resented being stationed in the United States when a war was being fought. Weaver didn't understand how the army could send so many to Vietnam who did not want to go, when he was eager to enter the fight. A disgruntled Randy Weaver left the army after completing his three-year commitment, receiving an honorable discharge in 1971. He and Vicki married that November.

The Weavers moved to Cedar Falls, Iowa, and Randy enrolled at Northern Iowa University. Weaver planned on getting a degree in criminal justice; with his training as a Green Beret, he hoped to join the FBI. When he could no longer afford the tuition, Weaver dropped out of college, selling Amway products for a time, then working for John Deere. Vicki worked for Sears, and with her modest income and the low cost of living in Iowa, they maintained a comfortable middle-class lifestyle and soon purchased a small home.

The Weavers maintained a close relationship with God, whom they referred to as Yahweh. They studied the Bible together every night before bed, hoping that the secrets of the Scriptures would be revealed to them.

In the 1970s, following the latest Arab-Israeli war, the Weavers came to believe that biblical doomsday prophecies were being fulfilled. They viewed Egypt's attack on Israel as an attack against God's "chosen people," and a sign that Armageddon was imminent. In 1978, Vicki began to talk to Randy of a recurrent dream, an omen. Vicki Weaver saw a beautiful mountaintop retreat where her family—daughter Sara was born in 1976—would be safe from evil and the coming apocalypse. She also saw two other children in her vision, Samuel and Rachel. After the birth of their first son, named Samuel after Vicki's vision, the Weavers began planning in earnest. Randy started buying the weapons they felt would be necessary to protect the family during Armageddon.

In 1982, the Weavers' third child was born; they named her Rachel, hewing to Vicki's vision. The following year the Weaver family sold their house and most of their possessions, buying twenty acres of land in the Ruby Ridge area of northern Idaho. The Weavers built a rough cabin, without electricity or running water, and Vicki homeschooled the children, a violation of Idaho law. The Weavers made friends in the nearby towns, eventually taking in a troubled teenager, Kevin Harris.

During the mid- to late 1980s, paranoia grew in the Weaver household. Weaver could be hotheaded and speak before thinking, a characteristic that put him in the middle of several disputes. He and Vicki came to believe there was a conspiracy against them, accusing others of running a "smear campaign" and slinging false accusations against them to the FBI and the Secret Service. Vicki filed an affidavit in the Boundary County Courthouse that described a supposed conspiracy to harm them, orchestrated by the people with whom her husband had argued.

Weaver ran for sheriff in 1988; his platform included protecting the public from the government, and he handed out "get out of jail free" cards, saying that anyone arrested for a nonviolent crime would get a second chance. Weaver lost the election.

The Weavers—self-described white separatists, rather than white supremacists—soon began sporadically attending events like the local neo-Nazi summer campouts. At one such meeting, Weaver met undercover informant Kenneth Fadeley, working under Agent Herb Byerly of the Bureau of Alcohol, Tobacco, and Firearms (BATF).

The Setup

In the late 1980s, the media began running stories featuring camouflage-clad families, with children brandishing military-style weapons. The stories often failed to detail the differing goals and philosophies of the various groups, the media portraying them as radical right-wing extremists bent on destroying the traditional American way of life. The public, frightened and angry, called upon legislators to control, if not destroy, these groups.

The FBI and the BATF began sending undercover agents—such as Fadeley—to infiltrate these organizations, to evaluate whether a threat to public safety existed, and to prosecute lawbreakers. Randy Weaver would occasionally leave his mountain retreat and attend meetings, where Fadeley pegged him as a potential informant. The former Green Beret had credibility when discussions turned to weapons, and the agent viewed Weaver as someone other members trusted, even though Weaver refused to join any of the organizations.

Slowly, Weaver grew to trust the undercover operative and regard him as a friend. Agent Byerly saw an opportunity and initiated a plan for Weaver to sell Fadeley some shotguns, which Weaver was to cut down to an illegal length. After continued requests from his "friend" and in need of money, Weaver reluctantly agreed to modify and sell Fadeley two sawed-off shotguns.

Eight months after the guns changed hands, criminal charges were filed against Weaver for sale of the illegal guns. Weaver was then approached and offered a deal. If he would become an informant and help infiltrate the neo-Nazi group, the charges against him would be dropped.

There was a real incentive to cooperate. The criminal charges carried a stiff penalty, and if convicted, Weaver would serve time in prison. Despite the potential punishment, Weaver didn't believe it was right to befriend someone only to betray him later, so he declined the deal.

The Weavers soon sent a letter to the U.S. attorney in Idaho, referring to him as the Queen of Babylon and urging him and other government officials to repent their lawless ways and choose to serve Yah-Yahshua (Jesus Christ). The letter said that the Weavers would not obey the lawless government, even if it meant their deaths.

Six months passed before an arrest warrant was issued on the gun charges, but the federal agents thought it was too risky to try to arrest Weaver at his home; they delayed serving the warrant because he and his family were armed and suspicious of government officials. Therefore, the feds devised a ruse. Law enforcement officials, pretending to be stranded motorists, arrested Weaver when, offering assistance, he approached an apparently broken-down van. While in custody, Weaver was brought before a federal magistrate, who found probable cause that he had modified the guns. After ordering Weaver to stand trial, the magistrate released him on his own recognizance, but not before implying—incorrectly—that if Weaver was convicted, he would have to surrender his home, his twenty acres of land, and his truck to the government to pay for the costs of the trial, a falsehood the magistrate later admitted. Weaver was released and assigned to a parole supervisor.

A trial date was set for February 19, 1991, but through some miscommunication, the parole officer told Weaver the trial was on March 20. Randy and Vicki discussed what the magistrate had told him. They believed there was no way they could win; he had sold the sawed-off shotguns and the Weavers knew nothing about the legal concept of entrapment. After Weaver failed to appear in court—on either February 19 or March 20—a bench warrant was issued for his arrest. The confusion about dates, once discovered, confirmed Weaver's fear that government agents were conspiring to take his life, liberty, and property. Weaver and his family withdrew even further from society, staying at their home and having friends deliver supplies, patiently awaiting the coming Armageddon.

Watching and Waiting

Eighteen months passed without any open action by the feds. However, the BATF had started surveillance shortly after Weaver missed his trial date. BATF agents spoke to the Weavers' neighbors and acquaintances, trying to ascertain what it would take for Weaver to surrender. In April

1992, well over a year from the onset of surveillance, a team of six U.S. marshals set up video cameras and took aerial pictures of the Weaver house. They had installed a sophisticated audio system throughout Weaver's yard and house, even putting speakers under his kitchen floor. The marshals had generators, solar panels and batteries, surveillance cameras with three thousand feet of wire, a medevac helicopter, and camouflaged gear.

Between April and August 1992, different plans were considered as to how to bring the Weavers in. The federal agents wanted an arrest warrant for Vicki as well as Randy, because they believed that she was the strongest member of the family, and her arrest would bring the Weaver situation to a peaceful resolution. The team had been told by a government psychiatrist hired to assess the mental state of the Weavers that Vicki was the maternal center of the family, and would likely kill her children to keep them from surrendering. Some argue that Vicki was actually being targeted based on this assessment. Despite the agents' desire, the U.S. attorney had nothing to arrest her for and no warrant was issued.

The marshals considered and abandoned several plans that would have allowed them to arrest Randy Weaver. One idea was to cut the water line from a well to the cabin and refuse to allow friends to bring supplies to the cabin. Another discarded plan was to capture Sara, the Weavers' eldest daughter, when she was in the "birthing shed" during her menstrual cycle (the Weavers' religious beliefs required that they isolate the women during the time that they were "unclean"). The goal of this plan was to capture the Weaver children as they brought food to Sara, and this would certainly force Randy and Vicki to surrender. The federal agents, however, had no arrest warrant for Sara, so kidnapping her was not a viable option. Finally, the BATF agents developed a reconnaissance mission plan, and on the morning of August 21, 1992, eighteen months after Randy had missed the trial date, the agents closed in on the Weaver home.

The Shoot-out

Kevin Harris, the teenager who had been taken in by the family, Sammy Weaver, fourteen, and Striker, the family dog, were walking down the trail to their home. They heard noise coming from the brush, noise they hoped was a deer or a bear. Striker led the way down the Y-shaped path to investigate the sounds; they were actually made by federal agents, hiding in the bushes and trees on the Weavers' property. The agents were covered from head to toe in camouflage, only their eyes visible, no markings or insignia on their clothing to indicate they were federal agents.

What happened next is in dispute—the agents' account differs significantly from that of the Weavers.

As the dog approached the hiding spot of a federal agent, the agent opened fire, killing the dog. Sammy Weaver, gun in hand, shouted, "You shot my dog, you son of a bitch!" and shot at the place in the brush where Striker's killer hid. Sammy's shots drew return fire, and he was hit, first in the arm, and then in the back as he was running home. Sammy fell, his nearly five-foot-tall body hitting the grass facedown. Kevin Harris opened fire, hitting a hidden lawman in the chest. Marshal Degan would soon die from his wounds. Harris ran back to the house alone, and the family's cries could be heard as they realized their only son and brother, just fourteen, lay dead. Randy Weaver rolled on the ground and pounded the earth, then fired his gun into the air in rage and frustration. Ultimately, Vicki, the source of the family's strength, was able to calm her grieving husband.

According to the feds, Weaver was with Sammy and Kevin Harris as they approached the Y. The agents said they shouted to identify themselves, and Harris fired, hitting Agent Degan. The mortally wounded Degan then shot seven times toward the trio. One of the agents then shot Striker, claiming he was afraid the dog would attack. At this point, Sammy fired at the agents and was shot. Some even suggested that Weaver shot his own son to prevent his arrest. Officer Cooper denied that he was the one who shot Sammy, claiming instead that he shot Kevin; forensic evidence, though not conclusive, indicates that Cooper killed Sammy, and Harris left the scene uninjured.

The Standoff

The Weavers brought Sammy's body up the hill and placed it in the birthing shed—away from the rest of the family. By now, the agents had sent for reinforcements, claiming they were pinned down by gunfire and needed help. The agents claimed they did not know Sammy Weaver had been shot and killed; the intense level of surveillance ought to have revealed the Weavers crying and bringing the boy up the hill.

As a result of the reports that the agents were "pinned down" and under heavy gunfire, additional snipers and special agents were sent to the area near the Weaver residence. A hostage rescue operation was in place, but there were no hostages. Two people were already dead, and the Weavers were armed and dangerous. A crowd gathered at the base of the mountain to shout insults at the federal agents and try to stop them from taking further action against the Weaver family.

During the standoff, drastic changes were made to the FBI's standard rules of engagement. Normally, the "enemy" can only be fired upon if the shooter or other agents are in danger of bodily harm or death. This is a standard set in place by the government and relied upon in situations like the one at Ruby Ridge. In this case, however, the rules were changed. Now the agents and snipers could fire at "any adult male with a weapon, if the shot can be taken without endangering any children," without the existence of any threat to the agents. These revised rules were never officially agreed to by the FBI, but SAC Eugene Glenn later claimed that Larry Potts, the assistant director of the FBI's criminal division, told him that they were approved. Potts later denied this, and no explanation for the change was ever offered.

Weaver, Harris, and Sara got ready to pray over Sammy's body, out in the shed, before they buried him. As the three made their way to the shed, armed as usual, the snipers were ready to act under the new rules of engagement. As the three reached the door to the shed, Weaver was shot near his armpit by sniper Lon Horiuchi. Sara tried to shield Weaver from another shot and pushed him in front of her toward the house. The three ran to the house, where Vicki, with ten-month-old Elisheba in her arms, held the door open for them. Weaver and Sara made it safely inside, but as Harris was about to enter, Horiuchi fired again. Horiuchi claimed he was aiming for Harris, but the bullet tore through Vicki's face before hitting Kevin in the chest. Vicki screamed and fell to her knees, still holding the infant in her arms. By the time Weaver and Sara dragged her inside, Vicki was dead. They laid her body on the kitchen floor, where it would remain for several days. Harris was seriously injured and losing a lot of blood, begging Weaver to kill him and end his pain.

Following this second shoot-out, the federal agents used their equipment to communicate with the Weavers. "We had pancakes for breakfast today. How about you, Vicki, what did you eat today? . . . How did you sleep last night, Vicki?" they would taunt. Horiuchi and the other agents claimed they did not know she was dead, though it seems likely that they could hear the family mourning and Elisheba's repeated cries of "Mama" through their surveillance equipment.

Given the violent turn of events, face-to-face negotiations were not possible. The federal agents sent a robot with a phone up to the house, but the robot was armed with a gun—apparently not loaded, but standard equipment. The Weavers, having just lost two family members, were convinced this was a ploy to kill them, so they did not take the phone. They had also heard a radio news report that erroneously reported that Randy had killed a federal agent. The Weavers assumed from this false report that the government was trying to justify the

Weavers' deaths to the American people. They were sure the agents planned to kill them all and explain away their deaths. Weaver heard nationally syndicated radio personality Paul Harvey plead with him to use the government's phone to call the radio station. Harvey promised to get Weaver the best lawyer in the country. Weaver did not respond.

Inside the cabin, afraid to stand for fear of being shot through the windows, the remaining Weavers and Kevin Harris wrote down their version of events. All signed the statement, even Rachel. Bo Gritz, a former Green Beret known for his right-wing views, was called in to negotiate with Weaver. Weaver was thought to know of Gritz and therefore trust him; he was eventually allowed to approach the cabin, where he shouted to Weaver through the wall but was not allowed inside. Weaver said that he was willing to negotiate. Gritz announced Vicki's death, which enraged the onlookers.

The next day, Gritz returned with a minister and Vicki's best friend. Weaver and Sara told the trio that they didn't think they would make it out alive. Weaver was certain he would never get a fair trial. Gritz called famed trial lawyer Gerry Spence, who said he would seriously consider representing Weaver if he came down off the mountain, but wouldn't agree to represent him until he could speak with him man-to-man.

On Gritz's third day there, he was finally permitted inside and allowed to take Kevin Harris down the hill, where he was taken to Spokane, Washington, for medical treatment. Weaver also allowed Vicki's body to be removed by the coroner. With Harris gone, only Weaver and the three girls remained in the cabin. The federal agents planned to storm the house the next day. Sara held out the longest, not convinced that the feds—who had already killed her mother and brother—would uphold their end of the bargain and let them leave together. Finally convinced, Weaver, Sara, Rachel, and Elisheba left the cabin. Weaver was taken first to a hospital and then to jail. The girls were turned over to Vicki's parents.

Spence Takes the Case

That evening, Weaver had a jailhouse meeting with Gerry Spence, perhaps the best trial lawyer in the country. A large man hailing from small-town Wyoming, known for his homespun style and Western courtroom attire, Spence began by telling Weaver—quiet and dirty in jail overalls and sandals—that he did not share his political and religious beliefs. But Spence *did* believe in Weaver's right to a fair trial, and after hearing Weaver out, Spence agreed to defend him. In a letter to his Jewish friend Alan Hirschfield—in response to Hirschfield's trying to persuade Spence not to take Weaver's case—Spence said that the defense of Randy Weaver "transcends a white separatist movement or notions of the supremacy of one race over another, for the ultimate enemy of any people is not the angry hate groups that fester within, but a Government itself that has lost its respect for the individual."

Spence's team included his son, Kent, and an Idaho lawyer named Chuck Peterson, who faxed Spence an offer of his services as cocounsel, and Peterson's partner Gary Gilman. The lawyers did not expect to be paid for their services, though Peterson did receive the token fee offered to appointed counsel. Kevin Harris would be represented by David Nevin—who took the case largely for the chance to work with Spence— and Ellison Matthews.

Handling the prosecution was Assistant U.S. Attorney Ron Howen, who had been assigned Weaver's original weapons case, and Assistant U.S. Attorney Kim Lindquist. Howen had successfully prosecuted white supremacists in the past and was aggressive and confident. He had been the toughest prosecutor in Boise and was known as a perfectionist, a man who did not like to plea-bargain cases. Howen and Lindquist opted for a conspiracy theory to tie together the ten charges—including the original counts relating to the sawed-off shotgun and the failure to appear in court. Among the laundry list of charges was one for the murder of Federal Marshal William Degan. The FBI and the U.S. Marshals office were opposed to filing conspiracy charges, maintaining that they detracted from the murder charge. Ultimately, though, it was Howen's decision, and he believed that the wider scope of conspiracy would allow him to raise Weaver's religious beliefs and his peripheral involvement with groups like the Aryan Nation, which would strengthen his case. The U.S. attorney for Idaho even sought leave to seek the death penalty against both Weaver and Harris, but the judge ruled that capital charges were unwarranted.

The Trial Begins

The trial of Randy Weaver and Kevin Harris began in Boise on April 12, 1993, in a packed courtroom. Security at the eight-story marble courthouse had been upgraded; trouble was anticipated, and metal detectors, X-ray machines, and a number of federal marshals were evident. The jury consisted of seven women and five men, ranging in age from thirty-one to seventy-two, high school dropouts to MBAs.

Bo Gritz had warned skinheads to be respectful if they were to attend, so only a few showed up to observe. Some of the skinheads who had gathered at the base of the mountain during the standoff were disappointed that more government personnel had not been killed; there was good reason to be concerned that their behavior in the courtroom might be inappropriate.

There had been some protesters outside the courthouse; Kent Spence thanked them for their support and asked them not to return, concerned that Weaver's defense might suffer from their presence. Media coverage was intense, with daily updates on the Boise evening news. TV stations from Boise, Spokane, Seattle, and Portland sent full-time reporting teams to cover the trial, and news trucks filled the courthouse parking lot.

The lawyers split on dealing with the press. The defense attorneys spoke with the media each afternoon after the close of the day's proceedings, whereas the prosecution adopted Ron Howen's thirty-year custom of avoiding comment.

In the prosecution's opening statement, Howen and Lindquist painted Weaver as a racist who had been planning to wage war against the government since 1982. They portrayed Weaver as a hate-filled extremist, an incurable fanatic, a man whose religious zealotry was overshadowed only by the threat of violence he posed to others.

In his opening statement on behalf of Kevin Harris, David Nevin concentrated on a self-defense theory. Spence went last, and as is his custom, he spent much of his time personalizing Randy Weaver. If the jurors could understand Weaver and feel empathy for him, they would view events from his perspective. Spence set forth a compelling picture of a loving and devoted family man just trying to protect his family.

The government's case began with U.S. Marshal Larry Cooper, who witnessed the deaths of Agent Degan and Sammy Weaver. Cooper testified that Kevin Harris shot Degan first and that the rest of the shooting followed. According to Cooper, Degan knelt with his gun on his shoulder and said, "Stop, U.S. marshals." Then Harris "brought [his] weapon around to hip level and fired." Cooper denied shooting Sammy, testifying instead that he shot Kevin Harris, who "went down like a sack of potatoes." He testified that he did not shoot Sammy because he "decided that Bill didn't fire, that Samuel had not fired at Bill, and that he was a thirteen-year-old kid and [he] wasn't going to shoot him."

In response to a defense request on Cooper's second day of testimony, he came to the stand in his full camouflage uniform, the same type he'd worn on August 21, and carried the gun he had carried that day into the courtroom. The defense wanted the jurors to see what had confronted Sammy and Harris at the Y. When asked why he carried a silenced weapon, Cooper answered, "There was no specific reason we carried it; it was just there." But he was forced to admit on cross-examination that he had orders to lure the dogs away from the Weavers and shoot the dogs, taking them out of the picture. Nevin also stressed the fact that Cooper referred to the Weaver's cabin as a "compound."

Spence went straight to the heart of the matter in his cross-examination. He changed Cooper's language from "the compound" to "this little residence with the chickens, the zinnias, the dogs, and the kids." He also tore into Cooper about the dog. Spence asked, "Now, the dog's biggest crime was that he was following you, isn't that true?"

Howen objected, and Spence rephrased the question. "Let me put it to you this way. As a member of the Special Operations Group, had you in your training been taught that because . . . you had automatic weapons and you were wearing camouflage gear, you had the right to kill somebody's dog?" "No, sir," answered Officer Cooper. "That has never been taught to me." Spence later asked the question that had been on the defense team's minds since the prosecution's version of events had begun to unfold: "As a man who has thought about this case a lot, Mr. Cooper, does it make sense to you that Officer Roderick would be shooting the dog *after* Mr. Degan is dead, *after* Mr. Degan is shot?" Howen quickly objected.

Another key witness for the prosecution was Kenneth Fadeley, the undercover agent who had asked Weaver to illegally modify the shotguns. During cross-examination it came to light that not all the meetings with Weaver were recorded, a fact that could prove crucial to the credibility of Fadeley's testimony. Fadeley testified that he didn't know that Weaver was going to offer to sell the shotguns before the meeting, so it hadn't been recorded. The jury listened to some of the scratchy recording that had been made, mostly racist small talk, painting Weaver in a racist light. Fadeley, bald and wearing glasses, even apologized to the jury for the profanity on the tapes.

Fadeley admitted under cross-examination that it was difficult to get Weaver to break the law, and in a key exchange, Spence's cocounsel, Chuck Peterson, got Fadeley to admit that he did not receive payment for his undercover work unless there was a conviction. The defense hoped that jurors would believe that such payment offered Fadeley an incentive to lie.

Peterson began his cross-examination by checking off on a chart the lies Fadeley had told, starting with his name—Peterson called him Magisono before correcting himself. Fadeley testified he had taken down license plate numbers from cars at the Aryan Nation meetings. Peterson asked, "I used to live down there in Coeur d'Alene. There's a little Free Methodist Church down the road not too far from there, from Hayden

Lake [where the Aryan Nation headquarters is]. Did you stop there and get all the license plates, too?" Fadeley answered respectfully, "No, sir."

Peterson continued, asking about the Catholic church, the Episcopalians, the Baptists, the Quakers, and the Lutherans, and concluded by saying, "Those people were not considered by you worthy of taking their license plates. They weren't a danger, were they?"

Later, after Fadeley said he didn't know how much he would be paid for the case, Peterson asked, "It certainly would have something to do with the number of lies you told throughout the case, wouldn't it?" Fadeley responded, "I was told I'd be paid case by case . . . [and] after we concluded a case, there may be a monetary settlement possible." Peterson jumped on the implication here: "And you would assume that . . . you would have to get him convicted, right?" Fadeley answered, "If he was guilty." Peterson persisted, "Well, if you don't get a conviction, you don't get any money, right?" Fadeley considered before answering, "I assume so." Peterson responded, "And that's not just your assumption, sir. . . . If Randy Weaver gets acquitted of this gun case, you don't get paid, right?" Fadeley said, "I guess so."

At the end of the fourth day of trial, during Fadeley's cross-examination, Judge Lodge instructed the jury to disregard news reports coming from Waco, Texas. On that day, April 19, 1993, the FBI's siege of the Branch Davidian church ended with gunfire and flames. Eighty people were dead. The jurors were told to ignore events playing out in Waco even though some of the same government agents involved at Ruby Ridge were participants in the Waco siege.

Meanwhile, a man named Timothy McVeigh was watching in ever-greater anger as the Waco fires burned. As mentioned, exactly two years later to the day, McVeigh would detonate the bomb at the Oklahoma City federal building, killing 149 adults and 19 children. McVeigh made a pilgrimage to Waco during the fifty-day standoff between Koresh and the government, and a coworker said McVeigh also visited Ruby Ridge, conducting his own inspection of the grounds and cabin.

The government next called Weaver's parole officer from the original weapons charge, who had accidentally given Weaver the wrong trial date, and Stephen Ayers, the magistrate who had presided over that early hearing, who admitted that he had given Weaver erroneous information—including threats that if Weaver lost at trial, he could forfeit his home and possessions.

Throughout the pretrial proceedings and during the trial, it became apparent that the FBI was not fulfilling its legal obligation to provide the defense with all documents relating to the case in its possession. At times, especially late in the government's case, when it seemed the defense was beginning to make some headway, new evidence and new witnesses appeared.

It appeared that the FBI and the BATF did not want to cooperate with the prosecution or the defense, putting prosecutors Howen and Lindquist in a difficult position. The judge and the defense lawyers were screaming for full disclosure of all relevant documents, while the FBI and BATF appeared to be stonewalling. An FBI agent even said that he'd rather see a mistrial than give certain documents to the defense attorneys.

Meanwhile Spence and the defense team, without calling a single witness, continued to find and exploit gaps in the government's case. In addition to the "admissions" from Fadeley, a number of other smaller problems and inconsistencies had surfaced and were beginning to take their toll.

Ron Evans, Idaho's chief deputy inspector of the U.S. Marshals Service, was caught in a contradiction. When questioned during the trial, Evans said that he couldn't tell if the dog was friendly when they approached the Weaver home by car. He said that he could only see the dog's back. However, during his grand jury testimony, he had stated that the dog was "running and nipping at the wheels." Also, Evans had said that he wasn't sure if the girl had a gun (three people had come to greet those in the car, one of whom was a girl, likely Sara Weaver). At the trial, though, Evans said that all three had guns. Spence asked him point-blank, "Which time were you telling the truth?" Evans answered, "I believe I was telling the truth in both instances."

In addition to the government witnesses, the prosecution called people who knew the Weavers, to testify about their habits and beliefs. Some, like Bill Grider, had had some run-ins with Weaver and his family.

A reporter who had interviewed the Weavers in 1983, Dan Dundon, had reported that Weaver planned to build a "kill zone" around his property, but in testimony at the trial, he stated that he took Weaver's plan as a defensive one, Weaver having no desire to kill anyone. Michael Weland, another reporter who had interviewed the Weavers for a story in May of 1992, testified that when he was there, the children were clean, smart, and well read. The home was pleasant and the family and the dog were friendly. Weland also testified that he had contacted the FBI and told them that Vicki was the source of the family's strength and that Randy would not surrender unless separated from Vicki. The jurors could not overlook that Vicki was killed by the sniper's bullet the very next day.

Richard Rogers, the commander of the FBI's Hostage Rescue Team, was also called. Spence began the cross-examination: "The people that get on these [hostage rescue] teams are people who know they are going to be trained to shoot other human beings, aren't they?" Rogers replied, "Well, that's certainly part of it." Spence continued, "And they know when they volunteer that they may have to kill a citizen?" "Or a terrorist," Rogers replied. "Now listen," Spence interjected, "we're going to be here a long time. Just answer my question, and we'll get along."

Later, Harris's other defense attorney, Ellie Matthews, asked if Rogers had considered Idaho law. Rogers answered, "In what regards, sir?" Matthews responded, "In establishing your rules of engagement." Rogers said, "No, sir. I don't operate under state law. I operate under federal law, which supersedes state law."

When Arthur Roderick was called to the stand, Nevin tried to get him to admit that he shot the dog first, but Roderick would not relent. He repeatedly answered that he did not shoot the dog first, becoming annoyed by the repetition of the question. Spence then took Roderick on cross-examination:

SPENCE: You told the ladies and gentlemen of the jury that you came sneaking out there in the middle of the night—

RODERICK: I did not say anything about sneaking.

SPENCE: You did sneak, didn't you?

RODERICK: What do you call sneaking? You're putting words in my mouth.

SPENCE: (looking for a dictionary): *Sneak,* "to go stealthily or furtively."

RODERICK: Are you asking me what I said or what you said? I did not say I was sneaking. You said I was sneaking.

SPENCE: Now, don't get excited.

RODERICK: I'm not getting excited. I'm just explaining to you what your question was.

SPENCE: You asked me, didn't you? Or have you forgotten? You asked me what I meant by *sneak.*

RODERICK: Correct, but I did not say that.

SPENCE: I didn't ask you that.

RODERICK: Yes, you did.

Finally, at the end of Roderick's two days of cross-examination by Spence, Roderick said, "The truth is the truth." Spence paused, then replied knowingly, "Yes." And, after a moment's silence, he went on, "It is."

The last witness who had been at Ruby Ridge was Lon Horiuchi, the sniper who had shot Weaver and had killed Vicki, apparently while trying to kill Harris. Horiuchi entered the courtroom surrounded by a security detail of four FBI agents; a neo-Nazi group had made a poster with Horiuchi's picture and the caption WANTED: DEAD OR ALIVE. The handmade wooden door to the Weaver cabin had been brought into the courtroom and was displayed behind Horiuchi, the bullet hole in the window visible to all.

Horiuchi testified almost like a machine, showing no emotion and including *sir* with every answer. The sniper testified that he was trying to hit Harris when he shot Weaver, and Spence had the two men stand up to show their distinctly different builds. Spence asked Horiuchi about his gun, his orders, what bullets were used—basic questions to set the scene.

On Horiuchi's second day of cross-examination, Spence went on the attack: "You intended to kill both [Harris and Weaver], didn't you?" Horiuchi answered, "Sir, if they came out all at one time, we were intending to take them all out at one time, versus waiting for one individual to come out and take him piecemeal. Our normal procedures are whenever you have more than one subject, you try to take them out one at a time."

Spence asked, "Just before you shot, you knew the door was open, didn't you?" Horiuchi answered truthfully, "At that time, yes, sir." Spence continued, "Didn't you know that there was a possibility of someone being behind the door?" The sniper answered, "There may have been, yes, sir." Later, Spence focused on Vicki's death, asking Horiuchi, "You heard a woman screaming after your last shot?" "Yes, sir, I did." Spence continued, "That screaming went on for thirty seconds?" "About thirty seconds, yes, sir," Horiuchi agreed.

In a classic bit of courtroom drama, Spence said, "I want us to just take thirty seconds; now pretend in our mind's eye that we can hear the screaming," as everyone examined the door behind Horiuchi and watched in silence as the clock ticked off thirty long seconds.

Horiuchi testified that he believed that Harris and Weaver were shooting at a helicopter; he shot to protect the helicopter, not because of the new rules of engagement. Another hole in the prosecution's case became apparent during Horiuchi's cross-examination. He testified that the curtain was drawn and he did not see Vicki through the door's window. However, Horiuchi had made a drawing of what he had seen on a piece of hotel stationery shortly after the shooting. Horiuchi's hand-drawn illustration clearly showed two heads in the window and the crosshairs of the gun pointing at the window. However, the drawing was not available at the time of Horiuchi's testimony because the FBI, apparently having found it in a desk drawer in the D.C. office, mailed it fourth class to Howen, who didn't receive it until two weeks later.

Horiuchi was called back to the stand from Washington, D.C., where he had returned home. The sniper insisted that he could not see two heads but had instead drawn in the two heads where he thought they might be.

When all was said and done, the key question was, who fired the first shot? While all the agents testified that Harris had fired first, the defense's view was that Marshal Degan had begun the shoot-out. If the defense could establish that the dog had been shot first, then the rest of Weaver's and Harris's accounts of the incidents made sense. So far, the only support for the defense's position was that it seemed unlikely that Degan could have fired his gun seven times after being shot in the chest by Harris, even though a wound ballistics expert had stated that it was possible.

Another key piece of newly discovered evidence was a second bullet hole in Degan's backpack, the one he was wearing when he was shot. Kent Spence discovered a second hole that the prosecution had missed; apparently a bullet entered from the side and exited the pack without hitting Degan. Suddenly there was evidence that Degan had been shot by someone other than Kevin Harris, a theory that would be introduced in closing arguments by Nevin and Spence. And even if Degan hadn't been shot by someone other than Harris, the extra hole surely demonstrated the government's incompetence in reviewing its own evidence.

The Defense Conundrum

Spence, Peterson, and Nevin were struggling with whether to produce their own witnesses. Spence had already decided not to call Weaver; he knew Randy came with too much baggage that would be mercilessly exploited on cross-examination. Nevin had originally decided to put Kevin Harris on the stand, relying on the jury to see that Kevin was telling the truth and that he had done nothing wrong, trying only to protect himself and his friend. But Nevin was also worried about what the prosecutor would do to Harris on cross. Spence advised Nevin not to put Harris on the stand, and they debated the merits of putting him on the stand until Nevin agreed with Spence.

The defense had also considered calling Sara Weaver as a witness. Although she was young, she was smart, attractive, well-spoken, and honest. Her story was so compelling that Peterson figured that the jury couldn't help but believe her, but he ultimately concluded that cross-examination was too dicey. Spence disagreed. He was certain she should testify, wanting the story to come out in a way that no one would question. To resolve the dispute, the attorneys put Sara through a mock cross-examination. Sara answered honestly when asked about wearing a swastika, stealing from a neighbor, and calling some kids niggers. Realizing she might alienate the jurors, the attorneys agreed the risks were too great.

After the prosecution presented all of its witnesses, Spence and Nevin announced that they were not going to put on any case, and would instead rest on the state of evidence as presented by the prosecution. They could see the surprise in the eyes of the jurors and worried whether they had done the right thing. Had they just condemned Weaver and Harris to prison? There was no way to be certain, but they had to rely on the inconsistencies and holes in the prosecution's case, and on closing arguments.

On June 11, almost two months into the trial, prosecutor Ron Howen, in the middle of arguing a point to the judge, stopped and sat down. Judge Lodge called a recess and Howen left the courtroom. He did not return that day, or the next. No one knew where he was or exactly what the problem was, but it would be days before they would see Howen again. The prosecutor, exhausted and on edge, seemed to have decided he needed a break, posthaste.

Just four days later, closing arguments began. Sara and Rachel Weaver were in the courtroom with their aunt and uncle, and so was Spence's wife. Also in attendance were Bo Gritz, who had not been able to attend the trial because he was a potential witness, and his wife, Claudia. Vicki Weaver's friend Jackie Brown, who had first entered the cabin during the standoff, was there with husband, Tony.

The courtroom was packed; an adjacent court was wired with sound so the overflow crowd could still hear the arguments. Even with the additional space, people were turned away.

Kim Lindquist started first for the prosecution, Howen still conspicuously missing. Lindquist began by talking about the theme of the trial: people intent on breaking the law and resisting enforcement of laws by using violence. Lindquist said it was "utterly not true" that Weaver was being persecuted for his beliefs, yet he blamed the Weavers' religious beliefs and spoke of Weaver's anger and distrust of the government: "Their beliefs about Armageddon included the fact that government is satanic, and by being satanic, is evil. Those beliefs were beginning to strain the parameters of reasonableness and common sense. They believed the government persecutes—not in the future, but now."

Lindquist argued that Kevin Harris had murdered Bill Degan, and that Vicki Weaver's death was a tragic accident. He blamed the deaths of Sammy and Vicki Weaver on Randy Weaver and Kevin Harris, and the men's desire to attack the government: "This is a case of resolve on the part of Weaver and Harris to defy laws to the point of using violence. . . . This whole thing is a tragedy . . . but the cause of the tragedy was the resolve of the Weaver family, and that translates into murder." Lindquist said that by joining the Weaver family, Kevin Harris "became a son, [and] he joined the conspiracy." He painted Weaver and Harris as evil and determined to provoke a confrontation with the government.

Kevin Harris's defense attorney David Nevin was next. He pointed out the inconsistencies in the government's case, reminding the jurors about Marshal Degan's bullet-riddled backpack. He threw out possible reasons for Degan's actions, explanations not discussed during the testimony, and he tried to get the jury to think about the facts in a way that made logical sense, rather than taking everything the prosecution presented as truth. In all, Nevin gave a skillful closing argument, his soft-spoken voice and low-key mannerisms inspiring professorial believability.

After a short break for lunch, all eyes focused on Gerry Spence as he rose to address the jury.

CLOSING ARGUMENT OF GERRY SPENCE ON BEHALF OF RANDY WEAVER

Thank you, Your Honor. If the court please, counsel, ladies and gentlemen of the jury. I have been at this for forty years, over forty years, and I never begin a closing argument in an important case, in any case, [until] I feel like I feel now. And I should tell you that since my argument starts with me, that maybe I ought to tell you how I feel. I think to myself, can I do what I need to do? I feel afraid. I feel inadequate. I wish, instead of doing this for forty years, I had done it a lot more and was a much better lawyer than I am right now.

It is my great honor to talk to you, it is an honor for any lawyer to talk to an American jury, but it is a special honor to talk to this jury. You may be the most important jury that has come along for many a decade. It is an experience that you will never forget, and your efforts and your determination and your thoughts may change the history of this country. This is a watershed case. Sometimes maybe you feel like I feel, maybe I'm not up to that either, but the law understands that a jury that has twelve people, with an average age, let's say—well, would I insult you if I said forty years?—average age of forty years. That is forty times twelve, that is how much? Four hundred and eighty years of knowledge, and just like I don't know everything that happens in a case and I depend upon my colleagues to help me, it comes as a result of the collective thoughts of many people, so the law gives that to our juries and they become very insightful. I have never tried a case yet but what a jury saw things in a case that I didn't and had a perspective that I didn't have.

I want to say something to you, and then I'm going to quit flattering you and talk to you about the case, but you are entitled to some flattery. I want you to realize that few of us, me included, ever really know how important we are or where we stand in history. Go back to 1775 and the Continental Congress. Do you think they thought they were important? They were just the local guys doing their job, like you are local people doing your job, but as we look back on history, they did something permanent and magnificent and lasting, and that is what you will do with your verdict in this case, something permanent, magnificent, and lasting. Now, one of those fellows, Tom, made a statement. He said, "Eternal vigilance is the price of liberty." You know who Tom is that I'm talking about, of course. It's Thomas Jefferson. "Eternal vigilance is the price of liberty."

So I have to ask you, and you must ask yourselves, why are we here? Why were we chosen? How did I get chosen for this job? There were many other jurors here. Why was I left? Why? And the question is, is there something more here than simply finding the answer to some charges that have been leveled by the government? Is there something more than just watching lawyers play their games? You've seen the games that go on between lawyers. You'll see it before the case is over, again. And your purpose here isn't just to find who wins the case. It seems to me that you have a larger function here, a more noble function.

Can I start with the basic proposition that I think we would all agree with, and that is that government agents are bound by the law, the same as the rest of us. They're bound by morals and by justice and by decency, the same as we.

And government agents can't lie and say it's right because they're officers. And they can't come into court and play hide-and-seek with the facts and say that's all right because they are federal employees. And they can't persecute people, and they can't entrap people, and they can't state the wrong law, and they can't use their huge forces and their power because they are federal officers. And they can't turn a piddly little two-bit case into a major case and expend millions of taxpayers' money simply because they are federal officers. And they can't refuse to negotiate with citizens, as [Prosecutor] Howen refused to negotiate with Randy Weaver, because they have power; they can't attack us because of our religious or our political beliefs, simply because they have power; they can't come into Idaho from Washington, D.C., and claim that Idaho law is null and void, like [Hostage Rescue Team leader] Rogers did and say, "I am the law," simply because they are officers.

Now, ladies and gentlemen of the jury, there is something wrong here. Let me tell you at the very beginning what my worry is, why my heart pounds and my heart skips beats. I've been feeling it; it is skipping beats. And I've been wondering what that's about.

We have a task here of defending Randy Weaver on eight counts with a bunch of subcounts contained in the murder charge. My goal is, when we leave here, for us all to walk out together. This is what I am trying to do, this is the purpose of my final argument, to ask you to free Randy Weaver and to free that boy, and let us all walk out together in this case.

When the foreman comes in and hands your verdict to the clerk and to the judge and it is read, I want that verdict to be so that Randy Weaver can step right up and never have to put a shackle on again as long as he lives, never have to be taken to a prison and put in a cell. I want him to walk out and be free with his little children. I want you to—stand up, please [motioning to Sara and Rachel Weaver]. Thank you, Sara and Rachel. I want them to walk out together, this is what my goal is.

So my task is to get a not-guilty verdict on all charges, and how can I do that? That's why I'm afraid. That's the task that I face on behalf of Randy Weaver. And when I began to think about that, I think to myself, there is something wrong here.

I mean, what is going on in this case? I mean, we have a boy charged with murder, Kevin. And we have Randy charged as an aider and abettor with murder. And we have both of these people charged with multiple charges, and we have three people dead, we have Sammy Weaver shot in the back, a little boy whose voice hadn't even changed, shot in the back, and nobody says anything about it. Mr. Lindquist [the coprosecutor] says nothing about it.

It's like putting on your pants in the morning. Nobody seems to be concerned that Sammy Weaver was shot in the back and murdered. No excuses. No investigation. Nobody charged. What's going on here?

We have Vicki Weaver shot in the head. Nobody seems to care. It's like putting your shirt on in the morning. Nobody's charged. No investigation. Nobody seems to care. Now, what is this all about?

We have Kevin Harris shot. We have Randy Weaver shot. And you say, what is this all about, what is happening here in this case?

That's where I want to start my argument with you. I want to show you what's happening in this case. You are, let us say, the federal marshals, and you wake up on August twenty-second in the morning, and you realize that you've done something that you shouldn't have done. You weren't to have a confrontation in the first place, particularly not with a little boy.

Now, a little boy, a sweet little boy, a bright little boy, who could tell you all of the facts in the encyclopedia, who could read as fast as the judge himself, is dead, shot in the back, and the marshals are not supposed to shoot little boys in the back. He was shot running home. And we have his dog lying there shot in the back. And we've got Marshal Degan shot under circumstances that are extremely suspicious, and people are in trouble.

They bring in the Hostage Rescue Team that day, the twenty-second, and they surround this place, and they murder another woman intentionally, as I think the facts have shown. Killed a woman because she was supposed to have been a witness to what happened at the Y, and when they found out she wasn't a witness, they changed the rules of engagement, but it was too late.

And so if you are the federal government, what do you do? Do you come up to His Honor and say, "Sir, we're sorry, we killed Vicki Weaver and we shouldn't have," and go over here to the judge again and say, "We're sorry, we killed Sammy, shot him in the back, and we shouldn't have"?

What do you do? Well, you bring out the shotgun, and you charge Randy Weaver with everything you can find to charge him with. Then not only that, but you charge him with a conspiracy to do all of those things on top of that. And then you send the FBI out to find out what you can about the man, and you bring back evidence that starts back in 1983 and you try to do what psychologists call demonize him.

If you can make the people of the state of Idaho hate Randy Weaver. If you can make the people of the state of Idaho despise him because of his religious beliefs or his political positions. If you can demonize him in the press so that when the jury is brought together such as this one, every one of you has read something about him and start with a position of distrust and hatred because he's been called a Nazi and a member of the Aryan Nation and a far-right kook and cultist. If you can charge him with murder of a federal officer and charge him with all of the other charges and counts, then maybe we won't have to answer why Sammy Weaver was shot in the back and Vicki Weaver was shot in the face.

Now, you saw that happen in the courtroom not more than a few hours ago. You saw Mr. Lindquist put up a chart. By the way, Mr. Lindquist, I understand you don't have the chart anymore, is that right?

LINDQUIST: I have it.

SPENCE: You have it?

LINDQUIST: I do.

SPENCE: May I have it, please?

LINDQUIST: I'm going to use it when I rebut this, as you well know.

SPENCE: I have a right to use the chart to rebut. He's put things up here in front of the jury, I couldn't see what they were, I'm sitting back here; I have a right to see the chart, and I would like to have you bring it up here so that I can answer it.

THE COURT: The chart should be produced, but you should not write on it. It is Mr. Lindquist's product.

SPENCE: May I have it, please?

LINDQUIST: Sure.

SPENCE: What you do, and you'll see it soon in Mr. Lindquist's chart, is, you tell the jury that Mr. Weaver's political and religious beliefs are protected under the Constitution. And it's all right for him to have them. But by the time you finish telling the jury all of the things that you think he has done and all of the things that you think he's thought, and all are put down on the chart and all of the rest, the net result is that this is a man that we don't like, this is a man that believes different than me, this is a man that we can't trust, this is a man we don't care what happens to; that's the point, ultimately, of the demonization.

If we've demonized the man, then we can find him guilty, and if we find him guilty, it covers up the murders, and then we are all okay, and everybody's happy, and so that's what's happened in this case.

What is the relevance of whether somebody has an Aryan Nation belt buckle? What is the relevance about a child whose head is shaved? What is the relevance, ladies and gentlemen of the jury, hauling in the ammunition, piles of it, but they don't bring in the honey and the wheat and the canned goods and the supplies and the clothing?

I mean, what's the relevance of telling about the guns when they are all legal, and they had fourteen of them? I bet there are people on this jury who own fourteen guns, or who have in their past. I'd hate to have the ATF come look in all my closets. I've got guns I don't even know where they are. But if they hauled them out in the courtroom and laid them out here, it would make you distrust me.

What's the relevance of talking about them being satanic but to say that it's okay for them to believe that? What's the purpose of talking about their religious beliefs and all of the rest? Why? Because he isn't the sweetest-looking guy I've ever seen; I mean excuse me, Randy, but I mean, I've seen more innocent-looking fellows than Randy Weaver.

But if all you saw was all of the things they bring in, let's just think about what happens if they did that to us—supposing they brought in all your kitchen knives and laid them down—paring knife, cleaver, butcher knife, other knives—across the floor, some your kids gave you, some are dull and you can't use, some you use every day, but then they didn't bring out anything else.

And then they began to tell the world about your witchery, your crazy beliefs. "But don't hold it against them, don't hold their beliefs against them, you know you mustn't do that, but we want to tell you about them anyway." And they did. They sat on the stand, and you heard me object, and I cried about it, and I pounded the table about it, and they continued to say, "We'll tie it in, it's inextricably entwined." You heard that until you must have come home, you say to your spouse, "Darling, you and I are inextricably entwined."

But I will tell you this: if all of these things happened to you, they put an evil twist on everything, as they did in the argument, everything he did was because he hated the government. You heard the argument, there wasn't a thing that Randy Weaver did that was good and solid and decent and right, not one thing.

And when they started out, they began to tell you about all of the people in the Aryan Nation that he knew. No evidence came in on that, but they told you about it. They showed you Mrs. Weaver's little letters, which I thought were pretty gutsy. I would like to know her. If she was standing here today I would put my arms around her and I would squeeze her and I'd tell her how much I loved her. I think that this world could use people that are no longer afraid of the government.

So, ladies and gentlemen, the theme in this case is not the hatred of the government. To resist the law and to resist enforcement and to defy the law. That isn't the theme. [Lindquist] told you about themes. Well, it sounds to me like he has read a lot of Shakespeare and he has read a lot of *Hamlet* and he has read a lot of fiction, and you know that you can take facts and make them sound, turn fact into fiction; it's called verisimilitude, every novelist does it. The theme of this case, if you have to have a theme, counsel [turning to the prosecutor], the theme is, charge Randy Weaver and demonize him and make him into an ugly, hateful, spiteful person so that you can cover the murder of a little boy shot in the back and the murder of a woman shot in the head. That is the theme.

Now, somebody has to say "No!" to this, and guess who that is? I can't do it. The only thing I can do is ask you to do it. Somebody has to say, "No, you can't do this; that's clever tactics, but we are going to say, no, you cannot do this, federal government, to one of our citizens," because a jury has that power. Stop and think about it. You have more power than anybody, and that's the way it's supposed to be, because you're the only ones who can say no. You have more power than His Honor, and I don't know many people that's got more power than His Honor. You've got a lot more power than Mr. Lindquist and Mr. Howen. You've got a lot more power than the Federal Bureau of Investigation and the ATF, you've got more power than the marshals. You've got more power than anybody because you can say no. And not only that, but every one of you has that power—not collectively, each of you individually—because the verdict has to be unanimous, so you can say no, and that is the end of it.

When you heard counsel [Nevin] talk about George Washington and his desire to set up a federal government so you wouldn't have to be afraid of it, that's why they gave you that power, and that's why you are so special.

Now, after you kill a little boy at the Y, after you do that, how do you arrange to cover this up? How would you do it if you were of the mind, which I know you are not? You would do just what they did. You would tell the Hostage Rescue Team [HRT] half a story. You'd say, well, you would first start out, "This was a radical, Aryan Nation white-supremacist cult," that's what you were told. Do you remember that? I asked Mr. Rogers, were you told about them being an Aryan Nation white-supremacist cult? Yes. And that they killed a U.S. marshal? Yes. And that they fired indiscriminately? Yes. And they were heavily armed? Yes. And highly dangerous? Yes. And the place was full of—remember?—booby traps, and all the rest. There weren't any booby traps, and the marshals knew it, but the HRT was told that anyway.

We saw their tapes, didn't we? Hours of them, with little kids flying around on their bicycles and the old dog wagging its tail and the people walking and living all over that little place up there, and yet, when the HRT was told what was involved, they were told there were booby traps.

What is the HRT doing with this kind of input? They're getting excited, because they've got a war, they can bring in their airplanes, and they can bring in their helicopters, and they can bring in their snipers and their assaulters, and they can have themselves a big war up in northern Idaho. In August. Get out of that hot Washington, D.C., and have themselves a ball.

They were told that this man was a Green Beret and he had explosives training, and that his wife, Vicki Weaver, was crazy—do you remember?—that she would kill her children, do you remember that, she would kill her children? That's what they told them, that she would kill her children. *Likely* was the word, and Randy Weaver wouldn't surrender as long as Vicki Weaver was in control.

So did they tell them the truth? I mean, did they say these marshals shot the dog and then they shot the boy in the back? Degan [the marshal killed on day one] was shot by somebody, and I'm not sure who shot Degan yet. And the boys were just walking down the trail, the boys weren't wanted for anything, they committed no crime, they'd done nothing. The marshals were hiding, and the marshals were in camouflage, and they said no—they said the marshals were ambushed. That's what they were told—you remember that testimony—that the marshals were ambushed by Randy Weaver and Kevin Harris.

They didn't say that Randy Weaver wasn't even there, he wasn't even around when the shooting took place, that as soon as they said, "Back off, federal marshals," he took off running like he was supposed to. So they give the Hostage Rescue Team—I mean, who were hostages up there after all? That's funny—that's what they call themselves, Hostage Rescue Team, which is a euphemism, a nice word for expert killers, trained killers.

So some ROEs were formed, some "rules of engagement." Now,

I'm getting ready to talk about that. Could you find me that instruction on the rules of engagement that the judge gave, it's in your instructions there someplace, and I want to read it to the ladies and gentlemen of the jury.

What you're going to hear is from the court, when I read the court's instruction to you. Remember what they said, that federal law supersedes state law, takes away state law, sits on top of state law, is wrong. I said, "Well, now, what federal law are you referring to that supersedes state law?" Remember that question? What did he say? "The whole code," he said, "the whole federal code," remember that? I said, "Well, what federal code gives you that?" Let's see what the judge said.

[To cocounsel] Hurry up, because I ain't got too much time.

Then we put Horiuchi [the sniper] on the stand—and remember—he said, the determination of the issue of danger or—what was the word he used?

[Talking to cocounsel] Haven't you found that yet? I can't stall much longer.

Horiuchi gets up there and says all of the decisions had already been made for him, about whether there was danger or not, it had already been made by the rules of engagement, and the standard rules of engagement are that you shoot somebody only if a reasonable person believes they are in danger. That's the standard rules for the marshals, that's the standard rule for the FBI, it's the standard rules for every state in the United States of America.

[To cocounsel] Did you find it? Thank you.

Instruction No. 40: "Federal law as governs the conduct of federal officers, so far as the law of self-defense is concerned, does not supersede the law of the state of Idaho." Isn't that interesting? I mean, I guess Mr. Rogers didn't know what he was saying when he established rules of engagement that were contrary to the laws of the state of Idaho, and when he established rules of engagement that would guarantee the death and the killing of the adults that were remaining up there as witnesses to what took place at the Y.

I'm talking about a situation where there was a killing at the Y of Sammy Weaver, and those people want you to believe that they didn't know they killed Sammy, and they want you to believe that they didn't see Mr. and Mrs. Weaver coming down, wailing, crying, taking their son back up and putting him in the birthing shed. They want you to believe that it was a big surprise to them how that child turned up in that birthing shed. So they have a rule of engagement that will allow them to kill the other persons they thought were there.

And who else did they think were there? They thought Kevin Harris was a witness to Sammy's death, to his killing, and they were right. And they thought that Randy Weaver was a witness to the killing, which he wasn't, and they thought that Vicki Weaver was a witness to the killing, which she wasn't.

They decided that the way they were going to do this was to set up rules of engagement that don't comply with the law. A man who comes in as a federal officer in charge of the Hostage Rescue Team—these are the Waco boys—that come in here and tell this court and this jury and the legislatures of Idaho, and the people of Idaho, what the laws of Idaho are and are not. "They are nothing; my rules of engagement apply," he said. Any adult that comes out of that door with a gun could or should be killed.

Now, did you ever—I can't swim backwards, I can hardly swim at all—but I never saw a man trying to swim backwards so fast in my life. I mean, *could* and *should* are words that we use every day. When my daddy tells me what I should do, I'd better do it. When the court tells me what I should do, I'd better do it. And I know what I should do.

When they tell Horiuchi that any adult that comes out with a gun could and should be killed, anyway, you know what they meant. You ought to see them try and play and monkey with those words. The whole defense of this case, every time we've got a problem, it's monkeying with the words.

Well, you see, that's why we have juries, because juries won't monkey with the words. You know what words mean, you know the plain meaning of those words and you apply it.

And so, when it comes out that Kevin has a gun as usual—they know he's going to have a gun, he always has a gun, you saw the tapes, did he ever come out of the house without the gun? They knew it; they'd seen it, a hundred hours of tapes with the kids coming out, everybody coming out with the guns, and so it was a tailor-made rule of engagement. Tailor-made to kill that man, right there, that nice young man, tailor-made to kill Randy Weaver, and tailor-made to kill the mother of those two girls. When they walked out, they could and should be killed.

What does it say? "In attempting to effect an arrest, to execute a federal arrest, to execute a federal warrant in accordance with Idaho law, deadly force may be used if a federal agent reasonably believes that a person poses a significant threat of death or serious bodily injury to the agent." So they can only use deadly force if they believe that somebody is in significant danger, bodily harm or death. It's the standard rule everywhere. That wasn't the rule when these people came out.

Now, the thing that was bloodcurdling to me, I mean, I don't know how you felt, but how did it feel when you heard Horiuchi say, "Yes, we were waiting till they all got out, and then we were going to shoot them all"? Then we hear Mr. Lindquist say, "Oh, that's just because we didn't want to give away our position. We were going to shoot them all." And he tried to shoot them all. And he hit, with two shots, three people.

That ain't too bad of shooting, is it? I mean, I've shot a few doubles in my day, but not people; I shoot on the trap range. This guy was shooting doubles, he was capable of it. And you think he didn't know who was there?

Did you see the attempt to hide this document [the drawing Horiuchi made that showed two heads behind the window before he shot], and the court made him come back—remember that? There's the head. Do you see the head? Do you know who was there? See the crosshairs? He knew where the bullet was going to hit. Do you think he couldn't see Vicki there?

Well, the curtain when it's drawn back—you can play with it when you get it in the jury room—pull that back where the bullet hole lines up with the curtain, the rest of the bullet hole. And the other curtain was pulled back, and there's six, eight inches of open space there, and he's got a ten-power scope, and he can shoot a quarter-inch target from a ways. As a matter of fact, he testified that the scope was so good that he saw the bullet enter the birthing house. Do you remember that testimony? He saw the bullet enter the birthing house when he shot Randy.

So here is what we've got, we are going to get rid of the witnesses.

We've got Randy going to say his last good-byes to Sammy, who is lying in state in the birthing shed. They cleaned his body, and by the way, they cleaned his body while this so-called firefight was going on. The officers were saying there was this terrible firefight, everybody continued to shoot their weapons, there were hundreds of rounds fired, you know, and the firefight was happening as Randy and Kevin and Vicki were up cleaning the body of their dead son and brother. That's the firefight they were having.

Randy goes on the twenty-second, the evening, to open the latch of the door—remember the picture—they shoot him. It's supposed to be Kevin Harris, he says; he thought it was Kevin Harris. We had the two of them stand up. I would like you two guys to stand up again so we can see how much you look alike—I mean, really that's the similarity that you've got. [Weaver and Harris stand.] Thank you. He thought he was shooting Kevin Harris and he shot Randy Weaver, so that's his first mistake, right?

No, the first mistake was they shot Sammy, either intended to kill him or not, never heard anybody say, I guess maybe they intended to kill that little kid. Either that or it was a mistake. They shot at him, they're good shots, they must have intended to kill him. Nobody seems to criticize that, that's okay, it's just another—it's like the dog. I mean, there's this dog out there, they killed the dog. How do you kill the dog? I mean, it's just a dog, we have a right to kill the dog; you see an instruction in here by the court that says that—"Instruction No. 41: You are instructed under the law, a person may use reasonable force to protect his property." The dog was property, and Sammy had the right to shoot and try to scare the marshals away, or maybe they were shooting at him already when he shot. He didn't hit anybody. So we've got a mistake or an intentional killing, one or the other, with Sammy.

Then we got a mistake or an intentional killing when they were shooting at Kevin Harris and hit Randy at the birthing house. They thought it was Kevin Harris.

Then we got a mistake or an intentional killing when Vicki Weaver was shot in the head. Now, that's pretty good shooting, and you will recall that the officers said that they had to get rid of Vicki because Randy wouldn't come down, she was the head of the house, she was the powerhouse there, get rid of her first. Remember? Remember the testimony about how she was the power—remember that?

So we've got a mistake with Vicki and then, just by mistake, hit Kevin, so everybody that was up there was either intentionally shot or shot by mistake and nobody's told us, nobody seems to care, nobody's investigated, nobody's charged with anything, all they want you to do is to forget this, put it aside, wash it under the carpet, and do away with this man.

You want to know what a conspiracy is? That would be to ask you to help them cover up their crimes by finding him and this young man guilty of something, if you can just find them guilty of something.

I will tell you what Randy is guilty of. Randy, you are guilty of being one stubborn mother. I will tell you that. He was guilty of being afraid. And aren't we all guilty of that? Aren't we all afraid? Wouldn't all of you, under the circumstances that existed in this case, be afraid? He is guilty of talking a lot. He's guilty of having the courage of his convictions. He is guilty of standing up to authority. Maybe he's even guilty of using poor judgment. Probably there isn't one of you on the jury that would have done what he did. That doesn't make him a criminal.

You're going to judge another human being. And you may not have done it that way; you may not have thought the way he thought, believed what he believed, or done what he did, but it doesn't make him a criminal if he did what he did. It doesn't make him a criminal for having poor judgment; it only makes him a criminal if he violates the law.

We are all guilty of using poor judgment. When I get through here, Imogene—this is my wife, Imogene, over here, this one that smiled at me. Would you just stand up, Imogene? I want the jury to see her. When I get home, she's going to say to me, "You used poor judgment. You shouldn't have had me stand up like that," and she's going to say a lot of other things. But it does not mean that I'm a criminal, except in her eyes.

He may be guilty of being a human being, of caring a lot; he may be guilty of having wrong ideas, he certainly has ideas that are different than mine. He may be guilty of loving his family too much and being a parent, and he may be guilty of fearing the federal government. But that doesn't make him guilty of any one of the crimes.

Now, why didn't I call Mr. Weaver to the stand? When I said I rested, I saw some of the jurors look disappointed, because the jurors wanted to hear his story. I mean, we've been sitting here for two months, we want to hear his story. But there is a price I have to pay for letting you hear his story. The price I have to pay is to pit this simple man against him [pointing at Lindquist]. What would you think if I represented you and I turned you over to him? How would you like that?

I mean, a lawyer is always faced with this dilemma in every case. I mean, if you put your witness on the stand, people say, "Well, he'll have to prove him guilty of every charge beyond a reasonable doubt." He can't defend himself, nobody can defend himself against this sort of thing. But I can defend him because I have cross-examined, along with my cocounsel, fifty-six witnesses in this case, and after fifty-six witnesses—we put on no defense, not called a single witness—you would think that the testimony would be overwhelming, that somewhere it is beyond any reasonable doubt of any kind, that this is a criminal of the worst kind, and that *isn't* what the evidence is. The evidence is that this is a man who has been the victim of a smear, who has had his wife and his child murdered. And I say he has been hurt enough and smeared enough and I don't want any more of it. Your decision may have been different, but I don't think you would want me to do that. He has been shamed, belittled.

And what did the court say? This is a constitutional case, I told you, this is a watershed case, this is a case that kids in law school are going to read about and your grandchildren and your great-grandchildren are going to be part of. It's a constitutional case, ladies and gentlemen.

A defendant has the right to remain silent and never has to prove innocence. Now, isn't that a blessing in our country today, that we don't have to prove our innocence? How could we ever prove our innocence?

In Nazi Germany you had to prove your innocence; nobody would listen to you, you couldn't prove your innocence. A defendant has the right to remain silent and never has to prove innocence or present any evidence; that a defendant may not testify is not to be held against a defendant.

Do you think we put on any evidence? I'd call it witnesses. Do you think we've put on any evidence? How about our cross-examination? Do you think our cross-examination helped you understand the truth of this case? Would you have liked to decide this case unless we cross-examined and brought out the other side? You wouldn't want to do that, would you? Any of you wish that we'd never gotten up?

I think there were times when you said you wished that Spence would be quiet, we've had enough of him. But I don't think you would ever want to decide this case without cross-examination. How would you like to decide it without the cross-examination of Marshals Cooper and Roderick? You couldn't decide the case, could you? You couldn't have. The right of cross-examination is absolutely essential, and it's guaranteed by the Constitution.

Ladies and gentlemen of the jury, this is a murder case. But the people who committed the murder have not been charged, the people who committed the murder are not here in court.

The question is, how did all of this get started, and why did there have to be murders committed here? Well, let's ask how it did start. Let's ask [BATF Special Agent] Byerly. How did it start, Mr. Byerly?

Did Randy Weaver come up to you or your agent and say, "I want to get involved in undercover," or "I want to get involved in illegal shotgun operations"? Did he approach you? Mr. Byerly knows the answer. I mean, Mr. Byerly represents a new twist in America today, it's called Big Brother. Big Brother has come.

The worst of our fears are here, and thank God, I'm in a courtroom where I can say this with protection. I can point my finger at a government agent in America and say, "This man and that agency are the new gestapo in this country." Only in America could I do that, and do you know why? Because it's protected, my speech is protected under the Constitution.

What does he do? Let me tell you what you'd better *not* do, don't you ever go anyplace where the ATF or the FBI is surveilling, don't you go to anyplace where you think there might be agents, because you will be seen there.

How would you like to live in a country like that—do you want to say no to that? I mean, don't you dare go to a meeting, a political meeting of some other kind than what the government's interested in, because they'll take your license number down, just like they took the license numbers of Randy Weaver. And they'll watch, and they did watch, and their undercover agents are there, and they make files on us, and they set us up, and then they send their Big Brother undercover agents to us who are bounty hunters.

You know, we're talking about the big shots of this case; the top dogs in the ATF were here testifying, the top dogs in the marshals, the big shot from the FBI—these are the top government people that your verdict is going to talk to, and it's going to say either yes or no.

They can spy on us with video cameras. You know, I go home and I say to Imogene, "My God, honey, they have cameras up on the hill that are run by sun—what do you call those things? Solar power—and they have pen registers on the phones, on public phones." Go to a public phone, they have a pen register on it to see who you call, and they have surveillance teams with airplanes up there, flying over while what you say to somebody is broadcast to the airplane, and they have undercover agents lying and sneaking and peering and recording, and they purchase witnesses like Fadeley, and they put bugs in cars, in your cars, and they have a mail cover so they know exactly who you get your mail from. Are you telling me this isn't Big Brotherism? I mean, they have infrared spots and night-vision equipment and aerial photos and listening devices, to the point that they even know when that little girl was going to have her period. They even know that.

These are government officials who don't have anything better to do. You know, our streets are covered with crimes and dopers and all kinds of people. We've got a man here who was curious about what was going on, was looking for the religious truth. I commend him for that. I've spent a lifetime wondering and wondering, and looking and looking. Why can't a citizen look, hear, and wonder and go and inquire? Why can't he do that?

Well, I will tell you an old story my mother told me, it's about the crows and the swan. She says, "Gerry, there was a farmer who set out his nets to catch the crows. And there was a swan who played with the crows. And so the farmer caught the swan with the crows. And when it came time to kill the crows, the swan said, 'Please, Mr. Farmer, you can see very, very, very plainly that I am not a crow, I am a swan.' And the farmer said, 'You must be a crow, I caught you in my net with the other crows.'"

Now, how many days did you hear these people over here try to make this man a member of the Aryan Nation church when he plainly was not, and try to connect him in some way or another with their beliefs?

And you heard horrid things that turn my stomach that he does not subscribe to at all. You heard witnesses say he is not a racist, he is not a white supremacist, he believes people of different races should live separately, that's separatism and not supremacy. And he did not subscribe to any of the theories of the Aryan Nation. As a matter of fact, that's why he didn't join the church, because he didn't believe in it, and you heard some testimony to that effect.

But he was caught up there—they took his license number. These ATF who are supposed to be taking care of crimes, and their excuse is "Well, we were checking out the Aryan Nation because they might have had some guns."

Well, everybody has guns. I mean, this was their excuse for an invasion of that group of people, who, as repugnant as they are to us, to me at least, I can't speak for you, nevertheless have their rights and the Constitution to protect them. And so, Randy Weaver made a mistake—he should never have gone up there. That's the mistake he made.

That's the first crime, that he went to a public gathering that was being infiltrated by the ATF, and Randy Weaver's crime, and I want you to hear me say this, Randy Weaver's crime was not that he sawed off a shotgun; Randy Weaver's crime was that he wouldn't snitch for Herb Byerly. And *you* know that, and *I* know that. Herb Byerly was perfectly willing to kiss him on both cheeks once he caught him and entrapped him, if he would just go snitch, and I heard Mr. Lindquist say that that was honorable—remember, he said in his statement— that's honorable, to snitch and betray and to lie.

To be a snitch you have to hold out yourself to somebody and not be who you are, and to encourage them and to make friends with them. And then, after you made friends with them, to lie to them, and to tell them things about yourself and your family that aren't true, and to try to get them to do things that are wrong, and to be wired so that you can do all that, and Randy Weaver said, "I'm not going to do that." That was his crime.

Sawing off the shotguns—they hold these awful-looking shot-guns out, and they're enough to scare anybody. I mean, when he holds them up, I think, "Oh, God, how can I ever deal with that with the ladies and gentlemen of the jury." But it's hardly more than a misdemeanor, hardly more. It's a two-hundred-dollar license tax, you fill out some papers.

And poor Randy Weaver, Randy isn't too smart. You ought to be able to understand that somebody, anybody, can cut off a shotgun, why do they need [Randy] to cut them off? Did you ever think of that? I mean, anybody that had thought about it very much would have known that this was an undercover agent setting him up. Randy Weaver's just a simple guy, an ordinary guy that needed the money, and he had been kind of sucked into this. You know, he had no propensity to do that before; he was going to find out how that was and Byerly was telling him how much money he was making, and how big a business it was.

And Randy kept saying, "I'd sure like to meet your family," because, you know, he thought that was the way you judged people, and I think he's right. You know how I could judge you better than any way in the world is to meet your family. Do you know how you can judge Randy Weaver? Judge him by those kids and see the kind of person Randy Weaver is: that's Sara and that's Rachel.

And so they got him to do this. Then they came to him and said, "Snitch!" and he said, "No," and they let him go. I mean, if it was such a terrible crime, you would think they would have arrested him immediately or something.

Snitch. No. They let him go.

And it was between October of 1989 until January of 1991, until he was arrested, that's fifteen months—big deal, right? Nobody was concerned about that. Then they go for fifteen months, and then one day they didn't have anything better to do, and so they put the truck across the road and they put this decoy out there, this poor woman, looking like she was having trouble, and they arrested him.

The entrapment instruction says the prosecution has to prove he had a propensity to commit the crime before you induced him to do it. In other words, it's sort of like a virgin soul; if you have a virgin soul—that is, you haven't done these crimes before—and the government induces you to commit the crime, you've been entrapped. In other words, that makes a criminal out of you.

The law tries to be fair. We've got enough criminals in this world without having our government agents out making criminals of our citizens. So, if a citizen has no propensity—that means that you wouldn't have done it otherwise—if you've had no propensity to commit crimes in your life and the government goes out and induces you to commit a crime, it's entrapment. And the government has to prove that you had a propensity to commit crimes; that you were a criminal to begin with.

I mean, if you're already a criminal, it's okay to induce you. You see it most often in dope cases, which I don't happen to represent, but I see it all the time with other lawyers in dope cases that are claiming entrapment, but if they've been selling dope all along, how can they claim they were entrapped? I mean, they were already criminals. But Randy Weaver was not a criminal. He had no propensity to commit crimes.

You have heard the testimony; they looked as hard as they could, and you know they looked. You know they looked to the bottom of the well for everything they could find against Randy Weaver. There isn't a thing that he ever did in his life that they didn't look up and try and smear him. If they would have found a crime, they would have brought it to your attention.

And this is a man who never had even a traffic ticket. Never been charged with a crime of any kind, and honorably served his country. Had no history of any kind of any criminal record. He had no propensity.

The judge will tell you, "The prosecution must prove beyond a reasonable doubt that the defendant was predisposed to commit the criminal act prior to first being approached by government agents."

Predisposed. Predisposed. That means he was a criminal beforehand, in effect. The person is entrapped when a person has no previous intention to violate the law and is persuaded to commit a crime by government agents.

On the other hand, where a person is already willing to commit a crime, the guy that's been selling dope, as an example, it is not entrapment if the government agents merely provide an opportunity to commit the crime.

Now, his failure to appear. He is told first by the judge something that was not true. He was told by the judge that if he lost the case, the money would have to be used, not because he didn't appear—remember that's contrary to what counsel said. Anyway, if you lose the case, you may lose your house to pay attorney's fees, the court-appointed attorney.

Now, what does that tell Randy? "If I lose, I'll lose my house." Now, if a judge makes a misstatement of the law, it's okay, it's just a mistake. If a judge makes a mistake, it's just a mistake.

No offense, Judge, I'm not talking about you. I'm talking about another judge. But if Randy Weaver makes a mistake, he's a criminal, right? And he gets charged. Now, when Richins [Weaver's parole officer from the original weapons charge] makes a mistake and sends him a letter that says you don't have to appear until the twentieth of March, it's just a mistake, right? Well, when Randy doesn't show up on the nineteenth or twentieth of February, he's guilty of a crime, right? And he gets indicted on the fourteenth of March, not on the twentieth of March, six days before the twentieth even rolls around.

They knew all about the mistake. They indicted him. They can't wait to indict him. They'd loved to indict him. Let's hope that he doesn't appear, then the indictment will stand up.

I don't think I would ever quite get over this situation. They're going to try to get Randy Weaver down—they left him up there for a long time, almost eighteen months, wasn't it? Never bothered him. He wasn't bothering anybody else either. And they knew the charge he had against him was no good, and he told the marshals, "When you arrest him and bring him in, I will probably have to dismiss it."

Now, you've got a no-good charge that you know you're going to have to dismiss, and it becomes the basis of a major case that results in the death of Sammy and Mrs. Weaver and Bill Degan. And brings in the whole Hostage Rescue Team and all the rest. On a charge they knew was no good in the first place.

Now, what are we going to teach? Are we going to send you off? We are going to tell the whole world something here by our verdict here of justice. Are we going to approve the prosecution doing this when they know that their case isn't any good?

Mr. Howen never came into court and told us why he continued to force that thing. I mean, this is a two-bit, no-good charge, and all [Weaver] is saying is "Don't take my kids away from me and I will come down. Don't take my house away from me, don't leave my children homeless." This isn't a welfare recipient. This is a guy that's making his living, making his way. Taking care of himself, taking care of his family, and he says, "Don't take my home; don't take my kids." You know how long it would have taken me to get him down off the hill? About five minutes. Just walk up there and say, "Randy, we're not going to take this house and we're not going to take these lovely kids. And if you want to work out something so you can have a fair trial, I will do the best I can to guarantee you that. Because I am the United States attorney, and you know what I do as the United States attorney? It is my job to see that you get a fair trial. It is not my job to set you up. It isn't my job to do something to hurt you. It's not my job to do something unfair. I will do it, I will take care of it."

What do we get from Mr. Howen? "Pursuant to our phone conversation of October fifteenth, 1991, concerning the proposed negotiated surrender of Randall Weaver. I cannot authorize further negotiations or discussions along these lines with the defendant or his agents for two reasons. First is that the defendant is represented by Hofmeister" [Weaver's attorney for the original weapons charge].

Now, we're talking about a big deal; well, you can take Hofmeister up there. Come on, pal, you're both members of the board, let's go up there together. Secondly, "That the areas proposed are either not within my power to grant or bind the government in the broad scope or the type of matters properly addressed in a plea agreement." That means after you've pled guilty. So what he's saying to him is "Plead guilty and I won't take your kids from you. Plead guilty and I won't take your home from you."

This is a two-and-a-half-month trial, do you think that is right? I think after you sat here as a juror you realize how important this right is, not to have to plead guilty to crimes that you haven't committed and that you've been set up for and have good defenses to.

You've heard the witnesses give their defenses and you know they're just and you know they're honest. And why shouldn't he have the right to present those defenses? And Mr. Howen says, "No, not until you plead guilty."

They could have set another trial date. Hofmeister said that Randy would come down, but the government agents demanded to know exactly when, so they could get the credit for the arrest.

Imagine that. You remember that testimony that came from the cross-examination of one of the witnesses. Mr. Willey [Weaver's friend from the Aryan Nation] said Randy was afraid they were going to kill him. I mean, it just makes me sad. The government will use all the power they have. They don't realize that this is a human being.

They saw him at an Aryan Nation conference and they're going to get him. And then they make a major case out of this. A major case out of a case where the underlying indictment would have to be set aside if it ever came to trial. Make a major case out of it—it's the only case they had. I mean, it's just sad. And I know that you feel sad about it and I know that you don't want to put your stamp of approval on it.

You know, so much has been made out of trying to demonize this man. But when finally the facts get laid out and they called Mr. Willey to the stand—I don't know if you were touched, but I saw a man up there who felt sad, too, about this.

"You had known Randy Weaver and you liked him?"

"That's true."

"Known his family and you liked and admired him?"

"Yes."

"You knew Randy Weaver to be an honest man who worked hard to try and support his children; is that true?"

"Yes."

"And his wife?"

"Yes."

"And you knew Randy Weaver to be a man more concerned about his family than anything else in the world; is that true?"

"That's true."

You remember how he [referring to the prosecutor] said I didn't think he cared about the kids.

"I want to ask you if in your entire life have you ever met a family that was more close-knit and more religious-oriented than the Randy Weaver family?" And he said, "I never. The family functioned as a unit. They are very well-disciplined, very well-educated. I have profound admiration for Vicki and her conviction and her stand with her convictions in response to her family. She was a very strong and lovable person."

"Did these people as a family have a moral foundation?"

"Yes, it was the Bible. They were a God-fearing family that frequently prayed together. They were loving children. They were always watching out for each other."

I said, "Can you tell the ladies and gentlemen of the jury the relationship between Randy and Vicki?"

"It was a love story. Every time I seen them together, they were holding hands. They often embraced each other, they hardly fought. They did everything by consensus."

It makes you sad.

We are unique. This government is our servant, not our master. They brought in this reporter/policemen who told you that all Randy wanted to do was stay on the mountain isolated—remember how they asked or were looking for the kind of reading materials he had. Why did he want to know that? I want to know that.

He said, "I will be happy with a well-worn King James," and then Howen wanted to know from Willey what he read. The *Turner Diary* and the *Silent Brotherhood*? No, they didn't see those books up there. Then about the big, yellow dog, said the dog was just attached to the boy, was just like Old Yeller in the movies.

Then, here's the key. I guess he forgot. Kill zone, kill zone. I mean, how would you like to be in a situation where a newspaper reporter—there's a whole bunch of them sitting over there—one of these very nice people, but they're like everybody else, they want a story. They write a story about a kill zone. That really upset Randy.

And they go back to 1983 and dig out a newspaper in which there was a kill zone article written that becomes the basis for the conspiracy that started in 1983 between Vicki, Randy, and their children; that little girl that was standing there was five years old, and she's a named coconspirator. That started in 1983.

Now, what did Weland [the reporter who interviewed the Weavers for a story] say about that? I didn't talk to him. He took the stand the first time I ever saw him, and I cross-examined him. He said Randy was upset about the kill zone misquote. The story the other reporter had published wasn't true; he wanted to make sure he wasn't misquoted this time when he gave a story to Weland. That's the testimony. One statement in the press and you're guilty of a conspiracy that began in 1983. That's their evidence. Rebutted by their own witness.

Now, something is very horrid that's happening here, and I want you to hear this. I told you this is a watershed case, and I want you to hear this. What is happening in America, when the government begins to point, not to criminals who are joining into conspiracies like dope dealers who join up and bankers who do behind-the-scene conspiracies and cheat old ladies out of their savings, but to families?

The new low in American jurisprudence is to attack the American family and to say that the American family now can be guilty of a conspiracy by virtue of the fact that they are a family. And unnamed conspirators, too.

The indictment, beginning at the unknown dates of approximately January of 1983 and continuing to August 31, 1992, within the District of Idaho and elsewhere, Randy C. Weaver, Vicki Weaver, husband and wife. Kevin L. Harris and others known and unknown before the grand jury, including some other members of the Weaver family.

This time the little child Rachel entered the conspiracy. They saw her coming out with her gun. I suppose Rachel, now as she tries to protect her daddy and is afraid something is going to happen to her daddy. Vicki was trying to protect them from this crazy stuff that's going on down there. All those people are now guilty of conspiracy. So now, be careful, because if you have a family, you could be guilty of a conspiracy.

One other thing I can't let go unsaid. The business of calling this little house a compound. Now, is that a compound up there? I mean, everybody fought for that. I mean, Roderick fights to the end calling it a compound. Cooper, why not call it a compound? The FBI people want to call it a compound. Why? Because if you kill them in the compound, it's okay, but if you kill them in the house, it might not be okay. Those are the kinds of demonizing uses of language.

So let's go back. It's a conspiracy to provoke a violent confrontation, and I say they were preparing to try and raise a family, be left alone. You know what the judge said, people are presumed innocent in this country, instruction No. 2 or 3. Read it. "They are presumed innocent." There wasn't any conspiracy. Do you want to say, "Yes, he's guilty of conspiracy"? Well, I sure hope you don't do that.

Count two, the sale of illegal firearms, you have seen that entrapped. Failure to appear, ask Howen. Count four, assault on a federal officer. Did Randy assault anyone out at the Y? Is there any evidence of that? They knew there wasn't any evidence of it, but they charged him with it anyway. He wasn't even there when the shooting occurred; he ran long before the shooting occurred. He ran when Cooper says, "Back off"—yes, he ran.

Count five, murder, same. Except my client is charged with aiding and abetting. What did he do? What did he aid and abet? Look at the instruction: you have to help before the commission of the crime. You have to help commit the crime before the commission of the crime, before the shooting. Assuming Kevin shot Degan and he didn't shoot him in self-defense, he just did it because he's a mean man. That's where you have to be. That Kevin is a mean man. That he's a murderer. And that Randy Weaver helped him murder Degan. I submit it.

Now, how far does it get? How far do they go? They even charge the kid with harboring Randy Weaver, how crazy can you get? That he harbored him. I mean, make him the harborer and this is the guy he harbored. If it's anything, it was Randy Weaver who was keeping Kevin Harris, not Kevin Harris keeping Randy Weaver, but that's how it's charged.

Count eight was thrown out by the court, as was count six. Count nine, crimes of a person on release—if he didn't commit any of these crimes, then this one is out. Count ten is that the crimes were committed with a firearm. Well, he didn't commit those crimes. They're gone, too.

I hate to go through each one of those because, you know what, it's very scary for me to do that. The reason it's scary is this: it's, like, you know, you want to get rid of this. The more you talk about it, the worse it gets, but I think I made a clean presentation of a defense to every one of those. There isn't a single iota of evidence that supports a crime committed by this man. I told you the crime he committed was the use of bad judgment. Maybe it was the best judgment he had. Maybe it was the best judgment that this family had when they sat together and prayed together.

I will tell you who really used bad judgment, the [Hostage Rescue Team] that came in and violated all the laws of the state of Idaho and killed the wife, and those officers who came out and killed Sammy. Those are people that used bad judgment.

Then they come in here with this shotgun charge, and I'll tell you what it's like—how much time do I have? Ten minutes. I am about ready to quit then, whether or not I want to. I'm always afraid to quit, because when I sit down, I can't say anything more, and I have to let loose of my case and I don't want to do that. It is my case, I love this case, and I love my client. And I love the causes, so I don't want to quit talking and I have to quit.

I will tell you what it is like, it's like if there is a cop that wants to get you. You know in a little town and the cop wants to get you and he is tailing you, you stop at the stoplight and the guy hasn't been watching and the cop is not watching and he runs into the back end of your car. Now, it is his fault. You were stopped properly, but what does he do? He charges you with everything but the kitchen sink. He charges you with stopping too quick, with your headlights off, with no evidence of insurance, driving too fast for conditions, with having a broken headlight, with having poor tires, everything that he can think of.

Then he charges you, like they did here, with the conspiracy to do all of those things, because your wife was along or your husband. Conspiracy to violate all of those crimes—that's what Randy is charged with is a conspiracy to commit all of those crimes that started back in 1983. So the cop charges you with that, and then you go to a jury, and the jury says, "Yeah, I don't think that's right. Let's just do him a favor and we'll only find him guilty of one."

And that lets the cop off the hook. That is what's going on here. Find him guilty of one so they can get off the hook. He has been shot with a shotgun. You want to know who was dealing with deadly shotguns in this case? I'll tell you the shotgun they put at Randy Weaver and this poor boy over here, Kevin Harris, is the most deadly shotgun that's ever been fired at anyone.

The jury will remember that the defendant is never to be convicted on mere conjecture or suspicions.

Well, I have to quit. I can't say anything more. I want you to turn this man loose, please. I want you to send him home with his children. It is time, he has been punished enough. He has been in that jail up there for ten months now, wearing that yellow plastic suit. And he's shackled every morning and every night.

I tell you something, he has been punished enough. You're not supposed to think about punishment, the court instructs you about that. I want to talk to you about another kind of punishment.

Randy Weaver would willingly go to the penitentiary for the rest of his life if he could have his boy back. Randy Weaver would go to the penitentiary for the rest of his life and willingly walk into it and say, "Lock me up forever," if he could have Vicki back.

Hasn't he been punished enough? Doesn't this terror and this horror have to end sometime? Shouldn't it end with you, and shouldn't it end without having to compromise? Shouldn't this jury have the courage to stand up and say, "No, they overexercised their power"? I ask you to do that.

I want to tell you a story. I want to tell you a story of the times, it's one of my favorite stories. It's a story about an old man and a smart-aleck little boy. The smart-aleck boy had decided he was going to show the old man up, show him what a fool he was. The smart-aleck boy caught a little bird on the porch and his plan was to go up to the old man and say, "Old man, what have I got in my hand?"

And he figured the old man would say, "Well, you've got a bird."

And the smart-aleck boy's plan was to say, "Well, old man, is the bird alive or is it dead?" And if the old man said, "The bird is dead," then the smart-aleck boy would open his hands and the little bird would fly off into the forest.

Or if the old man said, "The bird is alive," then the smart-aleck boy would crush it and crush it, crush it, crush it. And say, "See, it's dead."

So he went up to the old man, the kid did, and he said, "Old man, what do I have in my hand?" And the old man said, "You have a bird, my son."

He said, "Old man, is the bird alive or is it dead?"

The old man said, "The bird is in your hands, my son."

And justice, truth, and the future, but not only of this country, but this family, is in *your* hands.

The Jury Deliberates

The jury began deliberations on Wednesday, June 16, sequestered in a windowless room with institutional-green walls. Television news trucks filled the parking lot, waiting for word.

Thirteen days later, on June 29, a juror—suffering from post-traumatic stress disorder and a chronic heart condition—could not continue deliberating and was replaced by an alternate juror. This was a blow to the jury; they now had to start over with their deliberations. This was the same day that Ron Howen reappeared in court, with no explanation offered for his absence. The jurors soon asked to hear the entrapment testimony again.

Finally, on July 8, the jury sent word that they had reached a verdict.

The packed, tension-filled courtroom was silent as the verdicts were read aloud. Randy Weaver and Kevin Harris, overcome with emotion, hugged each other tightly. Weaver was acquitted of all charges except the original failure to appear in court and for committing a crime while on bail release. Kevin Harris was found not guilty of all charges; when a deputy said he'd have to take Harris back to jail for processing, his attorney, Nevin, told the lawman, "The hell you will. He's going out the front door with me." Harris left the court that day holding his mother's hand.

Though Spence was feeling "bittersweet"—he had wanted Weaver to walk out with his daughters—he smiled widely as he signed copies of his new book outside the courthouse. Weaver had to go back to jail, but would likely be out by the fall.

Ultimately, Judge Lodge dismissed the second conviction, since it had been proven that Weaver had committed no crime during the standoff, and Lodge sentenced him to between eighteen and twenty-four months in federal prison for his failure to appear. Since Weaver had already served fourteen months, he would be released by Christmas. Weaver was finally freed in December 1993. He flew to Iowa to reunite with his daughters, eager to spend Christmas with his family. The girls went to Grand Junction with their father, happy to finally be with their dad.

Aftermath

In August 1994, Randy Weaver filed a lawsuit for the wrongful deaths of Vicki and Sammy Weaver. The case settled before trial for $3.2 million in August 1995. The government, however, refused to acknowledge any wrongdoing. A Department of Justice official told Spence that a jury would have given $100 million if the case had gone to trial. Kevin Harris also filed a lawsuit; the government settled his case for $438,000.

Today Weaver lives, as before, a life of near solitude with his three daughters. Weaver and Sara wrote their story of the events at Ruby Ridge. He tells visitors, "I don't want to be anybody's hero." Weaver told a reporter, "You have to continue to have faith in people, and I believe there are some good people in the government." Despite the loss of his wife and son, Weaver has said, "If any of these guys would just flat-out start telling the truth about what happened, you know, I could be very forgiving of a lot of them."

Gerry Spence represented Randy Weaver free of charge, but Weaver granted him exclusive rights to their story. Spence added a chapter to an earlier book, *From Freedom to Slavery,* and has worked since the conclusion of the trial to change public opinion about his client. Despite his acquittal, many Americans still believe Weaver is responsible for the death of a U.S. marshal.

Not satisfied with Randy Weaver's acquittal, Spence also wanted justice for the other victims of Ruby Ridge. Who was going to be held responsible for the deaths of Vicki and Sammy Weaver?

Following Weaver's trial, the U.S. Senate appointed a special commission to investigate the "incident" at Ruby Ridge. A committee drafted a five-hundred-page report documenting the wrongdoing of the government agents involved in the siege. Following the investigation, Danny Coulson, the founder of the Hostage Rescue Team, was given a letter of censure; Michael Kahoe, who had been involved in researching the rules of engagement, was censured and suspended for fifteen days; Richard Rogers, head of the Hostage Rescue Team, was censured and suspended for ten days.

Kahoe later pled guilty to a charge of obstructing justice for his destruction of an FBI report critical of the Ruby Ridge siege.

Larry Potts, the FBI man who allegedly approved the rules of engagement without his boss's knowledge, was censured, although a later investigation concluded that there was insufficient evidence to prove he had approved the revised rules. Eugene Glenn, Ruby Ridge field commander, was censured and suspended for fifteen days; and Lon Horiuchi, the HRT sniper who killed Vicki Weaver received no punishment.

Attorney General Janet Reno promoted Larry Potts to second-in-command at the FBI shortly after the Ruby Ridge investigation, outraging members of the public who saw this as a reward for his conduct. The promotion was short-lived, however, and Potts and four other FBI personnel were later suspended while being investigated for allegedly destroying documents related to the Ruby Ridge incident. Potts and the others denied the charges.

The U.S. Senate judiciary subcommittee on terrorism also criticized the Hostage Rescue Team. Originally created to help in military action in other countries, the team was now being used in the United States, even in situations where no hostages were present. The U.S. Marshals Service and the BATF also came in for criticism by the subcommittee as a result of their actions at Ruby Ridge. The Senate judiciary subcommittee also found that sniper Lon Horiuchi's actions were illegal and violated Vicki Weaver's civil rights.

Idaho prosecutors acted, appointing California civil rights lawyer Stephen Yagman as the special prosecutor in *Idaho v. Frank Horiuchi,* charging the sniper with involuntary manslaughter in the death of Vicki Weaver. Horiuchi moved for dismissal, arguing that because he was a federal agent who killed in the line of duty, he was immune from prosecution in Idaho. The federal appeals court rejected his argument and ordered that he stand trial. However, a new Boundary County prosecutor, Brett Benson, was elected and, for reasons never made public, fired Yagman and dismissed the charges against Horiuchi. Benson said he did not believe he could have obtained a conviction.

Benson was later investigated for forgery and falsifying documents; misdemeanor charges were filed against him for impersonating a notary public. Prosecutor Ron Howen filed charges against Benson, who has since resigned.

Horiuchi never spent a day in jail, didn't lose his job, and never lost a day's pay.

Some critics argue that Weaver's distrust of the government was unwarranted; if he had just shown up for court, his wife and son—as well as U.S. Marshal Degan—would be alive.

Since the events at Ruby Ridge, militia groups have used Ruby Ridge and Waco as rallying cries and recruiting tools. Efforts by groups like Handgun Control, Inc., to ban assault weapons and seek tighter controls on public ownership of firearms served to heighten the fears of the militias that government confiscation of their weapons was inevitable.

Today the FBI has shifted its focus from the militia groups in the aftermath of September 11, 2001. The same federal agencies responsible for the murders at Ruby Ridge have been entrusted with more power, via the Patriot Act, which permits the government to open wider the window into our lives, in order to keep out those who threaten us.

Randy Weaver lost his son and wife to the federal law enforcement machine. In the fight against international terrorism, their deaths serve as a reminder that the rules of engagement must always provide for the protection of the innocent—and the freedoms we defend.

CHAPTER FOUR

Defending the Despised

Founding Father fights to save British troops from the gallows after the Boston Massacre

The plain English is, gentlemen, most probably a motley rabble of saucy boys, Negroes and mulattoes, Irish teagues and outlandish jack-tars. And why we should scruple to call such a set of people a mob, I can't conceive, unless the name is too respectable for them. The sun is not about to stand still or go out, nor the rivers to dry up, because there was a mob in Boston on the fifth of March that attacked a party of soldiers.

—John Adams in his summation

Famed attorney Gerry Spence is fond of guiding critics of the legal system through a question-and-answer session, starting with "Shouldn't we have a trial before we hang a scoundrel?"; then asking if that scoundrel shouldn't have an attorney by his side to make sure he gets a fair trial; and shouldn't that lawyer make sure the state proves its case—beyond a reasonable doubt—before they hang his client? By the end of the exchange, even the most vociferous critics are grudgingly forced to admit that even the most reprehensible criminal, by having a fair trial with effective counsel, strengthens the legal protections enjoyed by all Americans.

This tradition, inherited from the English common law, has been an essential component of the American justice system, even before the Founding Fathers began their deliberations in Philadelphia. This American tradition can, in fact, be traced directly back to one of the most prominent of the Founding Fathers, in a trial that nearly cost him the opportunity to serve his newborn nation. In 1770, John Adams, who would later serve as the first vice president and second president, represented the British soldiers who killed five American patriots during the Boston Massacre.

The (Slowly) Gathering Storm

The seeds of American independence were haphazardly sown with the arrival of the first Europeans in North America, survivors of the dangerous voyage across the North Atlantic, seeking a new life. With every succeeding generation, descendants would increasingly come to view Europe as a distant entity to whom their allegiance would become more and more attenuated. Eventually, events began to hasten the separation.

In 1731, King George II appointed a new governor for the burgeoning New York and New Jersey colonies. Governor William Cosby, a political hack who had been dismissed from his previous appointment for absconding with funds, began running roughshod over the established political processes in New York. New Yorkers began complaining, airing their concerns in a newspaper started for just that purpose; their grievances not yet calls for independence from Great Britain, they merely sought fair and equitable treatment from London and its appointed representatives. Governor Cosby arrested John Peter Zenger, the publisher of the newspaper printing scathing antigovernment articles, and brought him up on charges of criminal libel. Zenger, in a landmark trial establishing the right of the developing colonial press to criticize the government, was acquitted. Zenger's triumph emboldened the colonists to speak and publish freely, thus providing the essential ingredients to eventually foment a revolution still years away.

In the two generations that would separate Zenger's acquittal from the signing of the American Declaration of Independence, relations between England and its American colonists became increasingly strained and tense. The causes were numerous, rooted primarily in resentment of rule from afar, peppered with a disdain for the ever-increasing monetary burdens imposed by Parliament. The French and Indian War left the English economy in tatters. London thought it right that the American colonies shoulder some of the debts incurred during that war on the American continent, even though it had been fought for the benefit of the mother country in its quest for world domination.

And so, beginning in 1764, Parliament began levying taxes on its American colonies. The measures were increasingly met with protests and outright boycotts. The epicenter for colonial resistance to all things British was Boston. And at the center of the opposition to the Crown were Samuel Adams and the Sons of Liberty.

Sons of Liberty

Sam Adams, a Boston native and the son of a wealthy brewer, attended Harvard, the only college in the area, obtaining a master's degree in 1743. His thesis, "Whether it be lawful to resist the supreme magistrate, if the commonwealth cannot be otherwise preserved?" answered in the affirmative. After graduation, Adams tried his hand at several endeavors; none succeeded. He ultimately joined his father in the brewing business, even though he was a teetotaler. After Adams's father died, he was unable to sustain the business and it, too, failed. He eventually found work as a tax collector, a position he held for eight years. But Sam Adams's true passion was politics, and in 1765 he became a founding member of the Sons of Liberty, a radical political group based in Boston calling for complete independence from England. The group, composed of several prominent merchants and lawyers from the Boston area, included John Hancock, Patrick Henry, and Joseph Warren. Adams rapidly became a leader, and although he shook from palsy and his voice quavered when he spoke, he developed into a passionate orator. His primary contribution, however, was as a writer, and he contributed often to the *Boston Gazette*. His editorials succeeded in converting many neutral colonists to the radicals' cause.

It was rumored that British officials tried to bribe Adams with lucrative political positions, if only he would disavow the separatists; although perpetually broke, he never deviated from the "cause."

In addition to passionate speeches calling for independence and scathing editorials damning the British at every turn, the Sons of Liberty often resorted to more physical persuasion, including riots. Bostonians were no strangers to rioting; each year, this was how the town celebrated the anniversary of "Pope's Day," which marked the attempt by Catholics to murder King James I of England. Boston's townsmen paraded each November 5, meeting in the center of town to demonstrate, or "riot." Adams convinced the gang leaders to use their riots to protest unpopular British policies. The rioters gave the illusion of unpredictability; the subject of the mob's wrath was uncertain how far the angered crowd would go. When protesting the Stamp Act, rioters ransacked the homes of government officials, looting all their possessions. The rioters were also effective at forcing resignations of unpopular government officials, occasionally going so far as to threaten their lives.

In 1767, reacting to the Sons of Liberty, and to enforce the various taxes and other royal edicts, the British moved troops into Boston. The occupation of Boston was a dicey affair, generating intense resentment toward London, exacerbated by the fact that the newly arriving troops had no housing. Even though the Quartering Act was in effect, most colonists refused to provide shelter for the troops; some soldiers were forced to sleep in warehouses and other government buildings. To further compound matters, because their salaries failed to cover the cost of living, many of the soldiers were forced to seek outside work, incurring the wrath of Boston citizens, who viewed the soldiers as competitors for their jobs. Altercations between the colonists and the soldiers occurred daily; usually the fights were verbal, confined to insults and taunts. Occasionally, the disagreements would become more intense, escalating to spitting, pushing, and an occasional beating.

The uneasy truce continued into late 1769, when a colonial boycott of British goods was due to expire on December 31. Sam Adams and the Sons of Liberty pressed Boston's merchants to extend the boycott. A handful of them loyal to the British refused and became the focus of harassment by the anti-British forces. Derogatory signs were posted outside their shops, and human excrement was smeared on their storefronts. One particularly harassed was Ebenezer Richardson, who had provoked the rebels before—he had been an informant for the customs agents. Richardson and his wife were in their house while a hostile crowd gathered outside. Soon the house was being pelted with rocks, eggs, and fruit, the front windows shattered. Richardson, crouching by the window with a rifle, saw something fly through the broken window and hit his wife, knocking her to the ground. He screamed at the crowd that he would shoot the next person to throw anything at the residence. Just then, eleven-year-old Christopher Seider bent over to pick up a rock. Richardson fired his gun, killing the boy.

The Boston rebels had a field day. The story of a Tory supporter killing a colonial boy was on the cover of Sam Adams's *Boston Gazette.* More than two thousand people marched as Seider's coffin was carried through the streets of an uneasy Boston on February 26, 1770.

In the week after Seider's death, skirmishes between soldiers and colonists intensified. On March 2, 1770, a fistfight erupted between some rebels and British troops when a British soldier sought work at a rope-making shop. Samuel Gray, a rope-making laborer, insulted the soldier, Mathew Killroy. Killroy challenged Gray to a fight, and the two scuffled in the street, the soldier running away when Gray appeared to be winning. A few minutes later, Killroy returned with some of his comrades from the Twenty-ninth Regiment and a brawl ensued; no one was killed, but the two instigators would again meet in three days—one would die, the other would be charged with his murder.

The next morning, another group of soldiers fought with another group of colonials, one soldier suffering a fractured skull. More scuffles broke out throughout that day and night, and the commander of the Twenty-ninth Regiment sent word to the governor that a serious clash was imminent.

The Boston Massacre

On the evening of March 5, 1770, British private Hugh White was the only sentry guarding the Custom House, where incoming ships declared their cargo and paid their duties. Because this was where the taxes were collected, the Custom House had become a symbol of British power and arrogance. Shortly before 9 p.m., Edward Garrick, a barber's apprentice, strode down King Street and stopped across from Private White at his post. Garrick began shouting at White; White responded in kind, and eventually the British private smacked Garrick with his musket, cutting him below the ear. The boy, blood dripping from his head, ran off screaming for help.

Garrick's screams roused the neighborhood and an alarm was sounded. Sam Adams and the rebels rushed to the street with rifles, bayonets, and farming tools, joined by twenty or thirty drunken colonial sailors led by Crispus Attucks. A frightened Private White ran to the guardhouse, yelling, "Call out the main guard!" The British officer on duty, Captain Thomas Preston, was a prominent member of Boston's social scene, generally seen as an honorable man, even by the Sons of Liberty and their comrades. Preston heard White's plea and ordered seven of his grenadiers, the tallest and strongest men in the unit, to come to White's aid, hoping such a show of force might disperse the crowd.

Preston would later testify that it was his intent to recover White and then march his troops back to the barracks. Instead he found himself and his men penned against the Custom House by as many as four hundred armed and angry rebels, yelling and throwing rocks. Insults, shouts of "Murder them," "Kill 'em," "Bloody backs," came from the mob. Preston paced in front of his men, attempting to keep the peace, putting his body between his troops and the crowd. The rioters pressed closer, until British trooper Hugh Montgomery was knocked to the ground, either by a shove or a hurled object. Scrambling to his feet, Montgomery fired into the crowd. Everyone stopped for just a moment, frozen in stunned silence. Then all hell broke loose. The soldiers began firing; the crowd panicked and broke for cover. Preston screamed for his troops to cease firing.

When the smoke cleared, five colonials lay dead or dying, six others wounded. No civilians had fired a shot. Samuel Gray, who just days before had sparred with trooper Mathew Killroy, was dead. He was seventeen. James Caldwell and Samuel Maverick, both also seventeen, were killed, as was Crispus Attucks. Patrick Carr died nine days later.

A Call for Justice

An outraged Sam Adams stormed to the governor's mansion and demanded that Governor Hutchinson have the soldiers arrested. Hutchinson, fully cognizant of the volatility of the situation, immediately sought out Captain Preston and, standing at the gate of the barracks, demanded to know why Preston had been on the steps of the Custom House in the first place. Preston responded that he had gone to save the life of Private White.

Hutchinson, forced to address the angry crowd that had gathered and watched the exchange with Preston, appeased them by promising that justice would be done, but that nothing more could happen until morning. He pleaded with the throng to disperse and go home. Around 2 a.m. that following morning, under orders from the governor, Captain Preston was quietly arrested and charged with murder.

At sunup that same morning, all British troops were withdrawn from Boston to a fort a few miles from the center of town, and the eight soldiers who had been at the Custom House—Corporal William Wemms, James Hartigan, William McCauley, Hugh White, Mathew Kilroy, William Warren, John Carrol, and Hugh Montgomery—were also arrested and charged with murder.

The Sons of Liberty Create a "Massacre"

The colonial press played up the tragedy, and within days the five slain men had become martyrs to the sacred cause of liberty. Any full factual account, including mention of the drunken state of many in the mob and the disproportionate number of colonists versus soldiers, was lost in hyperbole. The label *massacre* was most likely coined by Sam Adams himself, in an effort to inflame American passion. The account in the weekly *Boston Gazette and Country Journal* on March 12, 1770, read:

> On the evening of Monday, being the fifth current, several soldiers of the 29th Regiment were seen parading the streets with their drawn cutlasses and bayonets, abusing and wounding numbers of the inhabitants. Thirty or forty persons, mostly lads, gathered in King Street, Capt. Preston with a party of men with charged bayonets, came from the main guard to the commissioner's house, the soldiers pushing their bayonets, crying, make way! They took place by the Custom House and, continuing to push the people off. Some of the people, it is said, threw snowballs. On this, the Captain commanded the soldiers to fire. More snowballs were thrown. He again

said, damn you, fire, be the consequence what it will! One soldier then fired, and a townsman with a cudgel struck him over the hands with such force that he dropped his firelock; and, rushing forward, aimed a blow at the Captain's head which grazed his hat and fell pretty heavy upon his arm. However, the soldiers continued the fire successively till seven or eight or, as some say, eleven guns were discharged.

By this fatal maneuver three men were laid dead on the spot and two more struggling for life; but what showed a degree of cruelty unknown to British troops was an attempt to fire upon or push with their bayonets the persons who undertook to remove the slain and wounded!

The people were immediately alarmed with the report of this horrid massacre, the bells were set a-ringing, and great numbers soon assembled at the place where this tragic scene had been acted. Their feelings may be better conceived than expressed; and while some were taking care of the dead and wounded, the rest were in consultation what to do in those dreadful circumstances. But so little intimidated were they, notwithstanding their being within a few yards of the main guard and seeing the 29th Regiment under arms and drawn up in King Street, that they kept their station and appeared, as an officer of rank expressed it, ready to run upon the very muzzles of their muskets.

The lieutenant-governor soon came into the town house and there met some of his Majesty's Counsel and a number of civil magistrates. A considerable body of the people immediately entered the council chamber and expressed themselves to his honour. He used his utmost endeavours to pacify them, requesting that they would let the matter subside for the night and promising to do all in his power that justice should be done and the law have its course. Men of influence and weight with the people were not wanting on their part to procure their compliance with his Honour's request by representing the horrible consequences of a promiscuous and rash engagement in the night, and assuring them that such measures should be entered upon in the morning as would be agreeable to their dignity and a more likely way of obtaining the best satisfaction for the blood of their fellow townsmen. Tuesday morning presented a most shocking scene, the blood of our fellow citizens running like water through King Street. Our blood might also be tracked up to the head of Long Lane, and through other streets and passages.

Last Thursday, agreeable to a general request of the inhabitants and by the consent of parents and friends, were carried to their grave in succession the bodies of Samuel Gray, Samuel Maverick, James Caldwell, and Crispus Attucks, the unhappy victims who fell in the bloody massacre of the Monday evening preceding!

The Boston city fathers ordered their own account of events published and bound in pamphlet form, which they intended for publication throughout the American colonies. This narrative described not only the "massacre" but the political backdrop in Boston that preceded the events of March 5. The pamphlet, entitled "A Short Narrative of the Horrid Massacre in Boston," read:

It may be a proper introduction to this narrative, briefly to represent the state of things for some time previous to the said Massacre; and this seems necessary in order to the forming a just idea of the causes of it.

At the end of the late French and Indian war, in which this province bore so distinguished a part, a happy union subsisted between Great Britain and the colonies. This was unfortunately interrupted by the Stamp Act; but it was in some measure restored by the repeal of it. It was again interrupted by other acts of Parliament for taxing America; and by the appointment of a Board of Commissioners, in pursuance of an act, which by the face of it was made for the relief and encouragement of commerce, but which had a contrary effect. By the act the Commissioners were "to be resident in some convenient part of his Majesty's dominions in America." This must be understood to be in some part convenient for the whole. But it does not appear that, in fixing the place of their residence, the convenience of the whole was at all consulted, for Boston, being very far from the center of the colonies, could not be the place most convenient for the whole. Judging by the act, it may seem this town was intended to be favored, by the Commissioners being appointed to reside here; and that the consequence of that residence would be the relief and encouragement of commerce; but the reverse has been the constant and uniform effect of it; so that the commerce of the town, from the embarrassments in which it has been lately involved, is greatly reduced.

The residence of the Commissioners here has been detrimental, not only to the commerce, but to the political interests of the town and province; and not only so, but we can trace from it the causes of the late horrid massacre. Soon after their arrival here in November

1767, instead of confining themselves to the proper business of their office, they became partisans of Governor Bernard [Boston's former governor who had recently been replaced by Hutchinson] in his political schemes; and had the weakness and temerity to infringe upon one of the most essential rights of the House of Commons of this province, that of giving their votes with freedom, and not being accountable therefor but to their constituents.

These proceedings of theirs rendered them disgustful to people in general, who in consequence thereof treated them with neglect. This probably stimulated them to resent it; and to make their resentment felt, they and their coadjutor, Governor Bernard, made such representations to his Majesty's ministers as they thought best calculated to bring the displeasure of the nation upon the town and province; and in order that those representations might have the more weight, they are said to have contrived and executed plans for exciting disturbances and tumults, which otherwise would probably never have existed; and, when excited, to have transmitted to the ministry the most exaggerated accounts of them.

Unfortunately for us, they have been too successful in their said representations, which, in conjunction with Governor Bernard's, have occasioned his Majesty's faithful subjects of this town and province to be treated as enemies and rebels.

Thus were we, in aggravation of our other embarrassments, embarrassed with troops, forced upon us contrary to our inclination—contrary to the spirit of Magna Carta—contrary to the very letter of the Bill of Rights, in which it is declared, that the raising or keeping a standing army within the kingdom in time of peace, unless it be with the consent of parliament, is against law, and without the desire of the civil magistrates, to aid whom was the pretence for sending the troops hither; who were quartered in the town in direct violation of an act of parliament for quartering troops in America; and all this in consequence of the representations of the said Commissioners and the said Governor, as appears by their memorials and letters lately published.

As they were the procuring cause of troops being sent hither, they must therefore be the remote and a blameable cause of all the disturbances and bloodshed that have taken place in consequence of that measure.

The attack of a party of soldiers on some of the magistrates of the town, the repeated rescues of soldiers from peace officers, the firing of a loaded musket in a public street, the endangering of a great number of peaceable inhabitants, the frequent wounding of persons by their bayonets and cutlasses, and the numerous instances of bad behavior in the soldiery, made us early sensible that the troops were not sent here for any benefit to the town or province, and that we had no good to expect from such conservators of the peace.

It was not expected, however, that such an outrage and massacre, as happened here on the evening of the fifth instant, would have been perpetrated. There were then killed and wounded, by a discharge of musketry, eleven of his Majesty's subjects.

The actors in this dreadful tragedy were a party of soldiers commanded by Capt. Preston of the 29th regiment. This party, including the Captain, consisted of eight, who are all committed to jail.

Captain Preston is said to have ordered them to fire, and to have repeated that order. One gun was fired first; then others in succession and with deliberation, till ten or a dozen guns were fired; or till that number of discharges were made from the guns that were fired. By which means eleven persons were killed and wounded.

Supplementing these reports was Paul Revere's widely circulated engraving of the massacre.

Revere's engraving was nothing short of a call to arms. It was highly effective at stirring up the emotions of the colonists in distant cities, who heard about the "massacre" for the first time a week after it happened. The engraving was complete propaganda. The soldiers are depicted as standing in attack formation, when in fact they were in complete disarray and pressed against the Custom House. The engraving had Captain Preston's arm raised, as if commanding his soldiers to fire, when in reality Preston had placed himself between the crowd and the soldiers. Revere also took liberties with the Custom House itself, renaming it Butcher's Hall in the picture. Revere's drawing was not the only picture circulated in the weeks after the "massacre." Two other drawings appeared, both oddly similar to the depiction by Revere. Because Revere was not known for his great artistic ability, he may simply have "borrowed" one of the other drawings, added color and a few final touches, and submitted it to the *Gazette* for publishing.

Representing the Crown

Meanwhile, the vilified Captain Preston and his troops remained in custody, awaiting trial on capital murder charges. In an ironic twist, their prosecutor was a British loyalist, a staunch Tory, Samuel Quincy, the solicitor general of Massachusetts. Quincy, devoted to the British Crown, was also a distant cousin of John Adams's. Both men had been admitted to the state bar on the same day. Although Quincy never enjoyed the success and fame that John Adams obtained, Adams credited him as the finest legal mind in all of Boston.

Concerned that Quincy's British loyalties would color or even subvert his prosecution of the soldiers, Samuel Adams persuaded the town of Boston to pay for another prosecutor. Accordingly, Robert Treat Paine, a patriot, was enlisted for the prosecution. Sam Adams and the Sons of Liberty, along with the other Boston colonists, had no doubts as to where Paine's loyalties lay. Paine was so devoted to their cause that he would later be a representative to the Continental Congress, would sign the Declaration of Independence, and would ultimately be appointed a justice of the Massachusetts Supreme Court.

Willing Defense Lawyers Few and Far Between

While the prosecuting team was quickly assembled, it would remain a far more arduous task to find able representation for the accused. Captain Preston and his redcoats were the most vilified men in America, and few lawyers were eager to come to their defense. The task of finding defense counsel was made more difficult by the considerable risk of physical harm—Boston was a volatile town full of volatile people. Additionally, any would-be defense lawyer would in all likelihood suffer a loss of professional opportunity for years to come, if not for the balance of his career, tainted as one of the king's men.

Following the "massacre," James Forrest, a loyalist merchant, took it upon himself to find representation for Preston and his soldiers. After being rejected by a number of lawyers, Forrest approached Josiah Quincy, the brother of prosecutor Samuel Quincy, to beg for his representation. Given his close relationship with the lead prosecutor, Josiah seemed an odd choice; it was perhaps a commentary on the scarcity of defense counsel. Surprisingly, Quincy did not outright refuse Forrest's entreaty but rather insisted that he would consider representing the accused only if John Adams could be persuaded to become lead counsel. This was likewise a surprising reaction—Quincy was well aware that John Adams was a supporter of greater independence from England, and had become a thoughtful and respected voice of reason, raising legitimate questions about continued British authority over the colonies. Further, John Adams was Samuel Adams's cousin. Perhaps Josiah Quincy's unusual stipulation was simply a convenient manner of refusal. Nonetheless, a dogged and somewhat desperate and skeptical James Forrest would at least approach John Adams.

John Adams, unlike most of the other legal scholars and political activists in Boston, was not born into wealth. He was the first son to parents who earned their living as farmers and shoemakers. After an unremarkable childhood, Adams was accepted at Harvard and offered a partial scholarship, eventually graduating in the top three of twenty-seven students in the class of 1755. It was at Harvard that someone first told Adams that his penchant for public speaking would lend itself nicely to the study of law. To become a lawyer in prerevolutionary Boston, the would-be litigator had to pay a practicing attorney to take him in as an apprentice. To raise sufficient funds, Adams taught grade school to save up for his legal apprenticeship.

A year later, Adams arranged an apprenticeship with attorney James Putnam. Adams continued to teach during the day while studying law under Putnam at night, and was admitted to the Massachusetts bar in 1759, when he was twenty-four. Five years later, he married Abigail Smith, and thus began one of America's great love affairs. Abigail and John regarded each other not just as husband and wife but as best friends. With the birth of their daughter Abigail in 1765, and son John Quincy in 1767, Adams was an immensely happy family man. Just as Adams was finding satisfaction in his family life, his professional reputation was in full bloom as he became one of Boston's busiest and most prominent attorneys.

Shortly after Parliament passed the Stamp Act in 1765, Adams aligned himself with the American cause. With the publication of his essay "A Dissertation on the Canon and Feudal Law" in the *Boston Gazette,* Adams became one of the preeminent voices in America decrying the heavy hand of England. In his brilliant dissertation he argued that American rights were firmly established by law, not privileges to be doled out by a distant monarch.

In 1765, soon after the "Dissertation" was published to widespread acclaim across the American colonies, Adams was called upon to write the "Braintree Instructions," a letter to the British-controlled governing body of Massachusetts, damning British "taxation without representation." This work also resonated throughout Massachusetts and eventually across America. More than forty towns and cities sent word to the ruling bodies that they, too, supported Adams's views in the "Instructions." In the "Instructions," he wrote:

> In all the calamities which have ever befallen this country, we have never felt so great a concern, or such alarming apprehensions, as on this occasion. Such is our loyalty to the King, our veneration for both houses of Parliament, and our affection for all our fellow-subjects in Britain, that measures which discover any unkindness in that country towards us are the more sensibly and intimately felt. And we can no longer forbear complaining, that many of the measures of the late ministry, and some of the late acts of Parliament, have a tendency, in our apprehension, to divest us of our most essential rights and liberties. We shall confine ourselves, however, chiefly to the act of Parliament, commonly called the Stamp Act, by which a very burdensome, and, in our opinion, unconstitutional tax, is to be laid upon us all. We have called this a burdensome tax, because the duties are so numerous and so high, and the embarrassments to business in this infant, sparsely-settled country so great, that it would be totally impossible for the people to subsist under it, if we had no controversy at all about the right and authority of imposing it. Considering the present scarcity of money, we have reason to think, the execution of that act for a short space of time would drain the country of its cash, strip multitudes of all their property, and reduce them to absolute beggary. And what the consequence would be to the peace of the province, from so sudden a shock and such a convulsive change in the whole course of our business and subsistence, we tremble to consider.

We further apprehend this tax to be unconstitutional. We have always understood it to be a grand and fundamental principle of the constitution, that no free man should be subject to any tax to which he has not given his own consent, in person or by proxy. And the maxims of the law, as we have constantly received them, are to the same effect, that no freeman can be separated from his property but by his own act or fault. We take it clearly, therefore, to be inconsistent with the spirit of the common law, and of the essential fundamental principles of the British constitution, that we should be subject to any tax imposed by the British Parliament; because we are not represented in that assembly in any sense, unless it be by a fiction of law, as insensible in theory as it would be injurious in practice, if such a taxation should be grounded on it.

And so, when James Forrest, the British loyalist, tried to persuade John Adams to represent the very representatives of Great Britain whom Adams had so thoughtfully and thoroughly taken to task, he had severe doubts that Adams would take the case. Years later Adams would write in his journal about his initial meeting with James Forrest.

With tears streaming from his eyes he [Forrest] said, "I am come with a very solemn message from a very unfortunate man, Captain Preston, in prison. He wishes for counsel and can get none. . . . " I had no hesitation in answering that counsel ought to be the very last thing that an accused person should want in a free country, that the bar ought, in my opinion, to be independent and impartial at all times, and in every circumstance, and that persons whose lives were at stake ought to have the counsel they preferred.

Adams—in a decision that stunned Boston and perplexed people across the American colonies—did the unthinkable and took the case. Few at the time could or would recognize that this lawyer was looking beyond the immediate passions and emotions that gripped his contemporaries to a larger and grander view of a country where the dispassionate rule of law and the objective sanctity of trial should prevail. Adams undertook the representation of Captain Preston and his men in this death penalty trial, well aware of the consequences. First and foremost was a fear for his family's safety. The anger in Boston was white-hot, and Adams was a very visible target. The second consequence could be to his law practice—who would retain the services of someone who could represent the perpetrators of this "massacre"? Finally, Adams knew that he would be viewed as a traitor to the cause he so passionately believed in. And any thoughts or hopes he might have entertained about participating as a leading voice in American independence and establishing a new government were surely dashed. For all its consequences, Adams viewed his role as a lawyer as a calling of the highest nature. And the accused, who were without representation, surely needed a good lawyer.

Josiah Quincy, true to his word, joined the defense team once Adams agreed to represent the soldiers. The twenty-six-year-old Quincy, politically aligned with the Sons of Liberty, signed on against the wishes of his family, as expressed in a letter from his father:

My Dear Son,

I am under great affliction, at hearing the bitterest reproaches uttered against you, for having become an advocate for those criminals who are charged with the murder of their fellow-citizens. Good God! Is it possible? I will not believe it. . . .

Your anxious and distressed parent,
Josiah Quincy.

Quincy's response to his father avoids the reasons why two prominent Boston attorneys, supporters of the colonists' cause, would agree to take on these seemingly doomed and vilified clients:

Honored Sir,

I refused all engagement, until advised and urged to undertake it, by an Adams. I dare affirm, that you, and this whole people will one day rejoice, that I became an advocate for the aforesaid "criminals," charged with the murder of our fellow citizens.

I am, truly and affectionately, your son,
Josiah Quincy Jun.

The Trial of Captain Preston

Captain Preston was tried first and tried alone. Although two months had passed since the shootings, passions ran high and the courthouse and surrounding yards were full. Noticeably absent, however, was Samuel Adams, who for unknown reasons had decided not to attend Preston's trial. It made sense to try Preston separately from his soldiers because he had a defense separate and different from that of his men—that he did not command the soldiers to fire—while the soldiers' defense was that they were just obeying orders. Preston's trial, beyond the charges themselves, would be noteworthy for two reasons. It would be the longest trial in colonial history; heretofore trials had never lasted more than one day. Of greater significance, Preston, a man vilified in Boston and throughout colonial America, would, despite his notoriety, receive the finest legal representation available.

The practice in colonial Massachusetts was to have a panel, rather than a single judge, preside at trial. These men were appointed by the governor of the colony. Because the loyalist governor usually appointed his friends and supporters to office, only one of the five judges in Boston's circuit court was trained in law. Jury selection was also quite different than modern legal practice. To ensure impartial jurors, colonial-era laws mandated that the jury panel be created of men from all around the state. The statute specified how many men from each Massachusetts town were to be called. Ultimately, the availability of men to serve was decided in town meetings, and Sam Adams and the Sons of Liberty controlled those. Sam Adams had taken great care to ensure that only men who supported the colonial cause, and no Tory supporters, showed up at the critical meetings from which prospective jurors would be secured. He was successful; the town halls were packed with pro-independence men from whom the jury pool was chosen.

John Adams, in a deft countermove, thwarted his distant cousin's stratagem. Adams, using all of his allotted twenty-two juror challenges, so depleted the potential juror pool that additional prospective jurors were needed. John Adams knew that additional potential jurors would not be drawn from another town meeting, but rather, as custom dictated, would be selected by the sheriff from those present at and around the courthouse. Spectators were indeed selected, and they resulted in a jury no one could have anticipated. Five of the jurors were Tories; one of them was Preston's friend, who claimed that he "would sit till doomsday" before sending the captain to the gallows. Sam Adams failed to show up in court that day, and it is possible that his absence from the gallery is the only reason this particular jury was impaneled. Though the partiality of the jury was denounced by the Boston rebels, the trial began as scheduled.

Once the trial was under way, the prosecution set about its task to prove that Preston had ordered his men to fire, or at bare minimum to prove that Preston had had the time and the opportunity to order his men to cease fire after the first shot, but before any fatal injuries had been inflicted.

Although no verbatim transcript of the examinations of the various witnesses has survived, summaries of the various witnesses, testimony have, primarily through the meticulous notes of John Adams and Robert Treat Paine, written during the trial.

The prosecution first called Edward Garrick, the young man who had been struck by Private White with a bayonet. Garrick testified:

> I heard a noise about eight o'clock and went down to Royal Exchange Lane. I saw some persons with sticks coming up Quaker Lane. I told Captain Goldsmith he owed money to my friend Prentice. He said he was a gentleman and would pay. I said there were no gentlemen in the Army regiment. He struck me. Prentice and a young man came up to the guard and called him bloody back. The guard called to the main guard. About a quarter of an hour later Captain Preston came with his guard. They chased everybody they saw.

Thomas Marshall, a witness to the "massacre," was the prosecution's second witness and testified that Captain Preston could have ordered his troops to stop firing after the initial shot. He testified:

> About five minutes after nine o'clock, I came up Royal Exchange Lane. All was still. I went home and heard the cry of murder. I saw no one but the guard. At my door I saw a man rushing with naked sword from the guard crying, "Damn them where are they, let them come, by Jesus." Others came soon after up Quaker Lane crying fire. I heard the bells ring and the cry of fire became general. The people kept gathering. I saw no uneasiness with the guard. Some soldiers then joined the guard. I heard one shot. A little space and then another, and then several. Between the first shot and the second there was time enough for an officer to step forward and to give the word to stop if he was so minded.

Ebenezer Hinkley, the prosecution's third witness, was not as helpful to their case. He testified as to the hostile nature of the crowd, and perhaps most significantly, he put Captain Preston between the crowd and his troops, an unlikely position for an officer to be in to order his men to shoot. It is also noteworthy that Hinkley offered no testimony as to whether Preston gave any order to shoot:

> Just after nine, maybe a quarter of an hour after, I heard the cry of fire. When I turned Bowe's Corner, I saw some soldiers moving to the guard. I heard someone at the guard window cry, "Fire at 'em, damn 'em, fire at 'em." The soldiers drew up and presented their bayonets and one started forward and kept pushing his bayonet at the people to stab 'em. They drew back but came up again on his

retiring. Captain Preston was one of this party. He ordered them to hold their bayonets breast high and so remained a few minutes. I saw a stick, a few pieces of snow or snowballs thrown. The stick hit the soldier and he thereupon fired. The second gun about a half minute after the first. The third about as long after the second. The rest immediately one after another. The Captain stood between the people and the soldiers, I did not see him behind them at all.

At the end of the first day the trial was far from concluded; this was unprecedented—no trial on American soil, criminal or civil, had ever lasted longer than one day. In fact, the jurors were to be denied food or rest until they reached a verdict, no doubt to discourage long deliberations. Consequently, the judges did not know what to do. It was ultimately decided after considerable debate to sequester the jurors. Each side, prosecution and defense, was allowed to choose someone to keep an eye on them. These two watchers and the jury were fed and bedded overnight in the jail keeper's house.

On the second day of the trial, the prosecution called Daniel Calef, who testified that he heard Preston give the order to fire:

> I was present at the firing. I heard one of the guns rattle. I turned about and looked and heard the officer who stood on the right in a line with the soldiers give the word *fire* twice. I looked the officer in the face when he gave the word and saw his mouth. He had on a red coat, yellow jacket, and silver-laced hat, no trimming on his coat. The prisoner is the officer I mean. I saw his face plain, the moon shone on it. I am sure of the man though I have not seen him since before yesterday when he came into court with others. I knew him instantly.

Following Calef's testimony, the prosecution called Robert Goddard. Goddard was considered "slow," but his testimony was clear: Preston had given an order to fire.

> About nine o'clock I heard the bell ring and ran into King Street. I saw eight or nine soldiers coming down pushing their bayonets damning. The soldiers came up to the guard and the officer told them to place themselves and they formed a half moon. The Captain told the boys to go home lest there should be murder done. The boys were throwing snowballs. The Captain was behind the soldiers. The Captain told them to fire. One gun went off. A sailor

or townsman struck the Captain. He thereupon said, "Damn your bloods, fire. Think I'll be treated in this manner." This man that struck the Captain came from among the people who were seven feet off and were around on one wing. I saw no person speak to him. I was so near I should have seen it. After the Captain said, "Damn your bloods, fire," they all fired one after another about seven or eight in all, and then the officer bid prime and load again. He stood behind all the time. One soldier went up to the officer and called the officer by name Capt. Preston. I saw him coming down from the guard behind the party. I was so near the officer when he gave the word *fire* that I could touch him. His face was towards me. He stood in the middle behind the men. I looked him in the face. He then stood within the circle. When he told 'em to fire, he turned about to me. I looked him in the face.

Following Robert Goddard's adamant and seemingly overwhelming account of Preston's culpability, the prosecutors nonetheless called fifteen more witnesses. And, at the conclusion of an unprecedented second day of testimony, the prosecution rested, confident that they had proved their case: first, that Preston had given the initial order to fire, and, second, that he had an opportunity to order the shooting stopped after the first shot but had failed to do so.

John Adams and Josiah Quincy faced a daunting task as they began their case. Adams, who undertook all of the direct examinations, first called bystander Joseph Edwards. Edwards testified that a small crowd mistreated the lone guard, Private White, and that the crowd that had gathered was large and threatening. Edwards also testified that it was one of the grenadiers, not Captain Preston, who had given the order to fire:

I heard the bells and came down King Street. I saw some boys about the guard abusing him. I advised the boys to go off. They told me they would. They were calling for others and gave three cheers. There were about twelve or fifteen men who abused the guard. Presently the soldiers came and I heard the word prime and load given. I took it the grenadier on the left hand gave the word. He was dressed in red and had a gun in his hand for I saw him prime. I stood below the steps on the flat stones and he stood below me.

The defense next called a slave known only as Andrew, who proved to be a pivotal witness. Andrew described a hostile, aggressive crowd that had pinned the British grenadiers against the Custom House. Andrew also provided critical testimony that Captain Preston had not ordered his men to shoot:

Hearing the bells ring, I came out. I ran to Phillips' Corner. I went from thence to try to get to the Custom House and get through the people. When I was at the head of Royal Exchange, I heard the grenadier who stood next to the corner say, "Damn your blood, stand off, or back." The people were crowding in to see those within forcing themselves from the grenadier who was pushing his bayonet at 'em. A young fellow said, "Damn you, you bloody back lobster are you going to stab me." He said, "By God will I." A number said, "Come away, let 'em alone, you have nothing to do with 'em." Turning round to see who was there, I saw that the officer and two men were talking with him. Some jumping upon their backs to hear what was said. I heard somebody, I took to be the officer, say stand off and something I could not understand. I heard somebody say, "Damn him, he is going to fire," and then they all began to shout, gave three cheers, clapped hands, and said, "Damn them, they dare not fire," and began to pelt snowballs at the soldiers. I saw snowballs thrown and saw soldiers dodging and pushing their bayonets. I saw several snowballs hit them.

I was crowding to get as near to the officer as I could. A stout man forced his way through and came up between me and the grenadier. He had a stick in his hand. I saw him strike at the officer. Persons were talking with him. He then began to strike on the grenadier's gun who stood about a yard and a half from the officer on the right. I saw the grenadier attempt to stick him with his bayonet. The man pushed it aside with his left hand, stepped in, and gave a lick upon the grenadier's neck or shoulder with his club. It was a cordwood stick not very long. As he struck, I turned about and looked at the officer. There was a bustle. The stout man still had hold of the bayonet. While I was looking at the Captain, the people crowded me between the soldiers, "Kill 'em, kill 'em, knock 'em over." Thereupon the grenadier stepped back and began to pay on the people with his gun to beat them back. They rushed back very quick making a great noise or screeching huzzahing and bid the soldiers, "Fire damn you, you dare not fire." I jumped back and heard a voice cry, "Fire," and immediately the first gun fires. It seemed to come from the left wing from the second or third man on the left. The officer was standing before me with his face towards the people. I am certain the voice came from beyond him. The officer stood before the soldiers at a sort of a corner. I turned round and saw a grenadier who stood on the

Captain's right swing his gun and fire. I took it to be Killroy. I looked a little to the right and saw a man drop. The mulatto was killed by the first gun on the Captain's right. I was so frightened, after, I did not know where I was. The first place I found myself in was Dehone's entry.

Following Andrew's testimony that Preston did not give the fatal order to fire, Adams and cocounsel Quincy reached an impasse. Quincy, who was charged by Adams with preparing the witnesses to testify, was convinced it was necessary to characterize the crowd not just as hostile but as vicious—even bloodthirsty. Such a characterization, Quincy maintained, would bolster the defense case that the soldiers had no options but to use deadly force. Adams, however, was gravely concerned that such a broad, damning characterization would spill over from the actual participants and amount to a virtual condemnation of the whole of Boston as an unruly, riotous, and rebellious city. He maintained that such a characterization was unfair to the city of Boston and unnecessary in the defense of Preston. Adams argued to Quincy that the defense should narrow the focus to the few minutes prior to the shootings. He believed he could make Preston's case without castigating all of Boston.

The disagreement between Adams and Quincy became so heated that Adams threatened to quit the defense unless Quincy backed down. Quincy eventually deferred to lead counsel.

As the defense case wound down, Adams and Quincy would have preferred to have Preston take the witness stand to testify in his own defense; however, that was impossible. As strange as it may seem, those accused of crimes in the eighteenth century and indeed well into the nineteenth century were barred from testifying on their own behalf. Indeed, more than a hundred years later in 1872, Susan B. Anthony was unable to offer her testimony when she was in the docket for the crime of casting her vote in a presidential election. The rationale for such a counterintuitive law was that anyone accused of a criminal offense had such a vital stake in the outcome of the proceedings that his—or her— testimony was inherently untrustworthy. Consequently, the jury would hear from Preston only by his written deposition. In it, Captain Thomas Preston began by detailing the tensions between his troops and the Boston colonists:

It is a matter of too great notoriety to need any proofs that the arrival of his Majesty's troops in Boston was extremely obnoxious to its inhabitants. They have used all means in their power to weaken the regiments, and to bring them into contempt by promoting and aiding desertions, and with impunity, by grossly and falsely propagating untruths concerning them.

One of their justices, most thoroughly acquainted with the people and their intentions, on the trial of a man of the 14th Regiment, openly and publicly in the hearing of great numbers of people and from the seat of justice, declared "that the soldiers must now take care of themselves, nor trust too much to their arms, for they were but a handful; that the inhabitants carried weapons concealed under their clothes, and would destroy them in a moment, if they pleased." This, considering the malicious temper of the people, was an alarming circumstance to the soldiery. Since which several disputes have happened between the townspeople and the soldiers, the former being encouraged thereto by the countenance of even some of the magistrates, and by the protection of all the party against government.

On the second of this month, the rope-makers provoked the soldiers, and from words they went to blows. Both parties suffered in this affray, and finally the soldiers retired to their quarters. The officers, on the first knowledge of this transaction, took every precaution in their power to prevent any ill consequence. Notwithstanding which, single quarrels could not be prevented, the inhabitants constantly provoking and abusing the soldiery. The insolence as well as utter hatred of the inhabitants to the troops increased daily, insomuch that Monday and Tuesday, the 5th and 6th of this month, were privately agreed on for a general engagement, in consequence of which several of the militia came from the country armed to join their friends, menacing to destroy any who should oppose them. This plan has since been discovered.

On Monday night about 8 o'clock two soldiers were attacked and beaten. But the party of the townspeople in order to carry matters to the utmost length, broke into two meeting houses and rang the alarm bells, which I supposed was for fire as usual, but was soon undeceived. About nine o'clock some of the guard came to and informed me that the town inhabitants were assembling to attack the troops, and that the bells were ringing as the signal for that purpose and not for fire. This, as I was captain of the day, occasioned my repairing immediately to the main guard. On my way there I saw the people in great commotion, and heard them use the most cruel and horrid threats against the troops.

In a few minutes after I reached the guard, about a hundred people passed it and went towards the Custom House where the king's money is lodged. They immediately surrounded the sentry posted there, and with clubs and other weapons threatened to execute their vengeance on him. I was soon informed by a townsman that their intention was to carry off the soldier from his post and probably murder him. On which I desired him to return for further intelligence, and he soon came back and assured me he heard the mob declare they would murder him. This I feared might be a prelude to their plundering the king's chest. I immediately sent twelve men to protect both the sentry and the king's money, and very soon followed myself to prevent, if possible, all disorder, fearing lest the officer and soldiers, by the insults and provocations of the rioters, should be thrown off their guard and commit some rash act. They soon rushed through the people, and by charging their bayonets in half-circles, kept them at a little distance. Nay, so far was I from intending the death of any person that I suffered the troops to go to the spot where the unhappy affair took place without any loading in their pieces; nor did I ever give orders for loading them. This remiss conduct in me perhaps merits censure; yet it is evidence, resulting from the nature of things, which is the best and surest that can be offered, that my intention was not to act offensively, but the contrary part, and that not without compulsion.

The mob still increased and were more outrageous, striking their clubs or bludgeons one against another, and calling out, come on you rascals, you bloody backs, you lobster scoundrels, fire if you dare, G-d damn you, fire and be damned, we know you dare not, and much more such language was used. At this time I was between the soldiers and the mob, parleying with, and endeavouring all in my power to persuade them to retire peaceably, but to no purpose. They advanced to the points of the bayonets, struck some of them and even the muzzles of the pieces, and seemed to be endeavouring to close with the soldiers. On which some well behaved persons asked me if the guns were charged. I replied yes. They then asked me if I intended to order the men to fire. I answered no, by no means, observing to them that I was advanced before the muzzles of the men's pieces, and must fall a sacrifice if they fired; that the soldiers were upon the half cock and charged bayonets, and my giving the word fire under those circumstances would prove me to be no officer. While I was thus speaking, one of the soldiers having received a severe blow with a stick, stepped a little on one side and instantly fired, on which turning to and asking him why he fired without orders, I was struck with a club on my arm, which for some time deprived me of the use of it, which blow had it been placed on my head, most probably would have destroyed me.

On this a general attack was made on the men by a great number of heavy clubs and snowballs being thrown at them, by which all our lives were in imminent danger, some persons at the same time from behind calling out, damn your bloods, why don't you fire. Instantly three or four of the soldiers fired, one after another, and directly after three more in the same confusion and hurry. The mob then ran away, except three unhappy men who instantly expired. The whole of this melancholy affair was transacted in almost twenty minutes.

On my asking the soldiers why they fired without orders, they said they heard the word fire and supposed it came from me. This might be the case as many of the mob called out fire, fire, but I assured the men that I gave no such order; that my words were, don't fire, stop your firing. In short, it was scarcely possible for the soldiers to know who said fire, or don't fire, or stop your firing. On the people's assembling again to take away the dead bodies, the soldiers supposing them coming to attack them, were making ready to fire again, which I prevented by striking up their firelocks with my hand.

Immediately after a townsman came and told me that four or five thousand people were assembled in the next street, and had sworn to take my life and the life of every man. On which I judged it unsafe to remain there any longer, and therefore sent the party to the main guard.

I immediately sent a sergeant with a party to Colonel Dalrymple, the commanding officer, to acquaint him with every particular. The lieutenant-governor and Colonel Dalrymple soon after met at the head of the 29th regiment and agreed that the regiment should retire to their barracks, and the people to their houses. It was with great difficulty that the lieutenant-governor prevailed on the people to be quiet and retire. At last they all went off, excepting about a hundred.

A counsel was immediately called issued a warrant to apprehend me and eight soldiers. On hearing of this procedure I instantly went to the sheriff and surrendered myself, though for the space of four hours I had it in my power to have made my escape, which I most undoubtedly should have attempted and could have easily executed, had I been the least conscious of any guilt. On the examination before the justices, two witnesses swore that I gave the men orders to fire. The one testified he was within two feet of me; the other that I swore at the men for not firing at the first word. Others swore they heard me use the word "fire," but whether do or do not fire, they could not say; others that they heard the word fire, but could not say if it came from me. The next day they got five or six more to swear I gave the word to fire. So bitter and inveterate are many of the malcontents here that they are industriously using every method to fish out evidence to prove it was a concerted scheme to murder the inhabitants. Others are infusing the utmost malice and revenge into the minds of the people who are to be my jurors by false publications, votes of towns, and all other artifices. That so from a settled rancour against the officers and troops in general, the suddenness of my trial after the affair while the people's minds are all greatly inflamed, I am, though perfectly innocent, under most unhappy circumstances, having nothing in reason to expect but the loss of life in a very ignominious manner, without the interposition of his Majesty's royal goodness.

And with that, the defense rested.

Unfortunately, no transcripts of Robert Paine's closing argument on behalf of the prosecution or of John Adams's closing argument in defense of Captain Preston exist.

At the conclusion of closing arguments and before the jury retired to deliberate, the circuit court justices, as was the custom of the day, made their remarks to the jury. Each of the justices was of the opinion that Preston never gave an order to fire, although their conclusions were not binding and the jury could reject them if they so chose.

The jury was then sent to deliberate and soon announced that they had reached a verdict. However, it was late in the day, so court did not reconvene until the next morning, when the jury returned and unanimously acquitted Captain Preston of murder.

Bostonians were shocked. How could the man who many believed had given the order to shoot and kill some of their own simply walk away free and exonerated? Would the city explode with new violence? However, there was surprisingly little reaction to Preston's acquittal from the notoriously volatile citizens of Boston. Sam Adams, under a pseudonym, wrote in the *Gazette* that Preston had gotten away with murder. Perhaps it is because the jury had been so obviously stacked in favor of the defendant that such a verdict was expected. However, at least one radical— William Palfrey—admitted that, after the trial, there was doubt in his mind that Preston had ordered his men to fire. The townspeople, although unhappy about the verdict, kept the peace. After all, the men who had actually done the killing were yet to be tried.

Redcoats in the Dock

The trial of the soldiers was delayed several times, the court citing the illness of a judge and then scheduling problems. The Sons of Liberty and much of Boston became increasingly agitated, believing the judges were deliberately stalling to allow tempers to cool. Rumors flew: if the authorities would not try the soldiers, it was for the mob to storm the jail and hang them; even if the soldiers were found guilty of murder, they would be pardoned by the Crown; all the more reason to take matters into the hands of the mob.

Just three weeks after Preston was acquitted, the soldiers' trial began. And, once again, the same team of lawyers represented both sides. This trial would prove more difficult for each. The prosecution, already under heavy criticism and intense scrutiny because of Preston's acquittal, had the complex task of proving which soldier shot and killed which victim, or in the alternative that all the soldiers aided and abetted one another in the shootings. This was no mean feat, considering the chaotic conditions that night. Additionally, the prosecution had to overcome the claim of self-defense raised by the soldiers as they were confronted by the hostile crowd.

Adams and Quincy also had a more formidable task this time around. Because Captain Preston had been acquitted, there was no hope of winning on a defense of following the commanding officer's orders. Additionally, and perhaps more important, the jurors were all aware of Preston's acquittal at the first trial, and the widely held belief was that someone must be held accountable for the deaths of the "brave" rebels.

Against such a challenging backdrop, the trial began. Fortunately, the transcripts from *this* trial survived.

When court was called to order on November 20, the same panel from which Captain Preston's jury had been selected was summoned. However, both sides raised concerns about their impartiality, and so the trial was delayed for a week to gather a new jury panel.

Once matters resumed, only nine jurors were selected before the new jury panel had been exhausted, and not one man was from Boston proper. Once again, the sheriff had to produce men from around the courthouse to complete the jury. Because most of the bystanders were from Boston, they were challenged and disqualified on the grounds of their suspected preconceived biases. After an exhaustive search for the last three jurors, three men from the neighboring town of Hingham were selected. Both sides were forced to compromise, recognizing that efforts to get a completely impartial jury for such a notorious trial was not possible.

Throughout jury selection Sam Adams railed against outsiders sitting as jurors, claiming that an important part of the jury's duty was to gauge the credibility of witnesses' testimony from their personal knowledge of the witnesses. To do this, Adams reasoned, the jurors needed to be local. This notion, of course, is at odds with contemporary trials, in which no juror can have knowledge of any of the parties, or even of any of the witnesses. All of Adams's complaining did not prevent the trial from starting. Having been absent for most of Captain Preston's trial, Sam Adams made a point of being very visible throughout this second trial.

On the first day, the prosecution called six witnesses; the first was Edward Langford, who testified that Private Killroy had shot and killed Samuel Gray:

Q: Were you in King Street, on the fifth of March?
A: Yes, the bell began to ring, and the people cried fire. I ran with the rest and went into King Street. I asked where the fire was. I was told there was no fire, but that the soldiers at Murray's Barracks had got out and had been fighting with the inhabitants. I went to the barracks and found the affair was over there. I came back, and just as I got to the town pump, I saw twenty or five-and-twenty boys going into King Street. I went into King Street myself and saw several boys and men about the sentry box at the Custom House. I asked them what was the matter. They said the guard had knocked down a boy. They crowded in over the gutter; I told them to let the guard alone. The guard went up the steps of the Custom House and knocked at the door, but could not get in. I told him not to be afraid, they were only boys and would not hurt him.
Q: Do you know the sentry?
A: Yes.
Q: Is he among the prisoners?
A: Yes, that's he [pointing to Private White].
Q: Do you know the rest?
A: Yes, that man [pointing to Killroy]. The boys were swearing and speaking bad words, but they threw nothing.
Q: Were they pressing on him [Killroy]?
A: They were as far as the gutter, and he went up the steps and called out, but what he said I do not remember.
Q: Did he call loud?
A: Yes, pretty loud.
Q: To whom did he call?

A: I do not know; when he went up the steps, he leveled his piece with his bayonet fixed. As I was talking with the guard, and telling him not to be afraid, the soldiers came down, and when they came, I drew back from the guard, towards Royal Exchange Lane, and there I stood. I did not see them load, but somebody said, "Are you loaded?" And Samuel Gray, who was shot that night, came and struck me on the shoulder and said, "Langford, what's here to pay?"

Q: What said you to Gray then?

A: I said, I did not know what was to pay, but I believed something would come of it by and by. He made no reply. Immediately a gun went off. I was within reach of their guns and bayonets; one of them thrust at me with his bayonet and run it through my jacket and greatcoat.

Q: Where were you then?

A: Within three or four feet of the gutter, on the outside.

Q: Who asked, "Are you loaded?"

A: I do not know whether it was the soldiers or the inhabitants.

Q: Did you hear the word given to load?

A: I heard the question asked, whether they were loaded, but I heard no orders to load.

Q: Somebody then said, "Are you all ready?"

A: I then heard the word given to fire, twice distinctly.

Q: How many people were there before the soldiers at that time?

A: About forty or fifty, but there were numbers in the lane.

Q: Were they near the soldiers?

A: They were not in the inside of the gutter.

Q: Had any of the inhabitants sticks or clubs?

A: I do not know.

Q: How many soldiers were there?

A: I did not count the number of them, about seven or eight, I think.

Q: Who was it fired the first gun?

A: I do not know.

Q: Whereabout did he stand that fired?

A: He stood on my right; as I stood facing them, I was about halfway between the sentry box and Royal Exchange Lane. I looked this man [pointing to Killroy] in the face and told him not to fire; but he immediately fired, and Samuel Gray fell at my feet. Killroy thrust his bayonet immediately through my coat and jacket. I ran towards the watchhouse and stood there.

Q: Where did Killroy stand?

A: He stood on the right of the party.

Q: Was he the right-hand man?

A: I cannot tell. I believe there were two or three on his right, but I do not know.

Q: You spoke to him you say before he fired; what did you say to him?

A: I said either "Damn you, or God damn you, do not fire," and immediately he fired.

Q: How many guns went off before he fired?

A: Two, but I saw nobody fall. Gray fell close to me.

Q: Did Gray say anything to Killroy before he fired?

A: He spoke to nobody but me.

Q: Did he throw any snowballs?

A: No, nor had he any weapon in his hand; he was naked as I am now.

Q: Did you see anything thrown?

A: No, I saw nothing at all thrown of any kind.

Q: Were you talking with Gray at the time the gun went off?

A: I did not speak with him at that instant, but I had been talking with him several minutes before that.

Q: Were you so near Gray that if he had thrown anything you must have seen it?

A: Yes, his hands were in his bosom, and immediately after Killroy's firing he fell.

Q: Did you hear any other gun at that time?

A: None, till I had got near to the watchhouse.

Q: How near were the people standing to the soldiers, at the time that gun shot Gray?

A: They were standing near the gutter.

Q: Did you see anything hit the soldiers?

A: No, I saw nothing thrown. I heard the rattling of their guns and took it to be one gun against another. This rattling was at the time Killroy fired, and at my right, I had a fair view of them; I saw nobody strike a blow nor offer a blow.

Q: Have you any doubt in your mind that it was the gun of Killroy's that killed Gray?

A: No manner of doubt; it must have been it, for there was no other gun discharged at that time.

Q: Did you see anybody press on the soldiers with a large cordwood stick?

A: No.

Q: After Gray fell, did he [Killroy] thrust at him with his bayonet?

A: No, it was at me he pushed.

Q: Did Gray say anything to Killroy, or Killroy to him?
A: No, not to my knowledge, and I stood close by him.
Q: Did you perceive Killroy take aim at Gray?
A: I did not; he was as liable to kill me as him.

Langford's testimony provided a strong foundation upon which the prosecution could build; specifically, that the crowd, though loud, was not necessarily threatening and that the actions of the grenadiers were unprovoked. Against this backdrop, the prosecutors followed up with Samuel Hemmingway, an acquaintance of Private Killroy's:

Q: Do you know any of the prisoners?
A: Yes, several; there is Killroy I know particularly well.
Q: Did you ever hear Killroy make use of any threatening expressions against the inhabitants of this town?
A: Yes, one evening I heard him say he never would miss an opportunity, when he had one, to fire on the inhabitants, and that he had wanted to have an opportunity ever since he landed.
Q: How long was that before the fifth of March?
A: A week or fortnight, I cannot say which.
Q: Did you ever hear any of the rest threaten anything?
A: No.
Q: What gave occasion for this?
A: He and I were talking about the town's people and the soldiers.
Q: Did he say it with any resentment?
A: No, none at all.
Q: Was it in jocular talk?
A: I do not know. I said he was a fool for talking so; he said he did not care.
Q: Had Killroy said that evening that he had been at the ropewalks?
A: No, he said nothing about the ropewalks.
Q: Was this conversation before or after the affray at the ropewalks?
A: I cannot say.

The prosecution also called twelve-year-old John Appleton, who described how he was battered by an unidentified soldier in an alley on that fateful night:

A: About nine I was sent on an errand into King Street. I had my brother with me, I heard a noise, I run out of the shop where I was to see what was the matter. I went into the middle of the street and

saw men talking to the guard. I thought they were going to quarrel and so I came away. I went to Jenkins's Alley, my brother with
me. Then we saw about twenty soldiers with cutlasses in their
hands. My brother fell and they run past him and were going to kill
me; I said, "Soldiers, spare my life." One of them said, "No, damn
you, we will kill you all." He lifted his cutlass and struck at my head,
but I dodged and got the blow on my shoulder.

Q: Was the cutlass drawn?

A: I believe it was not, for it rattled on my shoulder as if had been
   sheathed.

Through their witnesses, the prosecution continued to paint a picture
of the British soldiers—not just those on trial—as being brutal and
bloodthirsty men who wanted nothing less than to fight and even kill
Boston colonists. The prosecutors succeeded in producing compelling
testimony that Killroy had shot and killed Samuel Gray, that Montgomery had shot and killed Attucks, and that the British had fired the
only weapons that night. It would then remain for the government to fall
back on the legal concept that those who aid and abet are just as culpable
as the instigators, thus bearing the same penalty as Killroy if found guilty.
The prosecution, and most spectators, believed they had made their case.
And so, they rested and left it to the defense to attempt to prove that the
soldiers had acted in self-defense.

The first witness the defense initially planned to call was James
Thompson. Josiah Quincy had intended that Thompson testify that
many of the Boston citizenry had formulated a plan to prod the troops to
violence. John Adams, much as he had done during the trial of Captain
Preston, again refused to make such a wholesale assault on Boston and its
inhabitants and again threatened to quit if Quincy insisted. To the British
supporters, it seemed that Adams was more concerned with appeasing his
rebellious colleagues than saving his clients' lives, and some called for his
removal from the defense. Ultimately, Quincy again agreed to back
down, and again Adams continued as lead defense counsel.

Thompson was eventually called, but he was not questioned on the
generally riotous nature of the townspeople:

Q: What did you hear or see passing through Quaker Lane or
   Green's Lane, on the fifth of March last in the evening?

A: I came out of the Green Dragon Tavern about nine o'clock, and
   I met about fifteen persons walking on different sides of the
   street, and they had sticks in their hands.

Q: What sort of sticks were they?

A: They seemed to be pretty large sticks, rather too large for walking sticks. I passed on and went on board a vessel at Griffen's Wharf and said to people, I believed there would be mischief that night, for I had met several people armed with sticks. Just as I spoke, we heard the bells ring, and some said it could not be the usual bell for nine o'clock, they had heard that ring before. We all went on deck and heard a noise and cry of fire. I went aloft to see where the fire was, I heard the engines going along the street and then stop. I heard Mrs. Marston, who keeps tavern at the head of the wharf, say, "Good God! This is not fire, there will be murder committed this night." A little after I heard a huzzahing and guns go off in King Street.

Q: Did you count them?

A: Yes, I think there were seven; I remained there till a person came down the wharf, and I asked, what was the matter? He told me there were some people killed in King Street.

The defense team then called Patrick Keaton, a participant in the events of March 5, to paint a picture of the hostile crowd:

A: I was at my lodgings and heard a noise and went out towards Union Street and saw people coming from the North End with sticks and clubs in their hands; it was about nine o'clock. I followed them to Dock Square. Somebody asked what was the matter. He was answered that a boy and a soldier had been afoul of one another. They hallooed, "King Street." I went up to the foot of Jenkins's Lane, and there I saw a tall mulatto fellow, the same that was killed. He had two clubs in his hand, and he said, "Here, take one of them." I did so.

Q: What sort of clubs were they?

A: They were cordwood sticks. I went up to the head of the lane, and I dropped the stick in the snow; he went on cursing and swearing at the soldiers, down towards where the people surrounded the soldiers. I stood by the stone steps of the Custom House. There were people coming from all parts, calling out, "Bloody back!" and one thing and another. I could not distinguish what one-half of them said.

The defense's best evidence was from Dr. David Jeffries, who treated Patrick Carr, one of the men who was shot and later died. Jeffries had discussed the events of the fifth with the mortally wounded Carr. Statements made by one who is dying are admissible as an exception to the hearsay rule, the rationale being that a person would not die with a lie on his lips. As a result, Dr. Jeffries was permitted to testify to the following:

Q: Were you Patrick Carr's surgeon?

A: I was, in company with others. I was called that evening about eleven o'clock to him. After dressing his wounds, I advised him never to go again into quarrels and riots; he said he was very sorry he did go. Dr. Lloyd, who was present, turned round to me and said, "Jeffries, I believe this man will be able to tell us how the affair was, we had better ask him." I asked him then how long he had been in King Street when they fired. He said when he got to Walker's Corner, he saw many persons coming from Cornhill, who he was told had been quarreling with the soldiers down there. While he was standing there, he saw many things thrown at the guard. I asked him if he knew what was thrown. He said he heard the things strike against the guns, and they sounded hard. He believed they were oyster shells and ice. He heard the people huzzah every time they heard anything strike that sounded hard. He then said he saw the people pelt them as they went along; after they had got down there, he crossed over towards Warden and Vernon's Shop, in order to see what they would do; and as he was passing, he was shot.

I asked him whether he thought the soldiers would fire; he told me he thought the soldiers would have fired long before. I then asked him if he thought the soldiers were abused a great deal after they went down there; he said he thought they were. I asked him what he thought would happen if the soldiers had not fired; he said he really thought they would, for he heard many voices cry out, "Kill them." I asked him then, meaning to close all, whether he thought they fired in self-defense, or on purpose to destroy the people. He said he really thought they did fire to defend themselves. He did not blame the man, whoever he was, that shot him.

Q: Was he apprehensive of his danger?

A: He was told of it. He told me also, he was a native of Ireland, that he had frequently seen mobs, and soldiers called upon to quell them; whenever he mentioned that, he always called himself a fool, that he might have known better that he had seen soldiers often fire on the people in Ireland, but had never seen them bear half so much before they fired in his life.

Q: How long did he live after he received his wound?

A: Ten days.

Q: When had you the last conversation with him?

A: About four o'clock in the afternoon preceding the night on which he died, and he then particularly said he forgave the man, whoever he was that shot him; he was satisfied that the man had no malice but fired to defend himself.

Q: Did you yourself see any of the transactions that evening?

A: On the evening of the fifth of March, I was at my father's opposite Mr. Cooper's. About nine, one of the neighbors run in and said to my father, "Pray, sir, come out, there will be murder, the soldiers and people are fighting." I went directly towards Murray's Barracks. Before I got there, I found the passageway stopped up by a number of people of all sorts. I saw several soldiers. I think there were three; one of them had a pair of tongs in his hand, another had a stick. Behind them were several officers driving the soldiers towards the barracks' gate. As they went in, there were a great many snowballs thrown at them; they were called cowardly rascals, and that they were afraid to fight.

Q: What number of people do you think were there?

A: There were as many as could stand between the steps and the side of the way; I took the alley to be as full as it could be, for others were pressing to get into that street and could not. I judge not less than seventy or eighty could fill that space of ground. The officers told the people not a soldier would come out. There was a great deal of abusive language given to them, the soldiers were repeatedly called lobsters. While they were talking, I saw snowballs thrown at the officers, which struck the door before which they stood. The officers begged the people to go away. The people said they would not. The officers said they had done all they could, they had turned the soldiers in and shut the gate, that no soldiers should come out that evening. Somebody replied, "You mean they dare not come out, you dare not let them out." Many persons cried, "Let us go home"; others said, "No, we shall find some soldiers in King Street." A number of them passed up the alley; as they went up, they huzzahed and made a noise against the fences and side of the walls. I then passed up the alley myself into Cornhill. As soon as I got out of the alley, I heard the Old Brick bell ring. There were many in the street running, some with buckets, inquiring where the fire was. There were many answers given in the street. It is not fire, it is the soldiers fighting. At that time I heard a huzzah I thought from lower down King Street. I went to my father's. I had been but a little while in the house when the girl ran in from the kitchen and said there is a gun fired. I replied to the company, I did not believe it, for I had seen the officers put in the soldiers and shut the gate.

After Dr. Jeffries, the defense called just a few more witnesses. These examinations went quickly and added little to the defense's case, especially after the bombshell testimony by Jeffries that Patrick Carr believed his killer to have acted in self-defense. Interestingly, no depositions of any of the soldiers were read to the jury. And, given that defendants were precluded from testifying, the jurors were offered no accounts of events from their perspective.

As both sides prepared for closing arguments, certain points were beyond dispute. There was no doubt that bodies were lying in the streets as a result of gunshots. There was also no doubt that the shots had been fired by the British soldiers now on trial. However, unlike in Preston's trial, where the jury only needed to decide if Preston had given the order to fire, the jury here had to determine which soldier shot which victim and then determine if the soldiers fired in self-defense or with malice. And, if in malice, were all accessories and thus equally liable?

Adams's task during closing argument was to paint a picture of the confrontational and hostile nature of the crowd pushing those soldiers against the Custom House wall. And once he had sufficiently set up the general defense, he then had to turn to the particular circumstances of Private Killroy and the fight he had with victim Gray prior to the events of March 5. Finally, it was critical for Adams to rebut any prosecution claims that Killroy's actions should be imputed to the others.

The harsh language found in John Adams's closing argument shows that he did not fear the reaction of his fellow patriots. In his closing, which took the better part of two days, Adams refers to the colonists in the street as a "mob" and otherwise berates the unruly men who had initiated the bloody fight. In the end, the British supporters who had clamored for Adams to step down felt that the colonial mob had been exposed, and that the soldiers had their own fair day in court.

JOHN ADAMS'S CLOSING ARGUMENT

I, yesterday afternoon, produced from the best authorities, those rules of law which must govern all cases of homicide, particularly that which is now before you; it now remains to consider the evidence, and I will not trouble myself nor you with labored endeavors to be methodical, I shall endeavor to make some few observations, on the testimonies of the witnesses, such as will place the facts in a true point of light, with as much brevity as possible.

Witness Bridgham saw numbers of things thrown, and he saw plainly about a dozen persons with sticks, gave three cheers, and surrounded the party and struck the guns with their sticks. This is a witness for the Crown, and his testimony is of great weight for the prisoners. He gives his testimony very sensibly and impartially. He swears positively that he not only saw ice or snow thrown, but saw the guns struck several times. There are many others who swear to the same circumstances in favor of the prisoners. There were a dozen persons with clubs, surrounding the soldiers who were chained there by the order and command of their officer, to stand in defense of the sentry.

The soldiers could not defend themselves with their bayonets against so many people; it was in the power of the sailors to kill one-half or the whole of the party, if they had been so disposed. What had the soldiers to expect, when twelve persons armed with clubs—sailors, too, between whom and soldiers, there is such an antipathy, that they fight as naturally when they meet, as the elephant and rhinoceros—were daring enough, even at the time when they were loading their guns, to come up with their clubs and smite on the soldiers' guns. What had eight soldiers to expect from such a set of people? Would it have been a prudent resolution in them, or in anybody in their situation, to have stood still, to see if the sailors would knock their brains out, or not? Had they not all the reason in the world to think that they would proceed farther? Their clubs were as capable of killing as a sword, bayonet, or musket.

The witness told us that the soldiers were loading their guns when the sailors and the people surrounded them within the length of their guns. The soldiers were called cowardly rascals and were dared to fire. You will find evidence enough to satisfy you, these were some of the persons who had been arming themselves with sticks from the butchers' stalls and cordwood piles, and marched up under the command of [Crispus] Attucks. All the bells in town were ringing, the rattling of the blows upon the guns was heard, and it was violent.

There were fifty people near the soldiers pushing at them. Now what could the people expect? It was their business to have taken themselves out of the way. Some prudent people told them not to meddle with the guard, but you hear nothing of this from these fifty people. No, instead of that, they were huzzahing and whistling, crying, "Damn you, fire! Why don't you fire?" So that they were actually assisting these sailors that made the attack. The soldiers were pushing at the people to keep them off, ice and snowballs were thrown. There were some clubs thrown from a considerable distance across the street.

Mr. Langford, the watchman, is more particular in his testimony and deserves a very particular consideration, because it is intended by the counsel for the Crown that his testimony shall distinguish Killroy from the rest of the prisoners, and exempt him from those pleas of justification, excuse, or extenuation, which we rely upon for the whole party, because he had previous malice, and they would therefore conclude, he aimed at a particular person.

Hemmingway, the sheriff's coachman, swears he knew Killroy, and that he heard him say, he would never miss an opportunity of firing upon the inhabitants. This is to prove that Killroy had preconceived malice in his heart, not indeed against the unhappy persons who were killed, but against the inhabitants in general, that he had the spirit not only of a Turk or an Arab, but of the devil. But admitting that this testimony is literally true, and that he had all the malice they would wish to prove, yet, if he was assaulted that night, and his life in danger, he had a right to defend himself as well as another man. If he had malice before, it does not take away from him the right of defending himself against any unjust aggressor.

But it is not at all improbable that there was some misunderstanding about these loose expressions. Perhaps Killroy had no thoughts of what his words might import; many a man in his cups, or in anger, which is a short fit of madness, hath uttered the rashest expressions, who had no such savage disposition in general. So there is little weight in expressions uttered at a kitchen fire, before a maid and a coachman, where he might think himself at liberty to talk as much like a bully, a fool, and a madman as he pleased, and that no evil would come of it. Strictly speaking, he might mean no more than this, that he would not miss an opportunity of firing on the inhabitants if he was attacked by them in such a manner as to justify it. But still what he said amounts, in strictness, to no more than this: if the inhabitants make an attack on me, I will not bear from them what I have done already; or I will bear no more than what I am obliged by law to bear.

Some of the witnesses have sworn that Gray was active in the battle at the ropewalks, and that Killroy was once there, from whence the counsel for the Crown would infer that Killroy, in King Street, on the fifth of March in the night, knew Gray, whom he had seen at the rope-walks before, and took that opportunity to gratify his preconceived malice; but if this is all true, it will not take away from him his justification, excuse, or extenuation. The rule of the law is, if there has been malice between the two, and at a distant time afterwards they met, and one of them assaults the other's life and he kills in consequence of it, the law presumes the killing was in self-defense, or upon the provocation, not on account of the antecedent malice.

If therefore the assault upon Killroy was so violent as to endanger his life, he had as good a right to defend himself as much as if he never had before conceived any malice against the people in general, or Mr. Gray in particular. If the assault upon him was such as to amount only to a provocation, not to a justification, his crime will be manslaughter only. However, it does not appear that he knew Mr. Gray. None of the witnesses pretend to say he knew him, or that he ever saw him. It is true they were both in the ropewalks at one time, but there were so many combatants on each side that it is not even probable that Killroy should know them all, and no witnesses say there was any reencounter there between these two.

Witnesses have sworn to the condition of Killroy's bayonet, that it was bloody the morning after the fifth of March. The blood they saw, if any, might be occasioned by a wound given by some of the bayonets in the affray, possibly in Mr. Fosdick's arm, or it might happen in the manner mentioned by my brother before. One bayonet at least was struck off and it might fall where the blood of some person slain afterwards flowed. It would be doing violence to every rule of law and evidence, as well as to common sense and the feelings of humanity, to infer from the blood on the bayonet that it had been stabbed into the brains of Mr. Gray after he was dead, and that by Killroy himself who had killed him.

Young Mr. Davis swears that he saw Gray that evening, a little before the firing, that he had a stick under his arm and said he would go to the riot: "I am glad of a rumpus, I will go and have a slap at them, if I lose my life." And when he was upon the spot, some witnesses swear, he did not act that peaceable inoffensive part. They swear, they thought him in liquor, that he run about clapping several people on the shoulders saying, "Don't run away," "They dare not fire." Langford goes on, "I saw twenty or five-and-twenty boys about the soldiers and I spoke to him and bid him not be afraid." How came Langford to tell the guard not to be afraid. Does not this circumstance prove that the guard thought there was danger?

Langford goes on, "I saw about twenty or five-and-twenty boys that is young shavers." We have been entertained with a great variety of phrases to avoid calling this sort of people a mob. Some call them shavers, some call them geniuses. The plain English is, gentlemen, most probably a motley rabble of saucy boys, Negroes and mulattoes, Irish teagues and outlandish jack-tars. And why we should scruple to call such a set of people a mob, I can't conceive, unless the name is too respectable for them. The sun is not about to stand still or go out, nor the rivers to dry up, because there was a mob in Boston on the fifth of March that attacked a party of soldiers. Such things are not new in the world, nor in the British dominions, though they are, comparatively, rarities and novelties in this town. Carr, a native of Ireland, had often been concerned in such attacks, and indeed, from the nature of things, soldiers quartered in a populous town will always occasion two mobs, where they prevent one. They are wretched conservators of the peace!

Langford "heard the rattling against the guns, but saw nothing thrown." This rattling must have been very remarkable, as so many witnesses heard it, who were not in a situation to see what caused it. These things which hit the guns made a noise, but when so many things were thrown and so many hit their guns, to suppose that none struck the soldiers is incredible. Langford goes on, "Gray struck me on the shoulder and asked me what is to pay? I answered, I don't know but I believe something will come of it, by and by." Whence could this apprehension of mischief arise if Langford did not think the assault, the squabble, the affray, was such as would provoke the soldiers to fire? "A bayonet went through my greatcoat and jacket," yet the soldier did not step out of his place. This looks as if Langford was nearer to the party than became a watchman. Forty or fifty people round the soldiers, and more coming from Quaker Lane, as well as the other lanes. The soldiers heard all the bells ringing and saw people coming from every point of the compass to the assistance of those who were insulting, assaulting, beating, and abusing of them. What had they to expect but destruction if they had not thus early taken measures to defend themselves?

Witness Brewer saw Killroy and said the people had better go home. It was an excellent advice, happy for some of them had they followed it, but it seems all advice was lost on these persons, they would harken to none that was given them. They were bent on making this assault, and on their own destruction.

The next witness that knows anything was James Bailey. He is surely no friend to the soldiers, for he was engaged against them at the ropewalks; he says he saw twenty or thirty men around the guard, pelting him with cakes of ice, as big as one's fist; certainly cakes of ice of this size may kill a man, if they happen to hit some part of the head. So that, here was an attack on the guard, the consequence of which he had reason to dread, and it was prudent for him to call for the main guard. He retreated as far as he could, he attempted to get into the Custom House, but could not. Then he called to the guard, and he had a good right to call for their assistance. He did not know what was the matter, but he said, "He was afraid there would be mischief by and by"; and well he might, with so many shavers and geniuses round him capable of throwing such dangerous things.

Bailey swears that Montgomery fired the first gun. This witness certainly is not prejudiced in favor of the soldiers; he swears he saw a man come up to Montgomery with a club and knock him down before Montgomery fired, and that Montgomery not only fell himself, but his gun flew out of his hand, and as soon as he rose, he took it up and fired. If he was knocked down on his station, had he not reason to think his life in danger, or did it not raise his passions and put him off his guard, so that it cannot be more than manslaughter?

When the multitude was shouting and huzzahing, and threatening life, the bells all ringing, the mob whistle screaming and rending like an Indian yell, the people from all quarters throwing every species of rubbish they could pick up in the street, and some who were quite on the other side of the street throwing clubs at the whole party. Montgomery, in particular, was smote with a club and knocked down, and as soon as he could rise and take up his firelock, another club from afar struck his breast or shoulder, what could he do? Do you expect he should behave like a Stoic philosopher lost in apathy? Patient as Epictetus while his master was breaking his legs with a cudgel? It is impossible you should find him guilty of murder. You must suppose him divested of all human passions if you don't think him at the least provoked, thrown off his guard, and into the *furor brevis,* by such treatment as this.

Bailey "saw the mulatto seven or eight minutes before the firing, at the head of twenty or thirty sailors in Cornhill, and he had a large cordwood stick." So that this Attucks, by this testimony of Bailey compared with that of Andrew, and some others, appears to have undertaken to be the hero of the night; and to lead this army with banners, to form them in the first place in Dock Square and march them up to King Street, with their clubs; they passed through the main street up to the main guard, in order to make the attack. If this was not an unlawful assembly, there never was one in the world. Attucks with his myrmidons comes round Jackson's Corner, and down to the party by the sentry box. When the soldiers pushed the people off, this man with his party cried, "Do not be afraid of them, they dare not fire, kill them! Kill them! Knock them over!" And he tried to knock their brains out. It is plain the soldiers did not leave their station, but cried to the people, "Stand off." Now to have this reinforcement coming down under the command of a stout mulatto fellow, whose very looks was enough to terrify any person, what had not the soldiers then to fear? He had hardiness enough to fall in upon them, and with one hand took hold of a bayonet, and with the other knocked the man down. This was the behavior of Attucks, whose mad behavior, in all probability, the dreadful carnage of that night is chiefly to be ascribed. And it is in this manner, this town has been often treated; a Carr from Ireland, and an Attucks from Framingham, happening to be here, shall sally out upon their thoughtless enterprises, at the head of such a rabble of Negroes as they can collect together, and then there are not wanting, persons to ascribe all their doings to the good people of the town.

I will enlarge no more on the evidence, but submit it to you. Facts are stubborn things; and whatever may be our wishes, our inclinations, or the dictates of our passions, they cannot alter the state of facts and evidence. Nor is the law less stable than the fact; if an assault was made to endanger their lives, the law is clear, they had a right to kill in their own defense. If it was not so severe as to endanger their lives, yet if they were assaulted at all, struck and abused by blows of any sort, by snowballs, oyster shells, cinders, clubs, or sticks of any kind, this was a provocation, for which the law reduces the offense of killing, down to manslaughter.

The law, in all vicissitudes of government, fluctuations of the passions, or flights of enthusiasm, will preserve a steady, undeviating course. It will not bend to the uncertain wishes, imaginations, and wanton tempers of men. To use the words of a great and worthy man, a patriot, and an hero, and enlightened friend of mankind, and a martyr to liberty; I mean Algernon Sidney, who from his earliest infancy sought a tranquil retirement under the shadow of the tree of liberty, with his tongue, his pen, and his sword said, "The law, no passion can disturb. 'Tis void of desire and fear, lust and anger. 'Tis mens *sine affectu*; written reason; retaining some measure of the divine perfection. It does not enjoin that which pleases a weak, frail man, but without any regard to persons, commands that which is good, and punishes evil in all, whether rich, or poor, high or low. 'Tis deaf, inexorable, inflexible. On the one hand it is inexorable to the cries and lamentations of the prisoners; on the other it is deaf, deaf as an adder to the clamors of the populace."

Adams's closing argument was a deft blend of witness testimony and the law of self-defense, with vivid rhetoric castigating the mob that had menaced the soldiers against the Custom House wall:

> . . . What had eight soldiers to expect from such a set of people? Would it have been a prudent resolution in them to see if the sailors would knock their brains out? . . . Their clubs were as capable of killing as a sword, bayonet, or musket.

Adams directly challenged the notion that because one of the soldiers fired first, the rest of the troops were to shoulder the entire blame:

> . . . when that first gun was fired, the people fell in upon the soldiers and laid on with their weapons with more violence, and this served to increase the provocation.

Adams was careful to focus on the defense of Private Killroy, rebutting the theory that the prior confrontation between Killroy and Gray denied Killroy any claim of self-defense:

> . . . if there has been malice between the two, and at a distant time afterwards they met, and one of them assaults the other's life and he kills in consequence of it, the law presumes the killing was in self-defense.

Although Adams had delivered a skillful and eloquent defense of the "lobsterbacks," the prosecution had much to work with: there were many dead Bostonians, and the defendants were, after all, the hated British soldiers. It was now for prosecutor Robert Treat Paine to offer the rebuttal argument before the matter would go to the jury.

THE PROSECUTOR'S REBUTTAL

It now remains to close this cause on the part of the Crown, a cause which from the importance of it has been examined with such minuteness and protracted to such a length that I fear it has fatigued your attention as I am certain it has exhausted my spirits. However, gentlemen, it may serve to show you and all the world that the benignity of the English law, so much relied on by the counsel for the prisoners, is well-known and attended to among us and sufficiently applied in the cause at bar. Far be it for me to advance or even insinuate anything to the disparagement of that well-known principle of English law, in support of which the counsel last speaking for the prisoners has produced so many authorities. Nor should I think it needful to remark particularly on it but that it has been traced through so many authorities and urged with so much as though it were the foundation of their defense, or at least a principal argument relied on.

But, gentlemen, if you consider this sort of reasoning one moment, you will be sensible that it tends more to amuse than to enlighten and without due caution might captivate your attention and draw you entirely from justice. Justice, strict, is the ultimate object of our law. The last improvement of reason, which in the nature of it will not admit any proposition to be true of which it has not evidence, nor determine that to be certain of which there remains a doubt. If therefore in the examination of this cause the evidence is not sufficient to convince beyond reasonable doubt of the guilt of all or any of the prisoners, you will acquit them, but if the evidence be sufficient to convince you of their guilt beyond reasonable doubt, the justice of the law will require you to declare them guilty and the benignity of the law will be satisfied in the fairness and impartiality of their trial.

I am sensible, gentlemen, that I have got the difficult side of the question to conduct. I am arguing against the lives of eight of our fellow subjects, and the very thought of which is enough to excite your compassion and to influence my conduct. I am well aware of their advantage arising from the humane side of the question, have availed themselves of all the observations arising therefrom, and have pressed the defense by such appeals to the passions in favor of life as might be grating to your humanity should I attempt the like against life. Numberless are the observations that have been made in order to set the prisoners in a favorable point of light and bring them within the notice of your compassion. It has been represented "that the life of a soldier is thought to be less valuable among us than the life of a private subject," than which nothing can be more ill-founded. Whatever wrath and bitterness may have been expressed by some on account of the unhappy transaction now under examination, it was no more than would have been said had the persons who did it not been soldiers. Nay, the very appearance of this trial, the conduct of the witnesses and spectators and all concerned in it, must satisfy anyone that a soldier's life is by no means undervalued, but that they have as fair opportunities of defense as any other subjects.

I shall endeavor to address myself to your cool and candid reason and in the briefest manner I am able consider the evidence that has been offered in their defense, the arguments and law that have been applied to it, and then observing on the evidence against the prisoners and the law operating thereon, I shall rest the matter with you.

In the first place, gentlemen, you perceive that a very considerable part of the evidence produced by the prisoners is designed to prove to you that on the evening of the fifth of March the town was in a general commotion. That vast numbers of people were seen coming from all parts of the town armed with clubs and sticks of various sizes and some with guns, and that they assembled at and near King Street. That fire was cried and the bells rung in order to increase the collection, and from all this you may be induced to believe that there was a general design in a great number of the inhabitants to attack the soldiers. That it was the inhabitants who began the disorders that evening and that all the misfortunes of it was the effect of their disorderly conduct. But, gentlemen, if we recollect the evidence, we shall find that previous to all this collection, a number of soldiers had come out of their barracks armed with clubs, bayonets, cutlasses, tongs, and instruments of diverse kinds, and in the most disorderly and outrageous manner were ravaging the streets, assaulting everyone they met and even turning out of their way to assault and endanger the lives of some of the most peaceable inhabitants who were standing at their own doors and who did nor said anything to them.

The inhabitants had for a long while been fully sensible of the ill disposition and abusive behavior of many of the soldiers towards them, and the most peaceable among us had found it necessary to arm themselves with heavy walking sticks or weapons of defense when they went abroad. This occasioned that appearance of sticks in almost everyone's hand which has been testified and which in fact was little more than might have been seen on any other night.

In order to draw this affair to one point of view you will consider the account given you of the affray at the ropewalks at four or five different times some few days before of which three of the prisoners were present. It is clear that affray began first by the abuse of the soldiers and that previous to the unseemly answer given by one of the workmen. From this testimony of several of those present we have such an account of the riotous, barbarous, ungoverned, and ungovernable behavior of those soldiers as must necessarily fill the minds of the inhabitants with very alarming prospects, which when added to the behavior of the soldiers on the unhappy evening must naturally give rise to all that appearance.

There can be no doubt but that the collection of people that were seen that night was occasioned by many different causes. It evidently appears it was a bright moonlight evening the pleasantness of which increased by a new-fallen snow. Many persons to be walking the streets, and some of them hearing of the outrages of the soldiers, stopped to see and inquire of the matter, and some of them might join with those who were abused and make preparation to defend themselves. Such were those who being abused by the soldiers at Murray's Barracks ran down to Dock Square and began to pull the legs out of the butchers' stalls. Great numbers were brought by the ringing of the bells and cry of fire. Upon this, numbers came out of their houses from all parts with buckets and bags as is usual in case of fire, and many witnesses testify of a number of fire engines that were drawn out on the occasion of these. Great numbers went away. Some few tarried to see the end of those disorders of which they had had such repeated accounts.

But how does all this prove the grand point that there was a combination among the inhabitants to attack the soldiery? Does the threatening, rude, and indecent speeches of which so much pains has been taken to give you evidence prove anything like this? Is it to be wondered at that among a number of people collected on such an occasion there should be some who should rashly and without design express themselves in such a manner, and must the disposition and intention of the whole be collected from such expressions heard only by a few?

Was it lawful for the inhabitants of Boston to walk the streets that evening and with sticks? Was it lawful for them to run on the cry of fire? Was it lawful for them to stop to inquire into any disturbance that had happened, and while they were thus walking, running, or inquiring, must they be answerable for the rude speech of every person that happens to be near them, when it does not appear they assented to them or joined in putting them in execution? How many sailors and foreigners of the lower class may we well suppose there is in so populous a seaport who are fond of mingling with such commotions and pushing on a disorder of which they feel not the consequence? In all this I go upon the supposition that the witnesses who have testified of these threatening speeches are not mistaken or omitted some circumstance that might alter the force of them. To me it seems clear that if those speeches were made in the manner that has been testified, however rude and indiscreet, yet they are rather to be resolved into that frenzy of undisciplined resentment and those frantic transports of passion which naturally take place among a free people oppressed and galled with the ravaging of an ungoverned soldiery, than to be construed as evidence of an insurrection or a design to put in execution the supposed threats; and really when we trace the evidence to the end of the affair, we don't find an attempt to put them in execution.

What attack was made or pretended to be made on the main guard? Of the two hundred collected in Dock Square, who huzzahed for the main guard and ran several ways to King Street together with the large company from Murray's Barracks, some of whom ran toward the Town House as testified by others, we find but a very few that ever got into King Street; for by the best account we don't find above seventy or eighty, and some say about a hundred and as many boys as men, and of this it is clear from the current of the evidence that many came from elsewhere and but a small proportion had sticks.

Let us now inquire whether those few of them who did arrive in King Street or anybody else made an attack on the soldiery there. For this, gentlemen, is the purpose of all this evidence, the prisoners would have you believe that a number of men armed with clubs rushed down into King Street and first assaulted the guard there and then surrounded and assaulted the soldiers when they came to relieve and support him and endangered their lives in such a manner as they were obliged to fire on them for their own preservation, or else to what purpose has so much time been spent in producing this evidence? It was designed undoubtedly to give such a coloring to the appearance and behavior of the people in King Street as may render them a riotous and unlawful assembly and the proper objects of fear and resentment to the party.

Let us now draw the matter closer home and see how it will turn out. It appears from the evidence of many that King Street at nine o'clock was clear of people and free from disturbance, until Private White took upon him to strike a boy for speaking saucily of a captain.

The complaints of the boy engaged the attention of the people here-abouts as the abuses offered elsewhere had engaged others. Many are the witnesses who give some account of the supposed attacks on White, yet it was only a few boys that threw snowballs at him but none hit him, and some of the most intelligible persons agree in this. Some say that White called for the main guard. Others as likely to have heard nothing of it, and several of the witnesses tell you that the affair seemed subsiding. Some of the witnesses tell you there was not above twelve people by the guard when the soldiers came down, but the people who were collected by the ringing of the bells on the supposition of fire and who were standing in knots as some of the witnesses gathered round when the soldiers came.

The evidence must satisfy you that the people who composed this collection were of various kinds and various were their designs of coming. Some of them were people of fair characters and peaceable dispositions and who mingled with the rest to use their endeavors to prevent any mischiefs. These witnesses tell you they saw nothing of the violent abuses offered to the soldiers nor heard the threats and loud hallooings testified of by others. Some of this collection were boys and Negroes drawn there by the curiosity peculiar to their disposition, and without doubt might throw some snowballs, and it's quite natural to believe from the evidence and the nature of the thing that there were some there armed with sticks and clubs determined if the soldiers abused as they had done the inhabitants that evening to try the weight of them. They had not the least design or idea of attacking a party on duty. And many other peaceable people gathered there merely to see what was going on.

Can any person living from the history of this affair as it turns up in evidence suppose these persons were such dangerous rioters as to bring them within those rules of law which have been read to you that it is lawful to kill them? Shall the innocent and peaceable who by mere casualty are mixed with some of the ruder sort be liable to be shot down by a party of soldiers merely because they please to call them dangerous rioters? Are the actions of the whole and not a few that constitutes any riot and the agreement of the whole body that makes them parties?

No one will pretend to deny the numerous authority produced in the case by the defense. The grand question is whether they apply to the evidence, and in order to do this let us recapitulate the argument. It is proved to you, gentlemen, that all the prisoners at the bar were present in King Street at the firing. It appears by the current of the testimony that seven guns were fired, and it appears pretty certain that Wemms, the corporal, was the one who did not fire. It is certain that five men were killed by the firing, of which Montgomery killed Attucks and Killroy killed Gray.

But which of the other five prisoners killed the other three of the deceased appears very uncertain. But this operates nothing in their favor if it appears to you that they were an unlawful assembly, that every individual of an unlawful assembly is answerable for the doings of the rest. They are all considered as principals, and all that are present aiding, assisting, and abetting to the doing an unlawful act as is charged in the several indictments against the prisoners are also considered as principals. The defense counsel, aware of this, has endeavored to make it appear they were a lawful assembly, that the sentry was duly stationed at the Custom House, and that the party had a right and actually did come to support him and so were a lawful assembly. But it must be remembered that no man or body of men have a right to do a lawful action in an unlawful manner; if they do, they become an unlawful assembly. You recollect the evidence of the forcible manner of their going down, pushing all those who stood in their way, and of their behavior at their first arrival pushing their bayonets at several people standing peacefully there. Even though they were lawfully assembled when they got there, the moment they turned their arms on the people without just cause, they became an unlawful assembly and all are answerable for the doings of anyone. The king's troops have undoubtedly a right to march through the streets and as such are a lawful assembly. But if in such marching without just cause they fire on the inhabitants and but one man is killed, they surely are all answerable though it can't be proved who did the execution. What better is this case. If there was a just cause for firing, they will be acquitted on that plea and there will be no occasion to determine the legality of their assembling. If there was no just cause of firing, how will you excuse them all of the guilt though it is not proved who were the actual perpetrators? It appears to me you must be satisfied they were possessed of that wicked, depraved, malignant spirit which constitutes malice, that from the whole evidence taken together no just cause appears for such outrageous conduct, and therefore that they must be considered as aiding and assisting each other in this unlawful act, which the lawfulness of their assembling will not excuse. Will not the reason of the law impute guilt to all of them though at first lawfully assembled seeing they joined in doing an unlawful action?

It has been shown you, gentlemen, that all killing at the first blush is murder in the eye of the law, and that the prisoner must make out the facts which he relies on for his justification, excuse, or alleviation unless they appear from the witness who testify of the killing.

Does there appear sufficient evidence to justify or excuse the killing in order for which it must appear to be done to prevent the commission of a known felony? It seems Montgomery was not knocked down if at all until he pushed with his bayonet. Had the people intended any more than to resent the insolence of the party who were pushing and wounding them, they certainly would have executed their design on the discharge of the guns. But nothing of that kind appears. The plea of self-defense which is made for them must inevitably fail unless you can be satisfied there was no other possible way of saving their lives but by killing. No one can believe this to be the case, and if so, it was an unlawful act to kill, and as they were all combined in the firing, they are all answerable.

Neither, gentlemen, doth it seem by taking the evidence all together it will alleviate their crime to manslaughter, nor shall throwing a snowball from a distance alleviate the crime of firing a ball amidst a number of people. Is it not manifest that in that case the very assailant was killed, but here it appears that none of the persons killed were assailants. Attucks was fifteen feet off and leaning on his stick, Gray was twelve feet off with his hand in his bosom, and the other three had just turned into the street and scarcely knew of the affair before they were shot down. It is to human frailty and that only and not to such brutal rage and diabolical malignity as must have impelled the prisoners to fire as they did.

Indeed if you believe that Montgomery was knocked down in the manner asserted, his crime can amount to no higher than manslaughter; but what evidence is there that any of the rest received a provocation before firing as will alleviate their crime? The left wing of the party was uncovered by the people, the crowd was chiefly at the right. Andrew indeed supposes Killroy was struck, but when we consider he looked about and saw Attucks fall, he must have confounded this fact as in my opinion he has many others. The witness who testifies of Killroy's killing Gray puts it beyond dispute that he shot him deliberately and after caution not to fire and the witness must have seen the blow if he had received any. When you consider the evidence against Killroy, his previous threatening, and that express evidence of killing Gray and the manner of it, I think you must unavoidably find him guilty of murder. What you think of the rest though the evidence is undoubtedly the fullest against him, yet it is full enough against the rest.

Paine's argument deftly responded to the challenges and questions raised by Adams in the defense summation. The prosecutor moved to dispel the notion—so thoroughly stated by Adams—that the crowd gathered outside the Custom House had been a riotous mob, hell-bent on killing British soldiers. Paine instead insisted that the actions of the soldiers, as they'd blustered their way through town, had been the true cause of the escalating tensions. Having reframed the soldiers as the bad actors, Paine turned to the culpability of all the troopers, even though the evidence could only establish that Killroy had shot and killed Gray and that Montgomery had most likely fired the shot that killed Attucks. The prosecutor reduced the law of accessories and principles to an understandable concept, maintaining that "as they were all combined in the firing, they are all answerable."

Paine was no mere perfunctory foil for John Adams; rather he was a formidable adversary, armed with comparable force and skill. But these summations—and the trial itself—were not about glorifying the talents of either advocate, but rather teasing out a just result from chaotic and tragic events, and that task was now the province of twelve out-of-town jurors.

The Verdict

With the attorneys' work done, the circuit judges once again expressed their views that Adams and the defense had the argument. However, those opinions were merely advisory; it was for the jurors alone to render a verdict. They began their deliberations around one-thirty in the afternoon and were back with their decision by four o'clock that same day. The jury found Killroy and Montgomery guilty—not of murder, but of manslaughter—and acquitted the others. Adams's closing argument, that it would be better for eight guilty men to walk free than have one innocent man convicted, proved the linchpin of his case. The jurors later admitted that, although they knew that at least five soldiers had fired and wounded civilians, there was no evidence linking any of the acquitted soldiers with any specific victim's wounds. The jury had, it seems, taken the defense's advice and erred on the side of caution so that innocent lives would not be spent paying for these actions.

Sam Adams, livid after the verdicts, vented his anger on the pages of the *Boston Gazette,* writing a series of inflammatory columns under the pseudonym Vindex, lamenting the injustice done to the people of

Boston. His articles misstated—in some cases made up—witness testimony to favor the prosecution's case. One anonymous member of the Sons of Liberty fastened a letter to the door of the courthouse, urging the people of Boston to "rise up at the great call of nature and free the world from such domestic tyrants." The letter was immediately removed and a reward—unclaimed—offered for information about the man who had placed it there. But the nine months that had elapsed since the "Boston Massacre" had proved an effective cooling-off period, and civil unrest failed to materialize.

The lesser verdicts of manslaughter—rather than murder—were initially of small consolation to Killroy and Montgomery; both crimes carried the potential for a death sentence. However, there was a significant distinction: a person convicted of murder was routinely executed, whereas a manslaughter conviction typically resulted in some lesser punishment. In a bit of strategic skulduggery, John Adams and Josiah Quincy had secretly fired off a missive to London well before either trial, seeking pardons for any of the soldiers who might be convicted. Their efforts were, however, thwarted by the unpredictable North Atlantic transit, and the order of immunity they sought did not reach Boston in time for the soldiers' sentencing.

And so, without the insulation a pardon would provide, Adams and Quincy faced the court at the sentencing hearing. Adams begged the court to spare the lives of the two soldiers, invoking a medieval remnant, the "prayer for the benefit of the clergy." To invoke this right, the soldiers had to repeat Psalm 51, verse 1: "Have mercy upon me, O God, according to thy loving-kindness: according unto the multitude of thy tender mercies blot out my transgressions." The soldiers did as Adams requested, and the sentencing judges had mercy. The soldiers were branded on their right thumbs with an M for "manslaughter." Before sailing for England, Private Montgomery confessed that it was he, not Captain Preston, who had shouted the order to fire.

Surprisingly, the acquittal of six soldiers and manslaughter convictions for the other two, followed by lenient sentences for the killers, generated little outrage in Boston. The local newspapers provided scant coverage throughout this second trial, mirroring a decline in public attention. Following the trials, all British soldiers were removed from within the limits of Boston proper. However, the damage had been done, and the incident that would forever be known as the Boston Massacre fueled an increasing tide of resentment toward England. Many of those who would sign the Declaration of Independence just six years later referred to March 5, 1770, as the day that would signal the severance of the ties between Britain and America. John Adams himself later wrote of the event, "On that night the formation of American Independence was laid." The "massacre" was the beginning of the end of the British Empire in the Americas.

Although the urge for vengeance had cooled among most Bostonians, tempers still ran hot among the rebels. For his part in the trials, John Adams paid a heavy price, berated in the papers and harassed by the locals; some friends said he lost half of his business. It would be a long time before the people of Boston would forgive him. But he did have his defenders, even if they weren't exactly outspoken. Sam Adams, normally the most vocal of the Sons of Liberty, never condemned his cousin's representation of the hated troops. John Adams's once high standing among the rebels would eventually be regained, and he would go on to become the first vice president of the new republic and then serve as the second president of the United States of America.

Many years later, John Adams offered perhaps the ultimate judgment on the significance of the trial and verdict for the young republic:

> The part I took in defense of Cptn. Preston and the soldiers, procured me anxiety, and obloquy enough. It was, however, one of the most gallant, generous, manly and disinterested actions of my whole life, and one of the best pieces of service I ever rendered my country. Judgment of death against those soldiers would have been as foul a stain upon this country as the executions of the Quakers or witches, anciently. As the evidence was, the verdict of the Jury was exactly right.

Motivated by his understanding of the importance of zealous advocacy to the continuing survival of a just legal system, John Adams made the kind of efforts on behalf of the British troops that should be the standard to which all lawyers aspire, and to which all accused should be entitled.

CHAPTER FIVE

"You Have the Right to Remain Silent"

The rapist and the chief justice redefine the use of confessions and police interrogations

It is not sufficient to do justice by obtaining a proper result by irregular or improper means.

— Lord Sankey, Chancellor of England

Suspect confesses—case closed. Confessions mark the acknowledgment of an evil done—a purging of sorts—and perhaps the first act of remorse or even repentance. Confessions are frequently the best evidence of a crime, in that the actual perpetrator is disclosing his firsthand account of the act, often with details unobtainable through any other means. A suspect's confession is powerful evidence; more often than not, it is the deciding factor in his eventual conviction.

But what if the confession was physically coerced or psychologically induced? Is such a confession trustworthy? What if it was a lie? Even then, it has great significance, and given the importance of confessions at trial, should we be concerned that its admission into evidence might turn the end of justice on its head? A confession induced with a nightstick is suspect. But what about those "confessions" that are the product of more subtle "persuasion" techniques? Those confessions born of thirty-six-hour interrogations? Of false friends? Or lies? Are they trustworthy? Should they be used against the suspect at trial?

Since the eighteenth century, the criminal justice systems in both England and America have struggled with the trustworthiness—and ultimately the admissibility—of words from the mouth of the accused. The problem is not always one of police brutality; anything said in a police-controlled environment arguably has aspects of duress and coercion. But no matter what method is used, words uttered under duress may lack the trustworthiness required for trial.

Throughout American history, jurists and scholars alike have wrestled with the acceptability of confessions at trial. In a series of decisions prior to the Warren term, the U.S. Supreme Court was unable to find a constitutional framework to formulate a workable standard for determining when the words of the accused could be used against him.

No one foresaw that the long-awaited answer would be found in the confession of a twenty-three-year-old son of a Mexican immigrant, a man suspected of kidnapping and raping an eighteen-year-old girl.

A Sad and Sordid Life

To many visitors, the seclusion and sun made Arizona a desert paradise of freedom and leisure. But to some, Arizona's most appealing characteristic was that it was part of America, a nation of prosperity, of promise. Like so many immigrants before him, Manuel A. Miranda sought the American dream. Born in Sonora, Mexico, he emigrated to Arizona, marrying and fathering four sons, supporting his family as a housepainter. In 1940, Manuel and his wife had their fifth child, Ernesto Arturo Miranda.

The young Miranda's early years set the stage for what would become a troubled and turbulent life. His mother died when he was six; his father remarried less than a year later. Ernesto Miranda never developed a bond with his older brothers; he fought constantly with his stepmother and eventually became estranged from his father.

School was no more promising. Miranda was far from an ideal student at the Queen of Peace Grammar School; he rarely attended class, and when he did, he was a disciplinary problem. After he completed eighth grade, Ernesto Miranda's formal education ended. However, his "education" was far from over. Rapidly becoming a metropolitan area, Mesa, Arizona, offered free lessons in the arts of the streets. The pristine desert town began to take on the characteristics of an urban metropolis. With burglaries, rapes, and robberies on the rise, a now-teenage Miranda found himself surrounded by crooks and criminal enterprises. Unfortunately, Miranda was no better at crime than he had been at reading and arithmetic. In 1954, Miranda was arrested for his first felony: burglary. Receiving a slap on the wrist, he was sentenced to probation.

Less than a year later, he returned to the courthouse to face another burglary charge, landing him in the Arizona State Industrial School for Boys. At fifteen, Miranda was confused, angry, and far from reformed. Less than a month after his release, he committed his first sexual offense: attempted rape and assault.

Miranda was returned to the Industrial School for two more years. Following his release, the seventeen-year-old attempted a fresh start in Los Angeles, far away from Mesa's streets and temptations. Different place; same result. He was arrested for lack of supervision, curfew violations, and Peeping Tom activities. Miranda slipped through the cracks of an overtaxed system, spending only three days in the Los Angeles County Detention Home. He got work in a grocery store but within days was arrested for armed robbery. Subsequently convicted, he served forty-five days in the county detention home, before being packed off back to Arizona.

At eighteen, Ernesto Miranda could have been a poster boy for the recidivist criminal, with four convictions and imprisonment in three different facilities. Uneducated, broke, and alone, he decided that the U.S. Army might be a way out. However, as with his other endeavors, this was also short-lived and unsuccessful. During his year-and-a-half military career, Miranda spent more than a third of it at hard labor for going AWOL and being caught in another Peeping Tom act.

With a dishonorable discharge, Miranda had neither a plan nor a purpose. He aimlessly charted a course for a cross-country trip, traveling to Nashville and finally to Pecos, Texas, where he was arrested for vagrancy, spending two weeks in jail.

Following his release, he tried his hand at stealing cars. His ambition far exceeding his talent, Miranda was arrested while driving a car that had been stolen from Alabama. Arrested previously as a juvenile, Miranda was now an adult; consequently, he was sentenced to federal prison for a year. His time in the distant Ohio penitentiary further detached him from his already estranged family in Arizona. Citing his family ties, he applied for a transfer to the federal prison in Lompoc, California—closer to Arizona; the request was granted and Miranda spent the balance of his sentence in the California pen.

Miranda remained in California after his release and made another attempt at assimilating into civil society. This time things seemed to be working out. Now twenty-one, he met Twila Hoffman, a woman eight years his senior, who had recently separated from her husband, with whom she had both an eleven-year-old son and a ten-year-old daughter. Two months later, Miranda moved in with her and her children. The next year, the couple gave birth to their own child, a daughter. Miranda moved his new family back to Mesa and they found jobs; Twila worked at a nursery school and he was hired as a dockworker for a produce facility.

Miranda's employment provided a stark—and positive—contrast from his previous jobs. Until this time, he had never held a job for more than two weeks. Now he enjoyed a good relationship with his supervisor, who referred to him as "one of the best workers [he had] ever had."

The growth in both his personal and professional lives gave Miranda a new start. He had a family, a job. He was out of trouble. It seemed that he might become a responsible and law-abiding man. But the semblance of normality would soon be shattered.

Jane Doe

She was a fat girl, a slow girl, a girl whose consciousness of her unfortunate characteristics created an introverted personality. Her stepbrother once said that during the eleven years he knew her, he doubted if the two had exchanged a total of thirty words.

By the time she was eighteen, she lived in Phoenix with her mother, sister, and brother-in-law and worked at a local movie house.

On March 2, 1963, the Saturday-night rush at the concession stand finally began to dwindle. As the concluding frames of the D-day drama *The Longest Day* faded to black, hundreds of audience members walked through the exit doors and into the cool March evening. The picture's extended running time had forced her to remain on the premises far longer than she was used to. With her concession stand now closed, she and a coworker, a young man who took the same bus route, left at 11 p.m. They walked two blocks to the bus stop and boarded the northbound bus around 11:45, separating in northeastern Phoenix, when she had to switch routes. At 12:10, she reached her final stop in an area bordering the commercial district. Under the dark desert sky, she walked up Marlette Street, unaware that the next two hours would trigger a series of events that would profoundly reshape American criminal procedure.

The Unspeakable

She was nearly home when, suddenly, a car darted out of a driveway in front of her, the vehicle coming so close that she had to jump back to avoid being hit. The car stopped and a man jumped out and grabbed her. He forced his hand over her mouth and in a stern, low voice commanded, "Don't scream, and I won't hurt you."

She pleaded, "Let me go, please let me go." But her plea was stifled by the man's hand and went unheard and unanswered. The attacker dragged her to his car, tied her hands behind her back, and forced her to lie down on the backseat.

Her abductor sped along Marlette Street, veered onto Tenth, and then turned east onto Rose Lane. As the city lights became more distant, she watched the commercial buildings and houses give way to the darkness of the desert. The trip was punctuated by her desperate pleas for help, the man continuing to insist that if she remained quiet, he would not harm her.

After a twenty-minute drive, the car came to a stop. The man swung the door open and looked at the bound, terrified, and helpless girl. He crawled into the backseat and untied her, then ordered her to strip. Later on, she would offer different accounts of the following sequence of events. In one instance, she stated that she removed her own jacket and panties, while the man took off her skirt, slip, and bra. In another, she said that the abductor removed all of her clothing and, in the struggle, tore the shoulder straps off her slip.

The man removed his jeans and underwear, the only dialogue between the two a simple exchange:

"You can't tell me you have never done this before," the abductor said.

"No, I haven't," she replied.

The police report detailed her description of events:

> The man forced himself upon her and made penetration and reached a climax. However, again in questioning the victim more extensively, she told officers conflicting stories regarding the number of times the suspect had made penetration and reached a climax. Finally, she said that the suspect had attempted to make penetration and at first was unsuccessful. He then sat back on the seat and in a few minutes he tried again and was successful.

And then it was over. The man put his clothes on and told her to do the same. He then asked her for money and she gave him the $4 that she had. He told her to once again lie down on the backseat and started back to the city.

The car was silent. Paralyzed by fear, she lay still in the backseat; then, from the front seat, the man said, "Whether you tell your mother what has happened or not is none of my business, but pray for me."

The car came to a halt near Twelfth Street and Rose Lane, an intersection approximately four blocks from her house. He let her out of the car and drove off.

The girl was disoriented and shaken, but before long her slow gait gave way to a dead run. Finally, she approached the front door of her house. Her sister remembered her "pound[ing] on the door, her hair was all over like she had been in a fight, and her dress was brand-new, a new suit, and it was a mess, and she was crying and carrying on, and I asked her what was the matter, and she would not tell me."

She was in hysterics, her speech incoherent. Fifteen minutes later, she was able to tell her sister that a man had forced her into his car and taken her out to the desert. And finally, after a little prodding, Jane confessed to her sister that the man had touched her. Her sister called the police.

The Investigation

In the early hours of March 3, 1963, a policeman was dispatched to a home on Citrus Way to investigate the possible kidnapping and rape of an eighteen-year-old girl. Jane Doe relayed a condensed version of the events before the officer took her to Good Samaritan Hospital to be examined.

The Phoenix Detective Bureau was notified, and two detectives conducted a more thorough interview. However, almost immediately several problems concerning Jane Doe's account of events became evident. She was asked whether she had ever had sex prior to the alleged rape. She insisted that she had not. However, an exam at the hospital concluded that she had. In a later interview with Jane's sister, the sibling maintained Jane's assertion: she had been inexperienced, no matter what a medical test concluded; if the doctors said otherwise, they were obviously mistaken.

Jane also insisted that she fought her attacker. But the medical examination revealed neither abrasions nor bruises.

There were also problems with the ID of the rapist. At the hospital, Jane described her attacker as a "Mexican male, twenty-seven or twenty-eight years old, five feet eleven inches, 175 pounds, slender build, medium complexion with black, short-cut, curly hair, wearing Levi's, a white T-shirt, and dark-rim glasses." She added that he had a sparse mustache and the beginnings of a beard. When asked again later for a description, she was suddenly unsure about his nationality. He had no accent, she explained, and might have been Italian "or similar foreign extraction" or Mexican.

As for the rapist's car, Jane described a clean, old-model automobile, light green with good paint. Jane thought it might have been a Ford or a Chevrolet. She went on to describe a dated interior, with brown tattered upholstery that smelled distinctively of paint or turpentine.

Two days later, the detectives returned to her house on Citrus Way for yet another interview. They were skeptical that a rape had, in fact, occurred; maybe she was making it up for attention. Maybe she'd decided to file a report after a consensual sexual experience.

Neither scenario was uncommon in the detectives' experience, especially with an alleged victim in her age group. But whatever the reason, the various problems with her story pointed more toward a fabricated teenage tale than a rape. Perhaps, one of the detectives suggested, Jane had met someone with whom she became involved and for personal reasons decided to file a police report. She nodded her head in agreement and mumbled a quiet "Yes." But when Jane was once again asked to recount the events of March 3, she described a rape. This time, however, she said that she may have embellished the struggle she had with her attacker.

Two days later, Jane was brought to the police station. She was asked to tell her story again, only now while monitored by a polygraph machine. The results were inconclusive. The exam's administrator suspected that Jane had taken medication prior to the assessment. Further, the test gave some indication that she had lied while answering some of the questions.

The investigation was at a standstill. Any chance Jane Doe had of seeking justice against her abductor diminished by the day. Her vague and inconsistent accounts gave little concrete information to justify continuing the investigation. The sum of a week's worth of intense police work had produced only weary detectives ready to write the case off as an insecure girl seeking attention.

Then, seemingly out of the blue, the police and Jane Doe caught a break.

Since the incident, Jane—not surprisingly—had developed an insurmountable fear of walking home alone. In response, her brother-in-law began meeting her after work at her final bus stop. A week after the alleged abduction, as Jane's brother-in-law headed to meet her at the usual destination, he noticed an old Packard creeping along Marlette. The car seemed to be circling. As the brother-in-law watched the car slowly cruise along Seventh and then again on Marlette, he took note of the license plate number: DFL-312.

He contacted the police, and the license plate number—when run though the automobile registration database—revealed that the four-door 1953 Packard belonged to Twila N. Hoffman, of 210 North Labaron Street, Mesa, Arizona. When Detectives Carroll Cooley and Wilfred Young arrived at the address, they found a vacant house. They questioned neighbors and learned that Twila Hoffman had moved out only two days earlier. The residents further reported that Hoffman lived with her three children and her twenty-three-year-old boyfriend, a tall, slender Mexican man by the name of Ernesto Miranda.

The rapidly developing investigation revealed a change of address filed with the local post office. Hoffman and Miranda had moved to 2525

West Maricopa, Phoenix. As the officers approached the West Maricopa residence, they spotted a 1953 Packard parked out front.

The Interrogation

After a twelve-hour graveyard shift, a fatigued Ernesto Miranda returned home at 8 a.m. and went to bed. An hour later the detectives arrived. Twila answered the door and called for her boyfriend.

The detectives asked Miranda to accompany them to the police station to discuss a case under investigation. At the station, Miranda was placed in a four-man lineup. He was the only one with eyeglasses and visible tattoos. When Jane Doe stepped into the viewing room, she noted that Miranda had similar features to those of her attacker but could not positively identify him as the man who had raped her.

Following the inconclusive lineup, the officers led the nervous twenty-three-year-old Miranda into a small interrogation room.

"How did I do?" Miranda inquired, referring to the lineup.

"You flunked," one of the detectives lied.

Then the questions began. There was no rough stuff. The entire interrogation took two hours.

The detectives said they never threatened Miranda or promised him leniency. Miranda told a different story.

> . . . I haven't had any sleep since the day before. I'm tired. I just got off work, and they have me there interrogating me. . . . They mention first one crime, and then another one, they are certain I am the person. . . . They start badgering you one way or the other . . . "you better tell us . . . or we're going to throw the book at you" . . . that is what was told to me. They told me that they would throw the book at me. They would try to give me all the time they could. They thought there was even the possibility that there was something wrong with me. They would try to help me, get me medical care if I needed it. . . . Knowing what a penitentiary is like, a person has to be frightened, scared. And not knowing if he'll be able to get back up and go home.

No one except for the three men in that interrogation room knows for certain which version was true. Interrogation rooms in the 1960s were rarely equipped with tape recorders. Even so, that Miranda admitted to the rape and kidnapping was undisputed.

Following Miranda's brief oral confession, the detectives, in an attempt to solidify their case, brought Jane Doe into the room, hoping she would be able to identify his voice. However, immediately upon entry, one of the detectives surprised Miranda and asked if Jane was the girl he had raped. Miranda looked up at Jane Doe and said, "That's the girl."

Following this bizarre reverse lineup, Miranda went on to give a more detailed account of the rape and kidnapping of Jane Doe, closely corroborating Jane's story.

When asked to formalize his confession in a written statement, Miranda agreed and in a handwritten statement wrote:

> Seen a girl walking up street stopped a little ahead of her, got out of the car walked towards her grabbed her by the arm and asked to get in the car. Got in car without force tied hands & ankles. Drove away for a few miles. Stopped asked to take clothes off. Did not, asked me to take her back home. I started to take clothes off her without any force, and with cooperation. Asked her to lay down and she did, could not get penis into vagina got about [half] inch in. Told her to get clothes back on. Drove her home. I couldn't say I was sorry for what I had done. But asked her to say a prayer for me.

Across the top of the statement was a typewritten disclaimer stating that Miranda was confessing voluntarily, without threats or promises of immunity, and "with full knowledge of my legal rights, understanding any statement I make may be used against me." Miranda signed the disclaimer. Detective Cooley would later testify that the suspect "was not unknowledgeable about his rights. He was an ex-convict . . . and had been through this routine before." Given Miranda's impressive criminal résumé, the detectives did not fully explain to him his rights. At no time did the detectives inform Miranda that he had either the right to remain silent or the right to an attorney.

On March 13, 1963, at one thirty in the afternoon, Ernesto Miranda emerged from Interrogation Room Number 2 an admitted rapist and kidnapper. In fact, the interrogating officers' efforts had been so fruitful that Miranda had confessed to the attempted rape of another woman, the burglary of yet another woman's home, and a robbery in which he had made off with $8. So armed, the district attorney filed charges against Ernesto Arturo Miranda for the rape and kidnapping of Jane Doe. And with this action, the most-cited case in American legal history was born.

Interrogations Before Miranda

Miranda's interrogation was a marked departure from the method of police questioning popular during the first half of the twentieth century. In the years that followed World War II, the dropping of the atomic bomb, the birth of the suburbs, and the *Ed Sullivan Show,* the methodology of police interrogations had begun to soften, becoming less brutal.

But perhaps the most unexpected catalyst for the changing times was the U.S. Supreme Court. With the appointment of former California governor Earl Warren as chief justice, a sea change in criminal procedure was under way. And invariably, one aspect of that sea change would be the interrogation of criminal suspects.

To fully appreciate the breadth and scope of the Court's eventual decision in Miranda's case, it is important to step back a decade prior to Earl Warren's ascendancy to the Court and examine the prevailing practices used by law enforcement in attempting to obtain confessions from criminal suspects.

In 1942, law professor Fred Inbau, of Northwestern University, wrote a police manual that offered suggestions and recommended restrictions regarding station house interrogations and the use of lie detector tests. Aptly entitled *Lie Detection and Criminal Interrogation,* the guide soon became the unofficial standard in the field of police questioning. By the time the Inbau manual, as it is commonly known, reached its second edition in 1962, it had already played a major role in reshaping police interrogation practices.

The manual insisted that professionalized interrogation procedures would serve two essential functions: First, they would minimize interrogation abuses. Second, they would advance law enforcement's credibility by augmenting the interrogator's ability to obtain trustworthy and admissible confessions. With these twin goals in mind, officers were instructed to treat all suspects with respect and decency.

The centerpiece of the manual is a distinction between the specific tactics to be employed when dealing with suspects whose guilt is only possible, and with those whose guilt is reasonably certain. In the first scenario, interrogators are specifically directed to use deceptive questioning. In the latter, they are advised to appeal to the suspect's emotions. In appealing to emotion, interrogators were instructed to "sympathize with the suspect by saying anyone else under similar conditions or circumstances might have done the same thing," "to minimize the moral blameworthiness of the offense," or to "suggest a more morally acceptable motivation . . . for the offense." In dealing with nonemotional suspects whose guilt was reasonably certain, interrogators were encouraged to appeal to the suspect's rational side. To do this, the manual suggested themes that included "point[ing] out the futility of resistance to telling the truth" and playing multiple suspects against each other.

The manual prefaces these instructions with detailed techniques that detectives can use to assert psychological dominance over suspects. These directives include conducting the interrogation in absolute private; invading the suspect's personal space; directing him to remain seated if he tries to stand; and prohibiting him from smoking or fidgeting.

To protect the trustworthiness of confessions, the manual forbade the use of promising leniency in order to elicit a confession. This prohibition seems to somewhat contradict other sections that emphasize the need to tell the suspect that confessing will be in their best interest.

Given the manual's prominence—even today—the primary issue for policymakers has been in determining if any of these practices encourage police abuse. More important, for the U.S. Supreme Court, the principal question becomes, Do these practices comply with the requirements of the U.S. Constitution?

About sixty years before publication of the manual, the Supreme Court first considered the effect of police conduct during an interrogation on the validity of the resulting confession. Like the manual, the Court wrestled with the difficulty of balancing law enforcement needs with notions of fundamental fairness. After all, ruling a confession inadmissible may gut the prosecution's case. However, admitting a confession that is the product of threats, promises, or other means of coercion runs a serious risk of encouraging untrustworthy confessions and most likely unwarranted convictions.

The Court acknowledged that this conundrum was not of recent origin. In the sixteenth century, at the time of the infamous Star Chamber, the interrogator's sole charge was to obtain the confession at any cost, without regard to its trustworthiness. Those who initially refused to confess were beaten and tortured. This method of extracting confessions persisted for better than a century and a half, until the Star Chamber was abolished in 1641. However, not until the eighteenth century did English courts begin to exclude involuntary confessions. In doing so, the English adopted a "totality of the circumstances" test to determine whether a confession was voluntary. This test essentially undertook a hindsight analysis of the circumstances surrounding the interrogation. If the confession was found to be the product of coercion, it was deemed untrustworthy and therefore inadmissible.

The U.S. Supreme Court borrowed from the English precedent in adopting a form of this "voluntariness test." However, as opposed to the English court's focus on the causal connection between an officer's coercion and the confession's untrustworthiness, the U.S. Supreme Court placed the spotlight on the suspect's ability to exercise free will. Under this rationale, the Court held that confessions were inadmissible "when made in response to threats, promises, or inducements" that may have overcome the suspect's free will.

For instance, in *Brown v. Mississippi,* decided in 1936, a white deputy sheriff hung a black suspect from a tree, insisting that he confess to murder. The man refused. Frustrated, the officer whipped him. Still no confession. The irritated deputy then released Brown, only to rearrest him two days later. Brown was whipped again and finally gave a "confession." The Supreme Court held the confession was not the product of free will and was therefore inadmissible. This limited holding did not extend its reach to mere threats, promises, or other nonviolent methods of coercion, and even though the court did not single out racial animus as a factor, it most likely was a consideration. Nonetheless, the *Brown* decision was significant in that—for the first time—the actions of a state law enforcement official in obtaining a confession were limited by the federal Constitution.

In subsequent years, the Court began gradually extending the same protection to coerced confessions in nonviolent scenarios. In *Chambers v. Florida,* a case decided in 1940, the Court excluded a confession resulting from the five-day interrogation of uneducated "young colored tenant farmers" because the method employed was "calculated to break the strongest nerves and the stoutest resistance."

In 1940, the Court excluded a confession produced by a continuous thirty-six-hour interrogation. However, as opposed to the defendants in *Brown* and *Chambers,* the defendant in this case was white. This differing aspect placed the sole concern of the constitutional question on the interrogation itself—without any appeal to racial animus.

On into the 1950s, the Court further extended due-process protections to cases involving deceptive interrogation tactics. In *Spano v. New York,* an indicted suspect called a childhood friend—a police officer named Bruno—and indicated a desire to hand himself over to the authorities. However, after turning himself in, Spano sought the counsel of an attorney, who advised him not to confess. The defendant heeded the advice. Frustrated, the police officers had Bruno falsely tell the defendant that his initial phone call had gotten Bruno in a lot of trouble; further, that the defendant's failure to confess had placed Bruno's job in jeopardy. Returning to the "voluntariness test," the Court found the defendant's confession involuntary and therefore inadmissible. A particularly important factor in this case was the deceptive use of a childhood friend to evoke the sympathy and trust of the suspect.

Though the holdings in these cases condemned specific instances of unacceptable police conduct, the Court failed to establish practical guidelines for police officers to abide by—a framework consonant with the Constitution. This voluntariness test left a good deal of wiggle room for the lower courts to distinguish future cases. Without clear guidelines, even cases that closely resembled *Spano* could bypass the voluntariness test by the mere presence of other "factors." In short, this test provided only limited guidance to law enforcement.

Not only were there precedential problems, but also practical issues. Determining what happened inside interrogation rooms became a game of "cop said/crook said." Further, even assuming that police officers would testify truthfully at trial, appellate courts had little guidance to determine the coercive effect of certain tactics on interrogated suspects.

Law enforcement officials needed clearer, more understandable guidelines. Perhaps "due process" could not by its very subjective nature afford the degree of clarity essential in curbing abusive police interrogations. And indeed, in 1964, the Court, groping for solutions, turned from due process to the Sixth Amendment's guarantee of the right to counsel.

In *Massiah v. United States,* the Court held that the Sixth Amendment required exclusion of incriminating statements elicited from an indicted suspect in the absence of counsel. Essentially, once a suspect was indicted or formally charged, any confessions that resulted from police questioning without the suspect's attorney present could not be used in court.

And with the stroke of a pen, the focus had moved from the nebulous due-process voluntariness approach to a more readily applied test. The Court reasoned that if the suspect's lawyer was present, fewer abuses in the interrogation room would occur. And the Court got it right. Unfortunately, this right-to-counsel approach had limited application. By narrowing the rule to postindictment—or that phase when the suspect had formally been charged—the rule provided no guidance for the vast majority of all interrogations, those that would, in the ordinary course of affairs, occur prior to the bringing of formal charges.

How would the Court protect against coercive interrogation tactics at this stage? This was the question that the Warren Court would wrestle with for the two years following the *Massiah* decision.

The Court first addressed the issue by returning to the Sixth Amendment. In *Escobedo v. Illinois,* the justices looked to extend the right granted in *Massiah* to confessions made before indictment. The facts of *Escobedo* provided the perfect opportunity. Escobedo, a primary murder suspect being interrogated by the police, asked to speak with his attorney. Not only was his attorney in the station house at the time of the interrogation, but he had actually requested to see Escobedo. Nonetheless, the police continued to question Escobedo for three hours and got their confession—all the while denying Escobedo's attorney the chance to speak with his client. But this all took place before formal charges had been brought, and consequently, the right to counsel did not attach.

Obviously troubled by the circumstances presented in *Escobedo,* the Court wrote an opinion filled with emotional rhetoric. The following excerpt from the *Escobedo* ruling reveal the heart of an issue that had plagued prior courts for nearly a century.

> We have learned the lesson of history, ancient and modern, that a system of criminal law enforcement which comes to depend on the "confession" will, in the long run, be less reliable and more subject to abuses than a system which depends on extrinsic evidence independently secured through skillful investigation. We have also learned the companion lesson of history that no system of criminal justice can or should survive if it comes to depend for its continued effectiveness on the citizens' abdication through unawareness of their constitutional rights. No system worth preserving should have to fear that if an accused is permitted to consult with a lawyer, he will become aware of, and exercise these rights. If the exercise of constitutional rights will thwart the effectiveness of a system of law enforcement, then there is something very wrong with that system.

Though *Escobedo* demonstrated the urgency of fixing a system in contradiction with its founding principles, the scope of its holding did little to remedy the problem it so eloquently diagnosed. The Court did extend the Sixth Amendment right to counsel of *Massiah* to preindictment interrogations, but only when the criminal investigation had focused on a specific suspect. However, *Escobedo* failed to accomplish its primary goal of providing clear instruction to police officers as to when and how they could interrogate. The language of *Escobedo* was fraught with uncertainty. When has an investigation gone from a general inquiry to a focused investigation? *Escobedo* was plagued by the same nebulous tenor of the due-process voluntariness cases; it failed to provide clear and easily understandable guidelines. Though the Court had formally aired its concerns, it had still not devised a bright-line test that would protect suspects from the powers of police coercion in most preindictment scenarios.

This issue gained a new sense of urgency nearly a year after the *Escobedo* decision when influential law professor Yale Kasimar published "Equal Justice in the Gatehouses and Mansions of American Criminal Procedure." Kasimar showcased the problem with confessions through the clever use of a recognizable metaphor.

The courtroom is a splendid place where defense attorneys bellow and strut and prosecuting attorneys are hemmed in at many turns. But what happens before an accused reaches the safety and enjoys the comfort of this veritable mansion? Ah, there's the rub. Typically he must pass through a much less pretentious edifice, a police station with bare back rooms and locked doors. In this "gatehouse" of American criminal procedure the enemy of the state is a depersonalized "subject" to be "sized up" and subjected to "interrogation tactics" and techniques most appropriate for the occasion; he is "game" to be stalked and cornered. Here, ideals are checked at the door, "realities" faced and the prestige of law enforcement vindicated.

Kasimar's work highlighted a new philosophy that recognized the futility of constitutional protections at trial if those same safeguards were not also extended to the interrogation room. Kasimar argued that the Court had exhausted the power of the Sixth Amendment's right to counsel guarantees and that it was time for a different approach.

It had long been thought that the Fifth Amendment's protection against self-incrimination was limited to actual courtroom testimony. But perhaps not. Perhaps this right not to be compelled to be a witness against oneself was broader than long thought. Kasimar maintained that as long as interrogators did not advise a defendant of his rights or permit him to consult a lawyer, the average defendant would assume that his cooperation in the interrogation was compulsory. Other scholars also began to argue that the sought-after catalyst for change could be found in the Fifth Amendment's self-incrimination clause, which provides that no person "shall be compelled in any criminal case to be a witness against himself."

It now remained to be seen if a majority of the justices of the Supreme Court would opt for this Fifth Amendment "solution." The Court needed a case that would present it the option. Did the interrogation of Ernesto Miranda offer such an opportunity?

Miranda's interrogation presented the common occurrence that fell outside the constitutional protections granted under both the Sixth Amendment's right to counsel and the Fourteenth Amendment's due-process voluntariness test.

The Sixth Amendment right to counsel proved useless to Miranda, as the *Massiah* holding explicitly limited the amendment's protection to postindictment scenarios. Since Detectives Cooley and Young's interrogation of Miranda took place during the initial criminal investigation—long before formal charges were filed—the *Massiah* rule would not exclude Miranda's confession. And though *Escobedo* gave protection to a preindictment interrogation, who was to know if the interrogation of Miranda took place after the investigation had focused specifically on him?

Likewise, the voluntariness test did not protect Miranda: There was no evidence of his being tied to a tree and whipped. No use of a third party to extract the confession. No beatings. No spotlights. Though there was some contention as to the use of threats or promises, even the broadest reading of *Spano* would not rule this two-hour interrogation inadmissible.

With this legal framework, it seemed that Ernesto Miranda's confession—the key piece of evidence in the state's case—might be the right vehicle for the Court to strike off in a new direction. But that was just speculation at the time of Miranda's trial. The prevailing law made his confession very much admissible.

The Trial Attorney

Alvin Moore was born into a farming family on the dusty rangeland of the Oklahoma plains, near the turn of century. Moore began his adult life as a teacher, for nine years working in the classroom during the day and, with the aid of a correspondence school in Chicago, studying legal textbooks at night. He was admitted to the Oklahoma bar in 1922 and, in the years that followed, developed a successful criminal-defense practice. During this time, Moore defended thirty-five accused rapists; only one was convicted. Moore served as a lieutenant colonel in the infantry during World War II; when he returned home, he moved to Phoenix, where he hung his shingle.

Moore was appointed by the court to represent Ernesto Miranda. He was paid a total of $200 for the pretrial workup, the trial, and the appeal to the Arizona Supreme Court. Though he had experience in criminal law, Moore disliked those individuals he deemed responsible for the abhorrent crimes that offended society. He relayed his personal distaste for this aspect of his job to the jury during Miranda's trial:

> It is one of the cases that I don't like to be involved with; however, regardless of the type of case it is, the defendant is entitled to the best defense he can have. You know, perhaps a doctor doesn't enjoy operating for locked bowels, but he has to.

Though he was not fond of defending alleged rapists, his track record in Oklahoma indicated that he had a talent for it.

After reviewing the police report, reading Miranda's confession, and interviewing his client, Moore determined that Miranda's best interest lay in an insanity defense. Accordingly, Miranda was sent to two different doctors for examination. One psychologist described Miranda as "unable to control his sexual impulses and drives." The other diagnosed Miranda with an emotional illness of the "schizophrenic reaction, chronic, undifferentiated type." However, both doctors found Miranda aware of the charges made against him and found him competent to stand trial and assist in his own defense.

Precluded from an insanity defense, Moore faced the daunting task of confronting the state's case, armed as it was with Miranda's confession.

The Trial

After losing Miranda's robbery trial the previous day, Alvin Moore and his convicted client arrived at the Maricopa County Courthouse on a hot summer morning on June 20, 1963. The twenty-three-year-old stood accused of kidnapping and raping a retarded girl. The trial proceeded with grinding regularity. Far from the drama of television shows like *Law & Order* and *The Practice,* the proceedings were less than stimulating. A junior prosecutor trying another typical rape case. A passionless defense attorney. The actors unaware that their mediocre efforts would one day be scrutinized by the highest court in the land as a prelude to a monumental shift in American criminal justice.

Deputy Prosecutor Laurence Turoff called four witnesses: the victim, the victim's sister, and the two detectives. He submitted his one exhibit—Miranda's confession.

When Jane Doe took the stand, she spoke in a muted tone as Miranda sat directly across from her. At times, her voice became so faint that she was asked to speak up. And at one point, the judge took a recess so that she could regain her composure. Though the emotional effect of her testimony on the jury was powerful, the content of her statements unearthed another inconsistency. On direct examination she stated that Miranda had penetrated her with his finger. Then she expressed uncertainty. On further questioning, she stated that it had in fact been his penis. However, on cross-examination, she again acknowledged her uncertainty. This difference had the potential to alter the result of the case: Arizona rape laws required penile penetration.

There was, however, an additional aspect of Moore's efforts that merit comment. Although at the time it seemed little more than a futile grasp by a defense attorney facing overwhelming facts, Moore questioned Detective Cooley about the interrogation.

MOORE: Did you warn him of his rights?

COOLEY: Yes, sir. At the heading of the statement is a paragraph typed out, and I read this paragraph to him out loud.

MOORE: I don't see in the statement that it says where he is entitled to the advice of an attorney before he made it.

COOLEY: No, sir.

MOORE: It is not in that statement?

COOLEY: No, sir.

MOORE: It is not your practice to advise people you arrest that they are entitled to the services of an attorney before they make a statement?

COOLEY: No, sir.

With this less-than-shocking revelation, Moore brought a formal motion to exclude the confession. In misquoting the U.S. Supreme Court, Moore stated that current precedent guaranteed Miranda the right to an attorney at the time of his arrest. Though he was referring to the recent holding in *Gideon v. Wainwright,* which guaranteed an indigent defendant's right to counsel, this privilege extended only to trial proceedings. Moore's assertion was clearly erroneous. Further, not only was this contention made before both *Massiah* and *Escobedo,* but even under these later Sixth Amendment rulings, Miranda's confession would still be admissible.

Not surprisingly, the motion was denied.

At the conclusion of the prosecution's case, Moore opted not to put Miranda on the stand, and with good reason. If he did, Miranda's entire criminal history would be presented to the jury. The prosecutor would then be able to argue that Miranda had a pattern of sexual predation. Consequently, Moore did not produce a single defense witness. Not a piece of contradictory evidence. Moore would be forced to argue that the inconsistencies in the victim's testimony and her lack of resistance amounted to reasonable doubt.

The closing arguments were about as memorable as the previous parts of the trial. Deputy Prosecutor Turoff restated his case-in-chief. Alvin Moore stressed reasonable doubt.

And then it was over. Before the jury headed back into the deliberation room, Judge Yale McFate delivered the instructions in a professional, methodical demeanor. He offered the legal definitions of reasonable doubt and went through the elements of rape—specifically, that the jury would need to determine whether Jane gave her attacker the "utmost resistance" and whether penile penetration had occurred.

Judge McFate then succinctly restated the current law pertaining to confessions. He instructed the jurors that although he had allowed the confession into evidence, if they independently found it to be involuntary, they were free to disregard it. He delineated factors prevalent in cases like *Brown* and *Spano*. The judge then turned his attention to the confusion that Moore's motion to exclude the confession had brought to the courtroom. In explaining this facet of the law of confessions, McFate correctly stated the law.

The fact that a defendant was under arrest at the time he made a confession or that he was not at the time represented by counsel or that he was not told that any statement he might make could or would be used against him, in and of themselves, will not render such confession involuntary.

With these final words, the jury was sent to deliberate. And five hours later, the three women and nine men returned with their unanimous verdict.

Guilty.

For the next twenty to thirty years, Ernesto Miranda would pay his penitence at the Arizona State Prison. Or so he thought.

The Appeal

A little more than six months after Miranda's sentence, Alvin Moore filed a brief with the Arizona Supreme Court. In Arizona, all trial-court appeals were made to the state's highest judicial body. This lack of an in-between appellate-court filter created a logjam at the Arizona Supreme Court. Consequently, it was eighteen months until the court would review the case.

Moore's appellate brief contained a series of procedural and substantive objections to his client's trial. First, he believed that he had shown reasonable doubt as to a crucial component necessary to prove rape, that rape victims "resist [their attacker] to the utmost." Moore felt that this contention was his best shot at a new trial. However, he also slipped in two questions that would become the focus of scholarly debate for years to come: "Was [Miranda's] statement made voluntarily?" and "Was [he] afforded all the safeguards to his rights provided by the Constitution of the United States and the law and rules of the courts?"

Just before the Arizona justices began considering these issues, the U.S. Supreme Court handed down *Escobedo v. Illinois*. However, like the majority of state courts, the Arizona Supreme Court had difficulty deciphering the *Escobedo* opinion. After rigorous analysis, Justice Ernest W. McFarland, a former Arizona governor and U.S. senator, handed down an opinion that reflected the limits of both the due-process voluntariness test and the *Escobedo* decision. McFarland focused the analysis on Miranda's not having requested counsel at the time of interrogation. The court went on to find that not only had Miranda's confession been voluntary, but that *Escobedo* did not apply. The confession was properly admitted.

Regarding the due-process voluntariness test, the court found that Detectives Cooley and Young had acted reasonably when they assumed that a man with Miranda's criminal record would be aware of his rights.

However, in his discussion of *Escobedo* and the Sixth Amendment, Justice McFarland emphasized the importance of a suspect's right to counsel: no matter how heinous the crime, he explained, the protection of society from lawbreakers must not come at the expense of individual rights. McFarland's opinion echoed a growing sentiment in both academia and in some of the nation's courthouses: the due-process voluntariness test was not a sufficient protector of constitutional rights, and the confusing *Escobedo* opinion did little to alleviate these concerns. Nonetheless, Miranda's confession was valid and his conviction affirmed.

Ernesto Arturo Miranda seemed destined for a long stretch within the confines of the Arizona State Prison.

But he refused to give up. In the summer of 1965, Miranda, acting on his own behalf, filed a request for review (a writ of certiorari) to the U.S. Supreme Court. He felt that he had received an unfair trial in Maricopa County and sought relief before the high court. That year, as in every other year, the U.S. Supreme Court received hundreds of these inmate-written petitions. Most petitioners protested their innocence. None thought they had received a fair trial. One legal scholar recounted the nature of these requests:

> Some were handwritten in pencil or crayon on dime-store paper; others were painstakingly typewritten. Many were in stiff formal legalese, betraying the influence of the jailhouse lawyer. Some had merit; most did not, and the Supreme Court usually dismissed 70 percent of them without discussion. All were pathetic. Partly for the quality of the materials with which they were written and partly for the quality of the arguments they presented, law clerks to the justices referred to them as flimsies.

Miranda's petition was denied.

Around the same time, however, Miranda's case caught the attention of Robert J. Cocoran, the director of the Phoenix chapter of the American Civil Liberties Union. While sifting through the advance sheets of the *Pacific Reporter*—a digest of recent court decisions in the Pacific states—his attention was drawn to an Arizona Supreme Court decision involving the confession of an indigent, uneducated Mexican-American man. Cocoran wrote Miranda's attorney, Alvin Moore, and urged him to assist Miranda before the Supreme Court. Citing a lack of time, money, and energy, Moore declined. His role in *Miranda v. Arizona* had come to an end.

Cocoran, though, pressed on. After another failed attempt at hiring an appropriate attorney, he sought the assistance of John J. Flynn, a skilled trial lawyer at the prestigious law firm of Lewis, Roca, Scoville, Beauchamps & Linton. Flynn's firm had an ongoing arrangement with the ACLU to take two of its cases per year. Without hesitation, Flynn accepted the challenge, and the case soon became a firmwide event. Flynn sought the employ of his associate John P. Frank, a specialist in constitutional law, and the pair utilized the firm's younger associates in constructing their brief. Though they were not compensated, Frank later estimated that the cost of the case hovered around $50,000 in office time alone.

Flynn and Frank proved to be a dynamic duo. Flynn, a graduate of the University of Arizona Law School, was a compelling advocate. The forty-year-old attorney completed both his undergraduate and legal studies in only three and a half years. On the days that John Flynn presented his closing arguments at trial, lawyers and law students alike took the day off to listen; many times, the courtroom was standing room only.

Frank had been a professor prior to joining the ranks of Lewis & Roca. He received a BA, MA, and an LLB degree from the University of Wisconsin before getting his JSD from Yale Law School. His teaching credentials included time at both the University of Indiana and his alma mater in New Haven, Connecticut. Frank's personal studies focused primarily on the dynamics and decisions of the U.S. Supreme Court. The fruits of his education were reflected in several published writings. These ranged from a constitutional-law casebook to a biography of Supreme Court justice Hugo L. Black (whom he clerked for in 1942). He even published a composition entitled *The Warren Court*. In practice, Frank was an appellate attorney, a field that he felt reflected both his interests and talents.

With his scholarly credentials and meticulous style, John Frank would write the majority of the brief that the charismatic John Flynn would argue before the Supreme Court.

Upon word of his good fortune, Miranda wrote Cocoran a note of thanks from his prison cell.

> To know that someone has taken an interest in my case, has increased my moral [*sic*] enormously. . . . I would appreciate if you or either Mr. Flynn keep me informed of any and all results. I also want to thank you and Mr. Flynn for all that you are doing for me.

On to the Warren Court

In the dozen years preceding the *Miranda* decision, the U.S. Supreme Court under the leadership of Chief Justice Earl Warren handed down a series of cases aimed at protecting constitutional rights. Consequently, these decisions altered traditional power structures in radical ways: They desegregated the school system. They reapportioned voting districts. They ruled that all evidence that violated the Fourth Amendment would be inadmissible in court. They prohibited prayer in public schools.

In 1963, the Court began its delineation of the Sixth Amendment in *Gideon v. Wainwright*—the case that guaranteed a poor defendant's right to counsel. This decision had a significant impact on the states: they were immediately forced to find a way to pay the attorney's fees for every indigent defendant within their borders.

And in 1964 came *Massiah* and *Escobedo*.

By 1966, the insufficiency of *Escobedo* reached a near breaking point. The number of certiorari requests stemming from differing *Escobedo* interpretations had climbed to 150. As the 1966 Supreme Court session began, clerks were instructed to go through the petitions and mark *Escobedo* on the cases that cited a coerced confession. Chief Justice Warren then had the clerks divide the resulting stacks into four piles: those in which no warnings of rights were given; those in which possibly full warnings were given; those in which the record was silent on the issue; and those that questioned if a resulting decision should be made retroactive. After careful analysis, the clerks chose one case from each stack.

Out of the first pile—those cases where no warnings were given—the clerks' choice was an action arising from the Arizona Supreme Court in which an accused rapist had been interrogated for two hours without being informed either of his right to remain silent or his right to counsel.

For perhaps the first time in his life, Ernesto Miranda was a favorite.

The other three choices would be joined with Miranda's appeal under the single title *Miranda v. Arizona.*

John Frank, in his brief on behalf of Miranda, surprisingly shunned the newly emerging Fifth Amendment approach and instead proclaimed, "The day is here to recognize the full meaning of the Sixth Amendment."

Frank invoked the "right to counsel" decisions of *Gideon, Massiah,* and *Escobedo* to construct his constitutional claim.

The Arizona Attorney General's Office filed an answer within two weeks. The brief, written by Assistant Attorney General Gary Nelson, was a testament to fundamental legal reasoning—he distinguished the facts of *Escobedo* from those of *Miranda:* In *Escobedo,* the police made a concerted effort to deter the suspect from seeing his already present lawyer. In *Miranda,* the police did not. In *Escobedo,* the police lied to the defendant—saying that someone else had already ratted him out. In *Miranda,* the police used no such trickery. In *Escobedo,* the suspect had a completely clean record—indicating that he was unfamiliar with the criminal justice system. In *Miranda,* the defendant had a laundry list of offenses indicative of a thorough knowledge of interrogation.

Where Frank was looking to expand *Escobedo,* Nelson was looking to contain it.

The Court also received three amicus curiae (friend of the court) briefs. Of these, the most notable was authored by Professor Anthony G. Amsterdam, on behalf of the American Civil Liberties Union. As opposed to the other briefs, Amsterdam's developed the argument first outlined in Professor Kasimar's "Gatehouses and Mansions" article: It focused on the Fifth Amendment privilege against self-incrimination. Citing police interrogation handbooks such as the Inbau manual, Amsterdam asserted that these practices were aimed at getting a suspect to confess "by trapping him into it, deceiving him or by more direct means of overbearing will."

The Oral Argument

On a cold February morning, John Frank and John Flynn, on behalf of Miranda, and Gary Nelson, representing the state of Arizona, made their way up the marble stairs of the U.S. Supreme Court Building. Months of rigorous preparation had led them to perhaps the most intense hour of their lives. They settled into seats in the audience and watched the oral arguments that preceded their case. In that case, defense counsel F. Lee Bailey argued an appeal brought by Dr. Samuel Sheppard, the man whose infamous murder of his wife was the basis for the popular television series and movie *The Fugitive.* Bailey—the man who would later defend both Patty Hearst and O. J. Simpson—gave a rousing and ultimately successful performance, as the Court agreed that the massive press coverage of Sheppard's trial had denied him a fair trial. Bailey would be a tough act to follow.

The chief justice then called the case of *Ernesto Miranda v. the State of Arizona.*

CHIEF JUSTICE WARREN: Mr. Flynn, you may proceed.

FLYNN: Mr. Chief Justice, may it please the Court: This case concerns itself with the conviction of a defendant of two crimes of rape and kidnapping, the sentences on each count of twenty to thirty years to run concurrently. The issue before the Court is the admission into evidence of the defendant's confession, over the specific objections of his trial counsel that it had been given in the absence of counsel.

Now the petitioner's position on the issue is simply this: The Arizona Supreme Court, we feel, has imprisoned this Court's decision in *Escobedo* on its facts, and by its decision is refusing to apply the principles of that case, and for all practical purposes has emasculated it. Certainly every court desiring to admit a confession can find distinguishing factors in *Escobedo* from the fact situation before it.

I would like to very briefly quote from the transcript of the record which contains the Arizona decision [in Miranda's case]:

"It will be noted that the Court in the *Escobedo* case set forth the circumstances under which a statement would be held admissible, namely: one, the general inquiry into an unsolved crime must have begun to focus on a particular suspect; two, a suspect must have been taken into police custody; three, the police in its interrogation must have elicited an incriminating statement; four, the suspect must have requested and been denied an opportunity to consult with his lawyer; five, the police must not have effectively warned the suspect of his constitutional rights to remain silent. When all of these five factors occur, then the *Escobedo* case is a controlling precedent."

The Arizona Supreme Court, having indicated its clear intention to imprison the *Escobedo* decision, set about to do precisely that. First, as to the focusing question, it indicated that this crime had occurred at night. Consequently, despite the positive identification of the defendant by two witnesses, which the state urged were entirely fair lineups, the Supreme Court of

Arizona indicated that even then perhaps under these facts, attention had not focused upon this defendant. I think this is sheer sophistry and would indicate the obvious intent of the Arizona Supreme Court to confine *Escobedo* and to distinguish it whenever possible.

Next, the [Arizona Supreme] court found that the defendant was advised of his rights in the reading of the typed portion immediately preceding its transcript. They permitted that document to lift itself by its own bootstraps, so to speak, and to indicate that here was a man who was knowledgeable concerning his legal rights, despite the facts and circumstances of his background and education. They further found that he was knowledgeable because he had a prior criminal record, though in the decision he indicated this would be knowledge of his rights in court and certainly not his rights at the time of the interrogation.

I think the numerous briefs filed in this case indicating the substantial split in the decisions throughout the various states, the circuits, and the federal district courts indicate the interpretation that has been placed upon *Escobedo*. On the one hand, we have the California decision in *Dorado*. We have the Third Circuit decision in *Russo,* which would indicate that principle and logic are being applied to the decision, and in the words of Mr. Justice Goldberg, that when the process shifts from the investigation to one of accusation, and when the purpose is to elicit a confession from the defendant, then the adversary process comes into being. On the other hand, the other cases that would distinguish this have found and give rise to what I submit is not really confusion by merely straining against the principles and logic in that decision.

JUSTICE STEWART: What do you think is the result of the adversary process coming into being when this focusing takes place? What follows from that? Is there, then, a right to a lawyer?

FLYNN: I think that the man at that time has the right to exercise, if he knows, and under the present state of the law in Arizona, if he is rich enough, and if he's educated enough to assert his Fifth Amendment right, and if he recognizes that he has a Fifth Amendment right to request counsel. But I simply say that at that stage of the proceeding, under the facts and circumstances in this case of a man of limited education, of a man who certainly is mentally abnormal, who is certainly an indigent, that when that adversary process came into being, that the police, at

241

the very least, had an obligation to extend to this man not only his clear Fifth Amendment right, but to accord to him the right of counsel.

STEWART: I suppose, if you really mean what you say or what you gather from what the *Escobedo* decision says, the adversary process starts at that point, and every single protection of the Constitution then comes into being, does it not? You have to bring a jury in there, I suppose?

FLYNN: No, Your Honor, I wouldn't bring a jury in. I simply would extend to the man those constitutional rights which the police, at that time, took away from him.

STEWART: That's begging the question. My question is, what are those rights when the focusing begins? Are these all the panoply of rights guaranteed to the defendant in a criminal trial?

FLYNN: I think the first right is the Fifth Amendment right: the right not to incriminate oneself; the right to know you have that right; and the right to consult with counsel, at the very least, in order that you can exercise the right, Your Honor.

STEWART: Well, I don't fully understand your answer, because if the adversary process then begins, then what you have is the equivalent of a trial, do you not? And then I suppose you have a right to a judge, and a jury, and everything else that goes with a trial right then and there. If you have something less than that, then this is not an adversary proceeding and then you don't mean what you're saying.

FLYNN: I think what I say—what I am interpreting "adversary proceeding" to mean—is that at that time, a person who is poorly educated, who in essence is mentally abnormal, who is an indigent, that at an adversary proceeding, at the very least, he is entitled at that stage of the proceeding to be represented by counsel and to be advised by counsel of his rights under the Fifth Amendment of the Constitution; or, he has no such right.

STEWART: Well, again I don't mean to quibble, and I apologize, but I think it's first important to define what those rights are—what his rights under the Constitution are at that point. He can't be advised of his rights unless somebody knows what those rights are.

FLYNN: Precisely my point. And the only person that can adequately advise a person like Ernesto Miranda is a lawyer.

STEWART: And what would a lawyer advise him that his rights were?

FLYNN: That he had a right not to incriminate himself; that he had the right not to make any statement; that he had a right to be free from further questioning by the police department; that he had the right, at the ultimate time, to be represented adequately by counsel in court; and that if he was too indigent or too poor to employ counsel, the state would furnish him counsel.

STEWART: What is it that confers the right to a lawyer's advice at that point and not an earlier point? The Sixth Amendment?

FLYNN: No. The attempt to erode, or to take away from him, the Fifth Amendment right that already existed—and that was the right not to convict himself, and be convicted out of his own mouth.

STEWART: Didn't he have that right earlier?

FLYNN: If he knew about it.

STEWART: Before this became a so-called adversary proceeding?

FLYNN: Yes, Your Honor, if he knew about it and if he was aware— if he was knowledgeable.

STEWART: Then did he have the right to a lawyer's advice earlier?

FLYNN: If he could afford it, yes; and if he was intelligent enough and strong enough to stand up against police interrogation and request it, yes.

STEWART: What I'm getting at is, I don't understand the magic in this phrase of "focusing," and then all of a sudden it becomes an adversary proceeding. And then I suppose if you literally mean that it becomes an adversary proceeding, then you're entitled to all the rights that a defendant is given under the Constitution that would be given in a criminal trial. If you mean less than that, then you don't really mean it has now become the equivalent of a trial.

FLYNN: Well, I simply mean that when it becomes an adversary pro-ceeding, at the very least a person in Ernesto Miranda's position needs the benefit of counsel, and unless he is afforded that right of counsel, he simply has, in essence, no Fifth or Sixth Amend-ment right, and there is no due process of law being afforded to a man in Ernesto Miranda's position.

JUSTICE FORTAS: Is it possible that prior to this so-called focusing, or let's say prior to arrest—if those don't mean the same thing— that a citizen has an obligation to cooperate with the state, give the state information that he may have relevant to the crime; and that upon arrest, or upon this "focusing," that the state and the individual then assume the position of adversaries, and there is, at the very least, a change in that relationship between the individual and the state; and, therefore, in their mutual rights and responsibilities? I don't know whether that's what my brother Stewart is getting at, and perhaps it is unfair to discuss this through you—but if you have a comment on it, I'd like to hear it.

FLYNN: I think the only comment that I could make is that, without getting ourselves into the area of precisely when focusing begins, that I must in this instance limit it to the fact situation and the circumstances of Ernesto Miranda, because for every practical purpose, after the two-hour interrogation, the mere formality of supplying counsel to Mr. Miranda at the time of trial, is what, I would submit, would really be nothing more than a mockery of his Sixth Amendment right to be represented in court, to go through the formality, and a conviction takes place.

JUSTICE BLACK: May I ask you one question, Mr. Flynn, about the Fifth Amendment? Let's forget about the Sixth. The amendment provides that no person shall be compelled to be a witness against himself. It's disassociated entirely from the right to counsel. You have said several times it seems, during the case, that in determining whether or not a person shall be compelled to be a witness against himself, that it might depend to some extent on his literacy or his illiteracy, his wealth or his lack of wealth, his standing or his lack of standing—why does that have anything to do with it? Why does the amendment not protect the rich, as well as the poor; the literate, as well as the illiterate?

FLYNN: I would say that it certainly, and most assuredly, does protect. That in the state of the law today as pronounced by the Arizona Supreme Court, under those guiding principles, it certainly does protect the rich, the educated, and the strong—those rich enough to hire counsel, those who are educated enough to know what their rights are, and those who are strong enough to withstand police interrogation and assert those rights.

BLACK: I am asking you only about the Fifth Amendment's provision that no person shall be compelled to be a witness against himself. Does that protect every person, or just some persons? I am not talking about in practical effect; I am talking about what the amendment is supposed to do.

FLYNN: It protects all persons.

BLACK: Would literacy or illiteracy have anything to do with it if they compelled him to testify, whatever comes within the scope of that?

FLYNN: At the interrogation stage, if he is too ignorant to know that he has the Fifth Amendment right, then certainly literacy has something to do with it, Your Honor. If the man at the time of the interrogation has never heard of the Fifth Amendment, knows nothing about its concept or its scope, knows nothing of his rights, then certainly his literacy—

BLACK: He'd have more rights, because of that? I don't understand. The Fifth Amendment right, alone, not to be compelled to be a witness against himself? What does that cover?

FLYNN: Perhaps I have simply not expressed myself clearly.

BLACK: Does that cover everybody?

FLYNN: It covers everybody, Your Honor. Clearly in practical application, in view of the interrogation and the facts and circumstances of *Miranda*, it simply had no application because of the facts and circumstances in that particular case, and that's what I am attempting to express to the Court.

STEWART: Is there any claim in this case that this confession was compelled, was involuntary?

FLYNN: No, Your Honor.

STEWART: None at all?

FLYNN: None at all.

JUSTICE WHITE: Do you mean that there is no question that he was not compelled to give evidence against himself?

FLYNN: We have raised no question that he was compelled to give this statement, in the sense that anyone forced him to do it by coercion, by threats, by promises, or compulsion of that kind.

WHITE: "Of that kind"? Was it voluntary, or wasn't it?

FLYNN: Voluntary in the sense that the man, at a time without knowledge of his rights—

WHITE: Do you claim that his Fifth Amendment rights were violated?

FLYNN: I would say his Fifth Amendment right was violated, to the extent—

WHITE: Because he was compelled to do it?

FLYNN: Because he was compelled to do it?

WHITE: That's what the amendment says.

FLYNN: Yes, to the extent that he was, number one, too poor to exercise it, and number two, mentally abnormal.

WHITE: Whatever the Fifth is, you say he was compelled to do it?

FLYNN: I say it was taken from him at a point in time when he absolutely should have been afforded the Sixth Amendment—

WHITE: I'm talking about violating the amendment, namely the provision that he was—to violate the Fifth Amendment right, he has to be compelled to do it, doesn't he?

FLYNN: In the sense that Your Honor is presenting to me the word "compelled," you're correct.

WHITE: I was talking about what the Constitution says.

BLACK: He doesn't have to have a gun pointed at his head, does he?

WHITE: Of course he doesn't. So he was compelled to do it, wasn't he, according to your theory?

FLYNN: Not by gunpoint, as Mr. Justice Black has indicated. He was called upon to surrender a right that he didn't fully realize and appreciate that he had. It was taken from him.

WHITE: But in all the circumstances—I'm just trying to find out if you claim that his Fifth Amendment rights were being violated. If they were, it must be because he was compelled to do it, under all circumstances.

FLYNN: I would say that as a result of a lack of knowledge, or for lack of a better term, "failure to advise," the denial of the right to counsel at the stage in the proceeding when he most certainly needed it, that this could, in and of itself—and certainly in most police interrogations—constitute compulsion.

BLACK: Why wouldn't you add to that the fact that the state had him in its control and custody? Why would that not tend to show some kind of coercion or compulsion?

FLYNN: The whole process of a person, I would assume, having been raised to tell the truth and respect authority.

BLACK: Was he allowed to get away from there, at will?

FLYNN: No, Your Honor. He was in confinement and under arrest.

BLACK: The state had moved against him by taking him in to question him, did it not?

FLYNN: That is correct.

JUSTICE WARREN: Mr. Flynn, you would say that if the police had said to this young man, "Now you are a nice young man, and we don't want to hurt you, and so forth; we're your friends and if you'll just tell us how you committed this crime, we'll let you go home and we won't prosecute you," that that would be a violation of the Fifth Amendment, and that, technically speaking, would not be "compelling" him to do it. It would be an inducement, would it not?

FLYNN: That is correct.

WARREN: I suppose you would argue that that is still within the Fifth Amendment, wouldn't you?

FLYNN: It is an abdication of the Fifth Amendment right.

WARREN: That's what I mean.

FLYNN: Because of the total circumstances existing at the time—the arrest, the custody, the lack of knowledge, the—

WARREN: In fact, we have had cases of that kind, that confessions were had, haven't we, where they said it would be better for you if you do; we'll let you go; and so forth?

FLYNN: That, of course, is an implied promise of some help or immunity of some kind.

WARREN: Yes, but that isn't strictly compulsion that we have been talking about?

FLYNN: That certainly is not compulsion in the sense of the word, as Mr. Justice White had implied it.

BLACK: As I recall, in those cases—I agree with the chief justice— as I recall, in those cases that were put under the Fifth Amendment, and the words of the Fifth Amendment were referred to in the early case by Chief Justice White, I believe it was, and the fact that inducement is a compulsion and was brought in that category, and therefore it violated the amendment against being compelled to give evidence against yourself.

FLYNN: I am sure Mr. Justice Black has expressed it far better than—

BLACK: So it's a question of what "compel" means, but it does not depend, I suppose—I haven't seen it in any of the cases—on the wealth, the standing, or the status of the person, so far as the right is concerned.

FLYNN: Yes, I think perhaps that was a bad choice of words, in context, if Your Honor please, at the time I stated them.

I would like to state, in conclusion, that the constitution of the state of Arizona, for example, has, since statehood, provided to the citizens of our state language precisely the same as the Fourth Amendment to the federal Constitution as it pertains to searches and seizures. Yet from 1914 until this Court's decision in *Mapp v. Ohio,* we simply did not enjoy the Fourth Amendment rights or the scope of the Fourth Amendment rights that were enjoyed by most of the other citizens of the other states of this Union, and those persons who were under federal control.

In response to the amicus for New York and the amicus for the National Association of Defense Attorneys that would ask this Court to go slowly and to give the opportunity to the states, to the legislature, to the courts, and to the bar association to undertake to solve this problem, I simply say that whatever the solutions may be, it would be another forty-six years before the Sixth Amendment right in the scope that it was intended, I submit, by this Court in *Escobedo,* will reach the state of Arizona.

WARREN: Mr. Nelson?

NELSON: Mr. Chief Justice, may it please the Court, counsel:

I'm somewhat caught up in where to begin. I think perhaps the first and most important—one of the most important—things to say right now is concerning Mr. Flynn's last remarks. I, as a prosecutor, take serious issue—as strenuous issue as I can take—before this Court, in the statement that it will take another forty-six years in the state of Arizona for the right to counsel to become full-blown. I just simply think there is no reason for that statement to be made. If there is any reason for it to be made, or any possible justification for it to be made, then there is no point in going any further.

One issue that might be a good starting point is concerning the description of the Arizona court's supposed "off-the-cuff" referral to, or ignoring of, the *Escobedo* decision, or the attempt to void it clearly. There is no such thing in the Arizona Supreme Court opinion, and a reading of it shows that they agreed that they must follow this Court, not begrudgingly.

They simply stated that it's a fact, and then in exploring the case of *Escobedo* in the case of *Miranda,* they try to find out what happened in *Miranda,* what the case of *Escobedo* says, and apply those principles. There's no attempt to avoid, and I don't think you can read it, implicitly or otherwise, in the Arizona court's opinion. Clearly they did not base it on a request. They did not say we have A, B, C, D, and E, and F wasn't present, therefore it's not controlling. That is not what they said. They said other courts in that jurisdiction had gone off on that particular area. They mentioned that as a factor, but they discussed hundreds of—no, not hundreds—many other factors in *Miranda,* which differentiated it from *Escobedo*.

To get to the facts in *Miranda* I think it's very clear from the record that Mr. Miranda, as an individual defendant, does not particularly require any special rule. I certainly agree with Justice Black one hundred percent that the Fifth Amendment, the Sixth Amendment, and every part of our Constitution applies to everyone—poor, rich, intellectual, and so on. There is no possible difference for differentiation.

FORTAS: Mr. Nelson, in your brief you assert, "The petitioner was advised of his constitutional rights, specifically including his right to remain silent, the fact that his statement had to be voluntary, and that anything he did say could be used against him." Is the only basis for that the printed legend in the confession that he signed?

NELSON: No, I don't believe I would have put in as strong a statement concerning his right to remain silent had not we agreed to stipulate to this other portion of the other record. But I believe that as long as that's in the record, I can make this statement because it's supported in the finding of the court, based on the interrogation of the officers, the testimony of the officers in the trial that is actually before this Court concerning their advice to him, and the findings of the court based on his understanding, the reading of the statement, the testimony coupled with this. I believe, then, that the court below, which clearly found that to be true, that he had been fully advised, had a proper basis for finding all of these to exist, except that there is no quarrel that he was not specifically advised that he had a right to counsel.

FORTAS: Is it your position that the record shows that he was advised of these rights somehow, some way, in addition to the legend on his confession? That's my question.

NELSON: Yes.

FORTAS: How? Where is that?

NELSON: I believe the police officers testified to the fact that they told him of his rights and that they also, besides telling him—perhaps the record is a little unclear, in both cases, as to exactly when it took place—but I believe the record supports a statement that he was advised specifically by them of his rights and then he was alerted to the paragraph and perhaps even again the paragraph was read to him. But the record is not really all four-square. It is not that clear.

FORTAS: Let us assume he was so advised—and I understand you to say that the record is not clear on that point—let us assume that he was advised of his rights. In your opinion does it make any difference when he was advised? That is, whether he was advised at the commencement of the interrogation, or whether he was advised only when he was ready to sign the confession—the written confession? Does that make any difference in terms of the issues before us?

NELSON: Assuming for a moment that some warning is going to be required, or should have been given, then I would think that to be of any effect it must be given before he had made any statements. Perhaps he might have refused to sign the written confession. Certainly still, the oral statement could have been introduced against him.

FORTAS: So you think that the warning, if necessary, has to be given prior to the interrogation?

NELSON: At some meaningful time, right. I would think it would have to be at some time prior to the fact that after—if they used it before, of course the warning would mean nothing. If they could introduce what they had obtained from the time before they gave the warning, and not afterwards.

FORTAS: Is it your submission to us that a warning is necessary before a confession, in the absence of counsel, can be taken and subsequently introduced in the trial?

NELSON: No.

FORTAS: What is your position on that?

NELSON: My position basically is—concerning the warning—is that each case presents a factual situation in which the court would have to determine, or a court or a judge or prosecutor at some level, would have to make a determination as to whether or not a defendant, because of the circumstances surrounding his confession, was denied a specific right—whether it be right to counsel, the right to not be compelled to testify against himself—and that the warning, or age or literacy, the circumstances, the length of the questioning, all these factors would be important. But I don't think you can put it to one simple thing such as a warning, because there are perhaps many more situations that we could think of where a warning would be completely inadequate.

FORTAS: Well, tell me some of the factors that would be relevant in the absence of a warning.

NELSON: His age, his experience, his background, the type of questioning, the atmosphere of questioning, the length of questioning, the time of day, perhaps—all of these factors.

FORTAS: Do you think what we ought to do is to devise something like the *Betts and Brady* rule, special circumstances?

NELSON: Well, I think that's what the *Escobedo* case indicates. In other words, I am—of course my opinion is biased—if it's not something like that, then it is an absolute right to counsel. I don't think there can be any in-between unless some other theory. Under the way I read the decisions of this Court, if it is an absolute right to counsel, the same sort of right to counsel that attaches—

FORTAS: We're not talking about right to counsel. We're talking about the warning. When is the warning necessary? As I understand you, you say that if the warning is necessary, if it should be held to be constitutionally necessary in the absence of counsel, then the warning has to be given at a meaningful time.

NELSON: I would think so, certainly.

FORTAS: And I then proceeded to ask you to give us the benefit of your views as to whether a warning was necessary. As I understand it, you say that you have to look at the circumstances of each case?

NELSON: I would say, not absolutely.

FORTAS: I ask you what are the relevant circumstances in each case—the relevant circumstances to look for in each particular case? And how about this particular case?

NELSON: I don't think so. I'm not a psychiatrist, so I can't say. I think both [psychiatric] reports say, in effect, the man has an emotional illness that should be treated, but that he knew what was going on. Both the reports say his mental faculties, whatever they were, were sharp, acute, and that he had no psychotic disorders. They both say basically the same thing. I think the diagnosis in the other report said a "sociopathic personality."

FORTAS: So that if the *Betts against Brady* test were applied in the way that this Court did apply it prior to *Gideon,* I suppose it's quite arguable that Miranda, this petitioner here, was entitled to a warning. Would you agree to that?

NELSON: It's arguable. I have extensively argued the fact that he wasn't of such a nature, as an individual who because of his mental condition or his educational background, as to require any more than he got. In other words, I'm saying that he got every warning, except the right—the specific warning—of the right to counsel. He didn't have counsel. Counsel wasn't specifically denied to him, on the basis of a request to retain counsel. The only possible thing that happened to Mr. Miranda that, in my light, assuming that he had the capability of understanding at all, is the fact that he did not get the specific warning of his right to counsel.

FORTAS: Well, even if we assume that he got all the other warnings, and putting aside the question of the right to counsel, assume that the record does show that he got these warnings, still is there any evidence—and I have to ask you again—does the record show that he got it at what you would call a meaningful time?

NELSON: Yes. I think the police officers—they were never pinned down, in other words, as to whether at eleven thirty when they went into interrogation room two they immediately warned him. This was not pinned down by either side. But they did say he was warned.

FORTAS: Mr. Nelson, I certainly want your views and only your views, and I don't want to state anything unfairly, but am I correct in inferring from what you have just said, in answer to my questions, that the state of Arizona does agree that there are occasions when the United States Constitution requires that a warning as to the right to remain silent must be given to a person who is in custody, and must be given at a meaningful time? Do I correctly state the position that you are presenting to us here?

NELSON: Not completely. I don't think that the Arizona Supreme Court has worded its holdings, and I cite to the Court the case that followed *Miranda* and referred back to it concerning the point of waiver, and they go on to expand on their thinking. I don't believe the Arizona court has specifically said that warnings, as such, are of a constitutional dimension. The court has said that in some cases warnings may be required in a given case.

As I understand it, there is no right not to incriminate himself. The right is for him not to be compelled, whether it's subtle compulsion or direct, but it is still a right not to be compelled to incriminate yourself. At least this is my understanding, and he doesn't have a right not to incriminate himself. He has a right not to be compelled to incriminate himself by some means, either direct or devious. Now I think if the extreme position is adopted that says he has to either have counsel at this stage, or intellectually waive counsel, that a serious problem in the enforcement of our criminal law will occur.

First of all, let us make one thing certain. When counsel is introduced at interrogation, interrogation ceases immediately.

BLACK: Why?

NELSON: Well, for one reason: first of all there are several different situations, but assume counsel is immediately introduced and he knows nothing about the case. He has not talked to the defendant. He has been appointed, say, to an indigent defendant who says, "I want a lawyer. I need a lawyer right now. I don't want to talk to you without a lawyer."

He is given a lawyer. He talks to the defendant. First of all he stops the interrogation until he can talk with him. I would think, if he is going to represent him, he cannot allow him to say anything until he finds out what his story is, what he is going to say, and how it is going to affect him. So the interrogation would immediately stop, for that purpose. And after he has had an opportunity to confer with his client—let's assume another thing. Let's assume the client said, "Yes, I am guilty. I did it." He had all the requisite intents. He makes a statement to his lawyer in confidence that he did it and asks his lawyer what he should do.

Well, the lawyer maybe doesn't know his past history. Maybe the lawyer would want to find out what the police have, if he can. So maybe more time, in order to properly represent him, would be taken up here—time when there would be no interrogation. Let's further assume that he advises his client, "Well, I think you ought to confess. I think there's a possibility for a light sentence. You did it. They have other evidence; or maybe they don't have any other evidence"—let's say they don't have any other evidence—"and you can confess."

The fellow says, "Well, I don't want to confess. I don't want to go to the gas chamber if I don't have to. Is there anything else that you, as my lawyer, can do for me?" Well, what has he got to tell him? Under our system, he has got to tell him, "Yes, you don't have to say anything. And the fact that you don't say anything can't in any way hurt you, inferred or otherwise, and we can put the state to its burden of proof."

BLACK: Why does our system compel his lawyer to do that?

NELSON: He is compelled by the system to do this.

BLACK: Well, why does it do it? For what purpose? What's the object on the part of the lawyer?

NELSON: Because we believe that it's right, and proper, that the criminal defendant not be deprived of his life, liberty, or property, without due process of law.

BLACK: And something about giving testimony against himself.

NELSON: Right. I mean this is just one issue. The lawyer has to guard all these rights. But I'm saying that the practical effect of introducing counsel at the interrogation stage is going to stop the interrogation for any and all purposes, except what counsel decides will be in the best interest of his defendant. Otherwise, counsel will not be doing his job.

BLACK: Isn't that about the same thing as the practical effect and object of the amendment, which says he shall not be compelled to give testimony against himself? Is there any difference between the objects there, and purposes of the two—what the lawyer tells him, and what the Fifth Amendment tells him?

NELSON: Well, certainly that's the object of what his lawyer tells him.

BLACK: Isn't that the object of the amendment?

NELSON: Well, that is the question, of course. Under the Fifth Amendment he has the right never to be compelled to incriminate himself at whatever stage, and this, of course, involves a knowledgeable implementation of that right at this time, if he wants to.

What I am saying is that the state does not have to, at this stage, insist on that right being enforced or waived, because the pretrial police interrogation does more than just develop confessions. It develops incriminating statements. It develops exculpatory statements which pin a story down to a defendant very closely after the crime is committed, or very closely after he has been taken into police custody, which prevents or effectively makes it unprofitable for him to perjure himself or change his testimony at trial should he take the stand.

BLACK: Is there anything fantastic in the idea that the Fifth Amendment—that the protection against being compelled to testify against oneself—might be read reasonably as meaning there should be no pretrial proceedings when he was there in the possession of the state?

NELSON: Of course to me, I think there is. I think there is a valid interest—

BLACK: There is a valid interest, of course, if they can convict him—and that's their business, to try to convict him.

NELSON: Right. But I think this is another argument that I think must be made. Our adversary system, as such, is not completely adversary even at the trial stage in a criminal prosecution because the duty of the prosecution is not simply to go out and convict, but it is to see that justice is done.

FORTAS: Do you give defendants access to the state's evidence against him in your state?

NELSON: Mr. Flynn would tell you more about that at the trial level. I don't believe that the rule has been interpreted very broadly. I think it has been interpreted narrowly. I think he can get his own statements and perhaps he can get the police officers' reports.

There is a rule providing for motions, but the judges, as I understand it, have construed it fairly narrowly.

FORTAS: So that it is possible to speculate, isn't it, that the state has limitations—places limitations upon its obligation to cooperate with the defendant, as witnessed by the denial of discovery to the defendant, discovery of the evidence that the state has against him?

NELSON: Yes. Of course I'm sure the prosecutors would go along one hundred percent with full discovery for both sides.

FORTAS: Maybe the prosecutors that you know.

[Laughter.]

NELSON: The defendant, of course, is compelled to no discovery, no ordinary discovery procedures in the scope we think of them in a civil case. I just say that I am not sure that the analogy is completely—

FORTAS: What I was drawing your attention to is that there are, in our system, limitations upon the degree of cooperativeness on both sides. It's not just that the arrested person has, under the Constitution, a privilege against self-incrimination; it is also that the state, when it assumes an adversary position even before that time, takes advantage of certain "reticence," shall I say, with respect to disclosure to the accused.

NELSON: It surely does. But there is no compulsion. In fact, the compulsion is, to the contrary, on the defense side to cooperate, whereas there is complete compulsion—at least by my interpretation of the law—for the prosecutor to do as much, if it's available to him, to show that the defendant is innocent, as there is to prove he is guilty.

FORTAS: I think we have established, in this colloquy, that *complete* is a little bit of an overstatement.

NELSON: It doesn't always work that way. I am sure that's the case.

And with a brief statement from New York attorney general Telford Taylor, three years of litigation and appeals came to a close. The oral arguments from *Miranda v. Arizona* summed up an issue that had concerned the American justice system for nearly a century. John Flynn's argument on behalf of Ernesto Miranda combined the rights afforded to criminal suspects by the Fifth and Sixth Amendments. In response, Gary Nelson—arguing for the state—appealed to the necessity of keeping admitted rapists and murderers off the streets. How were prosecutors to effectively bring criminals to justice if one of their most crucial means of obtaining a conviction was seriously circumscribed?

It was the battle of constitutional rights versus the possibility of releasing dangerous criminals back onto the streets. It was the battle of good versus evil. But what was the ultimate good? And which was the worst evil? These questions would lie in the back of the minds of the nine men charged with formulating a workable, balanced, and constitutional standard.

Five to Four

On June 13, 1966, the Warren Court handed down what would become the most cited case in American history. The narrow decision was fairly predictable: The bare liberal majority—Warren, Brennan, Black, Douglas, and Fortas—that had pushed through the *Gideon* and *Escobedo* rulings prevailed. The conservatives—Harlan, Stewart, White, and Clark—filed their dissents.

Though the opinion comprised nearly sixty pages in the *United States Reports,* both the Court's holding and its basis for that holding were contained in the first paragraph.

> The cases before us raise questions which go to the roots of our concepts of American criminal jurisprudence; the restraints society must observe consistent with the Federal Constitution in prosecuting individuals for crime. More specifically, we deal with the admissibility of statements obtained from an individual who is subjected to custodial police interrogation and the necessity for procedures which assure that the individual is accorded his privilege under the Fifth Amendment to the Constitution not to be compelled to incriminate himself.

The Court indicated not only that it was about to definitively rule on the issue of coerced confessions, but also that it was following the approaches taken by Professors Kasimar and Amsterdam. The Sixth Amendment had been exhausted; it was the Fifth Amendment that was to be the backbone of the *Miranda* protections.

Chief Justice Warren, who wrote the opinion, began an exhaustive discussion of the current status of police interrogation practices with "This Court has recognized that coercion can be mental as well as physical and that the blood of the accused is not the only hallmark of an unconstitutional inquisition." Warren went on to describe the tactics described in various police handbooks, paying particular attention to the now ubiquitous Inbau manual.

The officers are told by the manuals that the principal psychological factor contributing to a successful interrogation is privacy—being alone with the person under interrogation. . . . The officers are instructed to minimize the moral seriousness of the offense, to cast blame on the victim or on society. These tactics are designed to put the subject in a psychological state where his story is but an elaboration of what the police purport to know already—he is guilty.

The manuals suggest that the suspect be offered legal excuses for his actions in order to obtain an initial admission of guilt. [According to the manual] the police may resort to deceptive stratagems such as giving false legal advice. It is important to keep the subject off balance, for example, by trading on his insecurity about himself or his surrounding. The police then persuade, trick, or cajole him out of exercising his constitutional rights.

Warren then placed these tactics into a constitutional framework:

It is obvious that such an interrogation environment is created for no purpose other than to subjugate the individual to the will of his examiner. Unless adequate protective devices are employed to dispel the compulsion inherent in custodial surroundings, no statement obtained from the defendant can truly be the product of his free choice.

And then, almost as if he had been taking dictation during John Flynn's oral argument, Chief Justice Warren wrote the most famous words in the history of American criminal procedure:

At the outset, if a person in custody is to be subjected to interrogation, he must first be informed in clear and unequivocal terms that he has the right to remain silent . . . that anything said can and will be used against the individual in court . . . that he has the right to consult with a lawyer and to have the lawyer with him during interrogation . . . [and] that if he is indigent, a lawyer will be appointed to represent him.

In response to both the argument presented by Assistant Attorney General Gary Nelson and the vehement dissent authored by Justice Harlan, Warren wrote:

We are not unmindful of the burdens which law enforcement officials must bear, often under trying circumstances. . . . This

Court, while protecting individual rights, has always given ample latitude to law enforcement agencies in the legitimate exercise of their duties. . . . Although confessions may play an important role in some convictions, the cases before us present graphic examples of the overstatement of the "need" for confessions. In each case, authorities conducted interrogations ranging up to five days in duration despite the presence, through standard investigating practices, of considerable evidence against each defendant.

Finally, the Court's focus turned to the interrogation of Ernesto Miranda:

It is clear that Miranda was not in any way apprised of his right to consult with an attorney and to have one present during the interrogation, nor was his right not to be compelled to incriminate himself effectively protected in any other manner. Without these warnings, the statements were inadmissible.

The U.S. Supreme Court had given the police a bright-line test: From now on, every time a suspect was taken into police custody, if he was not specifically informed of his constitutional rights, any subsequent confession would be inadmissible in court. From now on, if an officer failed to simply read the rights laid out in the *Miranda* opinion, the prosecution would lose a crucial piece of evidence, and admitted felons could go free. From now on—without proper warnings—when a suspect confessed, the case was no longer closed.

The Aftermath

Following *Miranda,* public outcry against the Warren Court intensified. For many, "Impeach Earl Warren" was not merely a suggestion, it was a mandate. How could the Court let a confessed rapist go free? Didn't they realize that Ernesto Miranda had preyed upon and violated a retarded girl? Didn't they care?

Aside from the immediate effect of the *Miranda* ruling, the more controversial issues lay in its effects upon future police interrogations. Scholars, prosecutors, and public officials alike voiced their passionate disapproval of the Warren Court's decision. Some said that the Court had not gone far enough; that the only way to fully protect a suspect during interrogation was to command that his attorney be present at all times. Others thought the Court had gone too far, stating that it had placed an undue burden on law enforcement officials. These critics produced the most vocal and scathing comments. One police chief declared that the Warren Court interpreted the Constitution as a "shield for criminals." Others contended that Miranda was "handcuffing police," "coddling criminals," and circumventing "law and order."

But the debate was not confined to the police station and the halls of academia. In 1968, as Richard Nixon prepared for his presidential bid, he issued a position paper that blamed the *Escobedo* and *Miranda* decisions for the nation's rising crime rate. In this statement, Nixon asserted, "The cumulative effect [of] these decisions has been to very nearly rule out the 'confession' as an effective and major tool in prosecution and law enforcement."

Not only had the *Miranda* decision filtered into presidential politics, but Congress reacted as well. The federal legislative body quickly enacted 18 U.S.C. § 3501, an act designed to confine the law of confessions solely to the pre-*Escobedo,* due-process voluntariness test. Essentially, Congress attempted to overrule the Warren Court's *Miranda* holding. However, even *Miranda*'s most ardent critics felt that Congress did not have the power to overrule a constitutional interpretation. Therefore, the immediate effect of § 3501 resembled more a congressional reprimand than an actual rule of law; *Miranda* was still intact—for the time being.

As the years passed, the real effect of the *Miranda* rule began to take shape. Studies conducted in the 1960s and 1970s indicated that—contrary to popular belief—*Miranda* had little if any effect on detectives' ability to solve crimes. Further, to aid police compliance, officers were issued *Miranda* cards, which had the infamous rights printed in English on one side and Spanish on the other.

Even so, as the Supreme Court came under the leadership of the decidedly conservative Chief Justice Warren Burger, many began to wonder if *Miranda* would survive. In a series of decisions, the Burger Court began to peck away at the scope of the Warren Court's holding. In fact, in its first ten cases pertaining to *Miranda*'s reach, the Court's opinions suggested an intention to limit *Miranda*'s scope as much as possible. Typically, when a *Miranda* interpretation came before the Burger Court, the subsequent ruling was in favor of admitting the contested evidence.

However, as the 1970s gave way to the 1980s, the Court's position on *Miranda* seemed to be changing. In 1980, the Burger Court handed down *Rhode Island v. Innis,* a decision that expanded the definition of an "interrogation" to include any words or conduct by the police that were reasonably likely to elicit an incriminating response. Regarding this attitudinal shift, Chief Justice Burger commented that "law enforcement practices ha[d] adjusted to [*Miranda's*] strictures" and that he had no intention of overruling it. With that statement, the *Miranda* debate seemed settled.

At the turn of the century, the Supreme Court had become what many claimed to be the polar opposite of its 1960s predecessor. The liberals who had once dominated the Supreme Court were replaced by a number of moderate or conservative Reagan and Bush appointees, including Justices Sandra Day O'Connor, Clarence Thomas, Antonin Scalia, and Chief Justice William Rehnquist. With the rise of the Rehnquist Court came increasing speculation that *Miranda* might be overturned.

In 2000, the Court gave a definitive answer to years of scholastic conjecture. In *Dickerson v. United States,* a man suspected of bank robbery confessed his involvement to FBI agents. However, he had not been given a *Miranda* warning. The District Court of Eastern Virginia granted the defendant's motion to suppress the confession on *Miranda* grounds. The government appealed. In overturning the district court's holding, the Fourth Circuit cited the thirty-year-old congressional law, 18 U.S.C. § 3501, stating that although the FBI agents had not met the *Miranda* test, they did meet the legislative voluntariness standard. The Fourth Circuit further asserted that *Miranda* was a judicial construct and not a constitutional interpretation. Therefore, Congress had the explicit power to overrule it.

The Rehnquist Court was faced with a difficult decision: overrule more than thirty years of precedent or hold a federal law unconstitutional. This was the Court's opportunity to overrule *Miranda,* and the conservatives had the votes to do it. However, in a surprising move, the conservative chief justice headed a majority comprising six of his colleagues. In the opinion, Rehnquist wrote:

> While Congress has ultimate authority to modify or set aside any such rules that are not constitutionally required, it may not supersede this Court's decisions interpreting and applying the Constitution.
>
> Whether or not this Court would agree with *Miranda*'s reasoning and its rule in the first instances, stare decisis weighs heavily against overruling it. Even in constitutional cases, stare decisis carries such persuasive force that the Court has always required a departure from precedent to be supported by some special justification. There is no such justification here. *Miranda* has become embedded in routine police practice to the point where the warnings have become part of our national culture.

Thirty-four years after Earl Warren drafted *Miranda v. Arizona,* the *Miranda* rights had become so intertwined with the American justice system that most Americans assumed that a reading of these rights was constitutionally required.

In short, *Dickerson* not only made the *Miranda* warnings an explicit constitutional right, but it seemed to forever shield the doctrine from congressional action.

And What of Ernesto Miranda?

Ernesto Miranda learned of the Supreme Court's decision while watching television in the Arizona State Prison. Did this mean he was free? Had a panel of nine strangers released the twenty-six-year-old felon from his confinement?

Not exactly. The Warren Court merely ruled that his confession was inadmissible during his trial. Consequently, the Maricopa County District Attorney's Office vowed to retry the case—this time without the confession.

Waiting for his trial, Miranda enjoyed his newfound celebrity. The most popular inmate at Arizona State Prison, he could frequently be seen telling his story, offering advice, and signing autographs.

Miranda's second trial was originally slated for October 24, 1966, just a few months after the Supreme Court decision. But with the consent of both parties, the trial was postponed for four months so that Jane Doe, who had recently been married, could give birth to her first child.

Miranda seemed assured to beat the prosecution this time around. He was represented by the now nationally prominent attorney John Flynn, taking over for Alvin Moore, and the prosecution would be without its most compelling piece of evidence: Miranda's confession. Without the confession, the District Attorney's Office was left with little more than Jane Doe's contradictory statements.

But the state pressed on; the prosecutor this time would be the district attorney himself, Robert Corbin. Just before trial, Corbin crossed paths with a confident John Flynn, who asked, "Why are you doing this? You haven't got a case." District Attorney Corbin knew that Flynn was probably right; nonetheless, he answered, "At least I'll go down fighting."

On the eve of the trial, Corbin received an unexpected visitor: Twila Hoffman, Miranda's former common-law spouse. Following Miranda's arrest in 1963, Twila and Miranda had become estranged. Now, with Miranda expecting his release from prison, he wanted custody of their daughter and had filed a complaint with the local welfare authorities, stating that because Twila had had a child with another man while Miranda was in prison, she was unfit as a mother.

Miranda had always been his own worst enemy. According to the furious woman, only a few days after his arrest for the rape and kidnapping of Jane Doe, Twila had gone to visit Miranda in county jail, where Miranda confessed to her that the charges against him were true. The twenty-nine-year-old woman sat and listened as her partner of two years told her that he had kidnapped and raped an eighteen-year-old girl. Miranda then asked that Twila pay a visit to Jane Doe's family and convey his vow to marry the victim if she dropped the charges against him. Of course, he added, he would go back to Twila later—he just needed to do this to stay out of jail.

Once the trial got under way, it seemed more like an appellate argument than a jury trial. Though the proceedings lasted for nine days, testimony took only one. For the first eight days, John Flynn battled the prosecutor on nearly every piece of evidence; most important, the admissibility of Twila Hoffman's testimony.

Flynn made two arguments. First, he contended that because Twila Hoffman was Miranda's common-law wife, she could not testify against him. Second, Flynn claimed that Miranda's confession to Twila was the "fruit of the poisonous tree"—meaning that if Miranda had not first confessed to the police, he would not have confessed to Twila.

Three years prior to this trial, the Warren Court had ruled that any evidence flowing from an invalid confession was inadmissible at court. However, after considerable research, Judge Lawrence K. Wren ruled against both assertions. Twila would be heard, and her testimony, coupled with Jane Doe's account of the attack, would prove devastating to the defense.

After only an hour and twenty-three minutes of deliberation, the four-man and eight-woman jury once again convicted Miranda of rape and kidnapping. Exactly one year after John Flynn's victorious argument before the U.S. Supreme Court, Ernesto Miranda was sentenced to remain in the Arizona State Prison for twenty to thirty years.

Flynn blamed himself. "I goofed this case," he admitted. "I forgot about the jury. I forgot about the question of guilt or innocence and a proper presentation on that point because I was so wrapped up in getting it dismissed on constitutional questions." Others agreed. In fact, Judge Wren later characterized the trial as a "nine-day game of constitutional chess."

Flynn appealed to the Arizona Court of Appeals, the Arizona Supreme Court, and finally to the U.S. Supreme Court, contending that common-law wives should not be allowed to testify against their husbands. This time, however, Earl Warren and his eight associates were unreceptive to his arguments; the Court refused to hear the case.

With this rejection, *Miranda v. Arizona* finally came to a close. The American criminal justice system would never be the same.

Epilogue

Earl Warren retired as chief justice only three years after the *Miranda* decision, at the age of seventy-nine. Although *Miranda* was the Warren Court's last landmark decision, it effectively propelled the chief justice from celebrity to infamy. Warren finished the 1968 session and handed in his resignation to President Nixon in 1969. Today, Earl Warren is remembered as one of the most influential figures in American legal history. Years after his retirement from the Court, his precedents remain—for the most part—intact. Although they remain controversial, it is difficult to discuss modern American law without an allusion to his name.

As to Miranda, after serving a third of his prison sentence, he was paroled in nine years. Less than two years after his release, Miranda was pulled over for driving on the wrong side of the road with a suspended license. A subsequent search produced amphetamines and a gun.

Prior to his trial, his attorney filed a motion to suppress the evidence, and the court held that the drugs and the gun were found in violation of Miranda's Fourth Amendment rights. Therefore, as a result of the Warren Court's ruling in *Mapp v. Ohio,* the evidence was excluded and the charges were dropped.

Having nearly landed in jail yet again, Miranda could make no more pretenses at starting anew. He did, however, keep a daytime job as an appliance deliveryman, but it was widely rumored that he also sold drugs.

By age thirty-four, Ernesto Arturo Miranda had become the man his juvenile rap sheet predicted. And on a cold desert evening in late January, his penchant for flophouses, booze, and poker brought him to La Amapola, a run-down dive bar in the Deuce section of Phoenix. He had some drinks while playing cards with two Mexicans who were in the country illegally. Soon after, Miranda and the other two players began to fight over a handful of change that sat atop the bar. After the fisticuffs ended and the brawlers withdrew to their respective corners, Miranda went into the bathroom to wash the blood from his hands.

When he returned, one of the men drew a six-inch knife and told the other, "Finish it with this." This would be one battle that Miranda—without the assistance of John Flynn or Earl Warren—would fight on his own. Miranda was stabbed once in the stomach and again in the chest. When the ambulance carrying him to Good Samaritan Hospital pulled into the emergency bay, he was dead.

Miranda's killer fled down a back alley; police caught up to his accomplice. As the arresting officers placed the man in the back of their cruiser, one of them pulled out a small card with words printed in English on one side and Spanish on the other. The officer began to read:

> You have the right to remain silent.
>
> Anything you say can and will be used against you in a court of law.
>
> You have the right to the presence of an attorney to assist you prior to questioning and to be with you during questioning if you so desire.
>
> If you cannot afford an attorney, you have the right to have an attorney appointed for you prior to questioning.
>
> Do you understand these rights?
>
> Will you voluntarily answer my questions?

CHAPTER SIX

The Black Doctor and the White Mob

Clarence Darrow puts racism on trial
and proves the home is *every* American's castle

The poorest man may in his cottage bid defiance to all the forces
of the Crown. It may be frail; its roof may shake; the wind may
blow through it; the storm may enter; the rain may enter; but the
King of England cannot enter—all his force dares not cross the
threshold of the ruined tenement!

—*William Pitt*

These despised blacks did not need to wait until the house was
beaten down above their heads. They didn't need to wait until
every window was broken. They didn't need to wait longer for that
mob to grow more inflamed. There is nothing so dangerous as
ignorance and bigotry when it is unleashed as it was here.

—*Clarence Darrow*

A man's home is his castle; a sanctuary sheltering, protecting, even nur-
turing a man's family, a haven for their privacy, an asylum apart from the
world. From the time English jurist Sir Edward Coke coined the phrase
in the early 1600s, to its first mention in North America in the late 1600s,
the concept of Americans having the right to be left alone in their homes
has been a constant in our culture. However, in 1925 Detroit, that same
home—that castle for a white man—could well have been a death chamber for a black family. In 1925, a black man didn't move his family into a
white neighborhood. In 1925, a black man's home was only his castle if
a white man said it was, unless that black man was named Ossian Sweet
and his lawyer was Clarence Darrow.

America in 1925 was booming; the war to end all wars had been won,
and with victory America had bounded onto the world scene, not only a

military power but an economic powerhouse as well, the coming Wall Street crash four years distant. Yet just beneath the glitz and facade of the Roaring Twenties was the specter of overt racial bigotry.

Not since Reconstruction had so many Americans joined the Ku Klux Klan. Membership in the KKK, revived in 1915, grew to 3 million by the mid-1920s. Its political power ran deep and wide. The Klan helped elect government officials across the country, including governors in Alabama, California, and Oregon.

Some whites justified their support for the Klan by saying they had to hold their ground; black Americans had steadily been moving into urban areas and competing for better homes and jobs. Racial tensions were at an all-time high. Jim Crow segregation laws flourished throughout the country, supported by the U.S. Supreme Court's 1896 decision in *Plessy v. Ferguson,* declaring constitutional the systematic racial segregation memorialized by the infamous phrase *separate but equal.*

Black Americans lived with the constant threat of violence; many black veterans who fought for their country in World War I faced new battles upon their return home. Their homeland struggles ranged from subtle discrimination in the workplace, schools, housing, and services, to the outright violence of lynchings and race riots.

A black man was lynched approximately every four days in America. The police—the criminal justice system itself—did little or nothing to prevent these murders or to bring the killers to justice. Lynchings were so pervasive in the 1920s that the National Association for the Advancement of Colored People (NAACP) made the issue its number one priority. They took out full-page ads in newspapers throughout the country to raise awareness of the black reality that was lynch law.

May 31, 1921, Tulsa, Oklahoma: the worst race riot in American history. It began when a seventeen-year-old white woman accused a nineteen-year-old black man of assaulting her. The black man had stumbled into an elevator where the white woman was an operator. Thinking she was being attacked, the woman started hitting the man with her purse. He restrained her in an attempt to shield himself from more blows. The woman screamed; the man ran. The woman told the police the man had attacked her. She declined to press charges, but the man was arrested anyway.

The headline of the local Tulsa newspaper read: "Nab Negro for Attacking Girl in Elevator." An editorial in the same paper unabashedly called for a lynching. The next evening four hundred white men surrounded the jail. A group of blacks also gathered at the jail, concerned for the youth's safety. But after receiving assurances from the sheriff that the prisoner was safe, the black crowd began to disperse. As they were leaving, the sheriff attempted to disarm one of the men. A shot was fired and all hell broke loose.

By the next day—when martial law was declared throughout the city—thirty-five square blocks of Tulsa lay in burned-out ruins. Nearly eight hundred blacks were victimized by white mobs: killed, raped, robbed, wounded, their homes completely burned to the ground. In the midst of the chaos approximately fifty whites were the victims of mob rule as well. The violence was so widespread that an accurate tally of the dead was impossible. There were persistent rumors of mass graves. More than six thousand blacks were arrested and placed in temporary camps. Twenty black men were indicted by a grand jury. Not a single white person was arrested, let alone prosecuted.

No White Picket Fences for Blacks

Individual states were busy enacting a vast series of discriminatory laws known as Jim Crow, which, among other things, permitted race-based restrictive housing covenants. In 1924, a black man, Samuel A. Browne, bought and attempted to move into a house in a white district in Staten Island, New York. The white residents, in an attempt to "protect" their neighborhood, offered to buy him out. Browne had paid $8,500 for the house; the initial offer from the white neighbors was $9,000. A second offer followed for $9,500, then a third for $10,000. Browne didn't budge. The offers turned to threats. A letter marked "KKK" advised Browne that he would regret moving into the neighborhood. The local police scoffed at the suggestion that the letter came from the KKK—it must be a prank.

Browne, frustrated at the lack of police concern, sought the help of the NAACP, which in turn requested help from the New York Department of Justice, as well as the federal Department of Justice. Browne received the following reply from the federal Department of Justice after a cursory review: "After consideration of the carefully prepared statement of facts submitted with your letter, the Department does not feel that a prosecution could be successfully maintained under the Criminal Code." In the meantime, a frustrated Sam Browne was unable to secure fire insurance at any price because the insurance companies believed the risk to his home was too great. The insurers were right; days later, Browne's home was destroyed by a mob.

Is the Home a Castle?

The "castle doctrine," the principle that a man's home is his castle—an inviolate place of sanctuary—dates back to eighteenth-century English common law. In 1763, William Pitt, Earl of Chatham, expounded upon this fundamental concept in his speech to Parliament regarding searches of the home incident to the enforcement of a tax law. This doctrine survived the journey from England to the American colonies. The significance of the castle doctrine is perhaps best evidenced by its presence in the U.S. Constitution. The castle doctrine is embodied in the Third Amendment's prohibition against the quartering of soldiers and the Fourth Amendment's protection against unreasonable searches and seizures.

The castle doctrine overlaps with the concept of self-defense. The right to protect one's person, members of one's family, and to a lesser extent one's property from harm by an aggressor has long been recognized. In most jurisdictions, when a person who is not the aggressor reasonably believes he or a member of his family is in imminent danger of death or great bodily harm, he may respond with deadly force. Some jurisdictions, however, require that one retreat from the confrontation, if it is safe to do so, before resorting to deadly force.

However, under the castle doctrine, no one is required to retreat from his own home. Your home is your sanctuary; once you are in your home, you have retreated to the wall, so to speak, retreated as far as you must. As U.S. Supreme Court justice Benjamin Cardozo aptly stated, "Flight is for sanctuary and shelter, and shelter, if not sanctuary, is in the home."

In short, as a citizen of the United States of America, under the castle doctrine and the doctrine of self-defense, if you are attacked in your home and you have a reasonable belief that you or your family members are in imminent danger of death or great bodily harm, you are entitled to use deadly force to protect yourself and your family.

While the laws of this country are meant to protect and empower all of its citizens, in 1925 the law and those entrusted with its enforcement and execution were only concerned with protecting and empowering a select group of citizens—white citizens. In 1925, a white man could shoot a black intruder who threatened his safety, his home, his sanctuary, and be absolved of all wrongdoing under the castle doctrine. However, would a black man who shot a white intruder who threatened his safety, his home, his sanctuary, be afforded the same absolution?

An Ugly Scar and the Qualified American Dream

Only seven years old, Ossian Sweet made his way home, walking leisurely along the banks of the Peace River in his hometown of Bartow, Florida. Sweet caught sight of a mob of angry white men marching toward him, with a young, bound black man in tow. The terrified youngster quickly hid behind a large cypress tree along the river's shore, where he remained hidden, silent and still, barely breathing, while the men administered justice under the prevailing law of the South, lynch law.

Under the boy's watchful eyes, the vigilantes methodically prepared a pyre. They set up a barrel, placed kindling around the barrel, and soaked the pile in coal oil to ensure it would quickly ignite. Fred Rochelle, a black man accused of murdering a white woman, was dragged on top of the flammable heap. The husband of the murdered woman stepped forward and had the "honor" of striking the match. Refreshments were served to the crowd as Rochelle begged for mercy. For more than eight minutes the screams of the dying man filled the air.

From his hiding place young Ossian watched as the flames slowly spread up Rochelle's body, swallowing his legs, his torso, his face. When the flames died down, young Sweet remained hidden, watching as members of the mob took souvenirs, pieces of Rochelle's charred remains. The images from that day would haunt the boy, a grotesque awakening to the harsh reality of life and justice in the turn-of-the-century South.

As Sweet grew to manhood, he came to believe that knowledge, discipline, and hard work were the keys to accomplishing one's goals—attaining one's true potential—values instilled by his father, Henry Sweet Sr., during Ossian's middle-class upbringing in the segregated town of Bartow. The town was strictly divided, white families living on the west side, black families on the east side. For the most part, the whites ignored the east side, which allowed the black neighborhood to flourish.

The Sweets' community was made up of teachers, miners, ministers, craftsmen, and woodcutters. Many of those who lived on the east side found work on the west side, where good wages and a steady demand for labor provided stability. The black workers brought their wages home, and soon the east side was booming, with its own hotel, a restaurant, a movie hall, a large church, and an Odd Fellows lodge. The white community's indifference helped lessen the sting of Jim Crow, giving rise to a black middle class, of which the Sweets were prominent members.

Henry Sr. was a proud, fiercely self-reliant man. He supported his wife and three children by working as a woodcutter, one of the few jobs without a white overseer. With only a seventh-grade education, he was determined to provide more for his children. Ossian and his siblings studied the violin and piano and sang in their school choir. Henry Sr. knew that culture and hard work were not enough to give his children the American dream—they needed an education, nothing short of the best. Ossian Sweet would attend the most prominent prep school for black children, Wilberforce Academy, just outside Cincinnati, Ohio.

Sweet had a highly successful six years at Wilberforce. He and seven of his fellow classmates organized a chapter of the fraternity Kappa Alpha Psi, the fourth chapter in the country, but the first on an all-black campus. During his time at Wilberforce he earned not only his high school diploma but a college degree as well. To prepare himself for medical school, Sweet maintained a rigorous schedule, completing 129 hours of physics, 240 hours of chemistry, organic and inorganic, and 180 laboratory hours in biology, plus lectures.

In the early 1900s, Howard University School of Medicine, in Washington, D.C., was the premier facility for training black doctors. An ambitious Ossian Sweet focused all his energies on gaining admittance. In addition to top grades, Howard demanded conversational French or German. Never one to settle for mediocrity, Sweet graduated from Wilberforce not only with outstanding grades but also speaking and reading both French and German and was accepted at Howard.

Sweet worked hard to put himself through college and medical school. He spent his summers in Detroit, where Wilberforce alumni provided him with steady work at various jobs. The money he made during the summer funded his studies the following year. When he graduated from Howard University, Sweet established his home and his medical practice in the city in which he had spent nearly a decade of summers.

His decision to move to Detroit was, like any other he made, deliberate and well thought out. The black community in the North had grown exponentially during the period referred to as the "black exodus" from the South. In Detroit between 1910 and 1926, the black population grew from six thousand to seventy thousand. During this time blacks fled the Jim Crow South in search of a better life in Northern cities. With such a boom in the black population, the city needed black professionals like Dr. Sweet. While in Detroit he met a young teacher named Gladys Atkinson. After a courtship of just under eight months, the couple married.

The newlyweds saved their money, planning a European honeymoon, an exciting adventure that would also allow Sweet to study abroad, observing and practicing the most modern medical techniques in the world. Sweet studied in Vienna, mastering the most innovative surgical procedures at the world-famous Allgemeines Krankenhaus. In France, Sweet deepened his knowledge of gynecology and pediatrics. While in Paris he studied radiology and its effects on cancer in women under the supervision of world-renowned scientist Madame Curie. His European studies brought much prestige to the ambitious young doctor, who eventually returned to the United States, a well-respected and successful gynecologist, with his wife and new baby, Marguerite Iva.

Since their return from Europe, Sweet and his family had been living with Gladys's parents. In early 1925, they began looking to buy a home of their own. Despite the thriving Detroit housing market, it was increasingly difficult for black middle-class professionals to find suitable housing. Many middle-class areas carried restrictive housing covenants promoting racially segregated neighborhoods: whites in the nicer ones, blacks in those less desirable—neighborhoods where the housing often violated health and safety regulations. Some real estate agents purposefully scattered one or two black families throughout the desirable neighborhoods, because black professionals, desperate for decent housing, would pay higher prices than white residents. But no one wanted more than one or two black families together; white residents feared property values would depreciate.

Despite the barriers, Gladys Sweet remained optimistic. She "had in mind only two things, first to find a house that was in itself desirable and, second, to find one that would be within our pocketbook. I wanted a pretty home, and it made no difference to me whether it was in a white neighborhood or a colored neighborhood. Only I couldn't find such a house in the colored neighborhood." Dr. Sweet wanted to please his wife. Yet the memories of racial violence from his childhood, coupled with the stories of Ku Klux Klan activity in nearby neighborhoods, kept him on his guard. He wanted his family to live in comfort but also in safety.

In May of 1925, the Sweets' real estate agent brought them to 2905 Garland Avenue, a two-story, brick-faced house on a corner lot with dormer windows, a front porch, and a three-car garage, in the Waterworks Park area on Detroit's east side. Across the street was a grocery store and an empty lot. Along the other side was a two-story apartment building. Kitty-corner was an elementary school.

The Sweets were impressed with the house, but Dr. Sweet knew he had to be careful. He made sure to ask the important question: Was the Klan active on these streets? He was assured that it was a safe neighborhood. Dismissing suggestions that the family use a white "middle party" to purchase the home, Sweet made his presence known. He openly visited the neighborhood several times, making himself as conspicuous as possible, testing the waters. He sat on the porch and walked the surrounding streets, wanting people to be fully aware that a black family was looking to buy 2905 Garland. After several visits, Sweet was satisfied that the house and location were both safe and suitable for a middle-class black family. Gladys was thrilled.

The first week in June, the couple agreed to the inflated price of

$18,500. They signed a contract and paid a $3,500 nonrefundable down payment. They were set to move in late July or early August.

A few weeks after signing the agreement, Sweet's colleague Dr. Alexander Turner, Detroit's most prominent black physician, moved his family into a new home across town. On moving day, Turner's van was met by more than two hundred angry white neighbors, calling themselves the Tireman Avenue Improvement Association, an association with one purpose: to maintain segregation—keep black families out. The mob began throwing food, garbage, and then bricks at Turner and his family.

The police arrived and made a single arrest, but they made no effort whatsoever to disband the crowd, which was growing into a mob. That evening, two of the mob's leaders barged into Turner's home, placed a gun to his head, slammed a deed on the table, and demanded he sign the house over. Turner complied. The mob threw the family's belongings into a van while Turner hurried his family into a car. As the Turner family drove away, rocks pelted the car, shattering one of the windows— shards of glass cutting Dr. Turner's face.

Spurred on by the success of the Tireman Avenue Improvement Association, the Sweets' own future neighbors—incensed by the Sweets' impending move—formed the Waterworks Park Improvement Association. The leader of the mob responsible for ousting the Turners was the keynote speaker at the newly formed association's first meeting. His message was simple, to the point: he urged them to keep their neighborhood pure—white. The meeting was held across the street from the Sweets' new home and attracted more than six hundred people.

The Sweets were greatly concerned by the news that the Turners had been forced out, and their anxiety only deepened when they heard of the new Improvement Association. But they were also determined. They had already invested a nonrefundable down payment of $3,500. They were not about to walk away—they couldn't afford to walk away. They wanted that house; they had earned that house.

The Mob

Ossian Sweet took great caution in planning the details of their move. He decided to postpone it from August to after Labor Day, optimistically thinking that the racist angst would subside, and hoping that the working families composing the Improvement Association would choose a day's wages over standing around harassing newcomers.

The morning of September 8, 1925, Ossian and Gladys Sweet began moving their belongings into 2509 Garland. The couple left fourteen-month-old baby Iva with Gladys's parents. Concerned there could be trouble, they were joined by Sweet's two brothers, Otis and Henry, as well as a couple of friends. It took two trips in the rented van to move their belongings. By that evening a group, a couple dozen or so, had begun to form across the street. There was no violence, only taunts. The taunts, however, were enough to frighten the Sweets and their guests. Everyone, including the guests, stayed the night, doors bolted, lights out.

The following day seven additional friends arrived to help the Sweets move in the rest of their belongings. As they worked, rocks, accompanied by shouted slurs—"Niggers," "Lynch 'em," and "Get the damn niggers"—started pelting the house. The city of Detroit dispatched four policemen, forcing an uneasy cease-fire.

Late on that second day, as dusk blanketed the neighborhood and Gladys began to prepare dinner, the crowd, now well over one hundred and growing, once again began throwing rocks. The police took no action. The throng, emboldened by their increasing numbers and the apparent indifference of the police, intensified their attacks. Rocks shattered windows; Sweet was cut.

The noise became louder, the mob frenzied; shattering glass, taunting, the mob closed in around the house. The Sweets and their friends checked the doors, turned off lights. Sweet ran upstairs and grabbed a gun, then peered through a bedroom window. A taxi pulled up and Otis Sweet got out, his arrival triggering cries of "Niggers, niggers, get the niggers!" The barrage of rocks increased as Otis ran for the house.

Inside, the men armed themselves. Sweet lay flat on the bed, images of mobs and lynchings filling his mind. What happened next is subject to dispute. The only known facts are these: A shot was fired into the mob and then another and another. The police, spurred to action, moved in, yelling for order. The mob moved back. One of the crowd, Leon Breiner, lay dead, another man lay wounded. The police called for reinforcements. Within the hour over one hundred officers and an armored car were outside the house. The mob was held back across the street. The police entered the Sweet home without resistance. One officer incredulously asked Sweet, "What in hell are you shooting at?"

"They are destroying my home and my life is in imminent danger," he answered.

Several policemen ordered all eleven occupants of the house into the living room, where each was handcuffed. Other officers searched the house and confiscated all of the firearms. The ten men were hustled into the armored car and taken to headquarters, Gladys Sweet driven separately. All eleven were charged with murder.

The Legendary Darrow

A white man was dead, the community was outraged, and the Sweets needed top-notch representation. Black leaders were convinced of the necessity of having a prominent white attorney handle the case. After all, it was white men who would judge the Sweets' actions. The judge and jury (almost guaranteed to be white—the norm in the 1920s) would have much more in common with those who made up the "improvement associations." A white attorney would be more palatable to such an audience. To receive a fair trial, the defense needed to connect with its white audience—understand where they were coming from—and who better to do this than a white attorney, someone they could relate to, someone they would respect, someone they would listen to.

Meanwhile the Sweets hired their own attorneys—Julian Perry, Ossian's close friend and fraternity brother, and two of his colleagues, three successful black attorneys. It took some serious talking to persuade the Sweets and their newly hired counsel that a white attorney was essential for a favorable verdict. The Sweets eventually agreed to let the NAACP set up the defense. The NAACP instructed their representative, Walter White, to find the right lawyer. Initially White wanted someone whom the local community would recognize; however, he had a far more difficult time than anticipated. Most of the candidates he approached, prominent Detroit attorneys, wanted no part of such a controversial case. The NAACP needed someone who would not shy away from controversy, someone up to the challenge—they wired Clarence Darrow in Chicago.

The legendary lawyer was exhausted. He had just completed his defense of John T. Scopes, who had been prosecuted for teaching evolution to his students in a Tennessee public school. Darrow was thinking of retirement—of writing, reading, and even travel. While he was renowned as dedicated to the pursuit of social justice regardless of the surrounding controversy or negative public opinion, Darrow had never tried a major case involving racial conflict. The NAACP had to work hard to convince Darrow to climb aboard. Finally, Darrow agreed to meet with Walter White to discuss the case. After eleven hours of intense discussion, Darrow asked White one final question: "Did the defendants shoot into that mob?"

Caught off guard and unsure of the appropriate response, White replied, "I am not sure."

The seasoned litigator was not one to accept an equivocal response: "Don't try to hedge, I know you were not there. But do you believe the defendants fired?"

"I believe they did fire."

"Then I'll take the case. If they had not the courage to shoot back in defense of their own lives, I wouldn't think they were worth defending."

And so Clarence Darrow, arguably the greatest trial lawyer in American history, agreed to defend the family and friends of Dr. Ossian Sweet.

Darrow's colleague Arthur Garfield Hays would assist in the defense, as he had in the recent Scopes trial. Julian Perry, the attorney previously hired by the Sweets, and his two associates agreed to stay on the case and work under Darrow as well.

Darrow was deeply committed to civil rights—he was a founding member of the NAACP. Commentating on race relations, Darrow wrote, "If the Negro is a man, then all people, high and low alike, should demand for him all the privileges and rights of every other citizen; should judge him for what he is, and not on the color of his skin." On another occasion he said, "Ever since I can remember, I have been possessed of the feeling of injustice that has been visited upon the Negro race—assuming you are a race. All races and colors are mixed with us, and why you are classified is because you are persons of chance. I have always thought the same ever since I have had any intellect or feeling on the subject."

At the time he was approached by the NAACP regarding the Sweet trial, Darrow was worn-out from more than forty years in the trenches, fighting and winning some of the most celebrated cases of his era, including his brilliant defense of Leopold and Loeb just a year before, and the just-completed Scopes "monkey" trial. The Scopes trial began when a teacher was arrested because he insisted on teaching the theory of evolution as part of his curriculum, in violation of Tennessee's antievolution law. The prosecution brought in William Jennings Bryan, a former U.S. secretary of state (and a fervent evangelist), who was responsible for drafting the antievolution law, as special counsel, anticipating that a star like Bryan could counter the skill and celebrity of Darrow.

After eight days of an extremely contentious trial, John T. Scopes was found guilty and fined $100. On appeal by the defense, the Tennessee Supreme Court reversed the lower court's decision and the case was eventually dismissed.

At the age of sixty-eight, Darrow needed time away from the intense pressure of the courtroom. Unpopular as unions were at the onset of the twentieth century, Darrow was one of the few lawyers who would represent union leaders and go head-to-head with large corporations. He unsuccessfully defended the head of the American Railway Union, Eugene V. Debs, who had been charged with contempt of federal court during the Pullman strike. His representation of the United Mine Workers Union before President Theodore Roosevelt's Anthracite Miner Commission during the Pennsylvania coal strike of 1902 brought to light the awful working conditions in the mines and resulted in a settlement that provided the workers with a 10 percent raise and several million dollars in back pay and established an eight-hour workday.

Darrow defended antiwar protesters charged with violating the antisedition laws following World War I. In 1924, he defended Nathan Leopold and Richard Loeb, two cold-blooded killers, offering perhaps the most compelling argument against the death penalty ever made in an American courtroom.

Almost as famous as—and more distinctive than—Darrow's oratorical skill was his disheveled look. Oversize suits, rumpled shirts, and haphazard hair were all components of Darrow's signature "style." Although he was wealthy, he dressed, much to his well-to-do wife's dismay, as one of the people. Darrow was, to his listeners, just the guy next door, and that allowed him to connect with his listeners in a way more meaningful than dollars or designer apparel ever could. Against the death penalty, against prejudice, against privilege, and for justice—Darrow was without a doubt the preeminent American lion in the courtroom Coliseum for the first two generations of lawyers of the twentieth century.

The Trial

As the trial approached, one prominent civil rights leader recalled that "a kind of hysteria swept over the city. The law-and-order leaders and organizations demanded that these Negroes be made an example." No judge wanted to try the case, except thirty-five-year-old Frank Murphy, who had been elected only two years earlier. For Murphy it was the first step of a remarkable career that would see him become the governor of Michigan, governor-general of the Philippines, U.S. attorney general, and eventually a U.S. Supreme Court justice. In one noteworthy decision while on the Supreme Court, he dissented from an opinion that upheld the internment of thousands of Japanese-Americans during World War II. At the conclusion of the Sweet trial, Murphy said of it, "This was the greatest experience of my life. This was Clarence Darrow at his best. I will never see anything like it again. He is the most Christlike man I have ever known."

The trial began on Friday, October 30, 1925. All ten of the men, as well as Gladys Sweet, were tried at the same time, and all except Gladys Sweet were denied bail before and during the trial. Though the trial did not receive an inordinate amount of national press coverage (the *New*

York Times printed only three articles on the case), it did receive a great deal of attention in the black press, and within the city of Detroit. The hometown newspapers covered the entire trial, and the local courthouse was not large enough to hold the hundreds of would-be spectators.

The state of Michigan was represented by prosecutors Robert M. Toms, Lester S. Moll, and Edward J. Kennedy. Toms was a respectful and polite trial attorney, never allowing Darrow to provoke him to anger. Toms described his approach to observers: "I was quite aware of Mr. Darrow's capacity for invective, and I did not propose to lay myself open by matching barbs with him. Accordingly I treated him throughout the trial with utmost reverence and deference."

After years of contentious courtroom battles around the country, Darrow was caught off guard by Toms's courteous, almost passive demeanor. A week into the trial Darrow vented his frustrations: "God damn it, Toms, I can't get going. I am supposed to be mad at you and I can't even pretend that I am." Darrow maintained throughout the trial that Toms's congenial demeanor was "purely strategic and that it was working a great hardship on him."

The prosecution maintained throughout the trial that there had been no mob outside the Sweet home, but rather just a few people milling around in the course of their daily activities. The prosecution further maintained that these harmless individuals posed no threat, and certainly no threat great enough to justify shooting. They went so far as to accuse the defendants of involvement in a deliberate conspiracy to kill their white neighbors. The prosecutors attempted to convince the all-white jury that race had absolutely nothing to do with the case: "Back of all your sophistry and transparent political philosophy, gentlemen of the defense; back of all your prating of civil rights, back of your psychology and theory of race hatred, lies the stark body of Leon Breiner [the man who had been shot] with a bullet hole in his back."

The prosecution's case, however, had two significant problems. First, they had no way of proving which one of the men inside the Sweet home had actually fired the shot that had killed Leon Breiner. And perhaps of even greater import, the prosecution, who insisted that only a few individuals (certainly not a mob) were outside the home, produced *sixty-four* eyewitnesses to the shooting. All sixty-four were, of course, white, and all sixty-four maintained that curiosity, not harassment, was the explanation for their presence.

On cross-examination, Darrow was able to distill the truth about the number of people milling around the Sweets' home. When Darrow questioned local resident Florence Ware as to her husband's whereabouts during the shooting, she slipped and answered that he went to see "the crowd of people—police on our corners."

> **DARROW:** Now, you first said "crowd of people," and you changed.
> **WARE:** I meant *policemen.*
> **DARROW:** You didn't mean *people?*
> **WARE:** No, sir.

Darrow encountered a similar response while questioning seventeen-year-old Dwight Hubbard.

> **DARROW:** When you first started to answer the question as to what you saw, you started to say a "great crowd" there, didn't you?
> **HUBBARD:** Yes, sir.
> **DARROW:** Then you modified to say a "large crowd," didn't you?
> **HUBBARD:** Yes, sir.
> **DARROW:** Then you said a "few people" after that?
> **HUBBARD:** Yes, sir.
> **DARROW:** Do you know how you happened to change your mind so quick?
> **HUBBARD:** No, sir.
> **DARROW:** Any officers talk with you about it?
> **HUBBARD:** No, sir.
> **DARROW:** What?
> **HUBBARD:** Lieutenant Johnson, if you consider him an officer.
> **DARROW:** When is the last time he talked with you about it?
> **HUBBARD:** I think it was yesterday morning.
> **DARROW:** When you started to answer the question, you forgot to say a "few people," instead of a "great many"?
> **HUBBARD:** Yes, sir.

In addition to casting doubt upon the prosecution's claim regarding the number of "curiosity seekers" present outside the Sweet home, Darrow set out to reveal the racial animus permeating the neighborhood, if not the city. As he continued to probe, it became painfully obvious that residents in the Sweets' new neighborhood had formed the Waterworks Park Improvement Association solely for the purpose of keeping black families out. For these white residents the key to improving their neighborhood was to band together and maintain racial purity. During the cross-examination of Eber A. Draper, one of the Sweets' white neighbors, Darrow asked, "Do you belong to the Waterworks Improvement Association?"

DRAPER: Yes, sir.

DARROW: When did you join?

DRAPER: I don't know. When it first started.

DARROW: When did it start?

DRAPER: I don't know.

DARROW: Well, now, don't you think you could tell us if you tried?

DRAPER: No, I don't think I could.

DARROW: Well, about when did you join it?

DRAPER: It must have been back in the middle of the summer.

DARROW: The middle of last summer?

DRAPER: Something like that.

DARROW: When did you hear Dr. Sweet was going to move into that neighborhood?

DRAPER: That was a long time ago, too.

DARROW: You joined the club at the time you heard it, didn't you?

DRAPER: No.

DARROW: You don't know whether you joined the club at the time you heard it or not?

DRAPER: No.

DARROW: Well, you think it was after you heard it that you joined the club?

DRAPER: I think it was.

DARROW: Did that have anything to do with your joining the club?

DRAPER: It possibly did.

DARROW: Oh, tell us now, don't you know? Is there any reason why you should not tell us if you know?

DRAPER: No.

DARROW: Well, did it?

DRAPER: Yes.

DARROW: And you joined the club so as to do what you could—I am not saying you did right or wrong—but to do what you could do to keeping that a white district?

DRAPER: Yes.

Racism was so prevalent during the 1920s that the witnesses felt no need to be circumspect about their desire to keep black residents out of their neighborhoods. Another property owner, William Goad, also admitted his reason for joining the association.

DARROW: You are a member of that association?

GOAD: Yes, sir.

DARROW: And you joined it with the idea that it might help keep colored people out of the district, didn't you?

GOAD: I joined for the good of the neighborhood.

Darrow also attacked the prosecution's claim that the people who had gathered about the Sweet home were simple curiosity seekers. During the cross-examination of thirteen-year-old Urlic Arthur, he asked, "Did you see anybody throw stones?"

ARTHUR: Well, there was four or five kids between the houses, they were throwing stones.

DARROW: Where were they throwing them?

ARTHUR: They were throwing them at the house where the colored people moved in.

Once Darrow felt he had sufficiently established that a mob was surrounding the Sweet home and that the mob was racially motivated, he directed the jury's attention to the big question: Did the Sweets have the right to shoot into the crowd to defend themselves? During the examination of Alfred H. Andrew, one of the Sweets' neighbors and a member of the Association, Darrow asked about a speech made at one of the Waterworks Park Improvement Association meetings. The speaker was one of the proud founders of the Tireman Avenue Improvement Association, the group responsible for driving out Dr. Turner's family.

DARROW: Did he [the Tireman Avenue speaker] tell you about any race-riot trouble they had in his neighborhood?

ANDREW: Yes, he told us about a Negro named Dr. Turner, who had bought a house on Spokane Avenue.

DARROW: Did he say his organization made Turner leave?

ANDREW: Yes, he said that they wouldn't have Negroes in their neighborhood and that they would cooperate with us in keeping them out of ours.

DARROW: Did the crowd applaud him?

ANDREW: Yes.

DARROW: Did you applaud?

ANDREW: Yes.

DARROW: You feel that way now?

ANDREW: Yes, I haven't changed.

DARROW: You know a colored man has certain rights?

ANDREW: Yes, I was in favor of keeping the Sweets out by legal means.

DARROW: Did the speaker talk of legal means?

ANDREW: No, he was a radical. I myself do not believe in violence.

DARROW: Did anybody in that audience of five hundred or more people protest against the speaker's advocacy of violence?

ANDREW: I don't know.

It was then the defense's opportunity to put on their case. Darrow first called an auto shop owner who worked nearby, and a woman who lived near the Sweet house; both testified that there had been at least five hundred people outside the home. Phillip Adler, a newsman, then testified, "I saw a considerable mob near the schoolhouse." After the prosecution objected to the use of the word *mob*, Adler qualified, "Well, I first noticed it as I slowed down. My estimate as I drove up was that there were between four hundred and five hundred persons. The street was somewhat congested with cars. I noticed a lot of people around Garland and Charlevoix, and I wanted to drive out on Garland, but the traffic officer made me go straight ahead."

With all the groundwork laid, Darrow called Dr. Ossian Sweet. Darrow first had Sweet describe the blatant racial prejudice he and his family had faced upon moving into their new home:

When my wife and I arrived home on the afternoon of September ninth, she received a telephone call. It was from a girl acquaintance who had been at our house all of the night before and who said she had heard a conversation on a streetcar and that we ought to know about it. She told of a white woman who told the motorman of the streetcar that the crowd around my house the night before was there because a colored family had moved in. She said we wouldn't be there after that night.

Darrow then moved Sweet to the night in question.

Something hit the house. Someone went to the window and looked out. Then I remember this remark: "The people, the people—we've got to get out of here; something's going to happen pretty soon."

I ran out to the kitchen to where my wife was. Everybody left what they were doing, and some of the fellows went upstairs. I went to see if the side door was locked. It was unlocked. I opened it. I could see people but they couldn't see me. Then I heard someone say, "Go to the front and raise hell, I'm going to the back."

I went to the closet and got a gun. I lay across the bed. Stones kept coming against the house. The intervals become shorter. After fifteen to twenty minutes a stone crashed through the glass and some of it hit me. I made a dozen trips up and down the stairs. It was a general uproar. Then I heard someone say, "Someone is coming. Don't open the door." I went to the door myself. It was my brother Otis, and William Davis. I heard someone in the mob say, "They're niggers, get them."

Just as they ran in, the mob gave a surge ten or fifteen feet forward. It looked like a human sea. Davis said, "What shall we do? What shall we do? I . . . " The stones were getting thicker and coming faster. Then I heard glass breaking upstairs. Almost immediately I heard one shot. Then there were eight or ten more in rapid succession. By this time it seemed to me stones were hitting the house on all sides, mostly the roof.

Somebody knocked at the door. It was Inspector Norton Schuknecht. "What in hell are you shooting at?" he asked. I said, "They are destroying my home and my life is in imminent danger." Then I took him up to the room where the window was broken. He dropped his head and said, "I didn't know they were throwing stones and breaking your house. I will drive them away and there will be no more stones thrown." Shortly after that more police officers came. They raised the blinds, turned on the lights, and handcuffed us in clear view of the mob.

To help the jury better understand the Sweets' state of mind as they were surrounded by the mob, Darrow asked Dr. Sweet to describe his thoughts at the time of the shooting:

When I opened the door and saw that mob, I realized in a way that I was facing the same mob that had hounded my people through its entire history. I realized my back was against the wall, and I was filled with a peculiar type of fear—the fear of one who knows the history of my race.

One striking aspect of the trial was the distinct difference in the witnesses called by each side. The prosecution witnesses were for the most part blue-collar, working-class residents with little or no education, often laboring with their words. The witnesses for the defense, on the other hand, held multiple degrees—doctors, dentists, teachers, lawyers, and clergymen, all highly articulate.

It was the Tuesday before Thanksgiving when the testimony was completed. Weeks and mountains of testimony—so convoluted at times the observation was made that "much of the testimony ran together like the foamy backwash of the waves returning to sea." The closing arguments extended late into Wednesday evening. In their two-and-a-half-hour summation, prosecutors Toms and Moll once again pounded home their main themes: conspiracy, murder, deliberation. They openly scoffed at the notion that the defendants were motivated by fear. Several conspicuous jabs were thrust in the direction of Darrow, characterizing his charming demeanor and down-home talk as nothing more than shadows and smoke screens attempting to cover sinister deeds. Darrow, his timing impeccable, interjected witty quips during the prosecution's closing, drawing laughter from the audience and frustrating his opponents.

Then it was Darrow's turn. He stood before the jury—hands shoved deep in his pockets, hair mussed, shoulders hunched. In his signature conversational style he leaned in and whispered to the jury, as he would to a longtime friend, "My clients are here charged with murder, but they are really here because they are black."

Darrow would speak for a great deal longer than two and a half hours. He described the scene outside the Sweets' home on the night of September 9 as it really was—terrifying. He talked of the castle doctrine and of self-defense—rights that should be basic to any American, white or black. Darrow was careful not to offend or alienate his white listeners. He masterfully portrayed racial prejudice as a social problem, not an individual problem—a problem they all needed to work together to fix and a problem for which no one was individually to blame. Word by carefully crafted word, he called upon each juror to fight the good fight—to stand up for justice.

Judge Murphy instructed the jury on the applicable law, paying special attention to the castle doctrine and self-defense. The jury left to deliberate mere hours before Thanksgiving Day. The process proved difficult; deliberations continued through Thanksgiving Day and into Friday. After forty-six hours it became apparent that the deadlock was unbreakable—the jurors were at an impasse. Judge Murphy had no choice but to declare a mistrial. A hung jury neither absolved nor condemned anyone—it was the most ambiguous of outcomes.

While at first the result seemed cause for celebration—after all, the Sweets had not been found guilty—the state was far from finished. Chief prosecutor Toms announced that there would be as many trials as necessary to "balance the scales of justice." This time around Toms intended to try each defendant separately, beginning with Henry Sweet Jr., Ossian's younger brother, the only defendant who admitted to firing a gun.

It was several months later, April of 1926, when the trial against Henry Sweet Jr. began, Clarence Darrow present once again for the defense. A jury was quickly impaneled, and in many ways this trial was, in terms of evidence and testimony, identical to the first. The only notable difference was Darrow's closing argument. It is widely agreed that this second closing argument was Darrow at his finest: his passion, his charisma, his skill, his conversational dialogue with the jury—all of those characteristics that attorneys across the nation have been attempting to emulate for decades can be found artfully woven into the fabric of the following plea made on behalf of not only a young man but an entire race.

CLARENCE DARROW'S CLOSING ARGUMENT ON BEHALF OF HENRY SWEET

My friend Mr. Moll [one of the prosecutors] says that this isn't a race question. This is a murder case. Race and color have nothing to do with this case. This is a case of murder.

I insist that there is nothing but prejudice in this case; that if it was reversed and eleven white men had shot and killed a black while protecting their home and their lives against a mob of blacks, nobody would have dreamed of having them indicted. I know what I am talking about, and so do you. They would have been given medals instead. Ten colored men and one woman are in this indictment, tried by twelve jurors, gentlemen. Every one of you are white, aren't you? We haven't one colored man on this jury. We couldn't get one. One was called and he was disqualified.

Now, let me ask you whether you are not prejudiced. I want to put this square to you, gentlemen. I haven't any doubt but that every one of you is prejudiced against colored people. I want you to guard against it. I want you to do all you can to be fair in this case, and I believe you will.

A number of you have answered the question that you are acquainted with colored people. One juror I have in mind, who is sitting here, said there were two or three families living on the street in the block where he lives, and he had lived there for a year or more, but he didn't know their names and had never met them.

Some of the rest of you said that you had employed colored people to work for you, are even employing them now. All right. You have seen some colored people in this case. They have been so far above the white people that live at the corner of Garland and Charlevoix that they can't be compared, intellectually, morally, and physically, and you know it.

How many of you jurors, gentlemen, have ever had a colored person visit you in your home? How many of you have ever visited in their homes? How many of you have invited them to dinner at your house? Probably not one of you. Now, why, gentlemen? There isn't one of you men who doesn't know just from the witnesses you have seen in this case that there are colored people who are intellectually the equal of all of you.

Am I right? Colored people living right here in the city of Detroit are intellectually the equals and some of them superior to most of us? Is that true? Some of them are people of more character and learning than most of us.

Now, why don't you individually, and why don't I, and why doesn't every white person whose chances have been greater and whose wealth is larger, associate with them? There is only one reason, and that is prejudice. Can you give any other reason for it?

They would be intellectual companions. They have good manners. They are clean. They are all of them clean enough to wait on us, but not clean enough to associate with. Is there any reason in the world why we don't associate with them excepting prejudice? I think not one man of this jury wants to be prejudiced. It is forced into us almost from our youth, until somehow or other we feel we are superior to these people who have black faces.

Who are we, anyway? A child is born into this world without any knowledge of any sort. He has a brain which is a piece of putty; he inherits nothing in the way of knowledge or of ideas. If he is white, he knows nothing about color. He has no antipathy to the black. The black and the white both will live together and play together, but as soon as the baby is born, we begin giving him ideas. We begin planting seeds in his mind. We begin telling him he must do this and he must not do that. We tell him about race and social equality and the thousands of things that men talk about until he grows up. It has been trained into us, and you, gentlemen, bring that feeling into this jury box.

You need not tell me you are not prejudiced. I know better. We are not very much but a bundle of prejudices anyhow. We are prejudiced against other people's color. Prejudiced against other men's religions; prejudiced against other people's politics. Prejudiced against people's looks. Prejudiced about the way we dress. We are full of prejudices.

You can teach a man anything beginning with the child; you can make anything out of him, and we are not responsible for it. Here and there some of us haven't any prejudices on some questions, but if you look deep enough, you will find them; and we all know it.

All I hope for, gentlemen of the jury, is this: that you are strong enough, and honest enough, and decent enough, to lay it aside in this case and decide it as you ought to. And I say, there is no man in Detroit that doesn't know that these defendants, every one of them, did right. There isn't a man in Detroit who doesn't know that the defendant did his duty, and that this case is an attempt to send him and his companions to prison because they defended their constitutional rights. It is a wicked attempt, and you are asked to be a party to it.

Now, let's see. I don't want to lean very much on your intelligence. I don't need much. I just need a little. Would this case be in this court if these defendants were not black? Would we be standing in front of you if these defendants were not black? Would anybody be asking you to send a boy to prison for life for defending his brother's home and protecting his own life, if his face wasn't black?

What were the people in the neighborhood of Charlevoix and Garland Streets doing on that fatal night? There isn't a child that doesn't know. Have you any doubt as to why they were there? Was Mr. Moll right when he said that color has nothing to do with the case? There is nothing else in this case but the feeling of prejudice which has been carefully nourished by the white man until he doesn't know that he has it himself.

While I admire and like my friend Moll very much, I can't help criticizing his argument. I suppose I may say what old men are apt to say, in a sort of patronizing way, that his zeal is due to youth and inexperience. That is about all we have to brag about as we get older, so we ought to be permitted to do that. Let us look at this case.

Mr. Moll took particular pains to say to you, gentlemen, that these eleven people here are guilty of murder; he calls this a cold-blooded, deliberate, and premeditated murder; that is, they were there to kill. That was their purpose. Eleven, he said. I am not going to discuss the case of all of them just now, but I am starting where he started. He doesn't want any misunderstanding. Amongst that eleven is Mrs. Sweet, the wife of Dr. Sweet. She is a murderer, gentlemen? The state's attorney said so, and the assistant state's attorney said so.

Pray, tell me what has Mrs. Sweet done to make her a murderer? She is the wife of Dr. Sweet. She is the mother of his little baby. She left the child at her mother's home while she moved into this highly cultured community near Goethe Street. Anyway, the baby was to be safe; but she took her own chance, and she didn't have a gun; none was provided for her.

Brother Toms drew from the witnesses that there were ten guns and ten men. He didn't leave any for her. What did she do, gentlemen? She is put down here as a murderer. She wasn't even upstairs. She didn't even look out of a window. She was down in the back kitchen cooking a ham to feed her family and friends, and a white mob came to drive them out of their home before the ham was served for dinner. She is a murderer, and all of these defendants who were driven out of their home must go to the penitentiary for life if you can find twelve jurors somewhere who have enough prejudice in their hearts, and hatred in their minds.

Now, that is this case, gentlemen, and that is all there is to this case. Take the hatred away, and you have nothing left.

Mr. Moll says that this is a case between Breiner [the man who was killed] and Henry Sweet. He is wrong. The question here is whether these defendants or this defendant is guilty of murder. It has nothing to do with Breiner.

He says that I wiggled and squirmed every time they mentioned Breiner. Well, now, I don't know. Did I? Maybe I did. I didn't know it. I have been around courtrooms so long that I fancy I could listen to anything without moving a hair. Maybe I couldn't.

I rather think my friend is pretty wise. He said that I don't like to hear them talk about Breiner. I don't, gentlemen, and I might have shown it. This isn't the first case I was ever in. I don't like to hear the state's attorney talk about the blood of a victim. It has such a messy sound. I wish they would leave it out. I will be frank with you about it. I don't think it has any place in a case. I think it tends to create prejudice and feeling and it has no place, and it is always dangerous. And perhaps—whether I showed it or not—my friend read my mind. I don't like it.

Now, gentlemen, as he talked about Breiner, I am going to talk about him, and it isn't easy, either. It isn't easy to talk about the dead, unless you "slobber" over them, and I am not going to "slobber" over Breiner. I am going to tell you the truth about it.

Why did he ask you to judge between Breiner and Henry Sweet? You know why he said it. To get a verdict, gentlemen. That is why he said it. Had it any place in this case? Henry Sweet never knew that such a man lived as Breiner. Did he? He didn't shoot at him. Somebody shot into that crowd and Breiner got it. Nobody had any feeling against him.

But who was Breiner, anyway? He was a conspirator in as foul a conspiracy as was ever hatched in a community; in a conspiracy to drive from their homes a little family of black people. Not only that, but to destroy these blacks and their home.

Now, let me see whether I am right. What do we know of Breiner? He lived two blocks from the Sweet home. On the fourteenth day of July, seven hundred people met at the schoolhouse and the schoolhouse was too small, and they went out into the yard. This schoolhouse was right across the street from the Sweet house. Every man in that community knew all about it. Every man in that community understood it. And in that schoolhouse a man rose and told what they had done in his community; that by main force they had driven Negro families from their homes, and that when a Negro moved to Garland Street, their people would be present to help.

That is why Mr. Breiner came early to the circus on September ninth, 1925. He went past that house, back and forth, two or three times that night. What was he doing? "Smoking his pipe." What were the rest of them doing? They were a part of a mob and they had no rights, and the court will tell you so, I think. And, if he does, gentlemen, it is your duty to accept it.

Gentlemen, it is a reflection upon anybody's intelligence to say that everyone did not know why this mob was there. You know! Every one of you know why. They came early to take their seats at the ringside. Didn't they? And Breiner sat at one point where the stones were thrown, didn't he? Was he a member of that mob? Gentlemen, that mob was bent not only on making an assault upon the rights of the owners of that house, not only making an assault upon their persons and their property, but they were making an assault on the Constitution and the laws of the nation and the state under which they live.

It was bad enough for a mob, by force and violation of law, to attempt to drive these people from their house, but, gentlemen, it is worse to send them to prison for life for defending their home. Think of it. That is this case. Are we human?

Did the witnesses for the state appearing here tell the truth? You know they did not. I am not going to analyze the testimony of every one of them. But they did not tell the truth and they did not mean to tell the truth.

Let me ask you this question, gentlemen: Mr. Moll says that these colored people had a perfect right to live in that house. He did not say it was an outrage to molest them. Oh, no, he said they had a perfect right to live in that house. But the mob met there to drive them out. That is exactly what they did, and they have lied and lied and lied to send these defendants to the penitentiary for life, so that they will not go back to their home.

Now, you know that the mob met there for that purpose. They violated the Constitution and the law; they violated every human feeling and threw justice and mercy and humanity to the winds, and they made a murderous attack upon their neighbor because his face was black. Which is the worse, to do that or lie about it?

In describing this mob, I heard the word "few" from the state's witnesses so many times that I could hear it in my sleep, and I presume that when I am dying, I will hear that "few," "few," "few" stuff that I heard in Detroit from people who lied and lied and lied. What was this "few"? And who were they, and how did they come there?

I can't tell you about every one of these witnesses, but I can tell you about some of them. Too many. I can't even carry all of their names in my mind and I don't want to. Anything is more interesting to carry in your mind than the names of that bunch, and yet I am going to say something for them, too, because I know something about human nature and life; and I want to be fair, and if I did not want to, I think perhaps it would pay me to be.

Are the people who live around the corner of Charlevoix and Garland worse than other people? There isn't one of you who doesn't know that they lied. There isn't one of you who does not know that they tried to drive those people out and now are trying to send them to the penitentiary so that they can't move back—all in violation of the law—and are trying to get you to do the job. Are they worse than other people? I don't know as they are.

How much do you know about prejudice? Race prejudice. Religious prejudice. These feelings that have divided men and caused them to do the most terrible things.

Prejudices have burned men at the stake, broken them on the rack, torn every joint apart, destroyed people by the million. Men have done this on account of some terrible prejudice which even now is reaching out to undermine this republic of ours and to destroy the freedom that has been the most cherished part of our institutions.

These witnesses honestly believe that they are better than blacks. They honestly believe that it is their duty to keep colored people out. They honestly believe that blacks are an inferior race, and yet if they look at themselves, I don't know how they can.

Gentlemen, lawyers are very intemperate in their statements. My friend Moll said that my client here was a coward. A coward, gentlemen. Here, he says, were a gang of gunmen, and cowards—shot Breiner through the back. Nobody saw Breiner, of course. If he had his face turned toward the house, while he was smoking there, waiting for the shooting to begin, it wasn't our fault. It wouldn't make any difference which way he turned. I suppose the bullet would have killed him just the same, if he had been in the way of it. If he had been at home, it would not have happened.

Who are the cowards in this case? Cowards, gentlemen! Eleven people with black skins, eleven people, gentlemen, whose ancestors did not come to America because they wanted to, but were brought here in slave ships, to toil for nothing, for the whites—whose lives have been taken in nearly every state in the Union—they have been victims of riots all over this land of the free. They have had to take what is left after everybody else had grabbed what he wanted. The only place where he has been put in front is on the battlefield. When we are fighting, we give him a chance to die, and the best chance. But, everywhere else, he has been food for the flames, and the ropes, and the knives, and the guns, and the hate of the white, regardless of law and liberty, and the common sentiments of justice that should move men.

Were they cowards?

No, gentlemen, they may have been gunmen. They may have tried to murder. But they were not cowards. Eleven people, knowing what it meant, with the history of the race behind them, with the knowledge of shootings and killings and insult and injury without end, eleven of them go into a house, gentlemen, with no police protection, in the face of a mob, and the hatred of a community, and take guns and ammunition and fight for their rights, and for your rights and for mine, and for the rights of every being that lives. They went in and faced a mob seeking to tear them to bits. Call them something besides cowards. The cowardly curs were in the mob gathered there with the backing of the law.

All right, gentlemen, call them something else. These blacks have been called many names along down through the ages, but there have been those through the sad years who believed in justice and mercy and charity and love and kindliness, and there have been those who believed that a black man should have some rights, even in a country where he was brought in chains.

There are those even crazy enough to hope and to dream that sometime he will come from under this cloud and take his place amongst the people of the world. If he does, it will be through his courage and his culture. It will be by his intelligence and his scholarship and his effort, and I say, gentlemen of the jury, no honest, right-feeling man, whether on a jury or anywhere else, would place anything in his way in this great struggle behind him and before him.

What are you, gentlemen? And what am I? I don't know. I can only go a little way toward the source of my own being. I know my father and know my mother. I know my grandmothers and my grandfathers on both sides, but I didn't know my great-grandfathers and great-grandmothers on either side, and I don't know who they were.

All that a man can do in this direction is but little. He can only slightly raise the veil that hangs over all the past. He can peer into the darkness just a little way and that is all. I know that somewhere around 1600, as the record goes, some of my ancestors came from England. Some of them. I don't know where all of them came from, and I don't think any human being knows where all his ancestors came from. But back of that, I can say nothing.

What do you know of yours? I will tell you what I know, or what I think I know, gentlemen. I will try to speak as modestly as I can, knowing the uncertainty of human knowledge, because it is uncertain. The best I can do is to go a little way back. I know that back of us all and each of us is the blood of all the world. I know that it courses in your veins and mine. It has all come out of the infinite past, and I can't pick out mine and you can't pick out yours, and it is only the ignorant who know, and I believe that back of that is what we call the lower order of life; back of that there lurks the instinct of the distant serpent, of the carnivorous tiger. All the elements have been gathered together to make the mixture that is you and I and all the race, and nobody knows anything about his own.

Gentlemen, I wonder who we are anyhow, to be so proud about our ancestry? We had better try to do something to be proud of ourselves; we had better try to do something kindly, something humane, to some human being, than to brag about our ancestry, of which none of us know anything.

Now, let us go back to the street again. The police department went up there on the morning of the eighth, to see that a family were permitted to move into a home that they owned without getting their throats cut by the noble Nordics who inhabit that jungle.

Fine, isn't it? No race question in this? Oh, no, this is a murder case, and yet, in the forenoon of the eighth, they sent four police-men there, to protect a man and his wife, with two little truckloads of household furniture, who were moving into that place. Pretty tough, isn't it? Aren't you glad you are not black? You deserve a lot of credit for it, don't you, because you didn't choose black ancestry? People ought to be killed who chose black ancestry. The policemen went there to protect the lives and the small belongings of these humble folks who moved into their home. What are these black people to do?

Suppose you were colored. Did any of you ever dream that you were colored? Did you ever wake up out of a nightmare when you dreamed that you were colored? Would you be willing to have my client's skin?

Imagine yourselves colored, gentlemen. Imagine yourselves back in the Sweet house on that fatal night. That is the only right way to treat this case, and the court will tell you so. Would you move there? Where would you move?

There were six or seven thousand colored people here sixteen years ago. And seventy-one thousand five years ago. Gentlemen, why are they here? They came here as you came here, under the laws of trade and business, under the instincts to live; both the white and the colored, just the same; the instincts of all animals to propa-gate their kind, the feelings back of life and on which life depends.

They came here to live. Your factories were open for them. Mr. Ford hired them. The automobile companies hired them. Every-body hired them. They were all willing to give them work, weren't they? Every one of them. You and I are willing to give them work, too. We are willing to have them in our houses to take care of the children and do the rough work that we shun ourselves. They are not offensive, either. We invited them; pretty nearly all the colored population has come to Detroit in the last fifteen years; most of them, anyhow. They have always had a corner on the meanest jobs. The city must grow, or you couldn't brag about it.

The colored people must live somewhere. Everybody is willing to have them live somewhere else. The people at the corner of Garland and Charlevoix would be willing to have them go to some other sec-tion. Everybody would be willing to have them go somewhere else.

Somewhere they must live. Are you going to kill them? Are you going to say that they can work, but they can't get a place to sleep? They can toil in the mill, but can't eat their dinner at home. We want them to build automobiles for us, don't we? We even let them become our chauffeurs. Oh, gentlemen, what is the use! You know it is wrong. Every one of you knows it is wrong. Can you think of these people without shouldering your own responsibility? Don't make it harder for them, I beg you.

They sent four policemen in the morning to help this little family move in. They had a bedstead, a stove, and some bedding, ten guns and some ammunition, and they had food to last them through a siege. I feel that they should have taken less furniture and more food and guns.

Gentlemen, nature works in a queer way. I don't know how this question of color will ever be solved, or whether it will be solved. Nature has a way of doing things. There is one thing about nature, she has plenty of time. She would make broad prairies so that we can raise wheat and corn to feed men. How does she do it? She sends a glacier plowing across a continent and takes fifty thousand years to harrow it and make it fit to till and support human life.

She makes a man. She tries endless experiments before the man is done. She wants to make a race and it takes an infinite mixture to make it. She wants to give us some conception of human rights, and some kindness and charity, and she makes pain and suffering and sorrow and death. It all counts. That is a rough way, but it is the only way. It all counts in the great, long, broad scheme of things.

I look on a trial like this with a feeling of disgust and shame. I can't help it now. It will be after we have learned in the terrible and expensive school of human experience that we will be willing to find each other and understand each other.

Now, let us get to the bare facts of this case. The city of Detroit had the police force there to help these people move into their home. When they unloaded their goods, men and women on the street began going from house to house. They went from house to house to sound the alarm, "The Negroes are coming," as if a foreign army was invading their homes; as if a wild beast had come down out of the mountains in the olden times.

Can you imagine those colored people? They didn't dare move without thinking of their color. Where we go into a hotel unconsciously, or a church, if we choose, they do not. Of course, colored people belong to a church, and they have a YMCA. That is, a Jim Crow YMCA. The black Christians cannot mix with the white Christians. They will probably have a Jim Crow heaven where the white angels will not be obliged to meet the black angels, except as servants.

Gentlemen, they say there is nothing to justify this shooting; it was an orderly, neighborly crowd; an orderly, neighborly crowd. They came there for a purpose and intended to carry it out.

How long, pray, would these men wait penned up in that house? How long would you wait? The very presence of the crowd was a mob, as I believe the court will tell you. Suppose a crowd gathers around your house; a crowd which doesn't want you there; a hostile crowd, for a part of two days and two nights, until the police force of this city is called in to protect you.

How long, tell me, are you going to live in that condition with a mob surrounding your house and the police force standing in front of it? How long should these men have waited? You wouldn't have waited.

Counsel say they had just as good reason to shoot on the eighth as on the ninth. Concede it. They did not shoot. They waited and hoped and prayed that in some way this crowd would pass them by and grant them the right to live.

The mob came back the next night and the colored people waited while they were gathering; they waited while they were coming from every street and every corner, and while the officers were supine and helpless and doing nothing. And they waited until dozens of stones were thrown against the house on the roof, probably—I don't know how many. Nobody knows how many. They waited until the windows were broken before they shot. Why did they wait so long? I think I know. How much chance had these people for their lives after they shot, surrounded by a crowd as they were?

They would never take a chance unless they thought it was necessary to take the chance. Eleven black people penned up in the face of a mob. What chance did they have?

Suppose they shot before they should. What is the theory of counsel in this case? Nobody pretends there is anything in this case to prove that our client Henry fired the fatal shot. There isn't the slightest. It wasn't a shot that would fit the gun he had.

The theory of this case is that he was part of a combination to do something. Now, what was that combination, gentlemen? Your own sense will tell you what it was. Did they combine to go there and kill somebody? Were they looking for somebody to murder? Dr. Sweet scraped together his small earnings by his industry and put himself through college, and he scraped together his small earnings of three thousand dollars to buy that home because he wanted to kill somebody?

It is silly to talk about it. He bought that home just as you buy yours, because he wanted a home to live in, to take his wife and to raise his family. There is no difference between the love of a black man for his offspring and the love of a white. He and his wife had the same feeling of fatherly and motherly affection for their child that you gentlemen have for yours, and that your father and mother had for you. They bought that home for that purpose; not to kill somebody. They might have feared trouble, as they probably did, and as the evidence shows that every man with a black face fears it, when he moves into a home that is fit for a dog to live in. It is part of the curse that, for some inscrutable reason, has followed the race— if you call it a race—and which curse, let us hope, sometime the world will be wise enough and decent enough and humane enough to wipe out.

They went there to live. They knew the dangers. Why do you suppose they took these guns and this ammunition and these men there? Because they wanted to kill somebody? It is utterly absurd and crazy. They took them there because they thought it might be necessary to defend their home with their lives and they were determined to do it.

They took guns there that in case of need they might fight, fight even to death for their home, and for each other, for their people, for their race, for their rights under the Constitution and the laws under which all of us live; and unless men and women will do that, we will soon be a race of slaves, whether we are black or white. "Eternal vigilance is the price of liberty," and it has always been so and always will be. Do you suppose they were in there for any other purpose?

Gentlemen, there isn't a chance that they took arms there for anything else. They did go there knowing their rights, feeling their responsibility, and determined to maintain those rights if it meant death to the last man and the last woman, and no one could do more.

No man lived a better life or died a better death than fighting for his home and his children, for himself, and for the eternal principles upon which life depends. Instead of being here under indictment, for murder, they should be honored for the brave stand they made for their rights and ours. Someday, both white and black, irrespective of color, will honor the memory of these men, whether they are inside prison walls or outside, and will recognize that they fought not only for themselves, but for every man who wishes to be free.

Did they shoot too quick? Tell me just how long a man needs wait for a mob? The court, I know, will instruct you on that. How long do you need to wait for a mob? We have been told that because a person trespasses on your home or on your ground, you have no right to shoot him. Is that true?

If I go up to your home in a peaceable way, and go on your ground, or on your porch, you have no right to shoot me. You have a right to use force to put me off if I refuse to go, even to the extent of killing me. That isn't this case, gentlemen. That isn't the case of a neighbor who went up to the yard of a neighbor without permission and was shot to death. Oh, no. The court will tell you the difference, unless I am mistaken, and I am sure I am not; unless I mistake the law, and I am sure I do not.

This isn't a case of a man who trespasses upon the ground of some other man and is killed. It is the case of an unlawful mob, which in itself is a crime; a mob bent on mischief; a mob that has no rights. They are too dangerous. It is like a fire. One man may do something. Two will do much more; three will do more than three times as much; a crowd will do something that no man ever dreamed of doing. The law recognizes it.

It is the duty of every man—I don't care who he is—to disperse a mob. It is the duty of the officers to disperse them. It was the duty of the inmates of the house, even though they had to kill somebody to do it.

Now, gentlemen, I wouldn't ask you to take the law on my statement. The court will tell you the law. A mob is a criminal combination of itself. Their presence is enough. You need not wait until it spreads. It is there, and that is enough. There is no other law; there hasn't been for years, and it is the law which will govern this case.

Now, gentlemen, how long did they need to wait? Why, it is silly. How long would you wait? How long do you suppose ten white men would be waiting? Would they have waited as long? I will tell you how long they needed to wait. I will tell you what the law is, and the court will confirm me. Every man may act upon appearances as they seem to him. Every man may protect his own life. Every man has the right to protect his own property. Every man is bound under the law to disperse a mob even to the extent of taking life. It is his duty to do it, but back of that he has the human right to go to the extent of killing to defend his life. He has a right to defend the life of his kinsman, servant, his friends, or those about him, and he has a right to defend, gentlemen, not from real danger, but from what seems to him real danger at the time.

Here is Henry Sweet, the defendant in this case, a boy. What had he to do with it? Why is he in this case? A boy, twenty-one years old, working his way through college, and he is just as good a boy as the boy of any juror in this box; just as good a boy as you people were when you were boys, and I submit to you, he did nothing whatever that was wrong.

Of course, we lawyers talk and talk and talk, as if we feared results. I don't mean to trifle with you. I always fear results. When life or liberty is in the hands of a lawyer, he realizes the terrible responsibility that is on him, and he fears that some word will be left unspoken, or some thought will be forgotten. I would not be telling you the truth if I told you that I did not fear the result of this important case; and when my judgment and my reason come to my aid and take counsel with my fears, I know, and I feel perfectly well, that no twelve American jurors, especially in any Northern land, could be brought together who would dream of taking a boy's life or liberty under circumstances like this. That is what my judgment tells me, but my fears perhaps cause me to go further and to say more when I should not have said as much.

Now, let me tell you when a man has the right to shoot in self-defense, and in defense of his home; not when these vital things in life are in danger, but when he thinks they are. These despised blacks did not need to wait until the house was beaten down above their heads. They didn't need to wait until every window was broken. They didn't need to wait longer for that mob to grow more inflamed. There is nothing so dangerous as ignorance and bigotry when it is unleashed as it was here.

The court will tell you that these inmates of this house had the right to decide upon appearances, and if they did, even though they were mistaken, they are not guilty. I don't know but they could safely have stayed a little longer. I don't know but it would have been well enough to let this mob break a few more windowpanes. I don't know but it would have been better and been safe to let them batter down the house before they shot. I don't know. How am I to tell, and how are you to tell?

You are twelve white men, gentlemen. You are twelve men sitting here eight months after all this occurred, listening to the evidence, perjured and otherwise, to tell whether they acted too quickly or too slowly.

A man may be running an engine on the railroad. He may stop too quickly or too slowly. In an emergency he is bound to do one or the other, and the jury a year after, sitting in cold blood, may listen to the evidence and say that he acted too quickly. What do they know about it? You must sit out there upon a moving engine with your hand on the throttle and facing danger and must decide and act quickly. Then you can tell.

Cases often occur in the courts, which doesn't speak very well for the decency of courts, but they have happened, where men have been shipwrecked at sea, a number of the men having left the ship and gone into a small boat to save their lives; they have floated around for hours and tossed on the wild waves of an angry sea; their food disappearing, the boat heavy and likely to sink and no friendly sail in sight. What are they to do? Will they throw some of their companions off the boat and save the rest? Will they eat some to save the others?

If they kill anybody, it is because they want to live. Every living thing wants to live. The strongest instinct in life is to keep going. You have seen a tree upon a rock send a shoot down for ten or fifteen or twenty feet, to search for water, to draw it up, that it may still survive; it is a strong instinct with animals and with plants, with all sentient things, to keep alive.

Men are out in a boat, in an angry sea, with little food, and less water. No hope in sight. What will they do? They throw a companion overboard to save themselves, or they kill somebody to save themselves.

Juries have come into court and passed on the question of whether they should have waited longer, or not. Later, the survivors were picked up by a ship, and perhaps, if they had waited longer, all would have been saved. Yet a jury, months after it was over, sitting safely in their jury box, pass upon the question of whether they acted too quickly or not. Can they tell? No. To decide that case, you must be in a small boat, with little food and water; in a wild sea, with no sail in sight, and drifting around for hours or days in the face of the deep, beset by hunger and darkness.

I say that no American citizen, unless he is black, need wait until an angry mob sets foot upon his premises before he kills. I say that no free man need wait to see just how far an aggressor will go before he takes life.

The first instinct a man has is to save his life. He doesn't need to experiment. He hasn't time to experiment. When he thinks it is time to save his life, he has the right to act. There isn't any question about it. It has been the law of every English-speaking country so long as we have had law.

Every man's home is his castle, which even the king may not enter. Every man has a right to kill, to defend himself or his family, or others, either in the defense of the home or in the defense of themselves. So far as that branch of the case is concerned, there is only one thing that this jury has a right to consider, and that is whether the defendants acted in honest fear of danger.

I know a little about psychology. If I could talk to a man long enough, and not too long, and he talk to me a little, I could guess fairly well what is going on in his head, but I can't understand the psychology of a mob, and neither can anybody else. We know it is unreasoning. We know it is filled with hatred. We know it is cruel. We know it has no heart, no soul, and no pity. We know it is as cruel as the grave. No man has a right to stop and dicker while waiting for a mob.

Now, let us look at these fellows. Here were colored men, penned up in the house. Put yourselves in their place. Make yourselves colored for a little while. It won't hurt, you can wash it off. They can't, but you can; just make yourself black for a little while; long enough, gentlemen, to judge them, and before any of you would want to be judged, you would want your juror to put himself in your place. That is all I ask in this case, gentlemen.

They were black, and they knew the history of the black. Our friend makes fun of Dr. Sweet and Henry Sweet talking these things all over in the short space of two months. Well, gentlemen, let me tell you something, that isn't evidence. This is just theory. This is just theory, and nothing else.

I should imagine that the only thing that two or three colored people talk of when they get together is race. I imagine that they can't rub color off their faces or rub it out of their minds. I imagine that it is with them always.

I imagine that the stories of lynchings, the stories of murders, the stories of oppression, is a topic of constant conversation. I imagine that everything that appears in the newspapers on this subject is carried from one to another until every man knows what others know, upon the topic which is the most important of all to their lives.

What do you think about it? Suppose you were black. Do you think you would forget it even in your dreams? Or would you have black dreams? Suppose you had to watch every point of contact with your neighbor and remember your color, and you knew your children were growing up under this handicap. Do you suppose you would think of anything else?

Do you suppose this boy coming in here didn't know all about the conditions, and did not learn all about them? Do you suppose he hadn't read the story of his race? He is intelligent. He goes to school. He would have been a graduate now, except for this long hesitation, when he is waiting to see whether he goes back to college or goes to jail. Do you suppose that black students and teachers are discussing it?

Anyhow, gentlemen, what is the use? The jury isn't supposed to be entirely ignorant. They are supposed to know something. These black people were in the house with the black man's psychology, and with the black man's fear, based on what they had heard and what they had read and what they knew.

I don't need to go far. I don't need to travel to Florida. I don't even need to talk about the Chicago riots. The testimony showed that in Chicago a colored boy on a raft had been washed to a white bathing beach, and men and boys of my race stoned him to death. A riot began, and some hundred and twenty were killed.

I don't need to go to Washington or to St. Louis. Let us take Detroit. I don't need to go far either in space or time. Let us take this city. Now, gentlemen, I am not saying that the white people of Detroit are different from the white people of any other city. I know what has been done in Chicago. I know what prejudice growing out of race and religion has done the world over, and all through time. I am not blaming Detroit. I am stating what has happened, that is all. And I appeal to you, gentlemen, to do your part to save the honor of this city, to save its reputation, to save yours, to save its name, and to save the poor colored people who cannot save themselves.

I was told there had not been a lynching of a colored man in thirty years or more in Michigan. All right. Why, I can remember when the early statesmen of Michigan cared for the colored man and when they embodied the rights of the colored men in the Constitution and statutes.

I can remember when they laid the foundation that made it possible for a man of any color or any religion, or any creed, to own his home wherever he could find a man to sell it.

I remember when civil rights laws were passed that gave the Negro the right to go where the white man went and as he went. There are some men who seem to think those laws were wrong. I do not. Wrong or not, it is the law, and if you were black, you would protest with every fiber of your body your right to live.

Michigan used to protect the rights of colored people. There were not many of them here, but they have come in the last few years, and with them has come prejudice. Then, too, the Southern white man has followed his black slave. But that isn't all. Black labor has come in competition with white. Prejudices have been created where there was no prejudice before.

We have listened to the siren song that we are a superior race and have superior rights, and that the black man has none. It is a new idea in Detroit that a colored man's home can be torn down about his head because he is black. There are some eighty thousand blacks here now, and they are bound to reach out. They have reached out in the past, and they will reach out in the future.

Do not make any mistake, gentlemen. I am making no promises. I know the instinct for life. I know it reaches black and white alike. I know that you cannot confine any body of people to any particular place; and, as the population grows, the colored people will go farther. I know it, and you must change the law or you must take it as it is, or you must invoke the primal law of nature and get back to clubs and fists, and if you are ready for that, gentlemen, all right, but do it with your eyes open. That is all I care for. You must have a government of law or blind force, and if you are ready to let blind force take the place of law, the responsibility is on you, not on me.

Now, let us see what has happened here. So far as I know, there had been nothing of the sort happened when Dr. Sweet bought his home. He took an option on it in May and got his deed in June; and in July, in that one month, while he was deliberating on moving, there were other cases of driving Negro families out of their homes in Detroit. This was accomplished by stones, clubs, guns, and mobs.

Suppose one of you were colored and had bought a house on Garland Avenue. Take this just exactly as it is. You bought it in June, intending to move in July, and you read and heard about what happened in another part of the city. Would you have waited? Would you have waited a month, as Sweet did?

Remember, these men didn't have any too much money. Dr. Sweet paid three thousand dollars on his home, leaving a loan on it of sixteen thousand dollars more. He had to scrape together some money to buy his furniture, and he bought fourteen hundred dollars' worth the day after he moved in and paid two hundred dollars down.

Gentlemen, it is only right to consider Dr. Sweet and his family. He has a little child. He has a wife. They must live somewhere. If they could not, it would be better to take them out and kill them, and kill them decently and quickly.

Had he any right to be free? They determined to move in and to take nine men with them. What would you have done, gentlemen? If you had courage, you would have done as Dr. Sweet did. You would have been crazy or a coward if you hadn't.

Would you have moved in alone? No, you would not have gone alone. You would have taken your wife. If you had a brother or two, you would have taken them because you would know that you could rely on them, and you would have taken those nearest to you. And you would have moved in just as Dr. Sweet did. Wouldn't you?

He didn't shoot the first night. He didn't look for trouble. He kept his house dark so that the neighbors wouldn't see him. He didn't dare have a light in his house, gentlemen, for fear of the neighbors. Noble neighbors, who were to have a colored family in their neighborhood. He had the light put out in the front part of the house, so as not to tempt any of the mob to violence.

Now, let us go back a little. What happened before this? I don't need to go over the history of the case. Everybody who wants to understand knows it, and many who don't want to understand it.

As soon as Dr. Sweet bought this house, the neighbors organized the Waterworks Park Improvement Association. They were going to protect the homes and make them safe for children. The purpose was clear, and every single member reluctantly said that they joined it to keep colored people out of the district. They might have said it first as well as last.

People, even in a wealthy and aristocratic neighborhood like Garland and Charlevoix, don't give up a dollar without expecting some profit; not a whole dollar. Sometimes two in one family, the husband and wife, joined. They got in quick. The woods were on fire. Something had to be done, as quick as they heard that Dr. Sweet was coming; Dr. Sweet, who had been a bellhop on a boat, and a bellhop in hotels, and fired furnaces and sold popcorn and worked his way with his great handicap through school and through college, and graduated as a doctor, and gone to Europe and taken another degree; Dr. Sweet, who knew more than any man in the neighborhood ever would know or ever want to know. He deserved more for all he had done. When they heard he was coming, then it was time to act, and act together, for the sake of their homes, their families, and their firesides, and so they got together.

I shall not talk to you much longer. I am sorry I talked so long. But this case is close to my heart. Gentlemen, who are these people who were in this house? Were they people of character? Were they people of standing? Were they people of intelligence?

First, there was Dr. Sweet. Gentlemen, a white man does pretty well when he does what Dr. Sweet did. A white boy who can start in with nothing and put himself through college, study medicine, taking postgraduate work in Europe, earning every penny of it as he goes along, shoveling snow and coal, and working as a bellhop on boats, working at every kind of employment that he can get to make his way, is some fellow. But Dr. Sweet has the handicap of the color of his face. And there is no handicap more terrible than that.

Supposing you had your choice, right here this minute; would you rather lose your eyesight or become colored? Would you rather lose your hearing or be a Negro? Would you rather go out there on the street and have your leg cut off by a streetcar or have a black skin?

I don't like to speak of it; I do not like to speak of it in the presence of these colored people, whom I have always urged to be as happy as they can. But it is true. Life is a hard game anyhow. But, when the cards are stacked against you, it is terribly hard. And they are stacked against a race for no reason but that they are black.

Who are these men who were in this house? There was Dr. Sweet. There was his brother, who was a dentist. There was this young boy who worked his way for three years through college, with a little aid from his brother, and who was on his way to graduate. Henry's future is now in your hands. There was his companion, who was working his way through college—all gathered in that house. Were they hoodlums? Were they criminals? Were they anything except men who asked for a chance to live; who asked for a chance to breathe the free air and make their own way, earn their own living, and get their bread by the sweat of their brow?

Gentlemen, these black men shot. Whether any bullets from their guns hit Breiner, I do not care. I will not discuss it. It is passing strange that the bullet that went through him, went directly through, not as if it were shot from some higher place. It was not the bullet that came from Henry Sweet's rifle; that is plain. It might have come from the house; I do not know, gentlemen, and I do not care. There are bigger issues in this case than that. The right to defend your home, the right to defend your person, is as sacred a right as any human being could fight for, and as sacred a cause as any jury could sustain.

That issue not only involves the defendants in this case, but it involves every man who wants to live, everyone who wants freedom to work and to breathe; it is an issue worth fighting for, and worth dying for; it is an issue worth the attention of this jury, who have a chance that is given few juries to pass upon a real case that will mean something in the history of a race.

These men were taken to the police station. Gentlemen, there was never a time that these black men's rights were protected in the least; never once. They had no rights because they are black. They were to be driven out of their home under the law's protection.

When they defended their home, they were arrested and charged with murder. They were taken to a police station, manacled. And they asked for a lawyer. And, every man, if he has any brains at all, asks for a lawyer when he is in the hands of the police. If he does not want to have a web woven around him, to entangle or ensnare him, he will ask for a lawyer. And, the lawyer's first aid to the injured always is "Keep your mouth shut." It is not a case of whether you are guilty or not guilty. That makes no difference. "Keep your mouth shut."

The police grabbed them, as is their habit. They got the county attorney to ask questions. What did they do? They did what everybody does, helpless, alone, and unadvised. They did not know, even, that anybody was killed. At least there is no evidence that they knew. But, they knew that they had been arrested for defending their own rights to live; and they were there in the hands of their enemies; and they told the best story they could think of at the time just as ninety-nine men out of a hundred always do. Whether they are guilty or not guilty makes no difference. But lawyers and even policemen should have protected their rights.

Some things that these defendants said were not true, as is always the case. The prosecutor read a statement from this boy, which is conflicting. In two places he says that he shot "over them." In another he said that he shot "at them." He probably said it in each place, but the reporter probably got one of them wrong. But Henry makes it perfectly explicit, and when you go to your jury room and read it all, you will find that he does.

In another place he said he shot to defend his brother's home and family. He says that in two or three places. You can also find he said that he shot so that they would run away and leave them to eat their dinner. They are both there.

These conflicting statements you will find in all cases of this sort. You always find them, where men have been sweated, without help, without a lawyer, groping around blindly, in the hands of the enemy, without the aid of anybody to protect their rights.

Gentlemen, from the first to the last, there has not been a substantial right of these defendants that was not violated. We come now to lay this man's case in the hands of a jury of our peers. The first defense and the last defense is the protection of home and life as provided by our law. We are willing to leave it here. I feel, as I look at you, that we will be treated fairly and decently, even understandingly and kindly. You know what this case is. You know why it is.

You know that if white men had been fighting their way against colored men, nobody would ever have dreamed of a prosecution. And you know that, from the beginning of this case to the end, up to the time you write your verdict, the prosecution is based on race prejudice and nothing else.

Gentlemen, I feel deeply on this subject; I cannot help it. Let us take a little glance at the history of the Negro race. It only needs a minute. It seems to me that the story would melt hearts of stone.

I was born in America. I could have left it if I had wanted to go away. Some other men, reading about this land of freedom that we brag about on the Fourth of July, came voluntarily to America. These men, the defendants, are here because they could not help it. Their ancestors were captured in the jungles and on the plains of Africa, captured as you capture wild beasts, torn from their homes and their kindred; loaded into slave ships, packed like sardines in a box, half of them dying on the ocean passage; some jumping into the sea in their frenzy, when they had a chance to choose death in place of slavery.

They were captured and brought here. They could not help it. They were bought and sold as slaves, to work without pay, because they were black. They were subjected to all this for generations, until finally they were given their liberty, so far as the law goes—and that is only a little way, because, after all, every human being's life in this world is inevitably mixed with every other life, and no matter what laws we pass, no matter what precautions we take, unless the people we meet are kindly and decent and human and liberty-loving, then there is no liberty. Freedom comes from human beings, rather than from laws and institutions.

Now, that is their history. These people are the children of slavery. If the race that we belong to owes anything to any human being, or to any power in this universe, it owes it to these black men. Above all other men, they owe an obligation and a duty to these black men which can never be repaid. I never see one of them that I do not feel I ought to pay part of the debt of my race—and if you, gentlemen, feel as you should feel in this case, your emotions will be like mine.

Gentlemen, you were called into this case by chance. It took us a week to find you, a week of culling out prejudice and hatred. Probably we did not cull it all out at that; but we took the best and the fairest that we could find. It is up to you.

Your verdict means something in this case. It means something more than the fate of this boy. It is not often that a case is submitted to twelve men where the decision may mean a milestone in the progress of the human race. But this case does. And I hope and I trust that you have a feeling of responsibility that will make you take it and do your duty as citizens of a great nation, and as members of the human family, which is better still.

Let me say just a parting word for Henry Sweet, who has well nigh been forgotten. I am serious, but it seems almost like a reflection upon this jury to talk as if I doubted your verdict. What has this boy done? This one boy now that I am culling out from all of the rest, and whose fate is in your hands, can you tell me what he has done? Can I believe myself? Am I standing in a court of justice, where twelve men on their oaths are asked to take away the liberty of a boy twenty-one years of age, who has done nothing more than what Henry Sweet has done?

Gentlemen, you may think he shot too quick; you may think he erred in judgment; you may think that Dr. Sweet should not have gone there prepared to defend his home.

But, what of this case of Henry Sweet? What has he done? I want to put it up to you, each of you, individually. Dr. Sweet was his elder brother. He had helped Henry through school. He loved him. He had taken him into his home. Henry had lived with him and his wife; he had fondled his baby. The doctor had promised Henry money to go through school. Henry was getting his education, to take his place in the world, gentlemen—and this is a hard job.

With his brother's help, he had worked himself through college up to the last year. The doctor had bought a home. He feared danger. He moved in with his wife and he asked this boy to go with him. And this boy went to help defend his brother and his brother's wife and his child and his home.

Do you think more of him or less of him for that? I never saw twelve men in my life—and I have looked at a good many faces of a good many juries—I never saw twelve men in my life that, if you could get them to understand a human case, were not true and right.

Should this boy have gone along and helped his brother? Or should he have stayed away? What would you have done? And yet, gentlemen, here is a boy, and the president of his college came all the way here from Ohio to tell you what he thinks of him. His teachers have come here from Ohio, to tell you what they think of him. The Methodist bishop has come here to tell you what he thinks of him.

So, gentlemen, I am justified in saying that this boy is as kindly, as well disposed, as decent a man, as any one of you twelve. Do you think he ought to be taken out of his school and sent to the penitentiary? All right, gentlemen, if you think so, do it. It is your job, not mine. If you think so, do it. But if you do, gentlemen, if you should ever look into the face of your own boy, or your own brother, or look into your own heart, you will regret it in sackcloth and ashes. You know, if he committed any offense, it was being loyal and true to his brother whom he loved. I know where you will send him, and it will not be to the penitentiary.

Now, gentlemen, just one more word, and I am through with this case. I do not live in Detroit. But I have no feeling against this city. In fact, I shall always have the kindest remembrance of it, especially if this case results as I think and feel that it will. I am the last one to come here and stir up race hatred, or any other hatred. I do not believe in the law of hate. I may not be true to my ideals always, but I believe in the law of love, and I believe you can do nothing with hatred.

I would like to see a time when man loves his fellow man and forgets his color or his creed. We will never be civilized until that time comes. I know the race has a long road to go. I believe the life of the Negro race has been a life of tragedy, of injustice, of oppression. The law has made him equal, but man has not. And, after all, the last analysis is, what has man done?—and not, what has the law done?

I know there is a long road ahead of him, before he can take the place which I believe he should take. I know that before him there is suffering, sorrow, tribulation, and death among the blacks, and perhaps the whites. I am sorry. I would do what I could to avert it. I would advise patience; I would advise toleration; I would advise understanding; I would advise all of those things which are necessary for men who live together.

Gentlemen, what do you think is your duty in this case? I have watched, day after day, these black, tense faces that have crowded this court. These black faces that now are looking to you twelve whites, feeling that the hopes and fears of a race are in your keeping.

This case is about to end, gentlemen. To them, it is life. Not one of their color sits on this jury. Their fate is in the hands of twelve whites. Their eyes are fixed on you, their hearts go out to you, and their hopes hang on your verdict.

This is all. I ask you, on behalf of this defendant, on behalf of these helpless ones who turn to you, and more than that—on behalf of this great state, and this great city which must face this problem, and face it fairly—I ask you, in the name of progress and of the human race, to return a verdict of "Not guilty!"

After seven and a one-half hours of closing argument, Darrow collapsed into his chair, spent. Already exhausted from his recent cases, he had somehow found the resources and passion to articulate not just the case for Henry Sweet but for all black Americans—indeed, for all Americans. Darrow accomplished a number of objectives in this brilliant summation. First and foremost, he reinforced for the jury the idea that racial prejudice was the sole motivation for the mob gathered outside the Sweet home. Darrow painted a vivid picture of the harsh reality of race relations in 1920s America. Perhaps most important, he convinced the jurors to place themselves in the shoes of young Sweet. What if a mob surrounded *their* houses, threatened *their* property, threatened *their* families, threatened *their* lives?

Typically, such an argument is prohibited as an unfair appeal to the jury's passion and sympathy. However, in a case involving a claim of self-defense, this type of argument is permitted. Darrow was aware of this narrow legal exception and took full advantage of such a rare opportunity: "Suppose a crowd gathers around your house, a crowd that doesn't want you there; how long, tell me, are you going to live in that condition with a mob surrounding your house, how long should these men have waited? *You* wouldn't have waited."

Darrow zeroed in on the Sweets' basic rights as American citizens—to protect themselves and their home: "The Sweets spent their first night in jail. Now the state wants them to spend the rest of their lives in the penitentiary. There are persons in the North and the South who say a black man is inferior to the white and should be controlled by the whites. There are also those who recognize his rights and say he should enjoy them. To me this case is a cross section of human history. It involves the future and the hope of some of us that the future shall be better than the past."

And finally Darrow argued that the castle doctrine, the right to defend oneself in one's own home, is universal. A man's home is his castle. What should have been among the most basic and fundamental rights for all American citizens was merely a hollow phrase for black Americans. Until the Sweet trial the castle doctrine would have been more aptly titled the *white man's* castle doctrine. For while a white man could shoot a black intruder who threatened his safety, his home, his sanctuary, and be absolved of wrongdoing, a black man who shot a white intruder would certainly not be afforded the same absolution.

Arthur Hays, Darrow's partner, said, "In his address to the jury Darrow showed his master hand. The ordinary lawyer collates facts, analyzes evidence, and makes his appeal. There are few who use history, psychology, and philosophy in order to show the real underlying facts. Darrow said to those men on the jury that if he had merely to appeal to reason, he would have little doubt of the result, but that the difficulty lay deeper. It arose from a prejudice which white men take in with their mother's milk. Darrow questioned whether it was possible for twelve white men, however they might try, to give a fair trial to a Negro."

Following Darrow's closing argument, the prosecution tried to redirect the jurors' focus on the victim and away from Darrow's emotional plea on behalf of the black community.

I do not think there is any panacea that you can apply to this situation. Maybe it is to be done by a process of mutual forbearance. Maybe it is to be done some other way. I do not know. Nobody else knows. I do not know whether anybody ever will know how this thing is to be settled.

I am willing to grant Sweet the right to live where he chooses, but why was not Breiner equally entitled to a right to merely live? Breiner has been allowed to lapse into an insignificant figure here, while the defense has taken us on a tour of "Darkest Africa" and the American cities where they say riots occurred that bred fear in Sweet.

I concede the right under the law of any man, black or white, to live where he likes or wherever he can afford to live, but we all have many civil rights which we voluntarily waive in the name of public peace, comfort, and security, and because we are ashamed to insist upon them.

I have a right to be a domineering, arrogant martinet to my subordinates; I have a right to remain seated in a streetcar while an elderly woman or a mother carrying a child stands; I have a right to keep my hat on in church or in the theater; I have a right to play the piano or honk my automobile horn when a woman next door is tossing on a sickbed—all these and many more civil rights which I may insist upon. But I would be shamed to insist upon them, and so would you.

But there is one civil right, more precious than all the others, which no man surrenders, except at the command of his God or his country, and that is the right to live.

[Darrow] himself is the perpetrator of one of the worst possible prejudices, that police officers and prosecutors are liars and twisters of facts. He has made liars out of the police wherever he has tried cases. It is not so important to us that Dr. Sweet was once an excellent waiter or that he could apparently cure lockjaw. This is all a smoke screen, gentlemen, thrown out to hide the real question to be decided. And that is, who is responsible for the killing of Leon Breiner?

Back of all your sophistry and transparent political philosophy, gentlemen of the defense; back of all your prating of civil rights, back of your psychology and theory of race hatred, lies the stark body of Leon Breiner with a bullet hole in his back.

All of your specious arguments, Mr. Darrow, all your artful ingenuity born of many years' experience—all of your social theories, all your cleverly conceived psychology, can never dethrone justice in this case. Leon Breiner, peaceably chatting with his neighbor at his doorstep, enjoying his God-given and inalienable right to live, is shot through the back from ambush. And you can't make anything out of those facts, gentlemen of the defense, but cold-blooded murder.

The lawyers had had their say; now it was the judge's turn to tell the jurors of the law, and how they should apply it. Judge Murphy instructed the jury that "under the law, a man's house is his castle. It is his castle, whether he is white or black, and no man has the right to assail or invade it." Darrow later said, "It was the first time in all my career where a judge really tried to help and displayed a sympathetic interest in saving poor devils from the extreme forces of the law, rather than otherwise."

Deliberations didn't last long, less than twenty-four hours. An onlooker described the scene: "When the jury came in, Darrow was seated with his hands grasping the arms of the chair, his great body stooped over, his head leaning forward, waiting to hear the verdict. When the verdict of not guilty was rendered, his great spirit almost seemed to have left his body. He had given his all, body, mind, and soul, to the trial." When the prosecutor tried to assist Darrow, he waved him off, saying, "Oh, I'm all right. I've heard that verdict before."

One contemporary news account summarized Darrow's impact on the case: "Without Clarence Darrow, the ten Negro men and [one] woman in that house would have been in the penitentiary today. Through the medium of one of the defendants who took the stand, and in his pleas, Darrow traced the Negro up through the eons of his evolution, traced him through the Gethsemane of Slavery, pictured him being tortured by the Simon Legrees of Puritanism, as the victim of mob vengeance, burning at the stake and finally emerging into the hope of a new day."

The NAACP held its annual meeting in June of 1926; Darrow and his wife, Ruby, attended, before finally taking their long-awaited vacation abroad. The attorney accepted one more case in 1929, then closed his practice for a quiet and secluded retirement. He died in 1938, at the age of eighty.

A year after Henry Sweet's acquittal, the charges against the remaining ten defendants were dismissed. Toms said later the prosecution's case was tough because "the colored people involved were so far superior to the white people involved."

While the Sweet trials represented a victory for black Americans in their historic struggle for racial equality, life for Ossian and Gladys Sweet would never be the same. They would never again live in their Garland Avenue home. Shortly after the trial, their daughter, Iva, was diagnosed with tuberculosis, a highly contagious disease that could lie dormant anywhere from months to years after exposure. It is likely that Gladys contracted the disease while in prison awaiting trial and then passed it to her baby. In the 1920s—before the discovery and widespread use of antibiotics—tuberculosis was not only highly contagious but fatal as well. Iva died in August 1926; shortly thereafter Gladys fought her own battle with the same illness, and one month after her twenty-seventh birthday she, too, succumbed. Within two years of his brother's trial, Dr. Sweet had buried his wife and his baby daughter, along with the life he had worked so hard to create for them.

Dr. Sweet lived out the remainder of his life in Detroit, never speaking publicly about the events of September 9, 1925. After years filled with death, failed marriages, and four failed campaigns for political office, Sweet was lonely, depressed, and in constant pain from debilitating arthritis. In March of 1960, at the age of sixty-five, Dr. Ossian Sweet took his own life.

And what of Dr. Sweet's home? The house at 2905 Garland Avenue, deemed a black family's castle by a jury of twelve white Detroit residents, is now a National Historic Site, a symbol of both the courage of the Sweets and their friends, and the long battle for equality.

CHAPTER SEVEN

The Trial of the (Nineteenth) Century

The killer congressman, the philandering district attorney,
and the first use of the temporary insanity defense

Should a woman who drowns five of her children go to prison? What about a would-be assassin who wounds a head of state? A Texas jury rejected claims that postpartum depression and a controlling husband drove housewife Andrea Yates to systematically drown her five children; they found that she was sane—responsible for her actions—and Yates was sentenced to life in prison without the possibility of parole. John Hinckley, who methodically planned his attack on President Ronald Reagan, nearly killing him and paralyzing presidential press secretary James Brady, was found to have been incapable of knowing right from wrong at the time of the crime; therefore, the jury found him not guilty of the attempted murders by reason of insanity.

The American legal system currently defines insanity as a disabling condition that leaves one unable to distinguish between right and wrong; a person so disabled is not legally responsible for his actions and therefore is to be treated medically, not punished. Defense attorneys alleged that both Hinckley and Yates suffered from long-term psychological problems, their vile deeds simply tragic symptoms—external manifestations—of the turmoil within their diseased minds. Furthermore, neither simply woke up one day and suddenly lost his or her mind or was presented with a situation that caused the loss of the ability to know right from wrong.

But what is society to do with an individual who does not suffer from a chronic, disabling psychological condition, yet, when presented with an extraordinary situation, temporarily loses his ability to distinguish right from wrong? Is he to receive the same legal protection given the insane? Is he blameworthy? These questions were raised—and answered for the first time—in the aftermath of a cold-blooded murder that rocked Washington, D.C., just a few years before the Civil War.

February 27, 1859, was an unseasonably warm day in the capital; families took advantage of the weather, attending church services and taking Sunday strolls through Lafayette Square, from which the White House could be seen a few blocks away.

A tall figure drew the eye of fellow pedestrians: District Attorney Philip Barton Key, enjoying the sunshine and doffing his hat to passersby. The fame of Key's father—Francis Scott Key, composer of "The Star-Spangled Banner"—as well as his own flair for style, made him a popular Washington figure. Six feet of elegance, Key was known as "the handsomest man in all Washington society," and today found him strolling the streets of the capital in his characteristic immaculate fashion, gray-striped trousers with matching vest, a smart knee-length jacket, and boots. He carried with him a pair of opera glasses, a white handkerchief, and two shiny brass keys.

Key was on his way to the home of his good friend New York congressman Daniel E. Sickles. A confidant of President Buchanan's, the congressman was said to have an "intelligence that fairly crackled" and had a reputation for always being ready to help a friend in need. Using both his friendship with the president and his influence over Washington, D.C., officials, Sickles helped District Attorney Key keep his job despite the lawyer's fast-paced lifestyle and a less-than-diligent focus on his official duties. The congressman's desire to help his friend led him without hesitation to recommend to others Key's talents as a lawyer—despite his professional lapses. The two men enjoyed each other's company, and Key was a frequent dinner guest at Sickles's home. However, not all of the visits to the Sickles residence were for male companionship. The district attorney often came calling on his lover, Teresa, who was also, to his later mortal regret, Mrs. Daniel Sickles.

Born in New York on October 20, 1819, Sickles was the only child of Susan Marsh and George Garrett Sickles. From an early age, he developed a desire to attend college and gain an education, fueled perhaps by a need to surpass his father's modest success as a real estate speculator. Sickles's parents obliged their son by allowing him to live and study in the household of Lorenzo Da Ponte, a professor of classics at the newly founded New York University.

The Da Ponte household was an exciting mix of family, visitors, lecturers, and friends from a wide variety of backgrounds, and Sickles loved it. Into that intellectual salon was born Teresa Bagioli, a charming baby whom the nineteen-year-old Sickles frequently bounced on his knee. As

Teresa grew, Sickles was busy expanding his knowledge under the tutelage of Professor Da Ponte. The two grew to be close friends, and Sickles did all he could to help the aging professor with his work. When Da Ponte died of tuberculosis in 1840, Sickles was so overcome with grief that he ran through the graveyard "shrieking" uncontrollably. Bystanders were so frightened by the outburst that they feared Sickles might do "some further violence to himself, and that his mind would entirely give way."

Unable to bring himself to continue studying at NYU after Da Ponte's death, Sickles turned to the study of law and the sport of politics. He became known for his zealous support of the Democratic Party, as well as for "sharp" dealing and a quick temper. On one occasion, a lender filed a lawsuit against Sickles, nearly ending his new career as a would-be politician. The suit revealed that Sickles had given the lender a mortgage in exchange for $800. Sickles asked for the mortgage note back momentarily to double-check one of the terms, then refused to return either the mortgage or the money. Sickles was acquitted based on a technicality; the mortgage wasn't filled out with sufficient precision. On another occasion, Sickles, a newly elected New York State representative, paraded a prostitute named Fanny White around the chamber of the New York Assembly. As a result of White's questionable character and occupation, the legislators promptly censured Sickles for his conduct. Sickles's notorious reputation prompted the remark that "one might as well try to spoil a rotten egg as to damage [Sickles's] character."

Sickles continued visiting his friends the Bagiolis, taking a special interest in their daughter, Teresa. In 1852, the thirty-two-year-old politician married Teresa Bagioli in a secret ceremony; the bride's and groom's parents objected on the same grounds: Teresa was only sixteen and too young to marry, much less to a man twice her age. Sickles's motivation for the secret ceremony soon became obvious: Teresa was pregnant with their child. Several months after the ceremony, she gave birth to a healthy daughter, Laura.

A few months after his daughter's birth, Sickles traveled to London to accept a position as assistant to the American minister, James Buchanan; concerned that his wife and daughter were not up to the journey, he left them in the care Teresa's parents. To his family's dismay, the newspapers reported that Sickles did not travel alone; he took longtime companion Fanny White with him to Europe. Sickles and Buchanan were soon fast friends, despite the future president's misgivings over the presence of his assistant's mistress. Sickles's relationship with his boss improved when he sent White home and asked that his wife and daughter come to London.

Teresa Sickles quickly made a positive impression on the queen, the

English court, and especially Buchanan himself. On one occasion, a Mrs. Thomas, the wife of an American diplomat, was to be presented to the queen, and Buchanan offered Teresa as an escort. Mrs. Thomas felt that Teresa, being so young, was not suitable and requested someone older and more distinguished. Buchanan took offense at the slight and canceled the scheduled visit. One of Buchanan's first acts as president was to remove Mr. Thomas from his post.

Through the many months Sickles spent in England, he often spoke to Buchanan of his love for and loyalty to the United States, even when propriety dictated he remain silent. Sickles demonstrated his devotion to the "red, white, and blue" at a dinner party given by George Peabody, a wealthy American expatriate turned London financier, thrown to foster friendly relations between the United States and England. Peabody chose July 4 as the day for his party and invited more than 150 guests, including Queen Victoria. When Sickles arrived, he noted that life-size portraits of Queen Victoria and her husband, Prince Albert, overshadowed a small portrait of George Washington. No picture of the current president, Franklin Pierce, adorned the walls, and—adding insult to injury—an edited version of "The Star-Spangled Banner" was sung, eliminating all less-than-charitable references to the British. This was too much for Sickles to bear, and to the mortification of most of his company, he conspicuously refused to stand for the toast to Queen Victoria's health and then walked out of the dinner.

Sickles's undiplomatic demonstration of patriotism may have embarrassed his fellow Americans in London, but it greatly impressed the voters in his district back home; he returned to New York and was elected to Congress by a wide margin.

Congressman Sickles's tenure in Congress was marked by a notable success—he chaired the committee responsible for the creation of one of the most famous landmarks in the United States: New York City's Central Park. The land chosen for the park was considered by some to be one of the "roughest and most forbidding spots on the face of the globe," an "irredeemable swamp." His fellow legislators had all but given up on the idea of creating anything useful out of such a place, but Sickles continued to pursue the idea with single-minded dedication.

He received much-needed support from a fellow committee member, James T. Brady, a brilliant criminal defense attorney who shared the congressman's vision. Brady would later become a valued friend and confidant to Sickles and his wife.

Sickles's efforts paid off. Although he is scarcely remembered today for the role he played in developing Central Park, without Sickles's efforts it is unlikely to have been built.

While Sickles busied himself with his congressional duties, his wife was often on her own, lonely and feeling neglected by her husband. Teresa complained of Sickles's frequent trips, but her husband, exceedingly ambitious and driven, was dismissive. Gossip about the congressman's reputation as a "lady-killer," as well as reports of extramarital affairs, left Teresa feeling as though their marriage was set dressing, to give Sickles credibility and respectability.

Although he took precautions to conceal his affairs from the public, newspapers reported that Congressman Sickles had signed into a Baltimore hotel several times with a woman identifying herself as Mrs. Sickles, a fact not ordinarily noteworthy. However, the papers also pointed out that at the time of these meetings, the real Mrs. Sickles was attending a dinner party hosted by one of Sickles's friends, standing in for her absent husband.

In 1856, Sickles was reelected to Congress. Tired of the constant travel between New York and Washington, D.C., he decided to move his family to the capital. This move had an added benefit: Sickles was sure he would be warmly welcomed by the newly elected president, longtime friend James Buchanan. This move also gave Teresa and their daughter, Laura, a house of their own, although at the cost of taking Teresa away from her parents and the Manhattan she had grown to love. She soon found herself in an unfamiliar city, trying to assimilate the local social mores and live up to expectations regarding the behavior of political wives. This situation was especially acute for Teresa because her husband had chosen a large home on Lafayette Square, an area of unsurpassed prestige. Teresa was required to manage the house and three servants, a task with which she had little experience. Nevertheless, Teresa quickly learned to give a dinner party, make conversation with the appropriate combination of polite inquiry and deference to her husband's views, and pay daily visits to other lonely wives, usually on the arm of a male escort.

Because Washington's power elite were regularly called away to nighttime meetings, using the services of one of the city's bachelors as an escort was seen as merely a convenience, ensuring that a woman arrived safely at a social function and returned home unharmed. Hosts rarely took notice of whose arm a political wife held upon her arrival, but Congressman Sickles's wife would change all that.

Oh, Say Can You See

Philip Barton Key may have had the most famous father in the United States: Francis Scott Key was best known for writing what became the national anthem, "The Star-Spangled Banner," during the War of 1812.

However, Key's life did not end with the poem he wrote by the rockets' red glare; he freed his slaves, married Mary Lloyd, and began raising a family in the Georgetown area of the District of Columbia. His seventh child, Philip Barton, was born April 5, 1818, and as they'd done at the births of their previous children, the Keys laid a small, circular bed of plants in the garden spelling out his first name.

The elder Key supported his growing family, which would grow to include eleven children, as the District of Columbia district attorney from 1833 to 1841. He encouraged Philip to follow him into the law, but the younger, less cerebral Key refused to study, preferring to rely on his natural talents as a fast-talker to make him a passable lawyer. When the country mourned the elder Key's death in 1843, his law library passed to Philip, who used it little and did even less to expand its contents.

Key married Ellen Swan in 1845, and together they had four children, three daughters and a son. Despite his spotty work ethic, Key was appointed to his father's former position as the district attorney for the District of Columbia in 1853. His marriage, though happy, lasted only nine years, until 1854, when Ellen died, leaving Key a thirty-six-year-old widower. After his wife's death, Key developed numerous phobias regarding his own health. Although his doctor could find nothing wrong, Key insisted that his heart was weakened and went to Cuba, hoping to strengthen it in the warm, clean air.

When Key returned, his colleagues thought he would bury his grief by throwing himself into his career as district attorney. But Key dealt with his loss in a different way, returning to his days as a ladies' man, often seen riding through the capital's streets on his iron-gray stallion, Lucifer.

According to his contemporaries, no other man in Washington was as popular with women or as "undoubted as a rival." Key's position as district attorney, the prestige of his uncle, U.S. Supreme Court chief justice Roger Taney, and his reputation for clever repartee assured his place on the guest lists of Washington's most exclusive social dinners, while allowing him to mix with the most prominent political players.

Teresa was first introduced to Key at President Buchanan's inaugural dinner in 1857. Because she was the wife of a congressman and Key was the district attorney, they moved in the same political and social circles and saw each other frequently. Initially, Key's relationship with Teresa was innocent, as he only escorted her to and from events, a duty that Sickles was comfortable entrusting to his friend when business called him out of town. Soon, however, Teresa developed an unwavering preference for Key's company, much to the chagrin of her other bachelor admirers.

One such admirer was Samuel Beekman, a young clerk in the Interior Department. Beekman was infatuated with the lovely young woman and enjoyed escorting her to the occasional dinner. He grew so jealous of Key's role as the preferred escort that he made several indiscreet comments about their relationship while drinking in a hotel bar. Beekman insinuated that Teresa and Key were lovers and said that Key "boasted that he only asked thirty-six hours with any woman to make her do what he pleased."

Beekman's accusations got back to Sickles, who was deeply offended that someone had provided the Washington rumor mill with grist about his wife. The congressman confronted Beekman, who denied saying anything derogatory about Teresa. The clerk's denials were not sufficient for the similarly slandered Key. When he discovered that rumors were flying regarding the nature of his relationship with a married woman, Key demanded that Beekman withdraw the accusations in writing; Beekman did so, adding a disclaimer that his statements were innocent and only assumed their unsavory character through the interpretations of the listeners. The ordeal so upset Beekman that he resigned his post and shortly thereafter left Washington.

In the aftermath of the recent rumors, Sickles asked his wife that Key not visit their house unless the congressman was home to issue the invitation. But Sickles remained troubled, believing Key had overreacted to Beekman's comments. Key had asked Congressman Haskin, Sickles's friend, to relay that Key viewed the twenty-two-year-old Mrs. Sickles as a child and had nothing more than paternal feelings for her, adding that, being nearly forty, he had four children of his own between three and eleven and that the fatherly instinct ran deep within him.

Sickles, suspicious but not seriously worried, was called away to New York on business the following weekend and asked Haskin to call on his wife from time to time and make sure that all was well. Haskin agreed, and he and Mrs. Haskin stopped by the next day for a visit with Teresa, whom they found drinking champagne and eating salad with Key.

An embarrassed Teresa jumped from her chair, blushing. Although she tried to recover by asking the Haskins to join her and Key for a glass of wine, her demeanor made it only too obvious to the visitors that she had been planning on spending the afternoon alone with Key. The Haskins hastily left; Mrs. Haskin never returned to the house, commenting as she climbed into her carriage that Teresa was "a bad woman." Congressman Haskin never mentioned the event.

Undeterred by the encounter with her husband's friends, Teresa was soon spotted at the theater and riding through Congressional Cemetery with the district attorney when her husband was out of town. Teresa and Key began seeing each other often, but attempted to conceal their growing attraction, to no avail.

Trouble for the pair began at a masquerade ball given by a California congressman. Although Sickles was in town the night of the party, he had fallen ill and could not attend. Teresa, however, was expected to attend, representing her husband.

Washington's elite came to the ball costumed as Greek goddesses, Turkish sultans, and druid priests. Teresa chose a more literary look, dressing as Little Red Riding Hood, and was so fetching in her red cloak that another guest wrote a poem about the evening, including her by name. Key wore an English-hunter costume with high-top boots and a jaunty cap, and carried with him a silver trumpet that he blew intermittently to draw attention to himself.

It appeared to many attending the ball that Teresa and Key were a couple, and while the festivities were in full swing, they took their leave. Teresa asked her coachman to drive them to the National Hotel, where, after a few minutes, Key left, whatever plans they had made giving way to caution and, perhaps, virtue.

However, just weeks later, Teresa and Key began meeting even more frequently. Once again, Sickles was out of town for a few days and Key had come to visit. Key and Teresa sat down in the study to chat, but wound up consummating their affair on a large red sofa near the door. There was little doubt that Washington society was rapidly becoming aware of their relationship. Even Teresa's own servants—having heard noises coming from the library and study on several occasions—rolled their eyes when Key came to visit, saying, "Here comes Disgrace to see Disgust."

Several months went by with Teresa and Key meeting nearly daily. Key would often slip into the house late at night after the streets had cleared of most passersby or wait at a prearranged location when Teresa went out visiting. Teresa would order the coachman to stop at a particular corner or a certain house, and her eager lover would hop in. They took minimal steps to conceal their relationship; Key would still greet Teresa with a formal "Good morning, madam," but would ride with her on nearly every social call and on every errand, climbing out of the carriage a mere block from Teresa's home.

After several months of careful scheduling and "accidental" meetings, Key decided that too many suspicions were being aroused by the series of coincidental encounters; he began looking to rent a small house a few blocks from Teresa's home, where they could carry on the affair without fear of discovery. It didn't take long to find a suitable place, a small brick house in a poor neighborhood where Washington politicians were unlikely to go. The owner of the house, a black named John Gray, rented the house to Key for $50 a month and handed him the shiny brass key.

That November of 1858, Sickles was reelected to the Thirty-sixth Congress, but took his time about returning to Washington. The congressman seemed unconcerned that he was spending little time with his wife, which seemed to be a permanent characteristic of their marriage. Despite Teresa's repeated complaints that she was lonely, Sickles's political ambition consumed him, and he spent his desire on other women in other towns.

Teresa learned of the house Key had rented after the New Year. Soon others knew as well. Observant neighbors noticed that a man would show up at the house and hang a white ribbon or string from the upstairs window. A woman, draped in a bugle-trimmed dark shawl, would arrive shortly thereafter and stay for a few hours. This signaling method worked well for the pair at first, but Key thought that it might be more discreet if Teresa did not have to leave her house to see if the signal for their rendezvous was present.

To remedy this situation, Key began signaling Teresa from the street in front of her house or from the clubhouse across the street by waving a white handkerchief and watching Teresa's upstairs windows through his opera glasses for a reply. Key tried to disguise this tactic by pretending that he was playing with the handkerchief, tossing it up in the air and catching it, or by waving it at a passerby's dog. Soon the entire neighborhood realized what was going on; that Sickles remained unaware is a testament to how often he found reasons to be away from his twenty-two-year-old wife.

When Sickles was at home, everything seemed normal. One day in early February, Sickles returned to the capital to host a dinner party at his Lafayette Square house. Teresa was in charge of the invitations, and Sickles asked that she invite Congressman George Pendleton and his wife, Alice, Key's sister; Teresa sent an invitation to Key as well. The dinner party was a success, and relations between Key and his friend Sickles were described as "of the most intimate character." It was apparent that Sickles had no idea that his friend and his wife were lovers.

Key and Teresa would have been mortified if they'd realized just how well-known their secret had become. Observers saw Key signal to Teresa on February 14, 16, 20, and 21, and each time Teresa would appear on the street, draped in her shawl with the bugle-trimmed edge, headed for the little brick house. The lovers had become so brazen about their meetings that on February 23, Key took the Sickleses' daughter, Laura, to Jonah Hoover's house for the afternoon. The Hoovers were only too pleased to watch their friends' small daughter so Key could meet Teresa. It seems appropriate that Jonah Hoover, the man who had first introduced Teresa to Key, would also help the pair this day, the last time they would ever make love.

As Key and Teresa were leaving the brick house following their tryst, a man cloaked in a dark shawl ran up to Key and handed him a letter before hurrying away. Key opened the letter to find that it was written in code, a simple one in which one letter was substituted for another. Key didn't have time to decode the letter until later that evening, because Laura had to be picked up from the Hoovers'. Sickles had returned home that night, so it was not until the following morning when he left the house that Key and Teresa met at the market to discuss the letter.

The exact contents are unknown, but it apparently dealt with the adulterous affair, because witnesses said that Teresa looked quite distressed as Key read her the letter. If there was any solace to be had, it was that Congressman Sickles did not know. Key and Teresa were confident enough of his ignorance that they made a stop at the confectionery before Mrs. Sickles went home to await her husband's return.

Betrayal

Philip Barton Key was walking through Lafayette Square on a sunny Sabbath day, once again ready to signal his lover with his handkerchief and look for her response with his opera glasses. Three days had passed since he had discussed the coded letter with Teresa, and nothing had come of it. A voyeur in the open street, Key stared at the upstairs window of the Sickleses' house, searching for a response from Teresa while nervously fidgeting with the key to their hideaway. The response he summoned forth was not the one he'd anticipated.

Key was not the only recipient of an anonymous letter. The same day Key had met with Teresa at the market, Sickles had received a note at his home. It read:

Washington, February 24th 1859
Hon. Daniel Sickles

Dear Sir with deep regret I enclose to your address the few lines but an indispensable duty compels me so to do seeing that you are greatly imposed upon.

There is a fellow I may say for he is not a gentleman by any means by the [name] of Phillip Barton Key & I believe the district attorney who rents a house of a negro man by the name of Jno. A. Gray situated on 15th Street btw'n K & L streets for no other purpose than to meet your wife Mrs. Sickles. he [*sic*] hangs a string out of the window as a signal to her that he is in and leaves the door unfastened and she walks in and sir I do assure you he has as much the use of your wife as you have. With these few hints I leave the rest for you to imagine.

Most Respfly [*sic*]
Your friend R.P.G.

Sickles was so agitated that night he did not sleep. A family friend recalled that he was acting strangely and had "a very wild, distracted look."

Sickles was indeed distracted, but he was also prudent. An adulterous affair was no small matter, and he did not want to mention the letter to Teresa—or any accusations against Key—until he could verify that they were actually having an affair. Sickles immediately placed an ad in the paper asking for R.P.G. to identify himself and then enlisted the help of his friend George Woolridge to find out if the accusations were true.

Woolridge began interviewing the neighbors around the house where Key and Teresa met and was ready with a description of the female visitor when he saw Sickles on Saturday at the Capitol. Although Sickles's ad was never answered and the identity of R.P.G. remains a mystery, Sickles had only to hear the neighbors' description of the bugle-trimmed shawl to know that Teresa was the woman who went almost daily to meet Key.

Sickles was crushed by his wife's betrayal—his own infidelities, unremarkable for nineteenth-century men of his station, were of no moment—and, just as with the death of Professor Da Ponte, his "exhibitions of grief" were so "violent" that a friend had to come to his aid. Woolridge offered his sympathy and led Sickles into another room to try to calm him.

After Sickles collected himself enough to leave the room, he headed for home, apparently attracting a great deal of attention on the way. Unable to hail a hack, Sickles set out on the mile-long walk to his house. Francis Mohum, an acquaintance of the congressman's, saw him pushing past other pedestrians and noted how disturbed he looked. Mohum was shocked by Sickles's appearance, describing him as looking "crazy or insane."

Sickles continued his near sprint all the way to Lafayette Square, where the Reverend Dr. Pyne and his son were passing by on their way home. Pyne had been to Sickles's house several times and was preparing to offer a greeting when he saw the "wild" look on Sickles's face. Though Sickles looked directly at him, Pyne said he saw no recognition register in Sickles's face, just a "mingled defiant air" about him. Without hesitation, Sickles pushed through the front door of his house, leaving the reverend standing in the street in disbelief.

Inside Sickles's home, dinner was just being served. Teresa was in the upstairs bedroom, but Sickles didn't wait and sat down at the table. Midway through the meal, which Sickles only picked at, he asked the maid to bring his dinner upstairs, then broke down in tears and fled the room. The maid, clearing the table, could hear shouts and recriminations coming from the bedroom as Sickles confronted his wife. After twenty minutes of yelling, the room fell eerily quiet.

Nearly two hours later, he called the maid to the upstairs bedroom. Teresa was sitting at her desk, pale hands carefully inking her words on the paper. Sickles, nervously pacing the floor waiting for her to finish, had stripped Teresa's wedding band from her finger and broken the ring, a symbol of their ruined marriage. When Teresa looked up, she asked the maid to witness the document she had signed; it was a confession describing her relationship with Key. In Teresa's own hand was an explanation of how Key signaled for her to join him, an admission of her repeated infidelity, and a detailed account of the adulterers' activities in the little brick house.

Teresa, in recognition of the current pro forma nature of her marriage to Sickles, signed the document with her maiden name, Bagioli. This same confession would soon be splashed across the country in every major newspaper, and nineteenth-century America would read in shock of Mrs. Sickles "undressing herself," being "kissed in the house a number of times," and "doing what is usual for wicked women to do."

Overwrought by the day's events, Sickles sobbed himself to sleep while Teresa slept on the floor, her head propped against a chair.

Morning dawned, bringing with it an incongruously cheerful sun beaming into the Sickleses' house. The maid, hearing church bells, left for Sunday-morning services. Teresa, still prostrate on the floor, could hear her husband sobbing uncontrollably in another room. When the maid returned an hour later, she tried to comfort the brokenhearted man of the house. Glancing out the window, the maid suddenly tensed, recognizing the tall figure of Philip Barton Key jauntily strolling down the street. One wonders if the maid considered warning him away, but given her station, it's unlikely she would have done anything other than what she did: said nothing and returned to the kitchen.

Just as the maid was leaving Sickles's side, Samuel Butterworth, superintendent of the U.S. Assay Office in New York and a close friend, dropped in to take her place. Sickles had sent a note to Butterworth the night before, asking him to come over right away, and Butterworth, concerned for his friend, obliged. Sickles was relieved to have a trustworthy male ear and related the events of the past four days. Butterworth first suggested Sickles send his wife to stay with her parents in New York, and that he himself should take a journey through Europe until the affair blew over. Sickles took little comfort from this suggestion, pointing out that all of Washington would be talking about the affair, while his absence would destroy his political career. Butterworth then changed tactics, saying, "There is but one course left you as a man of honor. You need no advice."

Sickles apparently found this course of action more appealing; when his guest departed, Sickles armed himself with two derringers and a five-shot revolver. Washington had no laws against carrying concealed weapons; Sickles, Key, and other well-to-do men regularly carried the highly inaccurate tiny derringers in their vest pockets for self-protection, while slipping a larger pistol into their coats.

As Butterworth and Sickles were finishing their discussion, Key was lingering outside Sickles's house, chatting with a young couple walking home from church, Bibles tucked under their arms. Although Key tried to appear attentive, he continued glancing anxiously at the upstairs window from which Teresa usually signaled back. The couple departed, but Key remained, now playing with the Sickleses' dog, Dandy. Key pulled out his white handkerchief and pretended to twirl it at the delicate greyhound, all the while watching the window to see if his lover had seen his signal.

Unfortunately, while Teresa did not see her lover hailing her, her husband did. Sickles looked out the window just in time to see Key waving his handkerchief with great vigor, assuming he could signal with impunity even though he knew that Sickles was home. This sight was too much for Sickles, knowing that his friend and his wife were lovers and that Key was even now standing in the open square in full view of the world, brazenly calling to Teresa to come and make love with him. In Sickles's mind he had been made the fool, and "the whole town knew it."

"Don't Murder Me!"

Sickles rushed from his house into Lafayette Square. At least seven other pedestrians were converging on the square, while neighbors, taking the opportunity to air out their houses on this unseasonably warm day, were watching through their open windows.

Sickles ran toward Key and, pulling a gun from his coat, shouted, "Key, you scoundrel, you have dishonored my house—you must die!" Sickles fired the gun, but the bullet only grazed Key. Key began shouting "Murder!" and charged Sickles and was able to knock the gun to the ground. The two men continued to grapple, but Sickles—nearly a full head shorter than Key—muscled his way out of Key's grasp and pulled a second gun out of his pocket. "Don't murder me!" shouted Key as he backpedaled, trying to escape the furious Sickles. Key pulled out his opera glasses and hurled them at Sickles; they hit and bounced off without effect, then fell to the ground, useless. Key was unarmed and defenseless.

Sickles leveled the gun at Key, took aim, and fired. The bullet hit Key two inches below the groin, entering his upper thigh and just missing the main artery. Key staggered as the impact of the bullet knocked him backward. He stumbled toward the sidewalk and begged Sickles not to shoot again. Sickles, in a frenzy, shouted at Key, "You villain, you have dishonored my house, and you must die!"

Key fell against a tree and wrapped one arm around it, the other hand pressed to his wound. He pleaded for his life as Sickles pulled the trigger; the gun misfired. "Murder! Murder!" Key yelled, but none of the stunned bystanders came to his aid. Sickles then stepped forward and stood directly over Key's body, aimed the gun at his chest, and fired point-blank. The bullet tore through his chest, and Key slid to the pavement, his chest filling with nearly four quarts of blood. His breathing became shallow and he could no longer call for help, but Sickles was not yet finished. He put the gun directly against Key's head and pulled the trigger. The gun misfired again, but Key's wounds were sufficiently serious to finish the job; two guns, five pulls of the trigger, two misfires, three bullets—it was merely a matter of time.

Bystanders carried Key into a nearby bar and propped him up on an overturned chair. Although his late-arriving rescuers tried to speak to him, Key gave no sign that he understood what they were saying. His breathing faded to a barely audible wheeze as he drowned in his own blood. He had no last words.

The Washington Tragedy

News of "the Washington tragedy" spread quickly. A young page named Bonitz ran to the White House to inform President Buchanan of the shooting. Buchanan listened to the news about his friend in grim silence and then lied. Buchanan, perhaps thinking Bonitz was the only witness, told the page that if he stayed in the capital to testify against Sickles, he would be held without bail until the trial was over. The president encouraged Bonitz to leave the capital and gave him a wad of money and a razor as a memento. Bonitz took the money, the razor, and Buchanan's advice, never to be heard from again.

Meanwhile, Butterworth—who was only a short distance from Sickles's house when the shooting began—took Sickles by the arm and slowly walked him toward Attorney General Jeremiah Black's house, where he planned to turn himself in. An acquaintance reported that Sickles was in a horrible rage and looked as if he "would kill every man, woman, and child" he saw. This was in marked contrast to his demeanor when he arrived at the attorney general's home. Sickles joined a conversation about Pennsylvania politics with other guests before pulling Attorney General Black aside and explaining what had just happened. Black, shocked by Sickles's composure, allowed him to return to his house, accompanied by two officers and Butterworth.

Although Sickles may have kept his composure in front of other politicians, once he was outside, the true import of his actions began to sink in. Bystanders waiting outside Black's home said Sickles emerged from his meeting with the attorney general wearing the mask of "a man frightened to death," his hair hanging limply over his face. The streets were so clogged with people seeking to offer Sickles support, condemn him as murderer, or satisfy their morbid curiosity that the carriage carrying Sickles to his house was barely able to move through the crowds. Looking across Lafayette Square, one could see souvenir hunters already cutting pieces from the tree under which Key had begged for mercy.

Once home, Sickles asked to see Teresa. The police made him promise he would not hurt his wife before allowing him to go upstairs, where Sickles found that Teresa had not moved since he'd last seen her. Sickles gazed at his wife, his face frozen, apathetic, and uttered one sentence before turning on his heel: "I've killed him."

Sickles's mood swings continued in his parlor; just before he was taken to jail, he was talking to Butterworth and another confidant when he suddenly threw himself on the sofa and covered his face with his hands in what appeared to be unbearable misery. Sickles wailed, as one observer said, "an agony of unnatural and unearthly sounds, the most remarkable" that he had ever heard, screaming and sobbing, while writhing about in convulsions. Witnessing Sickles descend into this "state of perfect frenzy," Butterworth feared "he would become insane" and tried to calm him before accompanying him to the jail.

These conflicting stories may be exaggerations on the part of creative witnesses, or they may be evidence that Sickles was driven to the edge, past the breaking point, entirely out of his right mind.

Sickles was escorted out of the house, whereupon he saluted the gathered crowds before being driven to the Washington jail. The jail was a mere three blocks from Key's fashionable home, where his funeral would be held two days later, but in terms of accommodations, the two places were worlds apart.

The jail was a three-story building erected in 1839 in an attempt at the Gothic Revival style. It was built of brick, but was plastered over and scored to look like stone. It had "no sewage, no bath, nor water, no ventilation" and "swarmed with vermin." The jail was known as a place that "combined all the disadvantages which have been gradually removed from every other place of confinement in Christendom."

Sickles waived a bail hearing, claiming he sought nothing but a speedy trial and complete vindication. Sickles no doubt questioned his hasty decision when he was led to the dingy cell reserved for prisoners charged with murder. It was crawling with insects, and aghast that he would have to sleep in such a place with only an iron pail for bathroom facilities, he asked the jailer if he had a better room. The jailer smugly quipped, "This is the best place you members of Congress have afforded us."

That night Sickles was visited by the Reverend Mr. Haley of the Unitarian Church, and although the two had just met, Sickles confided in the minister. Overlooking that his years of philandering had preceded Teresa's single love affair, Sickles vowed not to see her again and asked the reverend to dispose of Teresa's broken wedding ring, claiming that she had "sundered the bonds it pledged too cruelly."

The clergyman had also visited Teresa earlier that evening and, seeing her depressed state, asked permission of Sickles to return the ring to her. He agreed to return it as a token of comfort, explaining that the ring's broken state would serve as symbol enough to remind Teresa of their irredeemable marriage. Sickles passed a tortuous night with intermittent visits from the Reverend Mr. Haley, finally falling asleep for an hour or two just before dawn. He awoke to find himself covered with insects.

Two days after arriving—the same day Key was laid to rest next to his wife, Ellen—Sickles was transferred to a larger, nicer cell. Some suggested that President Buchanan, who could not visit Sickles in jail without committing an unprecedented breach of propriety, spoke to the jailer about providing better arrangements. Whatever prompted the change, the room that Sickles was given was unparalleled in the memory of jail administrators. The walls were whitewashed, the room fumigated, furniture was moved in, there was ventilation, a corridor in which Sickles could exercise, and he was allowed unlimited visitors, regardless of the hour. Sickles even had his dog, Dandy, stay with him in the cell.

Sickles was visited by many friends and acquaintances, but perhaps the most appreciated was his elderly father-in-law, Antonio Bagioli, who expressed support for Sickles and told him what "a good son, a true friend, and devoted, kind, loving husband and father" he was. Bagioli expressed regret that after all the "affection," "kindness," and "devotion" that Sickles had heaped on Teresa, she would have subjected him to such a humiliation. It is unknown whether Bagioli knew that his son-in-law had also been involved in adulterous affairs, but it would likely have made little difference, a result of the double standard that ruled the minds of polite society in the mid-1800s.

Though Americans condemned infidelity by either partner in a marriage, the results for each of the spouses were starkly dissimilar. The community looked down on extramarital affairs because they threatened what was viewed as the most stable societal unit, the marriage. Standards at the time dictated that the threat was greater if the wife committed infidelity than if the husband did. This belief was largely upheld by the inability to determine who fathered a child, thus leaving a living monument of a wife's infidelity and a constant doubt as to its lineage in the mind of her husband. A cheating husband would still be accepted in polite society; an adulterous wife was "condemned and ostracized." This was Teresa's plight, and Sickles's publication of her confession served only to make the public's ridicule of her more acute.

Sickles remained in jail and sought a speedy trial. On March 14, he was brought before a grand jury, and in ten days the grand jury issued an indictment for a single count of murder. Sickles's trial was set for Monday, April 4—a remarkably short thirty-six days from the Sunday on which Key was killed.

Assembling the Legal Dream Team

Sickles's defense began to take shape the day after the killing, when he hired two Washington lawyers to assist the police in gathering evidence of Teresa's adulterous affair. The lawyers were with the police when they searched Key's brick house on Fifteenth Street.

Sickles realized that he was going to be charged with murder, a hanging offense, and that his choice of defense attorney was a matter of life or death. He hired Philip Phillips, a local defense lawyer with a stellar reputation, then sought the help of two close friends, James T. Brady and John L. Graham. Brady and Graham both refused to accept any kind of payment for their services, offering them pro bono to help out a friend in need. Finally, Sickles enlisted the help of another friend, a powerful Ohio attorney who now practiced law in Washington, Edwin McMasters Stanton.

This nineteenth-century "dream team" was composed of skilled men who brought different—but valuable—talents to the table. Graham was known for his oratorical ability and convincing tone in front of a jury; for this reason he was chosen to make the first impression on the jury through his delivery of the opening statement.

Phillips was known for his ability to read a person's character, making him the perfect man to be in charge of jury selection. Brady was a renowned criminal defense attorney who'd won fifty-one of his fifty-two murder cases. Brady's only perceived fault? Verbosity, a weakness for ten words when one would do. Stanton made up for this with his "sledge-hammer earnestness" and skill in oral argument, earning him a reputation as a highly effective specialist in Supreme Court cases.

Brady, a bachelor nearing his forty-fourth birthday at the time of Sickles's trial, was in the prime of his career. His specialty was murder trials involving the insanity defense, and his ability to explain knotty legal concepts to the jury in a logical, plainspoken fashion made him an ominous opponent in the courtroom. He attracted the attention of trial watchers the moment he entered the room; his "massive head with its corona of curls" and his "graceful form, electric wit, ready rhetoric, and Irish enthusiasm" proved irresistible. Brady's courtroom demeanor was flawless, and he was unfailingly polite, preferring to allow an apparent erroneous ruling by the court stand rather than argue the point and create ill will between himself and the judge. Brady's reputation for etiquette was so well known that judges gave him the kind of deference usually reserved only for much older and more experienced attorneys.

Brady's defense was inspired not only by the intellectual challenge, but also by the depth of his friendship with his client. They had been close friends for many years, ever since Brady had stepped forward in support of Sickles's plan for Central Park, when other constituents were ready to abandon the idea. Whenever Brady visited Washington, he made sure to drop in on Sickles and was regularly a guest at the congressman's dinner parties.

Edwin Stanton, like Brady, had a long and impressive list of legal accomplishments, including winning a string of seemingly impossible cases, defending both the innocent and guilty. His legal arguments were so well reasoned that it was not uncommon for the judge to be seen nodding in agreement while listening to him. Stanton took on nearly every case offered him, regardless of topic, and was routinely successful.

Stanton had met Daniel Sickles at a social gathering in Washington, D.C. The two men had never worked together, but developed a solid friendship outside the professional arena. They enjoyed the differences in their personalities. Sickles was boisterous and energetic, not as experienced in law as Stanton. Stanton, typically somber, enjoyed hearing about the scrapes that Sickles had gotten himself into. Stanton tried to counsel Sickles, gently chiding him about his excesses, and willingly shared from his vast legal knowledge. The two got on wonderfully.

In 1855, Stanton joined several other attorneys—among them a lawyer by the name of Abraham Lincoln—to defend a patent for a reaping machine. The issue was one of first impression, the evidence complex. When the decision was made as to who would deliver the closing argument, the defense attorneys informed Stanton that Lincoln had been selected. Stanton was furious, calling the future president a "long-armed baboon." Stanton told the other attorneys, "If that giraffe appears in the case, I will throw up my brief and leave." The defense team yielded to Stanton, and Lincoln voiced no objection to Stanton delivering the close. The lawyers' efforts paid off, and thanks in no small part to Stanton's legal brilliance and thorough preparation, they won their case.

Later that year, Stanton was asked by the Pennsylvania Supreme Court to go to California on behalf of the government and settle a land dispute. This "dispute" would rocket Stanton to fame.

The United States had signed a peace treaty with Mexico in 1848, the terms of which bound the United States to give legal recognition to land grants given by Mexico before California joined the Union. There were 803 land claims brought by persons who had supposedly been granted them by Mexico during this time frame. One of the claims, held by a Jose Y. Limantour, appeared to be a valid grant certified by the signature of the Mexican governor. The problem for the United States was that this grant included all of San Francisco, San Francisco Bay, the islands in the bay, and Point Tiburon, where the American government was already spending $2 million on the construction of forts, lighthouses, and other strongholds.

Stanton accepted the daunting task, leaving his wife and newborn daughter behind, took a Spanish grammar book and his son Edwin for company, and headed out to the wilds of California. Armed with subpoenas, he began sifting through the papers left behind when the Mexican civil government had decamped during the settlers' revolt. Stanton found boxes of papers, all tumbled together, in countless warehouses and storerooms. He rose at seven each morning, working until nearly midnight each night. Ultimately, his research would contain four hundred folio volumes, including every law and decision relating to land in California dating back to the Spanish colonial administration, as well as a complete record of every land grant made by the Mexican government in California.

Stanton established that the Limantour claim was fraudulent, enabling the United States to legally claim the San Francisco Bay area. Stanton's research also showed many other grants to be forgeries, including that of the swindlers who tried to lay claim to the fabulously rich New Almaden quicksilver mine.

He returned to Washington in early February 1859, finally getting to spend time with his family. It wasn't long after his return, however, that he received word that his friend desperately needed his help.

Opposing the formidable Brady and Stanton was a man thrust into the limelight, selected for reasons having little to do with his legal acumen. Robert Ould, the newly appointed district attorney for the District of Columbia (the victim's former position), was to pursue the case against Sickles. Ould had two qualities of particular interest: He had been the assistant district attorney under Key and had been chosen to take his place and prosecute his killer. Second, Ould was put on the case by President Buchanan, Sickles's friend. Ould's appointment was the subject of much discussion; he was an inexperienced trial lawyer and seemed to many observers a prosecutor without much "grit." Ould had studied to be a minister before becoming an attorney and seemed to be "more like a friend to be honorably trusted than like a lawyer to be depended upon."

Key's family pleaded with Buchanan to appoint a more experienced prosecutor, but the president refused. Entirely dissatisfied with the president's decision, Key's family hired another prosecuting attorney, James M. Carlisle, a sometime city attorney for Washington, D.C., and a force to be reckoned with. The press reported that "he [was] sharp, forcible, and cautious," with a keen eye for detail that missed nothing. Despite President Buchanan's disapproval, Carlisle agreed to take a place at the prosecution table.

Ould began preparing for his first serious criminal trial, trying to concentrate on his duty to Key's family and his obligation to prosecute Sickles to the full extent of the law, while acknowledging that the president of the United States undoubtedly wanted an acquittal. Taking his seat at the prosecution table and glancing at Stanton and Brady, he drew a deep breath. Then he, and everyone else in the courtroom, fell silent as the "honorable and dignified" Judge Crawford took his chair, and the most talked about trial in recent history began.

Oyez! Oyez!

Jury selection took three full days. One hundred and forty-eight men were questioned and excused from jury service for bias. Most said they believed that Sickles was fully within his rights for killing Key; others openly admitted that if they were placed on the jury, they would vote to acquit. One man said that he would likely have done the same in Sickles's shoes, but if he happened to find Sickles guilty, he "would say hang him high as hell." In the end, twelve men—women were not allowed to serve—were selected: two farmers, four grocers, a shoemaker, a merchant, a tinsmith, a coachmaker, a cabinetmaker, and a dealer in "gents' furnishing."

The trial proper began on Monday, April 4—on what would have been the eve of Key's forty-first birthday—and Sickles's defense team began the proceedings in an unconventional manner. After announcing that Sickles's plea was not guilty, they delayed their opening statement until after all of the prosecution's witnesses had been called.

It's possible this was to keep their novel defense under wraps as long as possible, or perhaps it was to put additional time between the accusatory evidence against Sickles and deliberations, in the hope that the jurors would somehow forget the testimony given at the beginning of the trial. Whatever their reasons, it certainly seemed effective, for after Ould and Carlisle finished presenting the prosecution's evidence, John Graham got to his feet and delivered a spellbinding opening statement over two days, unveiling a defense strategy to the jurors that had never before been tried in U.S. history: the defendant was not guilty because he had been *temporarily* insane at the time of the killing.

Graham began by appealing to the jurors' emotions, highlighting the shocking betrayal of Sickles's trust by Key. Key was not only a dear friend of the defendant's, but a man who, like Sickles, had also made the solemn pledge of marriage and knew the value of the vows. Graham explained, "You are about to decide whether the defender of the marriage bed is a murderer—whether he is to be put on the same footing with the first murderer, and is to be presented in his moral and legal aspects with the same hue of aggravation about him. Gentlemen, the murderer is a detestable character, and far be it from me to defend him before this or any other jury. Society cannot, it ought not, to contain him."

The question, according to Graham, was not whether Sickles killed Key, but rather, "The question is, what was the influence of the provocation on the mind of the man who slew [Key]. What was the mental condition of the defendant at the time he took the life of the deceased? . . . The question I put to your minds is this: Whether when a man receives provocation which excites in him an amount of frenzy which he cannot control, he is responsible for what he does under the influence of that frenzy? It is folly to punish a man for what he cannot help doing?"

Graham then offered the jury an alternative to finding Sickles guilty of murder, a finding that Sickles had been temporarily insane at the time of the shooting.

> How far the provocation furnished by the deceased to the defendant acted upon or affected the defendant's mind in reference to exonerating him for all legal consequences for or by reason of the killing is the question; whether while the influence of the provocation remained it did render the defendant for the time being insane; whether it did not operate such a state of mental unsoundness as to relieve the defendant's alleged act of and from all criminality, supposing the act to have been immediately and directly prompted or occasioned by it. In other words, whether the case is one of pardonable or excusable unsoundness of mind, or of wanton or ungovernable passion; whether the defendant, not being to blame for the provocation, the frenzy, or its results, can be holden for a crime. This, gentlemen of the jury, is regarded as one of the most important items in this prosecution. We mean to say, not that Mr. Sickles labored under insanity in consequence of an established mental permanent disease, but that the condition of his mind at the time of the commission of the act in question was such as would render him legally unaccountable, as much so as if the state of his mind had been produced by a mental disease.

The defense was walking a fine line. Traditionally, insanity was defined as a long-standing mental condition that disabled a person from distinguishing right from wrong. If Sickles was found not guilty by reason of insanity, in this traditional sense, he would be sent to an asylum or held under house arrest for some unspecified time until he was once again adjudged sane.

Knowledge about the causes of mental disease and the treatment for it was in its most rudimentary form in the mid-1800s. It was common practice at the time to administer mercury and laxatives to insane patients, in an effort to keep them docile and free of stomach complaints. Patients with recurring stomach ailments, due in part to the diet of thin gruel and bread, were routinely forced to have enemas or have leeches applied to their anuses or genitalia. Doctors believed that digestive problems were caused by a swelling of the blood vessels in the lower intestine and that leeches would relieve this swelling by removing "bad blood." Patients who were believed to be violent, as Sickles would likely have been, were subject to a gruesome procedure called cupping. A patient's head would be shaved, and a glass or metal cup with a sharp edge would be pressed into the scalp and twisted to create a circular cut on the head. Doctors would allow the glass to fill with blood from the wound, believing that the patient's brain would cool off and would no longer cause violent outbursts.

Knowing that confinement in an asylum held these horrors for their client, Sickles's defense team would have to prove that the adulterous affair of his wife and his good friend was such extreme provocation that he became temporarily insane at the time of the shooting. The defense would then have to show that Sickles, no longer under the influence of this extreme provocation, was once again fit to rejoin society, now that the once-in-a-lifetime moment of madness had passed.

The origin of the insanity defense dated back as far as 1505, when a man on trial for the murder of an infant was acquitted due to his inability to distinguish between right and wrong. *M'Naghten's Case,* decided by the English House of Lords only sixteen years before the Sickles trial, was widely acknowledged as having provided the standard for determining whether someone was legally insane at the time of his crime. This rule required either that the defendant not know the nature and quality of his act, or if he did, that he did not know that the act was wrong. The defense of temporary insanity, however, was unheard of in the United States and had been tried only once before in England, unsuccessfully at that. Stanton and Brady knew that to prevent Sickles's execution or "incarceration" in a mental asylum, they would have to show that Sickles was insane at the time of the killing but had regained his sanity afterward.

Some legal scholars following the Sickles trial closely wondered why Brady and Stanton ruled out showing that Sickles was guilty of manslaughter, rather than murder. After all, manslaughter is a noncapital offense and would thus preserve Sickles's life, as would the temporary insanity defense. Why did the defense decide to risk the untried theory of temporary insanity instead? Brady and Stanton undoubtedly considered manslaughter as an option but rejected it for one reason: it would fail.

Manslaughter is a killing that occurs in the heat of passion, when one wishes to inflict harm on another and winds up killing him in the few moments of uncontrollable rage immediately following a severe provocation. The most common example is when a husband returns home to find his wife in bed with someone else. In the brief time of intense anger immediately following the viewing of this scene, the injured spouse might kill the man who had violated the home. This sounds similar to the Sickles case on its face, but with one crucial difference. Sickles's killing of Key lacked the immediacy required to classify the killing as manslaughter.

Sickles killed Key for "defiling" Teresa, yet he knew of the affair for at least a full day before the killing. Sickles saw Key outside his home, then took time to gather his guns and his ammunition before leaving the house. Sickles's act was not done in a few moments of passion, but rather was deliberate, occurring over several minutes and requiring multiple shots with more than one weapon as the wounded man struggled to escape. Even if Sickles was freshly provoked by the sight of Key signaling to his wife from the street below, the time Sickles took to prepare and execute the killing surely gave him a "cooling-off period," during which his passion would have waned. These facts would have invalidated any claim that Sickles was acting in the heat of passion at the time of the shooting. Abandoning the idea that manslaughter was a valid defense, Brady and Stanton turned all of their efforts toward proving that Sickles was temporarily insane at the time of the shooting.

At the time of Sickles's trial the assumption in every case was that the defendant was sane, thus avoiding unnecessary litigation over the defendant's sanity. Sickles's lawyers argued that this assumption was correct, but they also argued that when the issue of insanity was raised by the defense, it then became the prosecution's burden to disprove it. In other words, if the prosecution failed to prove that the defendant was sane, the defendant must be presumed to have been insane at the time of the crime. In a major blow to the prosecution, Judge Crawford agreed with Stanton's argument, ruling that Sickles was presumed to have been insane at the time of the killing.

Courtroom Drama

The trial attracted hundreds of spectators, most of whom had to be turned away at the courtroom doors. Many snuck in through open windows and stood in a crush against the wall, standing on tiptoe, straining for a glimpse of the defendant and the witnesses. The number of reporters covering the trial was unprecedented; to make room for them the courthouse staff removed all the writing tables from the front of the courtroom, replacing them with closely spaced chairs or long benches. The room was stiflingly hot, despite the frigid spring temperatures outside; Judge Crawford had to adjourn the trial in the midafternoon every day as a result.

Sickles remained composed, despite the heat and the crowds, immaculately dressed, back straight, head held erect, looking so calm onlookers might never guess he was on trial for his life.

Witness after witness walked to the stand. Some testified to Sickles's good character, some told of seeing the shooting, others talked about

Sickles's behavior after the killing. Through the examination of witnesses, the jury learned of Sickles's tormented screams upon the death of Professor Da Ponte, his breakdown after learning of his wife's adultery, the sleepless, tear-filled night following Teresa's confession, and his uncontrollable mood changes on the day of the shooting. The courtroom fell silent as the defense sought permission to describe the character of the adulterous relationship between Key and Teresa. Judge Crawford paused, then ruled, "At the time of the homicide the prisoner declared the deceased had dishonored his house, or defiled, or violated his bed. . . . This declaration is a part of the principal fact. It is important to the jury to have it explained, and it is the right of the defendant, in all justice, to have it explained."

In one move, the defense had succeeded in shifting the entire focus of the trial. It was no longer about Sickles killing Key; it was now about the victim's adulterous relationship with Teresa. Every sordid detail of their liaison was dragged before the jury—and across the front pages of the newspapers. Forty-three witnesses were called to testify about the illicit relationship. The prosecution team, Ould and Carlisle, sat dumbfounded as they watched their case crumble. Sickles broke down three times, weeping into his hands, until he finally had to be excused from the room, Stanton at his side for support.

The defense next tried to introduce Teresa's confession as physical evidence of the adulterous affair. Ould objected and Judge Crawford agreed, explaining that the marital privilege—the legal prohibition against a married person testifying against her mate—extended to written declarations of a wife or husband, and the confession was therefore inadmissible. The judge's ruling notwithstanding, the confession turned up on the front pages of major newspapers. Although Sickles's defense denied leaking it to the press, the damage was already done. The prosecution—on the theory that what's good for the goose is good for the gander—introduced evidence of Sickles's adulterous behavior. But Judge Crawford would have none of it, ruling that Sickles's moral character was entirely irrelevant.

The trial finally began to wind up, the weary jurors eager to leave the stifling courtroom and return to their lives after seventeen days of statements and testimony. It was time for the defense and the prosecution to sum up the merits of their respective cases; closing arguments would last for three days. The defense would go first, Stanton's precise, logical arguments and upright moral character immensely appealing to the Victorian-era jurors' sense of justice, honor, and integrity. The drama of the moment was heightened by a raging thunderstorm outside, the worst gale to lash the city in twenty years. Rain beat against the courthouse windows, lightning flashed across the sky, and thunder boomed as Stanton strode toward the jury, hands behind his back. He drew a slow breath and began.

CLOSING ARGUMENT OF EDWIN STANTON ON BEHALF OF DANIEL SICKLES

May it please Your Honor: It becomes my duty to present some considerations in support of the points of law which have been submitted by the defense, and which points are in conformity with those which may be given to a jury. The event which has brought the jury and the prisoner at the bar into solemn relations, and made the court and counsel participators in this momentous trial, is the death of Mr. Key at the hand of Mr. Sickles, which took place on Sunday, the twenty-seventh of February. The occasion of this event was an adulterous intrigue between Mr. Key and the wife of Mr. Sickles.

The law rising on the case must depend on the relations each held to the other at the time the occurrence took place. Two theories have been presented—one by the prosecution, the other by the defense. Those theories, as in all such cases, are opposite; and it will be for the court, by a comparison of those theories with the known principles of law, to give to the jury the instruction.

The act of taking human life is designated in law by the general term of *homicide,* which may be either with malice or without malice. The act of Congress which governs in this district designates two grades of unlawful homicide, namely, murder and manslaughter. "Murder," says Blackstone, "is now thus defined, or rather described, by Sir Edward Coke: 'When a person of sound memory and discretion unlawfully killeth any reasonable creature in being, and under the king's peace, with malice aforethought, either express or implied.'" The same author defines manslaughter to be "the unlawful killing of another without malice, either express or implied; which may be either voluntary, upon a sudden heat, or involuntary, but in the commission of some unlawful act."

There are two classes of cases in which a man may be exempted from judicial punishment for killing, namely, self-protection, which is a natural right, and, secondly, the defense of one's household from the thief or robber. But there is a third class, arising from the social relation, for the law holds family chastity and the sanctity of the marriage bed, the matron's honor and the virgin's purity, to be more valuable and estimable in law than the property or life of any man.

The present case belongs to that class. On it rests the foundation of the social system. As it involves the life of the prisoner, it cannot be too carefully considered. Indeed this principle has never come before a judicial tribunal in a form more impressive than now.

Here, in the capital of the nation, the social and political metropolis of thirty millions of people, a man of mature age, the head of a family, a member of the learned profession, a high officer of the government, entrusted with the administration of the law, and who for years at this bar has demanded judgment of fine, imprisonment, and death against other men for offenses against the law, has himself been slain in open day in a public place, because he took advantage of the hospitality of a sojourner in this city. Received into his family, he debauched his house, violated the bed of his host, and dishonored his family. On this ground, alone, the deed of killing was committed.

The instructions presented by the defendant bring to the view of the court two consistent lines of defense: one, that the act of the prisoner at the bar is justified by the law of the land, under the circumstances of its commission; the other, that, whether justified or not, it is free from legal responsibility by reason of the state of the prisoner's mind.

When the crime was committed against him by the deceased, in both points of view, the relations which the deceased and the prisoner at the bar bore to each other at the moment of the fatal act are to be observed: one, as a husband outraged in his house, his family, and his marital rights; the other, an adulterer in flagrante delicto. While counsel for the prisoner insist that the act is justified by the law, the counsel for the prosecution assert that the act is destructive of the existence of society and demand judgment of death against him as a fitting penalty.

The very existence of civil society depends not on human life, but on the family relations. "Who knows not," says John Milton, "that chastity and purity of living cannot be established or continued, except it be first established in private families, from whence the whole breed of men come forth?" "The family," says another distinguished moralist, "is the cradle of sensibility, where the first lessons are taught of that tenderness and humanity which cement mankind together; and were they extinguished, the whole fabric of society would be dissolved." In a general sense, the family may embrace various degrees of affinity, more or less near; but in a strictly legal sense, it embraces the relations of husband and wife, parent and child, brother and sister. The first and most sacred tie, however, is the nuptial bond.

"Eternal discord and violence," says a great moralist, "would ensue if man's chief object of affection were secured to him by no legal tie." No man could enjoy any happiness or pursue any vocation if he could not enjoy his wife free from the assaults of the adulterer. The dignity and permanence of the marriage are destroyed by adultery. When the wife becomes the adulterer's prey, the family is destroyed, and all family relations are involved in the ruin of the wife. When a man accepts a woman's hand in wedlock, he receives it with a vow that she will love, honor, serve, and obey him in sickness or in health, and will cleave only to him. This bond is sanctified by the law of God. "What God hath joined together, let no man put asunder." By a marriage, the woman is sanctified to the husband, and this bond must be preserved for the evil as well as for the good.

It is the blessing of the marital institution that it weans men from their sins and draws them to the performance of their duties. This seal of the nuptial vow is no idle ceremony. Thenceforth the law commands the adulterer to beware of disturbing their peace. It commands that no man shall look on woman to lust after her.

The penalty for disobedience to that injunction did not originate in human statutes; it was written in the heart of man in the Garden of Eden, where the first family was planted, and where the woman was made bone of man's bone, flesh of man's flesh. No wife yields herself to the adulterer's embrace till he has weaned her love from her husband; she revolts from her obedience and serves the husband no longer. When her body has been once surrendered to the adulterer, she longs for the death of her husband, whose life is often sacrificed by the cup of the prisoner, or the dagger or pistol of the assassin.

What, then, is the act of adultery? It cannot be limited to the fleeting moment of sexual contact; that would be a mockery, for then the adulterer would ever escape. But law and reason mock not human nature with any such vain absurdity. The act of adultery, like the act of murder, is supposed to include every proximate act in furtherance of, and as a means to, the consummation of the wife's pollution. This is an established principle in American and English law, established from the time of Lord Stowell, as will be hereafter shown.

If the adulterer be found in the husband's bed, he is taken in the act, within the meaning of the law, as if he was found in the wife's arms. If he provides a place for the express purpose of committing adultery with another man's wife, and be found leading her, accompanying her, or following her to that place for that purpose, he is taken in the act.

If he not only provides but habitually keeps such a place and is accustomed by preconcerted signals to entice the wife from the husband's house, to besiege her in the streets, to accompany him to that vile den; and if, after giving such preconcerted signal, he be found watching her, spyglass in hand, and lying in wait around a husband's house, that the wife may join him for that guilty purpose, he is taken in the act.

If a man hire a house, furnish it, provide a bed in it for such a purpose, and if he be accustomed, day by day, week by week, and month by month, to entice her from her husband's house, to tramp with her through the streets to that den of shame, it is an act of adultery, and is the most appalling one that is recorded in the annals of shame; if, moreover, he has grown so bold as to take the child of the injured husband, his little daughter, by the hand, to separate her from her mother, to take the child to the house of a mutual friend while he leads the mother to the guilty den, in order there to enjoy her, it presents a case surpassing all that has ever been written of cold, villainous, remorseless lust.

If this be not the culminating point of adulterous depravity, how much farther could it go? There is no one point beyond. The wretched mother, the ruined wife, has not yet plunged into the horrible filth of common prostitution, to which she is rapidly hurrying, and which is already yawning before her. Shall not that mother be saved from that, and how shall it be done? When a man has obtained such a power over another man's wife that he can not only entice her from her husband's house but separate her from her child for the purpose of guilt, it shows that by some means he has acquired such an unholy mastery over that woman's body and soul that there is no chance of saving her while he lives, and the only hope of her salvation is that God's swift vengeance shall overtake him.

The sacred glow of well-placed domestic affection, no man knows better than Your Honor, grows brighter and brighter as years advance, and the faithful couple whose hands were joined in holy wedlock in the morning of youth find their hearts drawn closer to each other as they descend the hill of life to sleep together at its foot; but lawless love is as short-lived as it is criminal, and the neighbor's wife so hotly pursued, by trampling down every human feeling and divine law, is speedily supplanted by the object of some fresher lust, and then the wretched victim is sure to be soon cast off into common prostitution, and swept through a miserable life and a horrible death to the gates of hell, unless a husband's arm shall save her.

Who, seeing this thing, would not exclaim to the unhappy husband, "Hasten, hasten, hasten to save the mother of your child. Although she be lost as a wife, rescue her from the horrid adulterer; and may the Lord, who watches over the home and the family, guide the bullet and direct stroke." [At this the audience broke into applause, which the bailiffs tried without success to stop.] And when she is delivered, who would not reckon the salvation of that young mother cheaply purchased by the adulterer's blood? Aye, by the blood of a score of adulterers? The death of Key was a cheap sacrifice to save one mother from the horrible fate which, on that Sabbath day, hung over this prisoner's wife and the mother of his child.

The law does not look to the degree of force; it looks to the forcible movement; and being an act of force, it follows that the right of the husband to resist that force is clear and undoubted on the highest principles of law. My friend here [the prosecutor] says he condemns the adulterer as much as anyone, but that he abhors lawless violence. So do I; but the question here is whether the violence be lawless? In undertaking to designate the act of the prisoner here as an act of violence, as an act of personal justice, he assumes the very question that is involved, because on no theory of law, on no system of jurisprudence recognized among men, has the defense of a right, the maintenance of possession in a right, the protection of a right, been recognized either as a revengeful act or an act of lawless violence. By the contemplation of law, the wife is always in the husband's presence, always under his wing; and any movement against her person is a movement against his right and may be resisted as such.

We place the defense here on the same ground and limited by the same means as the right of personal defense. If a man be assailed, his power to slay the assailant is not limited to the moment when the mortal blow is about to be given; he is not bound to wait till his life is on the very point of being taken; but any movement towards the foul purpose plainly indicated justifies him in the right of self-defense, and in slaying the assailant on the spot. The theory of our case is that there was a man living in a constant state of adultery with the prisoner's wife, a man who was daily, by a moral—no, by an immoral—power, enormous, monstrous, and altogether unparalleled in the history of American society, or in the history of the family of man, a power over the being of this woman—calling her from her husband's house, drawing her from the side of her child, and dragging her, day by day, through the streets in order that he might gratify his lust. The husband beholds him in the very act of withdrawing his wife from his roof, from his presence, from his arm, from his wing, from his nest; meets him in that act and slays him, and we say that the right to slay him stands on the firmest principles of self-defense.

It is not my purpose to pursue this discussion in reference to the other points. I shall leave them to my colleague [Mr. Brady]. I thank Your Honor for the patience with which you have heard me in the discussion of this question. I have endeavored to discuss it on principles which I believe, as a man, as a father, and as a husband, to be essential to the peace and security of your home and mine. I have endeavored to discuss it on principles which are essential to the peace and prosperity of the society in which my home is planted as well as yours; and I hope that, by the blessing of God, as it has been Your Honor's good fortune to lay down the law which secures the family, in one aspect, from the seducer of the sister, you may also plant on the best and surest foundations the principles of law which secure the peace of the home, the security of the family, and the relations of husband and wife, which have been in the most horrid manner violated in this case.

If the audience's applause was an accurate indicator of the closing argument's effect on the nonlawyer, the jurors' sympathy probably lay with Sickles. Stanton had done a brilliant job of defining the issue in terms tailor-made for the mid-nineteenth-century man: a husband, robbed of his wife's constancy, of his friend's trust, of the safety of his home, of his belief in womankind. A man left without recourse under the laws of the land, but shielded by the laws of morality. Sickles was left with no other choice but to defend his home and his marriage at the cost of a trespasser's life.

On the nineteenth day of the trial, James Brady rose to offer his argument on behalf of Sickles.

CLOSING ARGUMENT OF JAMES BRADY ON BEHALF OF DANIEL SICKLES

There was a great difference of opinion between the counsel for the defense and the counsel for the prosecution as to the principles on which this case rested, and the counsel for the prosecution was in error in saying that the instructions asked for by the defense were purely of an abstract character. The prosecution had commenced by showing a case which might be termed assassination, and which showed, in none of its aspects, mitigation or alleviation.

The district attorney had represented the prisoner as a walking magazine, an animated battery, going out from his house on the morning of the homicide determined to turn all his engines of destruction against Mr. Key. He is represented as knowing Mr. Key to be unarmed, and as having given the deceased no opportunity of defending himself, but in a cowardly manner shot him down. That statement, however, was utterly unsustained by the evidence adduced for the prosecution. Every man would have been surprised if the evidence had been allowed to stop there, showing only the mortal meeting of these two men, who had hitherto been fast friends. If the case had stopped there, would not the whole world say that in such a case there must have been either insanity or justification?

While the prosecution thus presented the case in the opening, the counsel for the defense had suggested that their defense rested on two grounds. He had seen in the newspapers criticisms of the defense, that the two theories were inconsistent, that if the act were justifiable, the defense of insanity should not have been set up. The defense, however, held that if the act was not held in law to be justifiable, they should have the benefit of the defense of insanity.

The extent of a court or jury is measured by what they may or may not decide with legal effect, and not by the correctness or error of their decision. The jury, in a criminal trial, have the legal right to decide the law as well as the facts involved in the issue; but this does not give them a right, by a wanton disregard of law, to decide arbitrarily.

I verily believe that next to the integrity of the judiciary, which I hope will always continue as it has done in the past, to adorn our national character, next to that is the importance of preserving the trial by jury, especially in criminal cases. I do not recognize in the Declaration of Independence, in the statement of all the abuses that led to the revolt of the American colonies, anything set up as the occasion for the War of the Revolution that compares in importance with the right of trial by jury as it now exists in this land, and much as I abhor the shedding of blood and cowardly as I might be found when the moment of danger approached, I would be willing to lay down my life and wade to any extent in the blood of the foe to prevent that palladium of liberty from being invaded for one moment.

Turning our attention now to that Sunday morning, and to that point of contact, let us see who the parties to it were. Each was in the rank of gentlemen, each a lawyer, each a man in public office. Looking at the relations that had existed between them as perfectly established in this case, we find that they had been close personal friends; we find that Mr. Sickles had, to the best of his capacity, urged the appointment or retaining in office of Mr. Key; that Mr. Sickles was desirous he should continue to discharge the duties of district attorney; we find that Mr. Sickles had recommended clients to him; had employed him as his own counsel; and had given him free access to his house in the exercise of that hospitality prevailing in this District, to which my associate [Mr. Stanton] has so ably referred, and to which, before I go away—perhaps never to return—I, as a stranger, want to bear cheerful and heartfelt testimony.

In view of all these facts, there is no man in the District, possessed of any intellect, who, knowing anything of the antecedents of Mr. Key and Mr. Sickles, could have supposed that Mr. Sickles walked out of his house that Sabbath morning, left his home and his wife, and that darling blossom of his heart—that child who has been polluted by the touch of the adulterer—could have walked out of his house in the light of day, under the blessed sunlight, and in the face of heaven, and committed an assassination on the person of his friend. Therefore Your Honor asks, the jury asks, and the whole world asks, how this thing was?

The whole world, Your Honor, has its eye on this case, and although there may seem to be egotism involved in the remark which I make, I cannot help saying, because I am here in the discharge of my duty, that, when all of us shall have passed away, and when each shall have taken his chamber in the silent halls of death, and while some of us would have been totally forgotten but for this unfortunate incident, the name of everyone associated with this trial, from Your Honor who presides in the first position of dignity, to the humblest witness that was called on the stand, will endure so long as the earth shall exist.

The whole world, I say, is watching the course of these proceedings, and the nature of the judgment; and I believe I know what kind of a pulsation stirs the heart of the world. I think I know, if the earth could be resolved into an animate creature, could have a heart, and a soul, and a tongue, how it would rise up in the infinity of space and pronounce its judgment on the features of this transaction.

It is for the jury to determine, under all the circumstances of the case, whether the act charged upon Mr. Sickles is murder or justifiable homicide. That it is for the jury, on all the evidence as to the husband slaying an alleged adulterer with his wife, to say whether it is murder or manslaughter.

The provocation, as we claim, was on the instant before Mr. Sickles went out, and if it had existed before that it would not detract from the influence of the last provocation, but make it the stronger and more controlling. The waving of the handkerchief was admitted—a white handkerchief. Mr. Key was unfortunate in its selection. A handkerchief of that color, even among the most savage nations of the earth, is regarded as emblematical of purity, peace, good faith; of regard for hospitality and protection against treachery. The color of the flag of truce is that which was selected in this case.

I hope I may be pardoned by my learned brethren for this remark, in passing, made not in anger, but sorrow, with all the feelings which belong to me. It would have been well if Mr. Key had attached as much importance to the dignity of a banner as did his distinguished sire, and had always within him a fresh recollection of those lines which identified him with the flag of our country wherever seen on earth. If he had remembered that the Star-Spangled Banner has been raised everywhere, in the wilds of Africa, and on the mountain height, by the adventurous traveler, he would never have forgotten these two lines:

Oh! thus be it ever, when freemen shall stand
Between their loved home and the war's desolation!

If his noble father inculcated in lines imperishable the duty of the American people to protect their homes against the invasion of a foe, how does it become less a solemn duty of the American citizen to protect his home against the invasion of a traitor, who, stealing into his embraces under the pretext of friendship, inflicts a deadly wound on his happiness, and aims also a blow at his honor? Now this raises up at once before us the question of adultery and its consequences, to which my learned associate so well referred—it brings to us, with regard to the use of that handkerchief, of that foul banner which polluted the atmosphere of Washington, the suggestion of our brother Stanton, that the common law to be enforced in this District was the common law that should be found to consist with our habits, customs, social condition, and institutions. It recalls to our mind what he said as to adultery being a crime generally recognized on the whole face of the earth, and punished by all nations as a crime.

"Jealousy is the rage of man." Thus speaks the Great God of the Universe to us. It is peculiarly the rage of a man, and in the wisdom of the inspired record, no estimate was ever formed of human nature more accurate as it now exists. I venture to say that if Mr. Key had possessed a wanton mistress, and that any man ventured within the house he had hired, to infringe upon his rights there, he would have been false to the instincts of humanity if that rage of jealousy had not taken possession of him.

If I could have the grave opened, if I could have summoned here a witness who has not been called, if I could put Philip Barton Key on the stand in this court, in which he once officiated as a prosecuting officer, if I could ask him in virtue of his birth, his education, of whatever manly characteristics belonged to him, and whatever opinions he may have derived from his association with gentlemen, what he would have done if any scoundrel had invaded his house, polluted and wronged his wife, and brought shame and reproach upon him, if I could have asked him what he would have done under such circumstances, I leave Your Honor, I leave the learned prosecutor, I leave his surviving friends, to say what would have been his answer.

"Jealousy is the rage of a man"; it takes possession of his whole nature; no occupation or pursuit in life, no literary culture or enjoyment, no sweet society of friends in the brilliancy of sunlight, no whispers of hope or promise of the future, can for one moment keep out of his mind, his heart, or his soul, the deep, ineffaceable, consuming fire of jealousy. When once it has entered within his breast, he has yielded to an instinct which the Almighty has implanted in every animal or creature that crawls the earth. I cannot speak of the amours or jealousies of the worm; but when I enter the higher walk of nature, when I examine the characteristics of the birds that move about in the air, I find the jealousy of the bird incites him to inflict death upon the stranger that invades his nest and seeks to take from him the love which the Creator has implanted in him and formed him to enjoy.

I read in the records of travelers who have penetrated the wilds of Africa that the most deadly engagement that can occur, an engagement which never permits both to pass away with that life, occurs between two lions when the lioness has proved wanton, or seduction has been applied to her. Yet man in his animal instincts is no more capable of controlling within him the laws which the Almighty has planted there than the inferior animals to which I have referred.

"Jealousy is the rage of a man," and although all the arguments that my learned opponents can bring, or that can be suggested, that a man must be cool and collected when he finds before him in full view the adulterer of his wife, to the contrary notwithstanding, yet jealousy will be the rage of that man, and he will not spare in the day of vengeance.

"Jealousy is the rage of a man!" It converts him into a frenzy in which he is wholly irresponsible for what he may do. I meet my learned friends distinctly upon the subject of insanity, relying upon the proposition which I have presented, drawn in strict conformity with the decisions already made by this court in other cases.

The counsel on the other side had remarked that he considered such a thing as instantaneous insanity almost impossible. Such a doctrine could be drawn from the rulings of the court. It was impossible for any human being to perceive the exact point when he passed from a state of wakefulness to a state of sleep, and it was just as impossible to fix the exact moment when the mind of a human being passed from a state of sanity to a condition of insanity. It was impossible, by the utmost exercise of the intellectual or mental power, to keep the thought fixed upon the circumstance of death even for the duration of a second.

We may, in a general philosophical way, declare that we must all die. But in reference to that sharp point of certain inevitable agony, of destruction, which is the thing called death, we cannot keep our minds upon it even for an instant.

To be capable of doing that for any considerable period of time would necessarily produce a tension of mind and spirit such as would inevitably result in the destruction of the intellect. Yet you might just as well attempt to discover the mysterious point of connection between life and death as between sanity and insanity. Insanity may be of greater or less duration. No man can measure it. It is not necessary to fix the exact point of time at which it commenced and at which it terminated.

All the emotions of his nature changed into one single impulse; every throb of his heart brought distinctly before him the great sense of his injuries; every drop of his blood carried with it a sense of his shame; an inextinguishable agony about the loss of his wife; an appreciation of the dishonor to come upon his child; a realization that the promise of his youth must be forever destroyed; that the future, which opened to him so full of brilliancy, had been enshrouded perhaps in eternal gloom by one who, instead of drawing the curtain over it, should have invoked from the good God his greatest effulgence in the path of his friend.

He remembered how, in a city where he had come to abide as the guest of the nation—in a city distinguished for its splendid hospitality—a city which for the time he had made his home, the man whom, above all others, he might have expected to cherish and sustain and protect him, had proved to be his implacable, hypocritical, treacherous, and detestable foe.

With that great sense of his injuries he rushes out on Pennsylvania Avenue, and, although a man who everyone knows, Your Honor knows, the jury and spectators know, is measured and steady and even in his gait at ordinary times, he passes with all possible rapidity down Pennsylvania Avenue—he attracts the attention of Mr. Mohum and of the Reverend Dr. Pyne, a learned and estimable gentleman; his eyes are observed—they are vacant in their stare; the expression of his countenance is all altered; each of these gentlemen perceive some great agony, some great affliction, some great change affecting his whole nature, and so he passes to his home.

How do you see him there? What are the incidents of the Saturday night? In feverish earnestness he paces that chamber of suffering more ferocious than the caged and starved tiger, thinking through the whole night of nothing but these reflections to which I have alluded and which darkened the past, the present, and the future.

Think how, on that Sunday morning, he made this exhibition to which the witnesses have referred, when he saw Mr. Key with his opera glass for inspection or for spying, with his handkerchief to make the adulterous signal, and with the keys in his pocket of the house in Fifteenth Street to which he was about to take Mrs. Sickles at that moment, if he could obtain her person.

There was Mr. Key, with all the weapons of moral death around him, going to make war upon Mr. Sickles and his wife and child. He is seen by Mr. Sickles. He is seen by Mr. Sickles to pass his house and to wave his handkerchief, and Mr. Sickles exclaimed, as Your Honor properly permitted to be proved, that "That scoundrel has passed the window and has waved his handkerchief." Then he disappears from the view of all the witnesses until he comes to the scene of the homicide. Just before Mr. Sickles thus passed out of that house, with the full knowledge that that iniquitous salutation was given to his wife to leave her child and husband on that Sabbath day and to go and be polluted again in that house of bad repute in Fifteenth Street.

Mr. Key had been standing in front of the clubhouse, or in the park, with his opera glass in his hand; he saw Mr. Sickles go out and pass up the street in which his house is; at that instant Mr. Key goes round the other way to go round Lafayette Square. Mr. Sickles is now gone and Mr. Key may be a little bolder; he may have a little less caution and more courage than ordinarily; he is now certain of his victim; he has the handkerchief, the opera glass, the keys, the locks waiting to receive them, the intent in his mind being exclusively to employ all his intellectual powers, of his physical and moral nature, to commit the act of adultery; Mr. Sickles sees him engaged in the act, as one of a set of burglars who watches at the corner while his confederate is breaking into the safe of an unsuspecting merchant, is, in the contemplation of law, engaged in the act of burglary.

Mr. Key, with the means of thus having the person of Mrs. Sickles, is there approaching the house of Mr. Sickles, supposing that he had entirely eluded the latter; he is eager, as he thought certain to obtain the wife. At that moment he is met by Mr. Sickles. If that be not taking a man in the act of adultery, I would like the learned counsel for the prosecution to tell me what it was. And if Mr. Sickles, having a weapon in his possession, which he had been accustomed to carry for reasons which we need not declare, with the realization of all these facts pressing down with terrific weight on his mind and heart and soul, thus meeting Mr. Key and understanding thoroughly the vile purpose of his heart, was not to shoot him, I ask my learned brother to tell me what he was to do? I would like to ask all assembled humanity, what he was to do? To bid him good morning, to pass him silently by, to avert his eye?

Daniel E. Sickles, a man of unblanching and unvaried courage, as I know from the past associations of our lives, let Philip Barton Key believe that he could not only seduce his wife, but cow him! If he had done anything more or less than became a man, under these circumstances, whatever may have been the intimacy of our past relations, I would have been willing to see him die the most ignominious death before I would venture to raise anything in his behalf but a prayer to heaven for the salvation which after death might come.

He did meet him; he met him under the influence of intense provocation fresh upon him; and here, Your Honor, unless I have totally misunderstood the indisputable facts in this case, this question of cooling time disappears entirely, if, indeed, there is any such thing as cooling time applicable to such a case.

We know just as well as we know that there is breath in our bodies it is idle to talk about cooling time in relation to the husband who knows that his wife has been seduced, whom he pressed closest to his bosom, and if the laws of the land do say that there is any time in a career of twenty millions of years when the indignation of the injured husband grows cool in relation to the adulterer of his wife, I hope I am not irreverent in saying that these laws of man are in direct hostility to the immutable laws of God.

In this connection, and in reference to the subject of malice, which here naturally associates itself with the question of cooling time, I refer to the exclamation made by Mr. Sickles at the moment of the homicide, that the deceased had defiled his bed; the presumption of malice was gone.

There was no evidence in this case that did not necessarily exclude the belief that Mr. Sickles could have had any preconceived motive, any malice, or any deliberate desire of revenge as against Mr. Key. In Blackstone's *Commentaries* it is said, "Of which life, therefore, no man can be entitled to deprive himself or another, but in some manner either expressly commanded in or deducible from those laws which the Creator has given us, the Divine laws—I mean of either nature or revelation. Second—in some cases homicide is justifiable, rather by the permission than by the absolute command of the law, either for the advancement of public justice, which without such indemnification could never be carried on with proper vigor, or in such instances where it is committed for the prevention of some atrocious crime which cannot otherwise be avoided."

It is a well-known principle of law that a man may be convicted of rape even on a prostitute, and that she may, in resisting the aggressor, take his life. But—hear it, men of the universe! Hear it, men of the United States!—it is claimed that a man is not permitted by law to do anything for the protection and vindication of his honor. He cannot be raped, but he can have the greatest affront put upon his right; he can have the relations between himself and his wife violated; he can have the legal contract between him and his wife made valueless to him by the ruthless hand of the adulterer; he can have his name made a byword and a reproach; and he can have his wife reduced to a thing of shame—and cannot raise his hand to prevent all this. He can have what more?

Look, Your Honor, at Daniel E. Sickles; look at Teresa, that was his wife; look at the woman whom I knew in her girlhood, in her innocence, and for whom in the past, as now, I pray the good and merciful interposition of heaven to make her future life a source of happiness, and of no more anguish than is inevitable for the repentance to which her life should be devoted!

Look at Mr. Sickles, and look at that poor girl—for positively, although the mother of a child, she is a girl, accessible to the influence of a master intellect, though the sphere of its mastery be even in a region of seduction! And look at that young child, standing between its father and its mother, equally influenced by the great laws of the Creator to go toward either, and destined to leave one! No judgment of Solomon can prevail here; but perhaps, as in the case of the rival mothers, it might be better to divide that poor child in twain and leave one-half at the feet of each parent, then let it live from the period it has now reached. Look at that case and the treasures of his home, betray the friend who confided in you, outrage his hospitality, bring shame upon him, leave him, leave him almost hopeless, a wanderer in the world.

This brings me to another of the instructions. The question as to whether, there being doubt on the question of sanity or insanity, that doubt belongs to the prisoner. It is fully and plainly determined that in making out a case of murder it is as necessary for the prosecution to prove that the prisoner was sane as to prove any further fact.

I grant that, there being no justification or excuse, the law presumed malice, and the presumption stood for proof; but when doubt was thrown on the question of sanity, that was a doubt affecting the case of the prosecution. Whether the doubt related to the fact of killing or to the sanity of the man who killed was utterly immaterial.

Immediately on the scene which occurred in this court, of which none of us have lost the recollection, he instituted a legal inquiry and made a suggestion which, as his construction to the cause of his client, I shall quote as quite germane to the matter in the discussion. In connection with this subject, the state of mind in which Mr. Sickles committed the act for which he stands arraigned, you recollect what occurred in court on Tuesday morning, the twelfth day of April. A distinguished gentleman was on the stand. In distinct and emphatic words, but, nevertheless, with an emotion which it was plainly perceptible he controlled with severe difficulty, he told us of the distraction, the bitter woe, the wild desolation, the frenzy, the despair, the strange, unutterable, unearthly agony in which he found Daniel E. Sickles on the afternoon of that memorable Sunday, the twenty-seventh of February.

"He seemed," said this distinguished witness, his own eyes and heart filling up and overflowing as he recalled the scene, "he seemed particularly to dwell on the disgrace brought upon his child." These words set free the tempest that had been so long pent up. As they fell from the lips of Robert J. Walker, there occurred here in this very court a scene which, from the memories of those who witnessed it, never will be, never can be, blotted out.

All eyes were turned to the dock, every eye was eager, fixed, dilated, quivering; and there was he—he who from the first hour of his imprisonment down to the utterance of those words had borne himself with a heroic calmness, suddenly overcome and racked with a relentless grief, struck down as though he were himself the motherless and houseless child for whom he wept, smitten to the quick and beaten to the dust, drenched in the gall and wormwood of a tribulation the depth of which no mortal hand can sound, and over the subsidizing flood of which no arch of peace can ever shine.

There was he, the avenger of the invaded household, of the more than murdered wife, of the more than orphan little one—there was he, in an appalling moment of parental agony, subdued at last. Talk of the mind diseased, talk of the circumstances which unhinge, upset, and madden it; talk of the distraction in which a ruthless perfidy had plunged my client and my friend; talk of his condition of irresponsibility when he dealt the fatal blow; talk of this, and with your worrying interrogations strive to elicit the recollection of it from those who, themselves the witnesses of it, were themselves agitated as they never were before. Nature, heaven, God Himself, in His heartbroken image, here became, here in this very court, became the witness of the torture by which, on that terrible day, the twenty-seventh of February, the prisoner was inflamed.

You beheld the scene of the twelfth of April. It was the same as that to which Robert J. Walker testified. Recall this scene. Think of how the proceedings of this court were suddenly arrested by the sobs of the prisoner, when the beautiful image of his poor child was revived by the words of Robert J. Walker, how he was bowed to earth, and how he writhed as though an arrow were buried in his heart; how, supported by his friends, he was led from this court, his vision quenched in scalding tears, his limbs paralyzed, his forehead throbbing as though it had been bludgeoned by some ruffian, and his whole frame convulsed. Recall this scene. Think of this—think of the tears you shed yourselves as this stricken victim was borne by—think, think of this—and then may we well say to the jury, If your love of home will suffer it, if your genuine sense of justice will consent to it, if your pride of manhood will stoop to it, if your instinctive perception of right and wrong will sanction it, stamp *murder* upon the bursting forehead that has been transpierced with the thorns of an affliction which transcends all other visitations, and for the scandal, the dishonor, the profanation, and, in the end, the devastation which provoked this terrible outburst, this tempest of grief, this agony of despair, as Robert J. Walker described it; for this incalculable wrong, I say, and for this irreparable loss, declare by a verdict for the prosecution, that so many thousand dollars, an appropriation from an economic, or swept right off from a lavish jury, can afford a soothing compensation. Do this, do it if you can, and then, having consigned the prisoner to the scaffold, return to your homes, and there, within those endangered sanctuaries, following your ignoble verdict, set to teach your imperiled wives a lesson in the vulgar arithmetic of compromising morality, and let them be inspired with a sense of womanly dignity by a knowledge of the value you attach to the sanctity of the household, to the inviolability of the wife, to the security of the honorable roof, and last of all, but above all, to the inherited traditions of an innocent but ruined offspring.

If the effect produced on the mind of strangers, who witnessed that scene, was so great that many were moved to tears, what must have been the nature of the agitation wrought on the mind of Mr. Sickles. And suppose that the condition in which Your Honor and my learned opponents have beheld Mr. Sickles since the trial had received no consolation, had found no vent, had had no alleviation. Suppose that the great, big, full, bursting heart of one oppressed with a sense of terrible wrong could not find in sobs and tears any relief, what would have become of his brain?

What did become of the brain of Mr. Sickles when the heart became sterile, except as a place of occupation for that sense of injury, for that desolating influence of mind as well as heart, to which the learned Dr. Pyne referred when he described the appearance of Mr. Sickles as "defiant and desolate." "Defiant," Your Honor, as poor Meg Merrilies was when she stood by the wayside and made that speech to the Laird of Ellengowan—"desolate" as the hearts which he had invaded, that the memorable outburst of her grief and despair might adorn the pages of him who was called a wizard in the fields of literature.

On this question of sanity, insanity, and provocation, we invite your careful deliberation and judgment. I wish to say, for all of the counsel on this side, and for our client, that none of us have forgotten the great command of our Maker, "Thou shalt not kill," any more than we have forgotten that other command, "Thou shalt not commit adultery."

We know, however, that our great Creator did not intend that homicide should be entirely excluded from the hand of man. We know it by the wars which desolate the earth, by the duels, by the killing of adulterers, ravishers, and criminals; we know of the right which the law gives, and which is sanctioned by home law, to kill him who in the silence of night comes as a burglar to rob and desolate our homes.

All that we appreciate and of all that we desire to have the benefit, and I will be permitted to say, whatever the consequences may result from the declaration that, in view of all that has transpired in the city of Washington, to whose citizens on this jury Mr. Sickles commits his life, his character, all that is to elevate or keep him in existence, for in our own confidence in the integrity and judgment of Your Honor and the jury, we are convinced that no harm can come to Mr. Sickles out of this trial.

In view, also, of the relations of Mrs. Sickles toward him before he came to this city, in view of what we know of her, of the extending of this shame from the mother to the child, which we suppose the evidence fixes on Mr. Key, Mr. Sickles might have gone anywhere else in the world but to New York if he had not resented that dignity. He could never have returned to the city of New York, and been accepted for one instant among any of his former friends.

Brady finished his closing argument exhausted, amid a thunder of applause. Then—whether for effect or out of genuine sorrow for Sickles's plight—he covered his face with his hands and wept.

Ould gave the prosecution's rebuttal argument, skillfully delivered; he tried to redirect the jury. The prosecutor agreed that adultery was an evil and wicked practice that violated one of the Ten Commandments, but pointed out that killing someone on the Sabbath, a day when all work is forbidden, is equally such a violation. Ould explained that the question at trial

is not one of adultery, but one of murder, and whatever vice and criminality may attach to adultery does not relieve the other and higher offense of murder from the condemnation which the law passes upon it. . . . [Perhaps Sickles had] the facility with which insanity may be simulated or feigned, and how wrong it would be to let the party accused thus escape the just punishment which his crimes should bring down guilt on his head.

The trial, after twenty days, was over; the case was ready to be placed into the jury's hands. The evidence having been presented and argued, the last remaining decision was what instructions should be read to the jury. Judge Crawford, from his chair high above the jury box, turned toward the twelve men, stood, and gave the instructions upon which Sickles's fate depended.

Gentlemen of the jury: The court is asked to give to the jury certain instructions, whether on the part of the United States or on the part of the defense. The first instruction asked for by the United States embodies the law of this case on the particular branch of it to which it relates and is granted with some explanatory remarks as to insanity, with a reference to which the prayer closes. A great English judge said, "That if the prisoner was laboring under some controlling disease which was, in truth, the acting power within him which he could not resist, then he will not be responsible."

The question is whether he was laboring under that species of insanity which satisfies you that he was quite unaware of the nature, character, and consequences of the act he was committing, or in other words, whether he was under the influence of a diseased mind and was really unconscious at the time he was committing the act that that was a crime. A man is not to be excused from responsibility if he has capacity and reason sufficient to enable him to distinguish between right and wrong as to the particular act he is doing, a knowledge and consciousness that the act he is doing is wrong and criminal and will subject him to punishment.

In order to be responsible, he must have sufficient power of memory to recollect the relation in which he stands to others, and in which others stand to him; that the act he is doing is contrary to the plain dictates of justice and right, injurious to others, and a violation of the dictates of duty.

On the contrary, although he may be laboring under a partial insanity, if he still understands the nature and character of his act and its consequences; if he has a knowledge that it is wrong and criminal, and a mental power sufficient to apply that knowledge to his own case, and to know that if he does the act, he will do wrong and receive punishment, such partial insanity is not sufficient to exempt him from responsibility for criminal acts.

There is, gentlemen, a presumption of malice in every deliberate killing, and the burden of repelling it is on the slayer, unless evidence of alleviation, mitigation, excuse, or justification arise out of the evidence adduced against him. The alleviation, mitigation, excuse, or justification must be such as the law prescribes.

It is for the jury to decide what was the state of Mr. Sickles's mind as to the capacity to decide upon the criminality of the homicide. The time when the insanity is to operate is the moment when the act occurred, with which the accused stands charged. If the jury have any doubt as to the case either in reference to the homicide or the question of sanity, Mr. Sickles should be acquitted. If a doubt is entertained by the jury, the prisoner is to have the benefit of it.

Whether a man is insane or not is a matter of fact. Murder can be committed only by a sane man. Everybody is presumed to be sane who is charged with a crime, but when evidence is adduced that a prisoner is insane, and conflicting testimony makes a question for the jury, they are to decide it like every other matter of fact, and if they should say or conclude that there is uncertainty, that they cannot determine whether the defendant was or is not so insane as to protect him, how can they render a verdict that a sane man perpetrated the crime and that no other can? The humane, and, I will add, just doctrine that a reasonable doubt should avail a prisoner belongs to the defense of insanity as much, in my opinion, as to any other matter of fact.

The jury listened attentively to the instructions, then left to begin their deliberations. The jurors asked for their chairs to be brought in, then for the stove to be lit. The faint buzz from the whispering audience was the only sound in the courtroom. In contrast to the practice in modern trials, the audience remained in the courtroom awaiting the jury's verdict. Murmured rumors soon filled the room. The jury wouldn't be able to reach a verdict. The jury was deadlocked at ten for acquittal, two for conviction—no! Eight for acquittal, four for conviction. An hour passed, the whispering slowly growing louder, the waiting crowd growing more impatient, uncomfortable on the unyielding wood of their chairs, reacting to the almost unbearable tension. Sickles remained in "perfectly unaffected calmness and self-possession," as the buzz gradually grew into a din. People were standing, moving their chairs around, chatting about what might happen; everyone had his eyes fixed on the jury room door.

Finally, after an interminable seventy minutes, the door opened. Members of the audience called out, "Here they come!" "Down in front!" The jury, led by the eponymous foreman Reason Arnold, was seated, and the courtroom fell silent. Impatient, the crowd listened to the court clerk ask the necessary procedural questions.

"Gentlemen of the jury, have you agreed upon your verdict?"

Reason Arnold replied, "We have."

Sickles was asked to rise and face the jury, to hear the words that would determine the remainder of his life's course.

The clerk continued drily, "How say you, gentlemen of the jury, do you find the prisoner at the bar, as indicated, guilty or not guilty?" The unfortunates in the back of the courtroom stood on tiptoe in anticipation, straining to see.

Slowly, deliberately, with perfect pronunciation, Reason Arnold spoke, "Not guilty."

The room exploded in pandemonium. People were shouting, slapping one another on the back, embracing. Some ran from the courthouse screaming the verdict, while reporters stood by, scribbling notes and asking questions. Over the uproar came Stanton's voice shouting at the bench, "I now move that Mr. Sickles be discharged from custody." Judge Crawford shouted back, "The court so orders."

Stanton, composed and dour throughout the entire trial, began dancing a jig in the aisle. Sickles's other lawyers were jumping up and down, congratulating their newly liberated client and proclaiming how "glorious" it was. Ould stood alone, watching the jubilant crowds. His "cocounsel" Carlisle was nowhere to be seen.

That evening, James Brady invited the jurors to his suite at the National Hotel to join him and the other defense attorneys in celebrating the verdict. The jurors admitted that they decided the case based not on the law but on the moral principle behind the killing. In their minds, "a man who violates the honor and desolates the home of his neighbor does so at the peril of his life." The jurors reasoned they had done the right thing, even though they'd disregarded Judge Crawford's instruction on insanity.

Outside, the Marine Corps band played tunes to entertain the lawyers inside the National Hotel. Reporters arrived at the home of Sickles's cocounsel Philip Phillips, demanding a statement. Phillips, drunk on the day's victory, proclaimed that the trial marked the beginning of a "new era" in the "jurisprudence of the world." He was right.

The Beginning of a New Era

Sickles's acquittal due to "temporary insanity," though relying on this theory merely as a pretext, marked the introduction of an entirely new affirmative defense for criminal acts. Although it was recognized at the time of the Sickles trial that, just as it would be unfair to punish an infant for pulling her mother's hair or a two-year-old for spilling his glass of juice, it would also be unjust to punish an insane person who either did not understand his act or was entirely without the ability to prevent it. Punishing the insane would thus neither deter criminal conduct nor punish the blameworthy. However, the notion that a person could be so insane as to lack understanding of his act, yet be completely sane afterward, was a more difficult concept to grasp. How insane does one have to be for his act to be shielded by the insanity defense, and how can a jury know if a defendant was actually insane at the time of his act or is merely using the defense as a ruse to escape punishment?

These questions are not easily answered, and the courts immediately began grappling with them. Unless facts are raised to rebut it, there is always a presumption that a defendant was sane at the time he committed the act for which he is on trial. Despite this presumption, there remains the issue of who bears the responsibility of providing evidence proving or disproving the defendant's sanity.

Even as late as the 1980s, many courts, like the one in the Sickles trial, placed the burden on the prosecution to prove the defendant's sanity. This was the scenario when John Hinckley, the man who tried to assassinate President Ronald Reagan, was tried in 1982. Hinckley was under the delusion that if he killed President Reagan, it would win him favor in the eyes of actress Jodie Foster. Though Hinckley managed to get off six shots and hit four people, including the president, his assassination attempt failed. When the prosecuting attorney could not satisfactorily prove that Hinckley was sane, the would-be assassin was found not guilty by reason of insanity. In the wake of the public outcry that followed, federal courts and most state courts reversed the burden, requiring the defendant to prove his insanity, reasoning that the defendant should have to prove any affirmative defense that shields his actions from the punishment.

To aid in fact-finding and to make trials involving the insanity defense more fair, many states, either of their own volition or under the Model Penal Code, and the federal system, under the Federal Rules of Criminal Procedure, require that notice of the insanity defense be given to the prosecuting party before the trial begins. This notice allows further fact-finding and permits a prosecutor to prepare for the sanity question, either in the case in chief or on rebuttal, depending on whether the burden of proof is placed upon the state. Even with a presumption of sanity and a requirement of disclosure, there remain two other pressing questions. How compelling does the evidence of insanity need to be, and what definition of insanity should be used to judge the defendant?

There are three general standards of proof. One is the "preponderance of the evidence," in which the defense had the burden of proving that the defendant was insane at the time of his crime. The preponderance of the evidence standard, sometimes phrased as "more likely than not," requires that the defense produce sufficient evidence to convince the jury that it is more likely than not that the defendant is insane. This standard of proof requires the least rigorous evidence and is also applied in civil suits, where the defendant will not face incarceration.

The second standard of proof is "clear and convincing evidence." This standard is somewhat difficult to define, but requires that the defense give evidence showing that it is strongly probable that the defendant is insane.

The third standard of proof, difficult to satisfy, is the "beyond a reasonable doubt" standard. This standard applies to all criminal charges, because the defendant faces the possibility of incarceration, and requires that the defense show beyond a reasonable doubt that the defendant is insane. Under this standard, if there is any reasonable doubt as to the defendant's insanity, the defense would have failed to meet their burden of proof and the defendant would be declared legally sane.

Currently, most states—both those that put the burden of proof on the prosecution and those that place it on the defense—apply the preponderance-of-the-evidence standard to the insanity issue. Federal courts, however, raise the stakes by requiring that the defense prove insanity by clear and convincing evidence. As of 2005, no state requires that insanity be proven or disproven beyond a reasonable doubt. However, this was once the standard for the federal system.

At the time of the Hinckley trial, the burden of proving that the would-be assassin was sane beyond a reasonable doubt was on the prosecution. Given that high threshold, the verdict is less surprising; it would be difficult for any juror to believe beyond a reasonable doubt that a man was sane when he thought killing the president would get him closer to Jodie Foster.

Looking beyond the burden of proof, what constitutes insanity? At what point is a person not responsible for his acts? Initially, the U.S. courts, just as Judge Crawford did in the Sickles case, looked to England for a standard by which to judge insanity. The 1843 decision of *M'Naghten's Case* set forth the first widely followed standard. M'Naghten was charged with shooting Edward Drummond, secretary to Prime Minister Robert Peel. M'Naghten mistakenly believed that Drummond, who was riding in Peel's carriage, was the prime minister and shot him. M'Naghten explained, "Tories in my native city persecute me wherever I go and have entirely destroyed my peace of mind." M'Naghten apparently had a severe and violent persecution complex and shot Drummond while under the influence of it. The standard promulgated by this case was the same one applied in Sickles's case. The test requires either that the actors did not know the nature and quality of their act, or, if they did know it, that they did not know that the act was wrong.

The M'Naghten test, while offering a definition of insanity, also introduces additional terms that must be defined, such as *nature and quality* and *know*. If a defendant throws a rock at a person believing that person to be a rat, then the defendant does not understand the "nature and quality" of his act. The defendant does not grasp that his act may affect another person at all, much less injure one. Such a person would be insane. However, if a defendant "knows" that he is throwing a rock at a person and that this act is considered "wrong," he is sane even if he does not understand that a rock may inflict pain to or injury on the person it hits.

This test has been widely accepted as *the* test for insanity, yet it has drawn frequent criticism. First, the test's requirement for the total lack of cognition has been attacked. Under the M'Naghten test, the defendant must be entirely unaware of the nature and quality of his act or the wrongness of the act. In reality, psychological states are a continuum without a clear, demonstrable line beyond which one understands the "nature and quality" of his acts. A continuum does not have black and white anywhere but at the extremes; the middle is mostly gray.

Second, M'Naghten fails to address persons who know that their actions are wrong, but are entirely unable to control them. Persons laboring under a mental disease that makes them unable to curtail their actions are just as undeterred by reason and the law as persons who are insane by the M'Naghten standard, thus making punishment just as problematic.

Third, the M'Naghten rule fails to distinguish between legal wrongs and moral wrongs. People who know that murder is legally wrong but genuinely believe that they are doing the will of God will not know that they have committed a moral wrong and will thus be judged insane if the test is meant to apply to moral wrongs. If, however, the test was intended to apply to legal wrongs, then the defendant will be judged sane since he knew his action violated the laws of mankind.

Some opponents of the M'Naghten test advocate expanding the definition of insanity to include all persons who commit acts under the influence of an "irresistible impulse." This test asks whether the defendant was subject to an irresistible impulse at the time of the crime that made him unable to avoid commission of the act or deprived him of the ability to choose not to commit the act. This test corrects one of the inadequacies of the M'Naghten test by providing for those who understand that their actions are wrong, but are incapable of resisting those actions due to mental disease.

Critics of this test are quick to point out that "the line between an irresistible impulse and an impulse not resisted is probably no sharper than between twilight and dusk." The trial of Mary Harris, just six years after the Sickles case, followed his lead by relying on the temporary insanity defense for the accused, who had shot and killed her ex-lover.

Harris's claim, which was substantiated at trial, was that her ex-lover had promised to marry her, ruined her, and then run off to marry another. She waited at a corner where she knew her ex-lover would pass and shot him dead. She was acquitted based on the legal theory of temporary insanity under the irresistible impulse test, primarily because she experienced strange and violent desires while suffering from premenstrual syndrome.

Some court watchers celebrated her acquittal, crowing that her ex-lover deserved what he got, but others believed the irresistible impulse test provided far too large a loophole for acquittal without requiring the showing of a serious mental defect. In any event, Harris's lawyer must have been convinced that her temporary insanity was gone for good, because a few years after the trial he married her.

A third definition of insanity is the Model Penal Code test. This standard is essentially an amalgam of the second prong of the M'Naghten rule and the irresistible impulse tests. This standard states that "a person is not responsible for criminal conduct if at the time of such conduct as a result of mental disease or defect he lacks substantial capacity either to appreciate the criminality [wrongfulness] of his conduct or to conform his conduct to the requirements of law." This definition provides several improvements over both the M'Naghten and the irresistible impulse test.

First, it is less narrow than the M'Naghten test, requiring only the lack of "substantial capacity" to appreciate wrongful conduct, rather than a total lack of knowledge. The Model Penal Code test, however, is more restrictive than the irresistible impulse test, requiring that the impulse be the result of a mental disease, rather than a mere physical ailment or mood swing. Further, the requirement of a lack of "substantial capacity" is more in tune with the realistic continuum of psychological states than the M'Naghten's total lack of cognizant ability.

Critics of this approach point to the trial of Hinckley as an example of the way this rule should not work. They argue that if the M'Naghten standard had applied, Hinckley would have been convicted, because he knew he was shooting a person—thus failing the first prong—and certainly knew that his action was considered legally wrong, thus failing the second prong. Critics of this approach also argue that straight application of the irresistible impulse test would likewise have failed to shield Hinckley from punishment, because there was evidence introduced at trial that he had President Reagan in his sights for nearly five minutes, but restrained himself, waiting to get the best shot at the president. The application of the Model Penal Code standard, however, resulted in Hinckley being found not guilty by reason of insanity, the logic being that anyone as delusional as Hinckley probably lacked substantial capacity to conform his actions to law.

A fourth definition of insanity was implemented in federal courts by the U.S. Congress in 1984. This definition, probably an attempt to prevent a reoccurrence of the Hinckley verdict, requires that a person "prove by clear and convincing evidence that, at the time of the offense, as the result of a severe mental disease or defect, she was unable to appreciate: (1) the nature and quality of her conduct; or (2) the wrongfulness of her conduct." This test allows a defendant to be found insane only if he suffers from a severe mental disease or defect and satisfies one of the modified prongs of the M'Naghten test. This rule also lowered the burden of proof that must be met to prove insanity.

A more recent application of the standards for determining whether a defendant is insane can be found in the 2002 Texas trial of Andrea Yates, a woman sentenced to life in prison for drowning her five young children. Yates suffered from a well-documented history of psychological problems, including severe postpartum depression, and had long been on prescription medications for this disorder. Yates claimed a voice told her to kill her children lest they suffer the torments of eternal damnation. Acting on this instruction, Yates drowned each of her children in the bathtub of their family home, even wrestling with her struggling seven-year-old to hold him underwater. Yates then lined the bodies up on her bed and promptly called the police to turn herself in.

Yates went on trial in the Harris County District Courthouse in Texas and pled insanity. By statute, Texas requires that a defendant show that "at the time of the conduct charged, the actor, as a result of severe mental disease or defect, did not know that his conduct was wrong." This standard narrows the definition of insanity to the second prong of the M'Naghten test, but leaves the jury without any definition of what it means to "know." The jury in the Yates case found that Yates did know that her act was wrong and rejected her insanity defense. The jury found that not only did Yates appreciate the nature and quality of her actions, being aware that she was killing her children and not merely giving them a bath, but that she showed knowledge of wrongdoing by waiting to kill her children until the short period between her husband's departure for work and her mother's arrival for baby-sitting.

Given the various tests for insanity available, one might wonder what happens to defendants who are found legally insane. Contrary to popular belief, dangerous persons who suffer from permanent insanity are not commonly released into the community. The U.S. Supreme Court has ruled that dangerous, insane defendants found not guilty by reason of insanity may be confined for an indeterminate term, to be treated for their disease. This confinement may, though not always does, exceed the prison term that the defendant would have received if he had been convicted of the crime.

The flip side of the Supreme Court's ruling is that persons who are either no longer dangerous or no longer insane *must* be released from custody. Thus, defendants found not guilty by reason of insanity must be freed if it is found that they are dangerous but not insane, or insane but not dangerous. This necessarily means that in temporary insanity cases the defendant found not guilty by reason of insanity must be set free once it is determined that his insanity was only temporary and no longer impairs his judgment.

Although states are constitutionally required to free defendants for either of the above reasons, they are permitted to implement automatic commitment laws, which require that all persons found not guilty by reason of insanity be immediately taken to a psychiatric hospital. Once the defendant is there, if it is found that he is indeed no longer insane or no longer a danger, the state must release him.

A discussion of the insanity defense would not be complete without some mention of the way juries must apply it in a practical setting. When the defense raises an insanity defense, the jury has three possible verdicts: guilty, not guilty, and not guilty by reason of insanity. Ideally, a jury should first decide if the defendant did the act that resulted in the crime. If there is inadequate evidence that the defendant even committed the act, then he should be acquitted regardless of his mental state. Only after a jury decides that a defendant committed the act should the insanity defense be considered as a possible excuse.

Many jurisdictions utilize a bifurcated trial when dealing with insanity cases. First a trial on the merits is held to determine if the defendant is guilty. Only after a guilty verdict will the court then begin the second half of the proceeding, to determine the sanity of the defendant. This not only assures that juries address the issues in the correct order, but eliminates the need for expensive psychiatric examinations if the defendant is acquitted in the trial on the merits.

Finally, some critics think that the insanity defense—defined, refined, and expanded as a result of the Sickles case—should be abolished. Some proponents of an end to the insanity defense believe "mental illness" is merely a deviation from the normal, complex, and not entirely understood thought processes of humans. Viewing insanity in this way, abolishment of the defense serves to acknowledge that the insane should be treated the same way as sane persons, rather than ostracizing them as persons who are too different to be considered a functional part of society.

Similarly, some believe that conditions not related to mental illness, such as abject poverty, should be just as valid an excuse for aberrant behavior as insanity, and that until these alternative conditions are recognized as legal excuses for crime, insanity should not be either. Other proponents of abolishing the insanity defense include those who view incarceration not as a form of punishment but as a form of protecting society from dangerous persons. According to this school of thought, an insane person who commits a crime poses just as much of a future threat as would a sane person committing the same crime and should thus be given the same sentence.

And what of Daniel Sickles? Cheered on by newspapermen, friends, and curious onlookers, Sickles left the criminal courthouse a free man. The prosecutor said the case had "given him a headache." President Buchanan was "delighted" by the verdict, and Sickles, vindicated, was welcomed back into respectable society with open arms.

Before leaving for New York, Sickles went walking with two friends to the spot on Lafayette Square where the shooting had taken place. The scars on the tree, where souvenir hunters had cut away pieces, were beginning to heal. Sickles told his friends of how he and Key had grappled, and the way the killing had played out. When asked if he had meant to kill his former friend, Sickles replied, "Of course I intended to kill him. He deserved it."

Sickles was on track to regain his political career, but he made a grievous error. He forgave Teresa. Up to the very end of the trial, Sickles had written an occasional letter to Teresa, and she had in turn responded. One of these letters convinced Sickles that he had condemned her too quickly. Teresa wrote:

> Do I now stand upon a footing with the other women I know you have loved? I have long felt like asking you what your love affairs have been—love of the heart, or love of their superior qualities such as you have often informed me I did not possess, or attraction of face and form, or an infatuation? If during the first years we were mar-

ried my good conduct did not keep you true to me, can I suppose for the moment the last year has? Ask your own heart who sinned first, and then tell me, if you will.

Sickles could never publicly admit that the mildly accusatory tone of her letter was justified; it would ruin his political future. He did realize that his estranged wife spoke the truth. He began writing to Teresa and occasionally visited her and their daughter. Although they would never again share a house, they maintained a civil and decent relationship.

Civil and decent was not what Washingtonians expected. The newspapers that once hailed Sickles as a hero now attacked him mercilessly. Teresa Sickles was as guilty of adultery now, after her husband's acquittal, as she had been before Key was killed. If Sickles could forgive Teresa now, the papers asked, why could he not have forgiven Key then and spared his life? It was as though Key's death was now meaningless and a talented man had needlessly been destroyed. Sickles had no answer for the papers. He had decided how he would deal with his wife and daughter, and he didn't need to—nor would he—try to justify it to anyone.

Teresa and Laura lived with Teresa's aging father until Teresa died of tuberculosis eight years later at the age of thirty-one. Victorian society had labeled Teresa an untouchable, and she was never again welcomed into the homes of Washington's ruling class. The last eight years of her life were lived in loneliness and isolation, spending warm afternoons at the market with a dark shawl covering her head to avoid recognition. Aside from her husband, who soon stopped visiting the house, Teresa had only one occasional visitor, James Brady. He remained a true friend to both of the Sickleses throughout his life and served as a pallbearer at Teresa's funeral.

Sickles paid little attention to Laura after Teresa's death, and the young woman soon began seeking the attention of men. Neighbors began saying that she was turning out just like her mother. Laura Sickles died at the age of thirty-eight in a Brooklyn slum, friendless, penniless, and alone, reportedly as a result of a severe drinking problem. Sickles paid little attention to the news of her death and did not attend her funeral.

Sickles barely won reelection to Congress in 1860. His previous hearty manner and vigor were diminished, a result of the constant barrage of bad press that dogged him month after month. Sickles became a kind of shadow figure, rarely speaking to his fellow congressmen, eating lunch alone. He, too, like his estranged wife, was an outcast, at least to the extent that a member of Congress can be considered a pariah. He abandoned the idea of running for a fifth term and moved into an apartment on Thirteenth Street. Sickles's career looked to be grinding to a halt, and then the bloodiest conflict in American history—the Civil War—changed his fortunes.

Before the war, Sickles had been an ardent opponent of slavery, yet he had also been a Southern sympathizer of sorts. Being a politician from New York, this was practically required; the harbors and docks of Manhattan handled almost the entirety of the Southern cotton crop. If the South did poorly, so did Sickles's constituents. Once the war began, however, Sickles could no longer reconcile his cotton-friendly beliefs with his Northern attitudes on slavery. He believed that the South had a right to peacefully secede, but when violence broke out over the issue, he thought that the South had gone too far. Sickles organized his own unit, christened the Excelsior Brigade, received a commission as a brigadier general, and marched against the Confederacy.

His friend and former defense counsel Stanton, meanwhile, had busily been organizing the Government Printing Office and had just been appointed attorney general by President Buchanan. Stanton— always an ardent opponent of slavery—still found time to follow the events taking place in the South. He gained a widespread reputation of being scrupulously honest and constant in his support of the North and his condemnation of the South. As a result, the newly elected president, Lincoln, appointed Stanton to his cabinet as secretary of war.

The secretary of war was indefatigable, working from seven in the morning until midnight, sometimes sleeping in the telegraph office waiting for news from the battlefield. Stanton took pride in keeping Union troops well cared for and placed enormous emphasis on the manufacture of blankets, shoes, guns, and clothing, pressuring the industries to keep the production lines rolling.

Meanwhile, the war raged on, and in 1863 both sides were preparing for a confrontation at Gettysburg. Sickles, now a major general, was to play a key role in the battle. Disobeying the direct orders of a senior officer, Sickles moved his men to a less strategic but more protected area in front of the Union line. This maneuver was later condemned by General George McClellan, who would later become commander of the Union Army, who said it was the reason that the casualties at Gettysburg were so high. But Sickles's disobedience earned him praise from other high-ranking officers. Union general Philip Sheridan—and others—quickly pointed out that if Sickles's move had not distracted Confederate general James Longstreet's initial attack, the battle of Gettysburg would likely have been won by the South. Longstreet himself, with whom Sickles became fast friends in later life, admitted to Sickles that the battle of Gettysburg would have had a different outcome entirely if Sickles had remained at his assigned position.

Sickles was struck by an artillery shell at Gettysburg; his right leg shattered, hanging by a small piece of ragged flesh, he pulled out a Havana cigar and lit up. Sickles was seen by his men industriously puffing away and barking orders as he was carried off the battlefield on a stretcher. Field surgeons were unable to save the limb, and Sickles would go every year to the Army Medical Museum in Washington to visit his leg, where the bones are still on display. Sickles received the Congressional Medal of Honor, the nation's highest military award, for his conduct at Gettysburg.

Sickles participated in only a few more battles, then returned to the North to be fitted for a prosthetic limb. He soon changed his mind about the prosthesis, refusing to wear it, preferring instead to display his war wound with pride. The aging war hero continued to attract the attention of the opposite sex; President Ulysses S. Grant appointed Sickles the American minister to Spain, where he met and married the dark-eyed, olive-skinned beauty Carolina Creagh. Together they had two children, George Stanton and Edith.

A few years before his death, he found himself staring down into the audience of a New York City playhouse. An observer watched Sickles curiously as the aging general leaned forward to see something in the boxes below. Looking down, the observer saw Philip Barton Key's son staring back at Sickles. "The pair recognized each other, undoubtedly," but neither one gave any sign of recognition.

It seems odd that significant portions of twenty-first-century criminal law, the complexities of the insanity defense, are based upon the outcome of an antebellum case in which the temporary insanity defense was used mainly as a pretext to excuse what the jury felt was justifiable homicide. Though the players in the Sickles case may not have known that their novel legal strategy would bring so much attention to the insanity defense in the coming centuries, surely Brady and Stanton knew that by representing Sickles as temporarily insane they would be forging a new precedent in American legal history and leaving a trail of footprints that others would follow.

CHAPTER EIGHT

Genius, Scoundrel, Traitor

Revolutionary War hero, former vice president Aaron Burr faces the hangman and lays the groundwork for treason prosecutions

Treason against the United States, shall consist only in levying War against them, or in adhering to their Enemies, giving them Aid and Comfort. No Person shall be convicted of Treason unless on the testimony of two Witnesses to the same overt Act, or on Confession in open Court.

—*U.S. Constitution, Article III, Section 3*

Imagine a scheme to steal the western United States and found an independent country. Imagine the resulting country with Texas, Louisiana, Kansas, Ohio, Kentucky, and all parts west as provinces of another nation. Increase the degree of improbability and imagine the mastermind behind this plan, a child genius; a war hero; a man who had served at the highest levels of American government. This scenario springs from the pages of early American history—May 22, 1807—when the former vice president of the United States stood accused of treason.

Betrayal—of a man, an idea, a nation—ranks high in the pantheon of sin; history and literature have long portrayed betrayal as the epitome of moral depravity. Sophocles had his Polynices; Goethe had his Faust; Shakespeare had his Iago, his Brutus, and his Claudius. In ancient Greece, betrayers and traitors were said to be destined for the inner circle of hell, and Christians have long alluded to the act of deceit at the core of their faith, referring to one who betrays a sacred trust as Judas Iscariot.

Benedict Arnold, Ethel and Julius Rosenberg, Robert Hanssen, Aldrich Ames—all Americans, all associated by history with the blue lining of a Revolutionary War–era coat turned inside out: turncoats, one and all.

Treason—the crime of betraying one's own country—violates and compromises the very fabric of society; it is a wholesale betrayal of the traitor's countrymen. It is also the only crime specifically designated in the U.S. Constitution. Fewer than fifty people have been prosecuted for treason in the history of the United States, and those have merited vast attention and wholesale damnation.

The Aaron Burr treason trial was the greatest criminal trial in American history—because of the breadth of the conspiracy; the many luminaries associated with the case; the triumph of law over public outrage; and because the judge crafted the law of treason for all such trials to follow.

The implications were staggering. Burr faced the hangman a mere three years after serving as the vice president of the United States and just seven years after nearly winning the American presidency itself. Burr's scheme allegedly involved senators, congressmen, commodores, and generals—the commander in chief was a coconspirator, and even future president Andrew Jackson had been consulted by Burr and seemed to approve of his actions. Burr's chief accuser was President Thomas Jefferson, who declared his guilt "beyond question." The president directed that charges be brought and was intimately involved in Burr's prosecution; the trial judge was the chief justice of the U.S. Supreme Court.

Public sentiment weighed so heavily against Burr during jury selection that he was forced to accept jurors who believed him guilty but said they were open to persuasion.

Aaron Burr lived a complicated life. He fought the British under Washington; he served as vice president under Jefferson; he killed Alexander Hamilton in a duel; and he was alleged to be America's great betrayer. To fully understand and appreciate his last and most notorious public drama, it is essential to study the man and the events that brought him to the precipice.

A Difficult Start, a Promising Future

Burr was born in Newark, New Jersey, on February 6, 1756; his mother, father, grandmother, grandfather, and great-grandfather succumbed to smallpox and other diseases before his second birthday. Custody of the young child went to his twenty-one-year-old uncle, Timothy Edwards, who imposed the strict discipline of his Puritan faith. Burr was often in open rebellion against his uncle, running away from home at the age of ten and securing a position as a cabin boy on an oceanbound ship. Discovered by his uncle just before the ship weighed anchor, Burr climbed to the safety of the masthead and negotiated a resolution: he'd return only if no punishment was imposed.

Burr's precociousness was matched by his brilliance. With the assistance of private tutors, he applied to Princeton University when he was eleven, only to be rejected because of his age. Undeterred, he spent the next two years studying, using the college's curriculum as a guide, and finally gained entry.

Burr attacked his studies while at Princeton, often working more than seventeen hours a day. He exhibited a fierce independence, rejecting the rigid puritanical values of many schoolmates. He believed that the dogmatic threats of hellfire and damnation, common during the religious "awakening" of the late eighteenth century, were more of an entertaining spectacle than actual religious expression. After graduation in 1772, and despite his reluctance to accept mainstream religious dogma, Burr enrolled in a seminary. However, he was coming "to the conclusion that the road to Heaven was open to all alike," and that the sacrifices and duties required of a minister could not be reconciled with his adventurous and independent spirit. While at the seminary, Burr began escaping to a nearby town, where he often enjoyed the company of local girls. He was eventually ostracized by his teachers and fellow students owing to his involvement with "those women" and decided to forgo the Calvinist discipline. He was, he decided, "much too sociable for that sort of life."

In May of 1774, Burr moved to Connecticut to study law.

A Call to Arms

The American Revolution was in full swing by late 1775, and accounts of skirmishes with the British interrupted Burr's studies; ready for adventure, he set off to enlist in the army, under the command of General George Washington. Burr's New England pedigree helped him secure letters of introduction to Washington: one from John Hancock, president of the Continental Congress, and the other from Colonel Lewis Morris, a delegate to the Continental Congress. Hancock's letter praised Burr and ended, "Your notice of this gentleman I shall esteem a particular favour." Morris's letter was far more straightforward: it called for Burr's commission as an officer in the Continental Army. But there was the problem of who was to foot the bill; the practice at that time was for each colony that sent troops to commission and pay for their own officers. Washington refused to give Burr a commission, maintaining it was too costly.

Burr took Washington's rejection personally. With his family connections and glowing recommendations, he assumed that his commission as an officer in the army was ensured. Undeterred, Burr became an uncompensated "gentleman volunteer," joining an expedition under the command of Colonel Benedict Arnold, a detachment of more than a thousand men preparing to march on Quebec City as a diversionary tactic for an American invasion of Montreal. Burr paid for his own equipment and even paid to outfit others for the Quebec expedition.

Burr looked every bit the soldier. He bought himself a pair of coarse woolen trousers that covered the top of his boots, and a rough jacket of the same material. His hat sported a large foxtail, intertwined with a black feather. Burr wrote that the hat was "meant to help [his] deficiency in size," as it added considerable height to his diminutive five-foot-six-inch frame.

The march to Quebec was arduous; the Kennebec River was navigable for less than the first fifty miles, cascades and waterfalls forming a series of barriers that could be surmounted only by the men hauling their barge around the obstacles. Equipment and provisions were damaged and lost; bad weather, floods, and dysentery set in. An early winter trapped the regiment along the river without adequate clothing and food. The men improvised, eating dogs, shaving soap, and shoe leather. Arnold wrote that the troops had less than five rounds of ammunition each, because the rest was lost or waterlogged during the journey. Further, "many of the men were invalids, and almost naked and wanting everything to make them comfortable." It was a haggard group that finally approached the outskirts of Quebec.

Desperate for reinforcements, Arnold sent Burr to find General Montgomery, the commanding officer of the Quebec expedition. Burr, disguised as a French priest, relying on his fluency in both French and Latin, traveled the French-Canadian underground and eventually reached Montgomery. The general was impressed by Burr's cunning and determination and made him an aide-de-camp, with the rank of captain. Soon after, Montgomery provided the supplies and ammunition Arnold needed to replenish his force.

Montgomery planned a two-pronged assault; while Arnold attacked from the opposite side of the town, he would charge the front gates. Montgomery's troops were met with intense cannon and musket fire, spraying grapeshot and bullets with horrific effect into the American troops. A ball struck Montgomery, instantly killing him before Burr's eyes, pitching his broken body into the pink snow. Montgomery's death destroyed morale, panicking the soldiers. Burr, with a few of the remaining officers, tried to rally the men, to collect the disorganized remnants of their formation. However, Colonel Campbell, the senior surviving officer, ordered a full retreat.

In an act that gained him fame, Burr braved hostile fire to return and retrieve the general's body. On the narrow, snow-covered road, Burr grabbed with the corpse but was unable to pull it back to the American lines. Years later, the story had been much burnished in the telling, Burr carrying Montgomery's body on his shoulders, running with it "down the gorge, up to his knees in snow, the enemy only forty paces behind him."

Burr's actions won him immediate recognition from his superiors, whose correspondence praised his bravery and gallantry. He earned respect as an officer with a reputation for determination and courage. Even those at home had got word that Burr had gained honor through his "intrepid conduct."

During the Quebec campaign, Burr met and befriended fellow officer James Wilkinson, who was a secret Spanish agent, entrenched deep inside the American military. The Burr-Wilkinson friendship would prove long-lasting, with profound significance years later.

Burr's gallantry during the unsuccessful assault won him an appointment as an aide to General Washington, whom Burr found unfriendly, stiff, and humorless. Washington himself acknowledged his wartime mind-set to his friend John Hancock: "I give in to no kind of amusement myself; consequently those about me can have none." Burr was reluctant to stay, writing to Hancock of his intention to leave the army if he had to remain with Washington. In response, Hancock arranged for Burr to be reassigned to General Putnam.

An American Hero

Burr added to the reputation he had gained at Quebec during his service with Putnam. When the British landed in Manhattan in 1776, the American troops retreated to Harlem. An isolated American brigade commanded by General Henry Knox was left at a small fort in the path of the advancing British forces. Burr and a troop of dragoons were dispatched by Putnam to contact Knox and escort his troops back to the main American force in Harlem. However, the general refused to abandon his position, concerned that his troops would be exposed to the British and massacred. The two men argued until Burr, ignoring Knox's authority, directly addressed the general's men, telling them "if they remained there, they would before night be all prisoners, and crammed in a dungeon, or hung like dogs." Burr proved persuasive; Knox and his troops abandoned their position and began the trek back to Harlem.

During their retreat, they encountered British troops. Burr "galloped directly at the Brits, hallooing to the men to follow him." The British soldiers turned and fled, as Burr and his dragoons followed and killed several of them. While there were a few other brief skirmishes, the entire brigade made it to the American lines with only minor casualties, earning Burr further praise.

Burr once again found himself under the direct command of General Washington; their relationship soon took a turn for the worse. One night, Washington sent for Burr and Colonel Robert Pawling, a fellow officer at the New York headquarters. According to Pawling, "the General had sent for Burr and me and was writing at his desk when we entered. Motioning at us to be seated, Washington continued to write for a few more moments, and then he left the room. Burr stood and slowly edged over to Washington's desk, and began reading the manuscript. Suddenly, General Washington returned, surprising Burr and catching him in the act of snooping." Pawling noted, "Burr was caught, and there was no escaping the consequences, which was a terrific reproof from the General."

Despite the enmity between the two men, Burr's unquestioned bravery and leadership resulted in his promotion to lieutenant colonel by Washington several months later, and he was given a regiment and ordered to defend and administer Westchester. He once again proved an effective commander; a contemporary describing his administration at Westchester said, "His humanity and regard to the security of the property and persons of the inhabitants from injury and insult were not less conspicuous than his military skill."

In late June 1778, Burr found himself under the command of General Charles Lee, who was preparing an attack plan for the Battle of Monmouth. Some historians have described Lee's strategy as the "most confusing in its movements and the most difficult to present or follow in detail of any of the battles of the Revolutionary War." Not surprisingly, the battle went poorly for the American forces, and General Lee eventually gave the order to retreat. Burr's regiment suffered heavy losses.

Afterward, General Washington, usually the most reserved of men, swore at Lee "till the leaves shook in the trees." Washington had Lee arrested and charged with "misbehavior before the enemy and making an unnecessary, disorderly, and shameful retreat." Burr testified at the court-martial on Lee's behalf, siding with anyone opposing Washington. Burr's actions further aggravated his relationship with Washington, and his continuing clashes with the future president led many to question Burr's judgment and character.

On March 15, 1779, following the Battle of Monmouth, Burr tendered his resignation, saying his health was "unequal to the undertaking." Burr was exhausted and felt he could no longer function effectively in the army.

The American Dream

Burr regained his health and resumed his legal studies. During his time in the military, New York had instituted a regulation requiring law students to study for a period of several years before taking the bar. Burr sought an exemption, maintaining that because he had begun his legal studies before the war, "long before the existence of the present rule . . . surely no rule would be intended to have such retrospect as to injure one whose only misfortune is having sacrificed his time, his constitution, and his fortune to his country." Burr's request was granted and he was admitted to the bar in April 1782.

Within the year he married and developed a successful practice, quickly establishing a reputation as a brilliant lawyer. The New York bar during this period was touted as one of the best groups of legal talent in the nation's history, with Alexander Hamilton as the premier member. Burr and Hamilton often squared off against each other, their courtroom styles dramatically different. Hamilton was intense and dramatic; Burr dispassionate with an uncompromising analytic style. At one point they found themselves jointly and successfully defending Levi Weeks, in what was America's first sensational murder trial. Weeks had allegedly abused his lover, killed her, then thrown her body into a public well. People were convinced of his guilt—chants of "Crucify him! Crucify him!" frequently interrupted the trial in the packed courtroom. However, by the time the formidable Burr-Hamilton team had finished attacking the government's case, the jurors—as well as the public—were forced to acknowledge the defendant's innocence.

When Burr first arrived in New York, politics were dominated by the Federalists, led by Hamilton, and the Anti-Federalists, led by Governor George Clinton. Burr's entry into the tumultuous political fray was tenuous. However, his intellectual prowess, coupled with his seemingly natural gravitas, led him to seek—and gain—a seat in the New York Assembly. His stances on controversial issues put him in the camp of the Anti-Federalists and afforded him immediate prominence. He championed the cause of the common man and fought against those in positions of power and authority, backing the abolition of slavery, extension of voting rights, and greater educational and political opportunities for women.

In his championing of women's rights, Burr parted ways with many of his contemporaries. In an era when political leaders like Thomas Jefferson and Alexander Hamilton believed that schooling was not for women, Burr believed in women's education and acted on his beliefs with his daughter. Not wanting her to be a mere socialite, he took personal responsibility for her education, requiring her to study Greek, Latin, French, literature, philosophy, and science. He told his wife, "If I could foresee that Theo would become a mere fashionable woman, with all the attended frivolity and vacuity of mind, adorned with whatever grace and allurement, I would earnestly pray God to take her forthwith."

Burr used his newfound influence to establish the Tammany Society—a group of tradesmen dedicated to social, patriotic, and charitable activities.

After finishing his one-year term in the New York Assembly, Burr returned to his legal practice, financial considerations playing a significant role in the decision. He had a penchant for the lavish and luxurious, often borrowing money to pay for his extravagant lifestyle. Despite his return to the law, the lure of politics was never far removed, and the 1789 New York gubernatorial campaign was too enticing to sit out. Burr and Hamilton worked together for Judge Robert Yates, the Federalist candidate, in an effort to oust Anti-Federalist Governor Clinton from office. This was a clear defection by Burr from the Anti-Federalist cause, and he was branded a political maverick, many claiming he lacked core convictions. Yet, to Burr, his support for Judge Yates was merely a demonstration of loyalty to a good friend, one who had been valuable in gaining his early admission to the New York bar. Despite the efforts of Burr and Hamilton, Clinton was reelected.

Following the election, Governor Clinton, concerned that the continued combined force of Hamilton and Burr would soon prove insurmountable, offered Burr the position of New York attorney general. Burr, despite his recent alliance with Hamilton and the Federalists, accepted the appointment. By seemingly realigning himself once again, Burr was subjected to harsh criticism, yet again as a man without real conviction, with Alexander Hamilton his most vociferous critic.

However, Burr's support among the working classes remained strong as he challenged Federalist senator Philip Schuyler for one of New York's Senate seats in 1791. Schuyler, as the incumbent, was expected to win, but Burr, under the banner of the Anti-Federalists, defeated Schuyler to become one of New York's two senators. Once again, Hamilton led the attack on Burr, blasting him as a man without principle, "for or against nothing but as it suits his interest or ambition." For Hamilton it was "to be a religious duty to oppose [Burr's] career."

Meanwhile, Hamilton's ambitions moved from the New York political stage to the national arena. President Washington appointed Hamilton secretary of the treasury, ensuring his position as the undisputed head of the Federalist Party. Hamilton believed in the principles that had worked for the world's greatest empires—the monarchical and elitist systems of aristocratic Europe—and therefore favored a strong central government. The Federalist Party was made up of large landholders, merchants, and lawyers—people whose objectives centered on commerce, trade, and overseas markets. The Federalists were strongest in the East in the rich port cities of New England.

Americans in the South and West distrusted a strong central government, being more concerned with land and the freedom to farm in peace. They supported the French Revolution, seeing the struggle as one for liberty and equality, similar to what America had undergone in recent years. Governor Clinton and his Anti-Federalist supporters began encouraging this ideal, coalescing into the Democratic-Republicans—forerunners of today's Democrats. Thomas Jefferson and James Madison soon emerged as the leaders of the new party.

However, Burr remained an enigma. Given his aristocratic background, many expected him to side with the Federalists. However, as a senator, while Burr tended to vote with the Democratic-Republicans, he occasionally broke rank and sided with the Federalists. As partisanship became more vicious, both sides began to view Burr as an unreliable ally, yet, despite his critics, he was mentioned as a possible vice presidential candidate in 1792. That notion, however, was quelled when many prominent politicians cautioned against him, claiming that Burr was politically unreliable and lacking in moral principle.

Nonetheless, 1792 would prove to be a watershed year for Aaron Burr, and it was the New York gubernatorial race that would push him into a party fold. Federalist John Jay and Democratic-Republican George Clinton were the candidates in what turned out to be a disputed election. Mistakes in the collection of ballots from several counties gave rise to the dispute. If the ballots were held to be invalid, Clinton would win; if the ballots were all validated, then Jay would prevail. The mistakes were purely procedural. The matter was to be settled by New York's two senators, Rufus King and Burr. King, citing the mere procedural nature of the errors, wanted to count the returns. Burr, in a blatantly partisan maneuver, sided with Clinton. This proved great fodder for Burr's critics, and predictably Hamilton and the Federalists again branded Burr as an unprincipled opportunist. Hamilton went so far as to write, "Mr. Burr's integrity as an individual is not unimpeached. As a public man, he is one of the worst sort—a friend to nothing but as it suits his interest and ambition. In a word, if we have an embryo Caesar in the United States, 'tis Burr." This incident proved decisive in pushing Burr into the Democratic-Republican fold.

Throughout the balance of his senatorial term he became the chief opposition leader to Hamilton's financial system and Washington's foreign policy. Burr and the Democratic-Republicans were pro-French, partly because of France's aid during the American Revolution and partly because their struggle mirrored America's struggle for independence. These efforts fueled public support for the Democratic-Republican Party and Burr. However, despite his rising popularity, he was unable to win the support of the Democratic-Republican party leader, Thomas Jefferson.

In 1794, the American ministry to France became vacant. Burr lobbied for the position; yet despite the recommendation from the Democratic-Republican caucus, President Washington, advised by Hamilton, responded that an important post would not be given to someone in "whose integrity he had not confidence."

It later came to light that Jefferson had also played a silent role in scuttling Burr's appointment. Jefferson would write in his diaries that "under General Washington's and Adams' administration, whenever a great military appointment or a diplomatic one was to be made, [Burr] came to Philadelphia to show himself." As Jefferson recounted, he "had never seen Colonel Burr till he came as a member to the Senate. . . . His conduct very soon inspired me with distrust." Historians have long debated whether Jefferson's efforts to thwart Burr were principled or because he viewed Burr as a national rival. It seemed that although his party coveted Burr's talents and popularity, it went to some lengths, even "insidious machinations," to keep him down.

As the presidential election of 1796 approached, Burr, conceding that Jefferson would be the Democratic-Republican presidential candidate, sought the vice presidency. Prior to the passage of the Twelfth Amendment in 1804, the president and vice president were not chosen on a single ticket. The electoral college did not distinguish between candidates running for president and vice president, but rather gave the top vote-getter the presidency and the runner-up the vice presidency. Jefferson needed strong support in New England, and Burr pledged to deliver electoral votes from New York, Pennsylvania, and elsewhere in New England. Jefferson and his Virginians, in turn, promised that if Burr delivered the New England states for Jefferson, they would do the same for him in the South. Despite their efforts, the presidency went to the Federalist John Adams, with seventy-one votes, to Jefferson's sixty-eight. Burr came in a distant third with thirty.

Burr had delivered his end of the bargain; however, Jefferson and his supporters did not reciprocate. Nowhere was Jefferson's lack of support for Burr more prevalent than in his home state of Virginia, where, despite Jefferson receiving all the electoral votes from the state, Burr received only one. Burr felt betrayed.

Following the vice presidential debacle Burr retired from the Senate and the following year was voted into the New York Assembly. Burr's return to the legislature proved disastrous. He proposed bills to remove barriers to land ownership for noncitizens. However, it soon developed that the proposed law would increase values in Burr's private lands in western New York. During that same tumultuous session, Burr helped introduce a charter to improve New York City's water supply, which had become a source of yellow fever. After it was passed, it was discovered that the bill included a clause stating, "The surplus capital might be employed in any way not inconsistent with the laws of the Constitution of the United States or of the State of New York." Burr had recently established the Bank of Manhattan, and his critics, including Hamilton, accused him of passing the water bill to fund the bank by using the surplus capital. New York's citizens, suspicious of bankers in general, turned on Burr, and he was voted out of office in 1799.

Despite his setbacks, Burr remained a power and once again surfaced as a national candidate as the election of 1800 approached. It appeared that the outcome of the race would again hinge upon the electoral votes in New York. New York had twelve electoral votes, comprising over 15 percent of the votes necessary for the electoral majority. Jefferson proclaimed, "If the city of New York is in favor of the Republican ticket, the issue will be Republican." Jefferson, in what must have been a difficult letter, wrote Burr asking him to "accept assurances of my high esteem and consideration." Burr agreed to help but made it clear to Jefferson that "his name was not being played the fool with."

Burr's task was to once again sway an overwhelmingly Federalist New York to the Democratic-Republican side. Largely owing to Burr's industry, all of New York's electors went to the Democratic-Republican ticket. When the electoral college convened and the votes were cast, the first electoral college crisis ensued. Each elector cast two votes without distinguishing between president and vice president. The Democratic-Republicans expected that their electors would cast one vote for Jefferson, electing him to the presidency, and that most would cast their second votes for Burr, giving him a second-place finish and the vice presidency. Although Jefferson would later admit that he once again did little to promote Burr in the South, this time the Southerners and Democratic-Republicans across the nation supported Burr as strongly as they had Jefferson. When the electoral results were announced, Adams and the Federalists had clearly been defeated, and Jefferson and Burr were tied with seventy-three votes apiece.

Article II, section one of the Constitution provided that "if there be more than one [candidate] who have such a majority, and have an equal number of votes, then the House of Representatives shall immediately choose by ballot one of them for president . . . each state having one vote." It was now left to the House of Representatives to choose the next president. However, the House making the decision was not the newly elected House, but rather the lame-duck House still controlled by the Federalists. Resigned to a Democratic-Republican victory either way, the Federalists were forced to pick between the lesser of two evils, Jefferson or Burr.

Many of the Federalists sided with Burr. After all, Jefferson was the leading Anti-Federalist. In contrast, Burr had never been an absolute partisan. Burr had, in fact, sided with the Federalists on a number of issues; in addition, he had been a soldier and was a New Englander by descent.

This was a seminal moment for Burr, who it seemed with minimal effort could gain the presidency. This maverick, this "opportunist," had only but to raise a finger; virtually any concession to the Federalists would assure his election. But instead, Burr did nothing. Despite being urged by many to negotiate with the Federalists, Burr refused. Instead, he replied that he would have nothing to do with a usurpation by the Federalists whether in his favor or against him. The only action put forth by Burr was a letter to Congressman Samuel Smith of Maryland in which he stated that he considered Jefferson to be the proper person for the presidency. In the letter, Burr had given Smith his proxy to make these views known to the members of the House of Representatives.

Although a majority of Federalists favored Burr, his old nemesis, Alexander Hamilton, quickly waded into the fray and began disparaging Burr. Hamilton proclaimed to various members of the House and to anyone else who would listen that Burr was "bankrupt beyond redemption except by the plunder of his country." Hamilton wrote that he "could scarce name a discreet man of either party who does not think Mr. Burr the most unfit man in the United States for the Office of President," that Burr was "selfish to a degree which excludes all social affections," and that "the truth seems to be that he has no plan but that of getting power by any means and keeping it by all means."

Despite Burr's passivity and Hamilton's assaults, when the House cast the first ballot in the tiebreaker procedure, most of the Federalists voted for Burr. Consequently, Burr received the vote of six states, and Jefferson received eight—just one short of a majority. The other two states could not muster a majority either way and therefore could not cast votes. The second vote bore the same results and continued on through thirty-five ballots without movement. As the state delegates prepared for the thirty-sixth vote, Hamilton's efforts finally bore fruit as James A. Bayard of Delaware switched his vote. Bayard had again and again voted for Burr but concluded that it was "a vain thing to protract the election as it had been manifest that Burr would not assist us, and as we could do nothing without his aid." Once Bayard had thrown his support to Jefferson, other Burr supporters agreed that the deadlock must be resolved in Jefferson's favor. Jefferson was elected president with ten votes, and Burr with four became the vice president.

Even after the vote, the attacks on Burr's character continued. Despite securing the election for the Democratic-Republicans due to his efforts in New York and throughout New England, Burr's failure to concede the presidency to Jefferson brought him contempt from his own party. Despite Burr's lack of affirmative action on his own behalf, it was widely thought that he had schemed to gain the presidency for himself, although this was contrary to the accounts of the Federalist members of the House who had been part of the process.

Although Burr was proclaimed an intriguer, his real "indiscretion" was that he did not vigorously renounce the presidency to Jefferson, an offense Jefferson would not forget; shortly after Jefferson was inaugurated, he set about to destroy Burr politically. Jefferson covertly enlisted the services of the editor of the newspaper *American Citizen* to attack Burr. The paper referred to Burr as "the most immoral, the most perfidious, the most unprincipled of men," who was "possessed of an evil of great magnitude." When Burr sought appointment in the new administration for many of his supporters and allies who had helped the party in New York, Jefferson was uniformly unreceptive. Burr was rarely allowed an audience with Jefferson or any cabinet member; he was locked out of the halls of power. Furthermore, since he no longer held an elected position in New York, the political machine that he had built there began to disintegrate. Aaron Burr had gone from the height of his political power in securing the presidency for his party to being virtually politically powerless in one year. As one writer noted, "Burr is completely an insulated man in Washington; wholly without influence."

Following the tumultuous events of the 1800 election, the Democratic-Republicans did not renominate Burr for the vice presidency in 1804. He tried to regain some political momentum by running in New York for governor that year, but was soundly defeated.

The Duel

Burr's final conflict with Hamilton began in the spring of 1804. A newspaper reported, "Gen. Hamilton and Judge Kent have declared in substance, that they looked upon Mr. Burr to be a dangerous man, and one who ought not to be trusted with the reins of government. . . . I could detail to you a still more despicable opinion which General Hamilton has expressed of Burr."

The comments proved too much for Burr, who fired off a letter to Hamilton demanding a "prompt and unqualified acknowledgement or denial" of the statements attributed to him. Hamilton's reply was evasive, trying to pass off the comment as legitimate and in the bounds "admissible between political opponents," declaring that "no interrogation" on this point should be necessary after fifteen years of competition.

Burr quickly responded, "Political opposition can never absolve gentlemen from the necessity of a rigid adherence to all the rules of honor," and he again inquired "whether you have uttered expressions or opinions derogatory to my honor."

Hamilton refused to answer.

In yet another message carried by Burr's close friend Peter Van Ness, Burr accused Hamilton of "a settled and implacable malevolence; that he will never cease in his conduct towards Mr. B. to violate those courtesies in life." Therefore, in Burr's eyes, there was no other alternative but for Hamilton to offer an apology or to stand and duel. The challenge was formally accepted by Hamilton's second, Nathaniel Pendleton.

Like many early American customs, dueling was imported from Europe. Since the Middle Ages, the European aristocracy had defended their honor in man-to-man battles. An early version of dueling was known as judicial combat—so called because spectators believed that God supported the righteous man and allowed him to win on the dueling ground. In 1777, a group of Irishmen codified dueling practices in the Code Duello, which contained twenty-six specific rules outlining various aspects of the duel, from the time of day during which challenges could be made to the number of shots or wounds required for satisfaction of honor.

In a typical duel, each acted through a second. The second's duty, above all else, was to attempt to settle the differences without resorting to violence. An apology would dissolve the disagreement and would end the matter and could be given at any time before combat. If an apology was not forthcoming, the recipient of the challenge would pick the weapons, the time, and the place of the encounter.

Most duelists chose guns as their weapons. Hamilton chose .56-caliber flintlock pistols; many American men owned and were often called to use a pair of such pistols during the eighteenth and nineteenth centuries. Even so, the chances of dying in a pistol duel were relatively slim. Flintlocks were unreliable and often misfired. The heavy, large-caliber guns were extremely difficult to aim and were notoriously inaccurate, even in the hands of an experienced shooter. Further, the Code Duello provided that pistols had to be fired within three seconds; aiming for a longer time was considered dishonorable.

Despite the finely honed etiquette, dueling in New York and New Jersey was a crime, the winner facing murder charges.

Before dawn on Wednesday, July 11, 1804, the longtime adversaries made their way to the Weehawken, New Jersey, wilderness in separate boats. The oft-used dueling ground across from modern New York's Forty-second Street was a ledge twenty feet above the waters of the Hudson. From the beach, a natural flight of stairs led up to the grassy ledge, which was about two yards wide and twelve yards long. The sheer cliff leading up to the ledge protected the duelists from being seen.

Van Ness and Pendleton, as the seconds, prepared and loaded the pistols, carefully weighing the powder and cutting the musket balls. Pendleton, as Hamilton's second, won the coin tosses for position and for giving the signal to shoot.

As custom dictated, both men paced to their designated positions, turned to face each other, and raised and aimed their pistols, awaiting the signal to fire. On Pendleton's command, both men shot. Hamilton's ball went through the branch of a cedar tree about twelve feet above the ground and four feet to the right of Burr. Burr's shot was accurate and deadly. It smashed into the right side of Hamilton's abdomen, clipped one of his ribs, and pulverized both the liver and the diaphragm before lodging in his spine. Hamilton immediately stiffened and fell, crying, "I am a dead man." Burr described Hamilton as looking "oppressed with the horrors of conscious guilt" as he lay on the dueling ground.

Hamilton was lucid on his way back to New York. Mortally wounded, he asked for his wife but requested that the news be gradually broken to her to "give her hope." The treating doctors told Hamilton that there would be no chance of recovery. The following morning, Hamilton's mind remained clear, even as he grieved for the family that he was going to leave behind. As he comforted his wife, he said, "Remember, my Eliza, you are a Christian." At two o'clock that afternoon, Hamilton succumbed to his wounds. He was reported saying during his last rites, "I have no ill will against Colonel Burr. I met him with a fixed resolution to do him no harm. I forgive all that happened."

Despite Hamilton's reported lack of animus, Burr became the most despised man in America, as public opinion quickly swelled against him. With that infamous shot, he killed both Hamilton and any chance of regaining political prominence. The Federalists despised Burr for killing their leader, and the Democratic-Republicans resented him for what they perceived as unfair competition with Jefferson for the presidency. Burr's political career was over.

In a letter to his son-in-law, Burr wrote:

> General Hamilton died yesterday. The malignant Federalists or Tories, and the imbittered [sic] Clintonians, unite in endeavouring [sic] to excite public sympathy in his favour [sic] and indignation against his antagonist. Thousands of absurd falsehoods are circulated with industry. The most illiberal means are practiced in order to produce excitement, and, for the moment, with effect.

Burr's concerns were well-founded: newspaper editorials and rumors spread by his political foes painted the duel as premeditated murder. The *Morning Citizen,* a New York newspaper, claimed that Burr had been honing his marksmanship in anticipation of the duel. There were rumors that Burr wore special silk clothing personally created for him by his tailor that was guaranteed to deflect bullets. With such talk swirling about New York, action was demanded.

Eight days later, a New York magistrate issued a warrant for Burr's arrest, charging him with murder. Burr fled to Pennsylvania, where he stayed for several weeks. When reports of possible extradition efforts reached him, he traveled incognito to Florida and was received and housed by friends.

With the passage of several months and sensing that much of the brouhaha over the duel was abating, Burr returned to Washington to resume his duties as vice president. On his arrival he learned that in addition to the pending murder indictment in New York, New Jersey had also brought an indictment for murder; although Hamilton had died in New York, he had been shot in New Jersey. As it developed, neither state actively pursued criminal charges beyond the indictment, and there was never an attempt to extradite Burr and have him face charges.

Although a lame duck, Burr resumed his vice presidential role as president of the Senate and in time found himself in the good graces of many in Washington. There was even a petition to New Jersey's governor to quash the murder charge. As president of the Senate, Burr presided over the impeachment trial of Supreme Court justice Samuel Chase, charged with high crimes and misdemeanors. Burr's efforts at conducting a fair and impartial trial even though Chase had formerly been a Federalist won him broad praise and further reduced some of the stigma he carried.

The conclusion of the trial coincided with the 1804 reelection of Jefferson and the election of the new vice president, George Clinton. Burr took his leave of the Senate and, prudently avoiding New York and New Jersey, prepared to travel to the West. His reputation tarnished, but with his ambition untamed, Burr looked to the turbulent and sparsely settled West for a new beginning.

The Unstable West

Burr's flight west came at an unstable time in the United States. The Union was aptly described as a loose federation of states rather than a single, coherent nation. Westernmost America lay primarily between the Tennessee and Ohio rivers. In fact, many territorial boundaries were still in dispute. In the Treaty of Paris that had ended the Revolutionary War in 1783, Britain had stipulated that the thirty-first parallel and the Mississippi River should be the southern and western boundaries of the United States, but Spain refused to recognize that arrangement. Instead, Spain claimed all of Florida and Louisiana and declared ownership over everything west of the Allegheny Mountains and south of the Tennessee River, as well as the entirety of Mexico.

The West of the early 1800s was the land of the frontiersmen. The typical Westerner farmed, fought Indians, grew corn, and distilled whiskey. It was a hard and tenuous life out on the frontier. While Virginia, North Carolina, as well as the federal government, all claimed jurisdiction in the West, they were not able to afford settlers much protection—the hardy folk had to depend on their own resources to survive.

Early American presidents feared that the West might secede from the Union. Thomas Jefferson wrote, "If [the Western settlers] see their interests in separation, why should we take sides with our Atlantic rather than our Mississippi descendants? God bless then both, and keep them in union, if it be for their own good, but separate them, if it be better."

Adding to the instability were the expansionist designs of Spain. Spain—citing military possession of the lower Southwest—seized property along the Mississippi River and denied passage to Americans. As the Mississippi River and its access to the ocean was the only route for trade, the settlers were infuriated. They demanded that the United States wage war with Spain.

The Spanish authorities in North America were hopelessly out of touch with their own colonists. Nonetheless, they attempted to increase their influence in America's Western territories. And to assist in such efforts, the Spanish government had years earlier enlisted the services of James Wilkinson of Kentucky, "a dreamer of strange dreams." This was the same James Wilkinson who had served with and befriended Aaron Burr as they'd fought the British some decades earlier. Wilkinson, a renowned scoundrel and schemer, had a history of intrigue and had secretly sworn allegiance to the Spanish crown. Spain rewarded him by granting him the exclusive right to use the Mississippi River to ship produce from Kentucky to New Orleans. Kentucky farmers and tradesmen, unable to bypass the Spanish blockade on the Mississippi, were desperate for relief. In return for the rights to clear passage, Wilkinson and his Spanish coconspirators urged Kentuckians to break away from the United States and become a Spanish colony. Their efforts failed when Western settlers refused to become subject to a nation and a civilization they loathed.

Later, while remaining secretly in the employ of the Spanish government, Wilkinson reenlisted in the American army and was commissioned as a lieutenant colonel. Over the next six years, he rose in the ranks and in 1796 was appointed commander in chief of the American army.

As the new century broke, Napoléon struck a deal with Spain that gave France possession of the Louisiana Territory. Spain had increasingly come to view the Louisiana Territory as an area of trouble—it was never a profitable colony, and its chief value was to act as a buffer zone between Spanish-held Mexico and the Americans. The Spaniards feared the lawlessness and aggression of the American settlers, believing that the Americans were after the gleaming silver mines of Mexico. The Americans, on the other hand, hated Spain for constricting trade and access down the Mississippi.

President Jefferson, conscious of his country's need for access to the Mississippi, was faced with a choice—he could either offer to purchase New Orleans from the French or ally the United States with the British in their war with the French and thus attempt to wrest New Orleans from them. Napoléon, in need of money and hoping to keep the United States on the sidelines, sold the entirety of the Louisiana Territory to the United States for less than five cents an acre.

Burr's Western Rebirth

In this volatile mix of international politics, internal intrigue, and rumors of war, Burr concocted the beginnings of a conspiracy. Even today, historians debate the true extent of Burr's intent and plan. Some believe that he wanted to mobilize the Western settlers to oust the Spanish. Others are convinced that Burr's design was to take over the Ohio and Mississippi river valleys and name himself president of the new nation. Still others theorize that Burr was about to stage a military coup against the United States. There were also those who believed that all these rumors that swirled around him were just vicious stories promulgated by Jefferson and others in an attempt to bury Burr once and for all.

What is known is that on April 10, 1805, Burr headed west. James Wilkinson provided Burr with a houseboat, sixty feet long and fourteen feet wide, opulently decorated, with a living room, kitchen, two bedrooms, and two fireplaces, for a trip down the Ohio and Mississippi rivers to New Orleans. As he headed west and south, Burr was received with pomp and circumstance—banquets and balls were held in his honor throughout his voyage.

An early stop was at Blennerhassett Island, a long, serpentine stretch of land in the middle of the Ohio River. Blennerhassett Island was a local legend. Purported to be its owner's vision of Eden, the island was home to exotic gardens, libraries of rare books, and the exquisite Blennerhassett Mansion. Harman Blennerhassett took Burr to be an influential man—one with pull and political power. Blennerhassett, hoping to align himself with such a luminary, told Burr of his waning fortune, of the costs of his little island kingdom, and his desire to recoup his losses and rise again to wealth and influence.

Burr even took a detour to Nashville, where he was feted by Andrew Jackson at his house. At Natchez, he was the center of attention at a series of parties at the newly minted plantations of the area. And then on to New Orleans, where Burr was received as a hero. To many in the South and West, Burr was the only one of the political elite to understand *their* needs and concerns.

With a potential war against Spain looming, people in the Western territories were looking for a dynamic man to lead them into conflict against the Spaniards. Burr was just their man—the instrument of America's manifest destiny to expand and conquer to the Pacific coast. From mid-November 1805 to August 1806, Burr was regarded as the "potential liberator" of Florida, Texas, and even Mexico.

Despite his popularity in the West, rumors began circulating in the East about Burr's movements and the reasons behind them. Newspapers hinted at future trouble, and many of Burr's old political adversaries were using every opportunity to taint his trip with intrigue and deceptive overtones. The *Gazette of the United States* wrote on August 2, 1805:

How long will it be before we shall hear of Colonel Burr being at the head of a revolutionary party on the Western Waters? Is it a fact that Colonel Burr has formed a plan to engage the adventurous and enterprising young men from the Atlantic States to Louisiana? Is it one of the inducements that an immediate convention will be called from the States bordering the Ohio and Mississippi to form a separate government? Is it another that all the public lands are to be seized and partitioned among these States, except what is reserved for the warlike friends and followers of Burr in the revolution? Is it part of the plan for the new states to grant the new lands in bounties to entice inhabitants from the Atlantic States? How soon will the forts and magazines and all the military posts at New Orleans and on the Mississippi be in the hands of Colonel Burr's revolutionary party? How soon will Colonel Burr engage in the reduction of Mexico by granting liberty to its inhabitants and seizing on its treasures aided by British ships and forces? What difficulty can there be in completing a revolution in one summer along the Western States, when they will gain the Congress' lands, will throw off the public debt, will seize their own revenues, and enjoy the plunder of Spain?

At the conclusion of his tour Burr met with Wilkinson in New Orleans to allegedly finalize plans to attack Mexico. Wilkinson, however, would later say that it was during this meeting that he feared Burr was involved in some dangerous conspiracy. Perhaps realizing that leading an unauthorized invasion against Mexico would cost him both his pension from Spain and his position as commander of U.S. forces, Wilkinson started to back away from what was in all likelihood a joint conspiracy with Burr and even sent a vaguely worded letter to the secretary of the navy warning of Burr's plans.

It was then that Burr, unaware of Wilkinson's fading support, set about refining his plans for the "Western Expedition." The full extent of the plan is unclear, but it certainly involved enlisting men, the purchase of boats and arms, and the movement of the men and armaments south toward New Orleans. Among the prominent Burr confederates were the Swartwouts of New York, ex-senator Jonathan Dayton of New Jersey, Senator John

Smith of Ohio, Harman Blennerhassett, and Burr's daughter, Theodosia, and her husband, Joseph Alston. Even General Andrew Jackson appears to have been in favor of the enterprise without actively engaging in it.

In July of 1806, Burr made a significant purchase, buying four hundred thousand acres of land on the Washita River. It was thought that he planned to use this land as a staging area after his force left Blennerhassett Island. This purchase marked the beginning of Burr's physical preparations for the "expedition."

It was also in July that Burr met with Colonel Morgan, a prominent citizen in western Pennsylvania, and disclosed in general terms his plans to attack the Spanish while en route to New Orleans. Morgan was the wrong man in whom to confide, and he promptly wrote to President Jefferson disclosing Burr's plans. This most likely was the first stimulus to any active measures on the part of the Jefferson administration to fully understand and thwart Burr's plans.

From Pennsylvania, Burr journeyed to Blennerhassett Island to continue preparations for the expedition, including the building and purchase of boats.

During this time Blennerhassett was busy recruiting men. To most of the recruits he said that settlement of the Washita land was the object, but to some he let on that the real destination was Mexico. Meanwhile, Comfort Tyler from New York was recruiting in Pittsburgh, and Davis Floyd was similarly employed in Ohio. Both groups planned to embark down the Ohio River to Blennerhassett Island.

In late July, Burr, still ignorant of Wilkinson's change of heart, dispatched Samuel Swartwout to Louisiana with a coded letter to Wilkinson. Swartwout journeyed nine weeks to reach Wilkinson and delivered one of the most infamous letters in American history. Burr wrote:

> I have obtained funds, and have actually commenced the enterprise. Detachments from different points under different pretenses will rendezvous on the Ohio, 1st November—everything internal and external favors views—protection of England is secured. T[ruxton] is gone to Jamaica to arrange with the admiral on that station, and will meet at the Mississippi—England—Navy of the United States are ready to join, and final orders are given to my friends and followers—it will be a host of choice spirits. Wilkinson shall be second to Burr only—Wilkinson shall dictate the rank and promotion of his officers. Burr will proceed westward 1st August, never to return: with him go his daughter—the husband will follow in October with a corps of worthies. Send forthwith an intelligent and con-

fidential friend with whom Burr may confer. He shall return immediately with further interesting details—this is essential to concert and harmony of the movement. . . . The project is brought to the point so long desired: Burr guarantees the result with his life and honor—the lives, the honor and fortunes of hundreds, the best blood of our country.

Burr's plan of operations is to move rapidly from the falls on the 15th of November, with the first five hundred or one thousand men, in light boats now constructing for that purpose—to be at Natchez between the 5th and 15th of December—then to meet Wilkinson—then to determine whether it will be expedient in the first instance to seize on or pass by Baton Rouge. On receipt of this send Burr an answer—draw on Burr for all expenses, &c. The people of the country to which we are going are prepared to receive us—their agents now with Burr say that if we will protect their religion, and will not subject them to a foreign power, that in three weeks all will be settled. The gods invite to glory and fortune—it remains to be seen whether we deserve the boon. . . . —29th July.

Historians have questioned the authenticity of the letter and of Wilkinson's assertions. The intriguing question is whether Wilkinson had been ignorant of Burr's plans as he claimed. It is difficult to fathom, however, why Burr would have sent such a damaging communication unless he was convinced of Wilkinson's full support.

Rumors and reports of Burr's activities became more common, leading the U.S. attorney in Kentucky to seek a court order requiring Burr to attend court and answer to the charge of "engaging in an enterprise against a power with which the United States was at peace." In all likelihood, the actions of the U.S. attorney, an ardent Federalist, were politically motivated. The magistrate refused to issue the order, yet upon hearing of the motion Burr voluntarily appeared. A grand jury was convened but, citing inadequate evidence, refused to indict. Burr's attorney for these proceedings was Henry Clay, then a young lawyer. Prior to undertaking Burr's case, Clay demanded and received from Burr an unequivocal denial that he was engaged in any actions against the United States. Wilkinson, meanwhile, wrote to Jefferson:

Sir, a numerous and powerful association, bordering on the Mississippi, has been formed with the design to levy and rendezvous eight or ten thousand men in New Orleans, at a very near period: and from thence to carry an expedition against Vera Cruz.

A body of the associates is to descend the Allegany River, and the first general rendezvous will be held near the rapids of the Ohio, on or before the 20th of next month; from whence this corps is to proceed in light boats, with the utmost possible velocity for the city of New Orleans, under the expectation of being joined in their route, by auxiliaries from the State of Tennessee and other quarters.

It is unknown under what authority this enterprise has been projected; from whence the means of its support are derived, or what may be the intentions of its leaders, in relation to the territory or Orleans; but it is believed that the maritime co-operation will depend on a British squadron from the West-Indies, under the ostensible command of American masters.

President Jefferson immediately sent a secret undercover agent—a State Department underling named Graham—to investigate. Graham was under orders to "consult Governors and arrest Burr, if he has made himself liable." Jefferson also issued an official presidential manifesto on November 27, 1806, advising Americans that illegal military activity might be possible in the West. Jefferson's manifesto did not mention Burr by name.

Based upon the information in Wilkinson's affidavit, Swartwout, the man who had carried Burr's letter to him, and Bollman, another Burr confederate, were arrested and immediately taken East and held on treason charges. Their lawyers immediately brought writs of habeas corpus before the Supreme Court. Hearing the news, Jefferson unsuccessfully tried to convince the Senate to suspend habeas corpus until the Burr business could be put to rest. He promised that Swartwout and Bollman would receive fair trials. Chief Justice Marshall, however, ruled that there was insufficient evidence to hold either man on treason charges and granted the writ releasing them.

Meanwhile Graham, Jefferson's loyal spy, quickly infiltrated Burr's group. Through Blennerhassett, Graham was able to uncover what appeared to be details of Burr's plot to separate the Western territories into an independent state. With this information, Graham convinced the governor of Ohio to raise a militia to capture Burr and seize his supplies. On December 9, 1806, Graham took over the remaining boats Burr had contracted for in Ohio—boats that had been scheduled to be delivered to Blennerhassett Island the next day.

The news quickly reached Blennerhassett Island, and the conspirators fled. Around midnight, four boats sped away from the island and down the Ohio River. When Graham's militia arrived the next day, they found the island deserted. They proceeded to demolish Blennerhassett's fine furniture, destroy his painted and gilded ceilings with musket fire, and celebrate with the whiskey that was stored in the cellar. When the militia was done, Blennerhassett's island paradise was in ruins.

Burr was in Nashville when news of the militia's action reached him. He reacted quickly and began making preparations to leave the country. He wrote to the remainder of his confederates, "If you are together, keep together and I will join you, tomorrow night; in the meantime put all your arms in perfect order. Ask the bearer no questions but tell him all you may think I wish to know . . . he does not know that this is from me or where I am."

New Orleans was placed under martial law and all of the towns along the Mississippi were alerted to prepare for possible trouble. Before long, Burr, disguised as a boatman, was captured near the Tombigbee River in Alabama and escorted with a nine-man military guard back to Richmond.

The Indictment

Shortly after Burr's arrival in Richmond, he was joined by Blennerhassett; the two men were charged with "Treason and Misdemeanor in preparing the means of a military expedition against Mexico, a territory of the King of Spain, with whom the United States were at peace."

Richmond instantly became the focus of the nation's attention. The rumors of the former vice president's Western activities had been swirling for months, and now the nation was stunned that this almost mythic figure stood charged with the capital crime of treason. Given the nature of the charge and the notoriety of the accused, U.S. Supreme Court chief justice John Marshall, exercising his considerable discretion, took the extraordinary step of presiding throughout the grand jury proceeding and the subsequent treason trial.

The chief justice's involvement further fueled the already compelling series of events leading up to and including the forthcoming trial. Marshall was a steadfast friend of George Washington's, and a prominent Federalist. He was also a veteran politician, having served in the Virginia assembly from 1782 to 1791 and 1795 to 1797. Marshall had been secretary of state under President Adams and in 1800 was appointed chief justice by Adams. Marshall, a lifelong Federalist, and Thomas Jefferson, the leading Anti-Federalist, were old adversaries by the time Jefferson assumed the presidency.

The legal talent produced on behalf of both sides was impressive. However, behind each remarkable set of lawyers were the old adversaries

Burr and Jefferson. Burr was the principal tactician on all defense decisions; without question, he ran the defense. And it was the president who made it his mission to see Burr convicted, who helped assemble the prosecution team, and who kept a keen focus on the day-to-day proceedings of the trial.

The lead prosecutor was U.S. district attorney for Virginia George Hay, the son-in-law of future president James Monroe and a zealous Democrat-Republican of the Jefferson school. He was ably assisted by William Wirt, who was personally recruited by Jefferson. Wirt, then thirty-five, was emerging as one of American's premier trial lawyers.

Burr also gathered about him some of the foremost legal minds of the day. His own considerable legal talent was supplemented by Edmund Randolph, John Wickham, Luther Martin, and Benjamin Botts. Randolph had served as U.S. attorney general and as secretary of state under Washington. Wickham was widely recognized as one of the leading trial lawyers in Virginia. Martin, an old friend of Burr's, was a seasoned practitioner and was regarded as one of America's premier legal scholars.

At the grand jury proceedings, the prosecution produced several witnesses who testified to a link between Burr and the boats and armaments found on Blennerhassett Island. From that evidence they argued that Burr planned to invade New Orleans by force and make it the capital of his new country. In rebuttal, the defense argued that no overt act of war had taken place. Without an overt act of war, they argued, there was no act of treason. Burr offered an innocent explanation for his actions:

> According to the Constitution, treason consisted in acts; whereas, in this case, His Honor was invited to issue a warrant based upon mere conjecture. Alarms existed without cause. Mr. Wilkinson alarmed the President, and the President alarmed the people of Ohio. If there had really been any cause of alarm, it must have been felt by the people of that part of the country; that the manner of descent down the river was a fact which put at defiance all rumors about treason and misdemeanor; that the nature of the equipment clearly evinced that the object was purely peaceable and agricultural; that this fact alone ought to overthrow the testimony against me; that my designs were honorable, and would have been useful to the United States.
>
> My flight, as it was termed, had been mentioned as evidence of guilt. At what time did I fly? In Kentucky, I invited inquiry, and that inquiry terminated in a firm conviction of my innocence; that the alarms were first great in the Mississippi Territory, and orders had

been issued to seize and destroy the persons and property of myself
and party; that I endeavored to undeceive the people, and convince
them that I had no designs hostile to the United States, but that
twelve hundred men were in arms for a purpose not yet developed;
the people could not be deceived; and I was acquitted.

There are three courses that might be pursued—an acquittal; or a
commitment for treason, or for a misdemeanor; that no proof
existed in support of either but what was contained in the affidavit of
Wilkinson, abounding in crudities and absurdities.

In December of 1806, Chief Justice Marshall agreed with Burr and
ruled that there was not enough evidence to go forward with the charge
of treason. Marshall's refusal to sustain the charge against Burr infuriated
President Jefferson, who suspected that the chief justice's decision was
influenced by his own Federalist political leanings.

The president was undeterred; he now saw Burr's conviction as his
personal mission and underscored his intentions in an extraordinary
message to a joint session of Congress on January 22, 1807:

I proceed to state therein expressed, information received touch-
ing an illegal combination of private individuals against the peace
and safety of the Union, and a military expedition planned by them
against the territories of a power in amity with the United States,
with the measures I have pursued for suppressing the same.

Some time in the latter part of September, I received intimations
that designs were in agitation in the western country, unlawful and
unfriendly to the peace of the Union; and that the prime mover in
these was Aaron Burr, heretofore distinguished by the favor of his
country. The grounds of these intimations being inconclusive, the
objects uncertain, and the fidelity of that country known to be firm,
the only measure taken was to urge the informants to use their best
endeavors to get further insight into the designs and proceedings of
the suspected persons, and to communicate them to me.

It was not until the latter part of October, that the objects of the
conspiracy began to be perceived, but still so blended and involved
in mystery that nothing distinct could be singled out for pursuit. In
this state of uncertainty as to the crime contemplated, the acts done,
and the legal course to be pursued, I thought it best to send to the
scene where these things were principally in transaction, a person, in
whose integrity, understanding, and discretion, entire confidence
could be reposed, with instructions to investigate the plots going on,

to enter into conference with the governors and all other officers, civil and military, and with their aid to do on the spot whatever should be necessary to discover the designs of the conspirators, arrest their means, bring their persons to punishment, and to call out the force of the country to suppress any unlawful enterprise in which it should be found they were engaged.

By this time it was known that many boats were under preparation, stores of provisions collecting, and an unusual number of suspicious characters in motion on the Ohio and its waters. Besides despatching the confidential agent to that quarter, orders were at the same time sent to the governors of the Orleans and Mississippi territories, and to the commanders of the land and naval forces there, to be on their guard against surprise, and in constant readiness to resist any enterprise which might be attempted on the vessels, posts, or other objects under their care; and on the 8th of November, instructions were forwarded to General Wilkinson to fall back with his principal force to the hither bank of the Mississippi, for the defence [sic] of the intersecting points on that river. By a letter received from that officer on the 25th of November, but dated October 21st, we learn that a confidential agent of Aaron Burr had been deputed to him, with communications partly written in cipher and partly oral, explaining his designs, exaggerating his resources, and making such offers of emolument and command, to engage him and the army in his unlawful enterprise, as he had flattered himself would be successful. It appeared that Burr contemplated two distinct objects, which might be carried on either jointly or separately, and either the one or the other first, as circumstances should direct. One of these was the severance of the Union of these States by the Allegheny mountains; the other, an attack on Mexico.

This was the state of my information of his proceedings about the last of November, at which time, therefore, it was first possible to take specific measures to meet them. The proclamation of November 27th, two days after the receipt of General Wilkinson's information, was now issued. Orders were despatched to every intersecting point on the Ohio and Mississippi, from Pittsburgh to New Orleans, for the employment of such force either of the regulars or of the militia, and of such proceedings also of the civil authorities, as might enable them to seize on all the boats and stores provided for the enterprise, to arrest the persons concerned, and to suppress effectually the further progress of the enterprise.

In Kentucky, a premature attempt to bring Burr to justice, without sufficient evidence for his conviction, had produced a popular impression in his favor, and a general disbelief of his guilt. This gave him an unfortunate opportunity of hastening his equipments. Some boats (accounts vary from five to double or treble that number) and persons (differently estimated from one to three hundred) had in the meantime passed the falls of the Ohio, to rendezvous at the mouth of the Cumberland, with others expected down that river. By information received yesterday I learn that on the 22d of December, Mr. Burr descended the Cumberland with two boats merely of accommodation, carrying with him from that State no quota toward his unlawful enterprise. Whether after the arrival of the proclamation, of the orders, or of our agent, any exertion which could be made by that State, or the orders of the governor of Kentucky for calling out the militia at the mouth of Cumberland, would be in time to arrest these boats, and those from the falls of the Ohio, is still doubtful.

On the whole, the fugitives from Ohio, with their associates from Cumberland, or any other place in that quarter, cannot threaten serious danger to the city of New Orleans.

Jefferson's address was a damning condemnation of Burr, and by it he brought pressure to bear on Chief Justice Marshall to revisit his decision to dismiss the indictment. Further, the president urged people throughout the Western territories to come forward and "communicate to the government any information he may possess" of the conspiracy. Jefferson dispatched deputies near Blennerhassett Island in hopes of gaining a damning deposition. Secretary of State James Madison wrote to Andrew Jackson, requesting more depositions from Tennessee that might help convict Burr. Largely through the efforts initiated by the president, the government assembled more than a hundred people, witnesses to the various events alleged as acts of treason.

Rearmed, the government once again took their case to the grand jury in an attempt to obtain an indictment, noting that the "evidence [was] different now." And this time, General James Wilkinson—described by the defense as the "alpha and the omega of the present prosecution"—arrived to testify before the grand jury. A spectator described Wilkinson's entrance, saying he "strutted into court" and "stood for a moment swelling like a turkey-cock." On Wilkinson's arrival, Burr "turned his head, looked him full in the face with one of his piercing regards, swept his eyes over the whole person from head to foot, as if to scan his dimensions, then coolly resumed his former position." Wilkinson's testimony, and the copy of the damning letter allegedly sent by Burr, led to an indictment against him and Blennerhassett for treason and high misdemeanor, a crime punishable by death.

On August 3, 1807, both men pled not guilty to all charges.

The Trial

Just three years removed from serving his country as vice president, this man who had so recently been but one vote short of the presidency itself was on trial for his life, accused of the only crime specifically condemned by the Constitution: treason.

Richmond, the site of the trial, was abuzz as the eyes and ears of America turned to the federal courthouse. The trial merited the vast attention, given the identity of the accused, the nature of his alleged offense, that the trial judge was the chief justice of the Supreme Court, and further that the president of the United States was in many respects the chief prosecutor. Newspaper coverage was intense and fiercely anti-Burr.

The courtroom was packed. Thousands of people had come from all over the country, sleeping in hastily erected tents, wagons, or in encampments along the riverbank and the hillsides. People packed into taverns, gathered on the courthouse lawn, or fought their way into the building, trying to catch a glimpse of the celebrated chief justice, and of the infamous former vice president.

The prosecutors were well aware that, despite Burr's notoriety, they faced significant obstacles. The charge against Burr was treason by levying war against the United States. However, the prosecution was confronted with the unfortunate fact that no shots had been fired, no military engagements had occurred. And, because it was specifically alleged that Burr's treasonable actions consisted of an act of war, they were forced to broaden the concept of what constituted such an act. A second substantial prosecution hurdle was that Burr was nowhere near Blennerhassett Island at the time the men, arms, and boats had been assembled. The defense maintained that even if there was an act of war at Blennerhassett Island, it could not be imputed to a man more than a hundred miles away. To further complicate the government's task, there was considerable legal authority that a person not immediately present at the site of the alleged crime was a mere accessory and, consequently, could not be convicted unless those present were first convicted. This presented a volatile issue: Must there first be a conviction of Blennerhassett or others before Burr could be convicted? This question, while not entirely novel, had not been fully addressed by the fledgling American courts as of 1807, and its resolution would create a precedent that would govern every treason trial to follow.

The government's first witness was General William Eaton. Eaton, a controversial figure throughout his long military career, had successfully led American troops against the British at Fallen Timbers, only to be later court-martialed for profiteering. He was later reinstated and dispatched to North Africa, where he defended American interests. Eaton paid for much of his North African campaign from his own pocket; on his return to the United States, Congress refused his demand for reimbursement. Eaton, not surprisingly, resented the government's actions, and many thought Burr had attempted to utilize Eaton's dissatisfaction to enlist him in the plot. Eaton testified about a conversation he had with Burr:

> I listened to Colonel Burr's mode of indemnity; and as I had by this time begun to suspect that the military expedition he had on foot was unlawful, I permitted him to believe myself resigned to his influence that I might understand the extent and motive of his arrangements. Colonel Burr now laid open his project of revolutionizing the territory west of the Allegheny, establishing an independent empire there; New Orleans to be the capital, and he himself to be the chief; organizing a military force on the waters of the Mississippi, and carrying conquest to Mexico.

The government next called Commodore Thomas Truxton, who had been one of America's foremost naval commanders. However, by the time he was approached by Burr, he, like General Eaton, had grown disillusioned with his country. After years of service, budget cuts had forced him to give up his command. Truxton felt cheated and held President Jefferson responsible. Truxton testified that Burr had tried to enlist him in an expedition against Spain and Mexico, and that Burr had asked him about the best strategy for attacking various Mexican cities. Truxton said that Burr gave him repeated assurances that General Wilkinson was prepared to assist in a Western expedition. Truxton—as had General Eaton—maintained that he was adamant in disassociating himself from Burr's plot.

The prosecution then called Blennerhassett's gardener to the stand. The gardener, Peter Taylor, recalled a conversation he had had with his employer:

> He made a sudden pause and said, "I will tell you what, Peter, we are going to take Mexico, one of the finest and richest places in the

whole world." He said that Colonel Burr would be the king of Mexico, and Mrs. Alston, daughter of Colonel Burr, was to be the queen of Mexico whenever Colonel Burr died. He said that Colonel Burr had made fortunes for many in his time, but none for himself; but now he was going to make something for himself.

William Love, another servant in the Blennerhassett household, offered the following testimony:

PROSECUTOR HAY: Were you on Blennerhassett's island?
LOVE: Yes; but I was not there at the time when Colonel Tyler's boats arrived there. I was then at Marietta; and it was on Sunday that I went down in a skiff with two barrels of salt.
HAY: How many boats were at the island?
LOVE: Four.
HAY: How many men?
LOVE: I cannot tell you, but I suppose about betwixt twenty and twenty-five belonging to Colonel Tyler's boats. When I arrived on the island, Blennerhassett met me.
HAY: Did you see any arms?
LOVE: I saw the men and rifles. I know that Mr. Blennerhassett took away with him one brace of horse pistols, a brace of pocket pistols, and a dirk. Some fuses were put in the boat, but not more than three or four, all belonging to him.
HAY: And what arms had Tyler's men?
LOVE: Pistols, dirks, and rifles, they brought there, but all were not armed with rifles. I know not whether they were armed with different things. Some of the men had guns, some had dirks. Being, as how, Mr. Blennerhassett's servant, that is, his groom, I went down the river with him.

The testimony of these witnesses and the several that followed all focused on Burr's plans and the specific activities on Blennerhassett Island. Before the prosecution could call another witness, Burr and his defense team moved to dismiss all charges, claiming the evidence had "utterly failed to prove that any overt act of levying war had been committed," and that even *had* an overt act been established, Burr was more than one hundred miles away from Blennerhassett Island at the time and could not therefore have been a party to it.

It was on this point that the trial would be decided; not by the jury, but by Chief Justice Marshall ruling on the defense motion. Burr and his defense team argued that the evidence produced had failed to establish that "an overt act of war" had taken place. Without an overt act of war there could be no treason. Burr and his team argued that in so failing to establish an act of war, all other evidence was rendered irrelevant; if the foundation (an act of war) was not laid, no other evidence mattered.

Marshall's findings and the rationale for his findings would not only determine the fate of Aaron Burr but would establish precedent for all such cases that would follow. It was for the prosecutors and defense counsel to argue as to the requirements essential to sustain a treason conviction. Even though the Constitution deemed treason a high crime, it did not set forth with any specificity its parameters. That remained for Marshall to do.

Burr began the defense argument:

Before the gentleman proceeds with his evidence, I will suggest that it has appeared to me that there would be great advantage and propriety in establishing a certain principle founded upon the facts which have been presented to the court. If the facts which had been presented were to be taken for granted; they utterly fail to prove that any overt act of war has been committed; and it was admitted that I was more than one hundred miles distant from the place where the overt act is charged to have been committed. No evidence was admissible to connect me with other persons, in acts done by them in my absence, and even done without my knowledge; or that facts brought from distant places could be connected with those done at Blennerhassett Island, to give to the acts done there the name of treason, when no overt act of war was committed at that place.

The defense had the right here to call upon the attorney for the United States to say whether an assemblage of men merely can be called or in any way tortured into an act of "levying war." This point must be inevitably determined at some stage of the examination, and therefore we have the right to require of the prosecutor to show that every witness will give testimony tending to prove an overt act of war, or his testimony would be irrelevant and immaterial.

Prosecutor Hay, answering for the government, argued that the motion was premature and should in any event be decided by the jury, not the judge:

I have no objection to any fair inquiry into these principles; but the motion is premature. Testimony would be introduced which would give a very different aspect to the transactions on Blennerhassett Island to what had appeared. Although there was not on that island what one would have called "open war," no "collision of arms," or "hard knocks," the government would prove that there was "military array"; that the men were collected for military purposes, and that a military object was in view. If the court after all that had been exposed, and with the uncertainty as to what might be brought to view, would undertake to say that an overt act of treason had not been proved. That was a fact to be ascertained by the jury.

Would common sense say, or would our statutes or Constitution require that the person who had produced all this commotion should be present when the battle was fought, or even when the troops were collected for the enterprise? He conceived the question to be, whether the accused was principally concerned with it—whether he did project and carry it on with a design to complete it? And how could this be ascertained, unless the prosecution were permitted to go on with the evidence?

Burr answered the prosecutor:

The gentlemen were about to proceed to connect me with the act. I deny, sir, that they can do so. They admit that I was not there, and therefore let the nature of the transaction be what it may, it cannot affect me. Again: I deny that there was war, at all, and no testimony can be brought to prove that there was war; and surely the article war is of imperious necessity in the charge of treason. Now, if this be true, will the court go on week after week, discovering nothing that can affect me? I was desirous that the court, the jury, and the country should know what was charged against me; this has been done, and it has been found that I cannot be connected with the facts. I demand the opinion of the court on these points.

This time, prosecutor Wirt responded to Burr:

This motion is a bold and original stroke in the noble science of defense. It marks the genius and hand of a master. For it gives to the prisoner every possible advantage, while it gives him the full benefit of his legal defense: the sole defense which he would be able to make to the jury, if the evidence were all introduced before them. It cuts off from the prosecution all that evidence which goes to connect the prisoner with the assemblage on the island, to explain the destination and objects of the assemblage, and to stamp beyond controversy the character of treason upon it.

Prosecutor Hay then picked up the argument from his colleague Wirt and continued on with the government's opposition to Burr's motion:

In answer to arguments on the other side, defense counsel all call aloud for an open deed of war. But neither the Constitution nor the law speak of an overt act of war. They speak of levying war. There was a real, essential difference between an open deed of war and an overt act of levying war. An open deed of levying war is an assemblage of troops. If you go beyond that line, if these troops employ force or fight a battle, it is folly to call it an overt act of levying war; it is an open act of war previously levied. Is not this distinction plain to the mind of every man of common sense? And is it not according to the obvious meaning of the Constitution? Why, then, should counsel call so loudly and vehemently for open deeds of war, when they must have known that the overt act of treason consisted in levying war against the United States, and not in making it?

The defense's first position was, that there is no treason in the United States but that which is defined by the Constitution. Agreed. This is sound doctrine. His next position was, that no man can be punished but he who does the act thus defined. This is conceded also. But when he says that this act of levying war against the United States cannot be performed but by a person present on the spot where the offense is alleged to be committed, I deny the correctness of the position, and aver that it is not founded in sound sense, or in the law of this country. A man may levy war without being present with the troops where the offense is alleged to be committed, or even without making actual war at all. It is unnecessary to press the distinction between levying war and war itself. The common sense of mankind has decided this question.

The man who levies war is he who projects the plan, provides the means, causes soldiers to be enlisted, and arms and other necessaries to be prepared, and directs and superintends the whole operation. He may sometimes be also master of means sufficient for the subversion of the liberty and happiness of a whole people. What would be the course of conduct which a man, at the head of a conspiracy to subvert the government of his country, and to raise himself on its ruins, would pursue, you may easily judge. Supposing him to be a man whose understanding was equal to his ambition, he would proportion the means to the end. He would use activity and enterprise. He would be confined to no particular scene of operations. He would be here and there and at every place, where and when it would be necessary to prepare for the accomplishment of his great object. The common understanding of mankind has decided this question. We find—and every expression used here may be soon verified—that George the Third levies war against the United States three thousand miles from us. It is he who declares the war, by whose directions the troops are raised and employed. It is he who levies the war, and not his subjects who fight the battles; his generals and soldiers who come hither for slaughter and murder, they make the war upon us, but they do not levy it.

Such is the case here: admit it to be true that Burr was not on the island, yet the men who went, met there by his procurement and direction; leave it by his direction. If the assemblage on Blennerhassett Island were an overt act of levying war, the person who procured that assemblage, by whom its movements to and from the island were directed, is emphatically guilty of levying war against the United States.

Are we to pronounce that the great projector, the prime mover of the whole conspiracy and plot, as constitutionally safe? Yet this is the language and this the doctrine of the defense. It appears to me, sir, that that construction of the Constitution which leads to such a conclusion is repugnant to common sense.

With this view of the subject, and believing the liberty, prosperity, and happiness of the people to be strongly connected with the decision of this case, I cannot conclude without expressing my hope that the motion will be rejected; that according to the opinion of this court on a late occasion, they will not stop the prosecution, but permit us to introduce the rest of our witnesses, in order to enable the jury to decide upon the facts coupled with the intention.

Luther Martin responded on behalf of Burr:

If a war has taken place, it was a mighty strange kind of war, which neither man nor woman nor child has ever seen or heard. Yet in this great war not a single act of violence can be proved by any human being to have happened.

We admit that there is in Great Britain one species of treason which consists in the intention, without any act consummating the guilt of treason. I mean that compassing the death of the king, where the crime is merely imagined; and nothing more is necessary than to write a letter to a man advising him to kill the king, and that fact being proved, he is guilty and liable to be punished for treason, though the king was not killed, and though the party advised took no steps to pursue it. But why is the intention to commit it treason in Great Britain? Because a special law is made for the safeguard of the life of the king, making it treason to conspire or imagine his death, when evidenced by some overt act such as I have just stated; a conspiracy against the life of the king, whether carried into execution or not, is made treason by special act of Parliament. But in America we have no species of treason except two: levying war against the United States, and adhering to their enemies, giving them aid and comfort. What is the treason charged on us? Levying war. According to the Constitution, no person can be convicted unless on the testimony of two witnesses to the same overt act. If there be twenty overt acts and each of them proved by one witness, nay, if there be fifty overt acts committed at different places, and each proved only by one witness, it will not suffice; two witnesses must concur in proving the same act at some particular place or the accused cannot be convicted.

But gentlemen must admit that the intention alone is not punishable. There must be an actual levying of war, and the overt act is proof of it. On an indictment for levying war they can give no evidence. Proof of the intention alone would be inadmissible; just as in the case of murder, the prosecutor cannot prove the murder without proving that the party has been killed; and so in a prosecution for stealing a horse, the taking of the horse must be proved; the malicious intention to kill in the one case, and the felonious intended appropriation in the other, must be established; but the intention in either case will not do without the act.

An overt act must be set forth in every indictment for treason, and proved in every instance. When the indictment is for levying war as a specific treason, it must specify the overt act which is to support it. They have on the present occasion proceeded on the principle that they could prove a conspiracy; but is there a particle of criminality proved? If some sort of connection between the person accused and those joined in the supposed conspiracy be proved, this is by no means sufficient on this indictment for levying war; but they must prove war actually levied—an act done. No person can be guilty of treason, though a thousand conspiracies to levy war were proved, without the existence of actual war.

The gentlemen [prosecuters] have said that agreeably to our Constitution they could not charge the accused otherwise than as they have done; that they must have charged him with levying war. I cannot see any difficulty in charging him according to the truth of the case. But however criminal or injurious his conduct may be, and however much he may deserve punishment, he ought not to be deprived of the benefit of law, or to be considered as guilty of treason, without legal proof of his having committed an overt act of levying war, or to be condemned unheard to subserve unworthy party purposes. If advising a man to levy war be treason and punishable under the Constitution in the same manner as actually levying war, I ask why should not the indictment be so drawn as to correspond with the evidence, and give full notice to the accused of the charge intended to be proved against him? I ask why was not the indictment in this case so drawn as to embrace the real facts? Why did it not state that A, B, and C—meaning those on the island—did levy war against the United States, and that Colonel Burr did advise, incite, encourage, and counsel them to levy it?

Having proved that under this indictment no evidence yet adduced is competent to convict the accused, I shall now make a few observations on one of the questions before this court. What is a levying of war? Why, gentlemen say that levying war is—levying soldiers—that it consists in preparing the means of war. I should rather suppose that the framers of our Constitution, who proceeded with so much caution, and endeavored in every part of that instrument to secure the rights and liberties of their fellow citizens, did not intend, by the terms "levying war," an unnatural and dangerous construction, unknown in common parlance, and unusual in history or judicial proceedings. They never could have intended that acts peaceable or innocent in themselves should constitute treason. If by "levying war" they meant enlisting of troops or raising an army, they would have said so in plain terms. They would have said that "treason against the United States shall consist in enlisting or levying troops, or raising an army, with intention to make war against them." If levying troops, embodying men, or enlisting soldiers, with intention to subvert the government of the United States, were intended as sufficient to constitute treason, why did not the framers of the Constitution say so? Why did they not say that levying of troops or raising an army had the same idea or meant the same thing as levying of war?

Levying of war implies force of some kind. The idea of violence of some kind is inseparable from that of war. But, sir, raising an army or levying troops is only a preparatory step towards levying war. You levy troops in preparation, in intention to levy war. But no act preparatory to levying war can be an actual levying of war. What is the technical meaning of *levying*? Whether derived from the French word *lever,* or the Latin word *levare,* "to raise," to levy war is to make it, according to its popular acceptation, as well as its meaning as used by some of the best writers. The meaning or true construction of both expressions, *to levy war,* and *to make war,* is precisely the same. Whatever is making war is levying it.

I beg leave to make a few observations on that part of our inquiries which relates to the great constitutional question: whether a person who would only be guilty of accessorial agency can be guilty of treason. He who advises, procures, or persuades another to commit treason is highly criminal and merits very severe punishment. The receiver of a traitor, knowing him to be such, is highly censurable and punishable. But we aver that neither of them is guilty of treason within the interpretation of the Constitution of the United States. Every preparation made for the purpose of making or levying of war is not an act of treason; because nothing but making war for the purpose of changing or subverting the government of the United States is treason. Every act of those who make those preparations to levy war is criminal; and the government has an undoubted right to use the force of the country and all the means which the laws allow for their suppression. The government has an unquestionable right to punish those persons and prevent their acts from being ripened into acts of treason. No person doubts the right of the government to punish those persons and prevent the maturity and success of their plans. The only question is, whether a person who advised or procured treason to be committed be guilty of high treason or not. No person doubts that he is guilty of a great crime or a high misdemeanor; but is the offense of which he is guilty of treason?

But gentlemen ask what a deplorable situation the country is in if such an offense be not treason. As if the people and government were bound hand and foot and could take no step to prevent the levying of war; as if, because he who only prepares to levy war cannot be punished as if he had actually levied it, he must escape entirely with impunity! As if, because preparation is not the same as consummation, there was no possibility of punishing it! This is begging the question entirely. Can a person who only advises war to be levied be said to have actually levied it? Gentlemen, say that he had all the intention, therefore ought to be considered as having the actual guilt of it. Let it be so, that he has all the guilt of giving the advice, but not of the act of levying the war, because he never committed it. The court is to decide according to the Constitution and laws. What prevented the framers of our Constitution from providing that persons who should counsel, commend, or procure levying of war against the United States should be guilty of treason? As they made no such provision, they did not intend it.

The Constitution states in plain terms that treason against the United States shall consist but in two acts: that it "shall consist only in levying war against them, or in adhering to their enemies, giving them aid and comfort." He who levies war against the United States, and he who adheres to their enemies, giving them aid and comfort, are traitors, and none other, by the very positive and plain language of this compact. Does the Constitution say that he who advises these acts, that he who receives or comforts any person who has done either of these acts, is guilty of treason? No person will say that he who counseled an act of war to be done is the person who actually did it. No person will say that he who advises another to adhere to the enemies of his country is the person who actually did adhere to them. He who advises, procures, or persuades, he who receives, comforts, or protects, or even he who has been active in aiding and assisting, but absent at a remote distance from the scene of action, is not the actor. The parts which these persons perform are all essentially different. Have the judges who judicially expound this Constitution any authority to make the act of advising or comforting treasonable by construction? Is it not by construction that a man is made guilty of having levied war who only advised it? Is it not by construction that he is rendered guilty of levying war who only gave a night's lodging to a person who did assist in levying it? Is it not by construction that giving a dinner to a man in distress is tortured into levying of war? Is it not by construction extravagantly extended that they make a party absent at a great distance constructively present and constructively guilty of the acts of others? Is the Constitution of the United States to be taken by construction contrary to its own plain and explicit words? It is the same as if the Constitution had expressly said that there should be no constructive treason, no constructive presence, no constructive agent.

Before concluding, let me observe that it has been my intention to argue the cause correctly, without hurting the feelings of any person in the world. We are unfortunately situated. We labor against great prejudices against my client, which tend to prevent him from having a fair trial. I have with pain heard it said that such are the public prejudices against Colonel Burr that a jury, even should they be satisfied of his innocence, must have considerable firmness of mind to pronounce him not guilty. I have heard it not without horror. God of heaven! Have we already under our form of government, which we have so often been told is best calculated of all governments to secure all our rights, arrived at a period when a trial in a court of justice, where life is at stake, shall be but a solemn mockery, a mere idle form and ceremony to transfer innocence from the goal to the gibbet, to gratify popular indignation, excited by bloodthirsty enemies! But if it require in such a situation firmness in a jury, so does it equally require fortitude in judges to perform their duty. And here permit me again, most solemnly, and at the same time most respectfully, to observe that, in the case of life and death, where there remains one single doubt in the minds of the jury as to facts, or of the court as to law, it is their duty to decide in favor of life.

When the sun mildly shines upon us, when the gentle zephyrs play around us, we can easily proceed forward in the straight path of our duty; but when bleak clouds enshroud the sky with darkness, when the tempest rages, the winds howl, and the waves break over us—when the thunders awfully roar over our heads and the lightnings of heaven blaze around us—it is then that all the energies of the human soul are called into action. It is then that the truly brave man stands firm at his post. It is then that, by an unshaken performance of his duty, man approaches the nearest possible to the Divinity. Nor is there any object in the creation on which the Supreme Being can look down with more delight and approbation than on a human being in such a situation and thus acting. May that God who now looks upon us, who has in his infinite wisdom called you into existence and placed you in that seat to dispense justice to your fellow citizens, to preserve and protect innocence against persecution—may that God so illuminate your understanding that you may know what is right; and may he serve your soul with firmness and fortitude to act according to that knowledge.

And with the conclusion of Luther Martin's brilliant and passionate remarks, it was left to Chief Justice Marshall to essentially render a life-or-death decision. There was little doubt that had all the prosecution's evidence been heard, an overwhelming case of Burr's activities would have condemned him in the eyes of the jury. Burr's very public and controversial life subjected him to critical scrutiny. However, Justice Marshall's task, as with all judicial rulings, was to rise above public sentiment, even rise above the public expressions of Burr's guilt as prejudged by President Jefferson, and fairly and evenly apply the law. The law of treason as evidenced by the arguments on both sides was anything but clear. Given the short history of the United States in 1807, there was not a great deal of American legal precedent for Marshall to draw upon. Consequently, he turned to the English common law and the leading English authorities for guidance in fleshing out the scant language in the Constitution concerning treason to resolve the complex questions raised by counsel on both sides.

Perhaps the central question was what constituted an act of war. The U.S. Constitution says "treason . . . shall consist only in levying war." Is this so specific and limited that it requires a person to pick up a weapon and strike at another? Or can it be extended to picking up a weapon and assuming a hostile posture in the face of an adversary?

A second equally compelling question confronting Marshall was whether an accessory, a person not physically in the act of levying war, but one who may have advised or even incited the act, would be as culpable as the actual participant. At common law and throughout the development of criminal law in the United States, an accessory has always been treated less harshly than a principal, aiding and assisting being viewed as less blameworthy than the actual commission of the crime. However, in English common law the lone exception to the principal/accessory distinction involved crimes of treason. As discussed by the attorneys, the law of treason in England often revolved around threats to the monarch; such threats were viewed as going to the heart of the nation and were dealt with most severely. Consequently, there were no accessories in treason—everyone was a principal and would be punished as a principal. Should then this quirk of English law be brought to bear against Burr?

Another question was whether a person far removed from the act of "levying war" could be held responsible for that act. As suggested by the presentation, when King George III dispatched British troops to America to quell the American Revolution, was he not levying war even though he was three thousand miles away? Burr was over a hundred miles away from Blennerhassett Island when those boats with armed men pushed off. Was he levying war from his remote local?

A final question to be dealt with concerned the language used in the indictment under which Burr was charged. The indictment said Burr had levied war at Blennerhassett Island, when in reality he was far away at the time the boats set out. This may at first glance seem a trivial concern in light of the other questions raised, but it is a critical tenet of English common law that the charging document set forth with particularity the specifics of the alleged offense, in order that the accused be able to adequately defend himself. Did the indictment of Burr meet that requirement? Was it specific enough to put Burr on precise notice as to the charges he faced? And so it was for Justice Marshall to pick through the arguments and render a decision.

Freedom or Death?

After due consideration and careful deliberation Chief Justice Marshall delivered his ruling on the defense motion to block further testimony of Burr's culpability, setting forth the essential elements necessary to convict a defendant of treason. To the assembled throng, to the lawyers, to the jurors, and most important, to the accused, Marshall issued his decision:

> The question which arises on the construction of the Constitution, in every point of view in which it can be contemplated, is of infinite moment to the people of this country and to their government, and requires the most temperate and the most deliberate consideration. "Treason against the United States shall consist only in levying war against them." What is the natural import of the words "levying war"? and who may be said to levy it? Taken most literally, they are, perhaps, of the same import with the words "raising or creating war"; but as those who join after the commencement are equally the objects of punishment, there would probably be a general admission that the term also comprehended making war or carrying on war. In the construction which courts would be required to give these words, it is not improbable that those who should raise, create, make, or carry on war, might be comprehended. There is no difficulty in affirming that there must be a war or the crime of levying it cannot exist; but there would often be considerable difficulty in affirming that a particular act did or did not involve the person committing it in the guilt and in the fact of levying war.
>
> It is a technical term. It is used in a very old statute of that country whose language is our language, and whose laws form the substratum of our laws. It is scarcely conceivable that the term was not employed by the framers of our Constitution in the sense which had been affixed to it by those from whom we borrowed it. So far as the meaning of any terms, particularly terms of art, is completely ascertained, those by whom they are employed must be considered as employing them in that ascertained meaning, unless the contrary be proved by the

context. It is, therefore, reasonable to suppose, unless it be incompatible with other expressions of the Constitution, that the term "levying war" is used in that instrument in the same sense in which it was understood in England. The understanding of such writers as Coke, Hale, and Foster, is to be considered. Coke does not give a complete definition of the term, but puts cases which amount to levying war. "An actual rebellion or insurrection," he says, "is a levying of war." In whom? Coke does not say whether in those only who appear in arms, or in all those who take part in the rebellion or insurrection by real open deed. Hale, in treating on the same subject, puts many cases which shall constitute a levying of war, without which no act can amount to treason; but he does not particularize the parts to be performed by the different persons concerned in that war, which shall be sufficient to fix on each the guilt of levying it. Foster says: "The joining with rebels in an act of rebellion, or with enemies in acts of hostility, will make a man a traitor. Furnishing rebels or enemies with money, arms, ammunition or other necessaries will prima facie make a man a traitor." Blackstone is not more satisfactory. Although we find among the commentators upon treason enough to satisfy the inquiry, what is a state of internal war? Yet no precise information can be acquired from them which would enable us to decide with clearness whether persons not in arms, but taking part in a rebellion, could be said to levy war, independently of that doctrine which attaches to the accessory the guilt of his principal.

The terms of the Constitution comprise no question respecting principal and accessory, so far as either may in fact be said to levy war. Whether in England a person would be indicted in express terms for levying war or for assisting others in levying war, yet if in correct and legal language he can be said to have levied war, and if it have never been decided that the act would not amount to levying war, his case may, without violent construction, be brought within the letter and the plain meaning of the Constitution. In examining these words, the argument which may be drawn from felonies, as, for example, from murder, is not more conclusive. Murder is the single act of killing with malice aforethought. But war is a complex operation, composed of many parts, co-operating with each other. No one man or body of men can perform them all if the war be of any continuance. Although, then, in correct and in law language, he alone is said to have murdered another who has perpetrated the fact of killing, or has been present aiding that fact, it does not follow that he alone can have levied war who has borne arms. All those who perform the various and essential military parts of prosecuting the war, which must be assigned to different persons, may with correctness and accuracy be said to levy war. Taking this view of the subject, it appears to the court that those who perform a part in the prosecution of the war may correctly be said to levy war and to commit treason under the Constitution.

In opening the case, it was contended by the attorney for the United States, and has since been maintained on the part of the prosecution, that neither arms nor the application of force or violence are indispensably necessary to constitute the fact of levying war. A force is supposed to be collected for an avowed treasonable object, in a condition to attempt that object, and to have commenced the attempt by moving towards it. If a rebel army, avowing its hostility to the sovereign power, should confront that of the government, should march and countermarch before it, should maneuver in its face, and should then disperse from any cause whatever without firing a gun—I confess I could not, without some surprise, hear gentlemen seriously contend that this could not amount to an act of levying war. A case equally strong may be put with respect to the absence of military weapons. If the party be in a condition to execute the purposed treason without the usual implements of war, I can perceive no reason for requiring those implements in order to constitute the crime.

Independent of authority, trusting only to the dictates of reason, and expounding terms according to their ordinary signification, we should probably all concur in the declaration that war could not be levied without the employment and exhibition of force. War is an appeal from reason to the sword; and he who makes the appeal evidences the fact by the use of the means. His intention to go to war may be proved by words; but the actual going to war is a fact which is to be proved by open deed. The end is to be effected by force; and it would seem that in cases where no declaration is to be made, the state of actual war could only be created by the employment of force, or being in a condition to employ it. Lord Hale supposed an assemblage of men in force, in a military posture, to be necessary to constitute the fact of levying war. The cases here put by Hawkins, of a constructive levying of war, do in terms require force as a constituent part of the description of the offence. Judge Foster, in his valuable treatise on treason, states that the cases of constructive levying of war all contain, as a material ingredient, the actual employment of force. He says "enlisting" and marching are sufficient overt acts, without coming to a battle or action.

Judge Blackstone, speaking of levying war, says: "This may be done by taking arms, not only to dethrone the king, but under pretense to reform religion or the laws, or to remove evil counselors or other grievances, whether real or pretended. For the law does not, neither can it, permit any private man or set of men to interfere forcibly in matters of such high importance." He proceeds to give examples of levying war, which show that he contemplated actual force as a necessary ingredient in the composition of this crime. It would seem, then, from the English authorities, that the words "levying war" have not received a technical distinction different from their natural meaning, so far as respects the character of the assemblage of men which may constitute the fact. It must be a warlike assemblage, carrying the appearance of force, and in a situation to practice hostility.

Several judges of the United States have given opinions at their circuits on the subject. Judge Chase, in the *Case of Fries,* has been particularly clear and explicit. In an opinion which he appears to have prepared on great consideration, he says: "If a body of people conspire and meditate an insurrection to resist or oppose the execution of a statute of the United States by force, they are only guilty of a high misdemeanor; but if they proceed to carry such intention into execution by force, that they are guilty of the treason of levying war; and the quantum of the force employed neither increases nor diminishes the crime; whether by one hundred or one thousand persons is wholly immaterial. A combination or conspiracy to levy war against the United States is not treason unless combined with an attempt to carry such combination or conspiracy into execution; some actual force or violence must be used in pursuance of such design to levy war; but that it is altogether immaterial whether the force used be sufficient to effectuate the object. Any force connected with the intention will constitute the crime of levying of war."

The judges of the United States, so far as their opinions have been quoted, seem to have required still more to constitute the fact of levying war than has been required by the English books. Our judges seem to have required the actual exercise of force, the actual employment of some degree of violence. This, however, may be, and probably is, because, in the cases in which their opinions were given, the design not having been to overturn the government, but to resist the execution of a law, such an assemblage as would be sufficient for the purpose would require the actual employment of force to render the object unequivocal.

Returning to the case actually before the court, it was argued: "A design to overturn the government of the United States in New Orleans by force would have been unquestionably a design which if carried into execution would have been treason; and the assemblage of a body of men for the purpose of carrying it into execution would amount to levying to war against the United States." The verbal communication said to have been made by Mr. Swartwout to General Wilkinson in which it was stated that Mr. Burr was levying an army of 7,000 men, and observing that the treason to be inferred from these words would depend on the intention with which it was levied, and on the progress which had been made in levying it. The question, then, is whether this evidence prove Colonel Burr to have advanced so far in levying an army as actually to have assembled them. Actually to assemble an army of 7,000 men is unquestionably to place those who are so assembled in a state of open force.

The position here stated by the counsel for the prosecution is that the army commencing its march by detachments to the place of rendezvous is sufficient to constitute the crime. This position is not admitted to be universally correct. Why? This act as it is argued, would be equivocal and have no warlike appearance. The act, then, should be unequivocal and should have a warlike appearance. It must exhibit the appearance of war. Now, a solitary individual traveling to any point, with any intent, could not, without a total disregard of language, be termed a marching detachment. There must be several individuals traveling together, and the words being used in reference to the position they intended to qualify, would seem to indicate the distinction between the appearances attending the usual movement of a company of men for civil purposes, and that military movement which might, in correct language, be denominated marching by detachments. The meeting of particular bodies of men, and their marching from places of partial to a place of general rendezvous, would be such an assemblage.

An assemblage of men who should constitute the fact of levying war must be an assemblage in force. Is it not to judge in some measure of the end by the proportion which the means bear to the end? Why is it that a single armed individual entering a boat, and sailing down the Ohio for the avowed purpose of attacking New Orleans, could not be said to levy war? Is it not that he is apparently not in a condition to levy war? If this be so, ought not the assemblage to furnish some evidence of its intention and capacity to levy war before it can amount to levying war? When speaking of an assemblage for the purpose of effecting a treasonable object by force, should that be understood to indicate an assemblage exhibiting the appearance of force? The definition of the attorney for the United States deserves notice in this respect. It is, "When there is an assemblage of men, convened for the purpose of effecting by force a treasonable object, which force is meant to be employed before the assemblage disperses, this is treason." To read this definition without adverting to the argument, we should infer that the assemblage was itself to effect by force the treasonable object, not to join itself to some other bodies of men and then to effect the object by their combined force. Under this construction, it would be expected the appearance of the assemblage would bear some proportion to the object, and would indicate the intention; at any rate, that it would be an assemblage in force. This construction is most certainly not that which was intended; but it serves to show that general phrases must always be understood in reference to the subject-matter and to the general principles of law.

On that division of the subject which respects the merits of the case connected with the pleadings, two points are also raised in defense of the prisoner: 1st. That this indictment, having charged the prisoner with levying war on Blennerhassett Island, and containing no other overt act, cannot be supported by proof that war was levied at that place by other persons in the absence of the prisoner, even admitting those persons to be connected with him in one common treasonable conspiracy. 2dly. That admitting such an indictment could be supported by such evidence, the previous conviction of some person, who committed the act which is said to amount to levying war, is indispensable to the conviction of a person who advised or procured that act.

As to the first point, the indictment contains two counts, one of which charges that the prisoner, with a number of persons unknown, levied war on Blennerhassett Island, in the county of Wood, in the district of Virginia; and the other adds the circumstance of their proceeding from that island down the river for the purpose of seizing New Orleans by force. In point of fact, the prisoner was not on Blennerhassett Island, nor in the county of Wood, nor in the district of Virginia. In considering this point, the court is led first to inquire whether an indictment for levying war must specify an overt act, or would be sufficient if it merely charged the prisoner in general terms with having levied war, omitting the expression of place or circumstance. The place in which a crime was committed is essential to an indictment, were it only to show the jurisdiction of the court. It is, also, essential for the purpose of enabling the prisoner to make his defense. That at common law an indictment would have been defective which did not mention the place in which the crime was committed can scarcely be doubted. This necessity is rendered the stronger by the constitutional provision that the offender "shall be tried in the state and district wherein the crime shall have been committed," and by the act of Congress which requires that twelve petit jurors at least shall be summoned from the county where the offence was committed. A description of the particular manner in which the war was levied seems, also, essential to enable the accused to make his defense. The law does not expect a man to be prepared to defend every act of his life which may be suddenly and without notice alleged against him. In common justice, the particular fact with which he is charged ought to be stated, and stated in such a manner as to afford a reasonable certainty of the nature of the accusation and the circumstances which will be adduced against him. In all criminal prosecutions the accused shall enjoy the right to be informed of the nature and cause of the accusation. Such information enables him to prepare for his defense. It seems, then, to be perfectly clear that it would not be sufficient for an indictment to allege generally that the accused had levied war against the United States. The charge must be more particularly specified by laying what is termed an overt act of levying war.

If it be necessary to specify the charge in the indictment, it would seem to follow, irresistibly, that the charge must be proved as laid. Might it be otherwise, the charge of an overt act would be a mischief instead of an advantage to the accused? It would lead him from the true cause and nature of the accusation, instead of informing him respecting it. But it is contended on the part of the prosecution that, although the accused had never been with the party which assembled at Blennerhassett Island, and was, at that time, at a great distance, and in a different state, he was yet legally present, and, therefore, may properly be charged in the indictment as being present in fact. It is, therefore, necessary to inquire whether in this case the doctrine of constructive presence can apply. It is conceived by the court to be possible that a person may be concerned in a treasonable conspiracy, and yet be legally as well as actually absent while some one act of the treason is perpetrated. If a rebellion should be so extensive as to spread through every state in the Union, it will scarcely be contended that every individual concerned in it is legally present at every overt act committed in the course of that rebellion. It would be a very violent presumption indeed, too violent to be made without clear authority, to presume that even the chief of the rebel army was legally present at every such overt act. If the main rebel army, with the chief at its head, should be prosecuting war at one extremity of our territory, say in New Hampshire; if this chief should be there captured and sent to the other extremity for the purpose of trial; if his indictment, instead of alleging an overt act which was true in point of fact, should allege that he had assembled some small party which in truth he had not seen, and had levied war by engaging in a skirmish in Georgia at a time when, in reality, he was fighting a battle in New Hampshire; if such evidence would support such an indictment by the fiction that he was legally present, though really absent, all would ask to what purpose are those provisions in the Constitution, which direct the place of trial and ordain that the accused shall be informed of the nature and cause of the accusation? But that a man may be legally absent who has counseled or procured a treasonable act is proved by all those books which treat upon the subject, and which concur in declaring that such a person is a principal traitor, not because he was legally present, but because in treason all are principals. Yet the indictment, speaking upon general principles, would charge him according to the truth of the case. Lord Coke says: "If many conspire to levy war, and some of them do levy the same according to the conspiracy, this is high treason in all." Why? because all were legally present when the war was levied? No. "For in treason," continues Lord Coke, "all be principals, and war is levied." In this case the indictment, reasoning from analogy, would not charge that the absent conspirators were present, but would state the truth of the case. If the conspirator had done nothing which amounted to levying of war, and if by our Constitution the doctrine that an accessory becomes a principal be not adopted, in consequence of which the conspirator could not be condemned under an indictment stating the truth of the case, it would be going very far to say that this defect, if it be termed one, may be cured by an indictment stating the case untruly.

This doctrine of Lord Coke has been adopted by all subsequent writers, and it is generally laid down in the English books that whatever will make a man an accessory in felony, will make him a principal in treason; but it is nowhere suggested that he is by construction to be considered as present when in point of fact he was absent. Foster is precisely in point: "It is well known that in the language of the law there are no accessories in high treason; all are principals. Every instance of incitement, aid, or protection, which in the case of felony will render a man an accessory before or after the fact, in the case of high treason, whether it be treason at common law or by statute, will make him a principal in treason." In point of law, then, the man who incites, aids, or procures a treasonable act, is not, merely in consequence of that incitement, aid, or procurement, legally present when that act is committed. If it does not result, from the nature of the crime, that all who are concerned in it are legally present at every overt act, then each case depends upon its own circumstances; and to judge how far the circumstances of any case can make him legally present, who is in fact absent, the doctrine of constructive presence must be examined.

Foster says: "When the law requireth the presence of the accomplice at the perpetration of the fact in order to render him a principal, it doth not require a strict actual immediate presence, such a presence as would make him an eye or ear witness of what passeth." The terms used by Foster are such as would be employed by a man intending to show the necessity that the absent person should be near at hand, although from the nature of the thing no precise distance could be marked out. Foster observes that "in order to render a person an accomplice and a principal in felony, he must be aiding and abetting at the fact, or ready to afford assistance if necessary." That is, at the particular fact which is charged. He must be ready to render assistance to those who are committing that fact. He must be ready to give immediate and direct assistance. All the cases to be found in the books go to the same point. Let them be applied to that under consideration.

The whole treason laid in this indictment is the levying of war in Blennerhassett Island; and the whole question to which the inquiry of the court is now directed is whether the prisoner was legally present at that fact. I say this is the whole question; because the prisoner can only be convicted on the overt act laid in the indictment. With respect to this prosecution, it is as if no other overt act existed. If other overt acts can be inquired into, it is for the sole purpose of proving the particular fact charged. It is evidence of the crime consisting of this particular fact, not as establishing the general crime by a distinct fact. The counsel for the prosecution have charged those engaged in the defense with considering the overt act as treason, whereas it ought to be considered solely as the evidence of the treason; but the counsel for the prosecution seem themselves not to have sufficiently adverted to this clear principle; that though the overt act may not be itself the treason, it is the sole act of that treason which can produce conviction. It is the sole point in issue between the parties. And the only division of that point, if the expression be allowed, which the court is now examining, is the constructive presence of the prisoner at the fact charged.

To return, then, to the application of the cases. Had the prisoner set out with the party for Blennerhassett Island, he would have been present at the fact. Had he not arrived on the island, but had taken a position near enough to co-operate with those on the island, to assist them in any act of hostility, or to aid them if attacked, the question whether he was constructively present would be a question compounded of law and fact, which would be decided by the jury, with the aid of the court, so far as respected the law. In this case the accused would have been of the particular party assembled on the island, and would have been associated with them in the particular act of levying war said to have been committed on the island. But if he was not with the party at any time before they reached the island; if he did not join them there, or intend to join them there; if his personal co-operation in the general plan was to be afforded elsewhere, at a great distance, in a different state; if the overt acts of treason to be performed by him were to be distinct overt acts—then he was not of the particular party assembled at Blennerhassett Island, and was not constructively present, aiding and assisting in the particular act which was there committed. The testimony on this point, so far as it has been delivered, is not equivocal. There is not only no evidence that the accused was of the particular party which assembled on Blennerhassett Island, but the whole evidence shows he was not of that party. In felony, then, admitting the crime to have been completed on the island, and to have been advised, procured, or commanded by the accused, he would have been incontestably an accessory and not a principal. But in treason, it is said, the law is otherwise, because the theatre of action is more extensive. He who counsels, procures, or aids treason, is guilty accessorily, and solely in virtue of the common law principle that what will make a man an accessory in felony makes him a principal in treason. So far from considering a man as constructively present at every overt act of the general treason in which he may have been concerned, the whole doctrine of the books limits the proof against him to those particular overt acts of levying war with which he is charged.

What would be the effect of a different doctrine? If a person levying war in Kentucky may be said to be constructively present and assembled with a party carrying on war in Virginia at a great distance from him, then he is present at every overt act performed anywhere. He may be tried in any state on the continent, where any overt act has been committed. He may be proved to be guilty of an overt act laid in the indictment in which he had no personal participation, by proving that he advised it, or that he committed other acts. This is, perhaps, too extravagant to be in terms maintained. Certainly it cannot be supported by the doctrines of the English law.

Here the indictment does not charge the prisoner to have been present. Yet if he caused the assemblage, he may be indicted as being present, and convicted on evidence that he caused the treasonable act. To counsel or advise a treasonable assemblage, and to be one of that assemblage, are certainly distinct acts, and, therefore, ought not to be charged as the same act. The great objection to this mode of proceeding is, that the proof essentially varies from the charge in the character and essence of the offence, and in the testimony by which the accused is to defend himself. The indictment must give notice of the offence; that the accused is only bound to answer the particular charge which the indictment contains, and that the overt act laid is that particular charge. A special overt act of levying war must be laid.

But suppose the law to be as is contended by the counsel for the United States. Suppose an indictment charging an individual with personally assembling among others, and thus levying war, may be satisfied with the proof that he caused the assemblage. What effect will this law have upon this case? The guilt of the accused, if there be any guilt, does not consist in the assemblage, for he was not a member of it. The simple fact of assemblage no more affects one absent man than another. His guilt, then, consists in procuring the assemblage, and upon this fact depends his criminality. The proof relative to the character of an assemblage must be the same whether a man be present or absent. In the general, to charge any individual with the guilt of an assemblage, the fact of his presence must be proved; it constitutes an essential part of the overt act. If, then, the procurement be substituted in the place of presence, does it not also constitute an essential part of the overt act? Must it not also be proved? Must it not be proved in the same manner that presence must be proved? If in one case the presence of the individual make the guilt of the assemblage his guilt, and in the other case the procurement by the individual make the guilt of the assemblage his guilt, then presence and procurement are equally component parts of the overt act, and equally require two witnesses. The presence of the party, where presence is necessary, being a part of the overt act, must be positively proved by two witnesses. No presumptive evidence, no facts from which presence may be conjectured or inferred, will satisfy the Constitution and the law. If procurement take the place of presence and become part of the overt act, then no presumptive evidence, no facts from which the procurement may be conjectured or inferred, can satisfy the Constitution and the law. The mind is not to be led to the conclusion that the individual was present by a train of conjectures, of inferences, or of reasoning; the fact must be proved by two witnesses. Neither, where procurement supplies the want of presence, is the mind to be conducted to the conclusion that the accused procured the assembly by a train of conjectures or inferences, or of reasoning; the fact itself must be proved by two witnesses, and must have been committed within the district.

If it be said that the advising or procurement of treason is a secret transaction, which can scarcely ever be proved in the manner required by this opinion, the answer which will readily suggest itself is, that the difficulty of proving a fact will not justify conviction without proof. Certainly it will not justify conviction without a direct and positive witness in a case where the Constitution requires two. The more correct inference from this circumstance would seem to be, that the advising of the fact is not within the constitutional definition of the crime. To advise or procure a treason is in the nature of conspiring or plotting treason, which is not treason in itself. The fact that the accused procured the assemblage on Blennerhassett Island must be proved, not circumstantially, but positively, by two witnesses, to charge him with that assemblage. But there are still other most important considerations which must be well weighed before this doctrine can be applied to the United States.

It is, then, the opinion of the court that this indictment can be supported only by testimony which proves the accused to have been actually or constructively present when the assemblage took place on Blennerhassett Island.

It is further the opinion of the court that there is no testimony whatever which tends to prove that the accused was actually or constructively present when that assemblage did take place; indeed, the contrary is most apparent.

The law of the case being thus far settled, what ought to be the decision of the court on the present motion? Ought the court to sit and hear testimony which cannot affect the prisoner, or ought the court to arrest that testimony? No person will contend that, in a civil or criminal case, either party is at liberty to introduce what testimony he pleases, legal or illegal, and to consume the whole term in details of facts unconnected with the particular case. Some tribunal, then, must decide on the admissibility of testimony. The parties cannot constitute this tribunal; for they do not agree. The jury cannot constitute it; for the question is whether they shall hear the testimony or not. Who, then, but the court can constitute it? It is of necessity the peculiar province of the court to judge of the admissibility of testimony. If the court admit improper or reject proper testimony, it is an error of judgment; but it is an error committed in the direct exercise of their judicial functions. The present indictment charges the prisoner with levying war against the United States, and alleges an overt act of levying war. That overt act must be proved, according to the mandates of the Constitution and of the act of congress, by two witnesses. It is proved by a single witness. The presence of the accused has been stated to be an essential component part of the overt act in this indictment, unless the common law principle respecting accessories should render it unnecessary; and there is not only no witness who has proved his actual or legal presence, but the fact of his absence is not controverted. The counsel for the prosecution offer to give in evidence subsequent transactions at a different place and in a different state, in order to prove—what? The overt act laid in the indictment? That the prisoner was one of those who assembled at Blennerhassett Island? No: that is not alleged. It is well known that such testimony is not competent to establish such a fact. The Constitution and law require that the fact should be established by two witnesses; not by the establishment of other facts from which the jury might reason to this fact. The testimony, then, is not relevant. If it can be introduced, it is only in the character of corroborative or confirmatory testimony, after the overt act has been proved by two witnesses in such manner that the question of fact ought to be left with the jury. The conclusion that in this state of things no testimony can be admissible is so inevitable that the counsel for the United States could not resist it. I do not understand them to deny that, if the overt act be not proved by two witnesses so as to be submitted to the jury, all other testimony must be irrelevant; because no other testimony can prove the act. Now, an assemblage on Blennerhassett's Island is proved by the requisite number of witnesses; and the court might submit it to the jury whether that assemblage amounted to a levying of war; but the presence of the accused at that assemblage being nowhere alleged except in the indictment, the overt act is not proved by a single witness; and, of consequence, all other testimony must be irrelevant.

The arguments on both sides have been intently and deliberately considered. The result of the whole is a conviction, as complete as the mind of the court is capable of receiving on a complex subject, that the motion must prevail. No testimony relative to the conduct or declarations of the prisoner elsewhere, and subsequent to the transaction on Blennerhassett Island, can be admitted; because such testimony, being in its nature merely corroborative and incompetent to prove the overt act in itself, is irrelevant until there be proof of the overt act by two witnesses. The jury has now heard the opinion of the court on the law of the case. They will apply that law to the facts, and will find a verdict of guilty or not guilty as their own consciences may direct.

In granting Burr's motion to preclude further testimony based on the prosecution's inability to produce adequate evidence of an overt act of levying war, Marshall set forth three principles that would guide future treason trials. First, Marshall adopted the English tradition that in treason there is to be no distinction between accessories and principals; all participants are considered principals.

Second, to be guilty of treason it need not be proved that the accused was actually present at the time the overt act of war was levied. An accused could be guilty if he were at some other place and procured or organized or incited the act of war. However, Marshall warned, that did not relieve the prosecution from proving that an act of war had actually occurred. It is interesting that, despite all Marshall's discussions of what constituted an overt act of war, he never resolved that question. That resolution, he opined, was unnecessary to the decision in this case.

The third principal to come from Burr's trial was the particularity required in charging an accused with the crime of treason. Putting the accused on notice of the precise nature of the criminal conduct is a fundamental principle of American law. In Burr's case, he was charged with treason in that he levied war. Marshall ruled that such a pleading was inadequate. The prosecutors argued that Burr, though not present at Blennerhassett Island, nonetheless levied war there. In reality, Burr may well have levied war and been guilty of treason; however, the government had to spell out with greater particularity Burr's overt act. While this may seem an irrational technicality, especially in light of the grave nature of the charge, it is nonetheless a critical precept of American law that the accused be alerted to precisely those alleged acts that render him criminally responsible.

Marshall's ruling effectively ended the government's case by precluding them from producing additional evidence. The only question remaining for the jury was whether the assembled men at Blennerhassett Island levied war and whether Burr and Blennerhassett were sufficiently connected to that assemblage.

The jury expressed their dissatisfaction with Marshall's ruling through the wording of their verdict: "We of the jury say that Aaron Burr is not proved to be guilty under this indictment by any evidence submitted to us. We therefore find him not guilty."

Jefferson was furious over Marshall's ruling. He wrote, "It now appears we have no law but the will of the judge," and considered either proposing a constitutional amendment limiting the power of the judiciary or asking Congress to impeach Marshall. In a later letter Jefferson wrote, "The scenes which have been acted at Richmond are such as have never been exhibited in any country, where all regard to public character has not yet been thrown off. They are equivalent to a proclamation of impunity to every traitorous combination which may be formed to destroy the Union."

Nonetheless, Burr, despite his often flagrant acts and undoubted guilt, walked away from the capital treason charges, any lingering stature as an American statesman completely dissolved.

The Aftermath

Harman Blennerhassett had been a man in over his head from the outset. By casting his fortunes with Burr he lost his fortune and his island. He went West after the trial and eventually found the money to buy a cotton plantation. It proved unsuccessful and he eventually sold it and moved to Montreal, where he practiced law until he returned to Great Britain, where he died in 1831.

General James Wilkinson, who, apart from Burr, was the most intriguing character involved in the fiasco that was Burr's "Western Expedition," for a time led a seemingly charmed life. But by the start of the War of 1812, Wilkinson had been investigated and then court-martialed in events that traced back to his "association" with Burr and even to his Spanish connections. Miraculously, Wilkinson survived the court-martial and remained the senior military officer of the United States during the war with Britain. However, his command of American troops proved ineffectual and he was once again court-martialed. Subsequently acquitted and forced to leave the military, he eventually made his way to Mexico City, where he died in 1825.

Burr, perhaps emboldened by his acquittal, continued his intrigues. His new objective was Cuba, and he looked to England for financial support; none was immediately forthcoming. Burr sailed for England, where he was—for a time—received as a celebrity, moving in elite social circles while seeking funds. But his welcome ran out, and by 1809 his creditors were once again bedeviling him. Burr moved on to Paris, with hopes of enlisting Napoléon's support in yet another scheme: the acquisition of Florida and Mexico. His plans were rebuffed, and by 1812 he was back in New York, the indictment for murder forgotten amid the general chaos of another war with Great Britain. His plans for conquest finally at an end, Burr once again took up the practice of law. Any thought of resurrecting his political career was met with disinterest and derision. After a lifetime of power, fame, and controversy his influence faded out. He was not even accorded distinction as an elder statesman. Years later, after hearing word of the Texas revolution, Burr was heard to laugh and say, "There! You see? I was right! I was only thirty years too soon. What was treason in me thirty years ago is patriotism now."

Index